THE COLLABORATOR

THE COLLABORATOR THE TRIAL & EXECUTION OF ROBERT BRASILLACH

ALICE KAPLAN

THE UNIVERSITY OF CHICAGO PRESS

CHICAGO AND LONDON

The University of Chicago Press, Chicago 60637
The University of Chicago Press, Ltd., London
© 2000 by The University of Chicago
All rights reserved. Published 2000
Paperback edition 2001
Printed in the United States of America
09 08 07 06 05 04 03 02 01   3 4 5
ISBN (cloth): 0-226-42414-6
ISBN (paperback): 0-226-42415-4

The University of Chicago Press gratefully acknowledges
the assistance of the John Simon Guggenheim Memorial
Foundation in the publication of this book.

Library of Congress Cataloging-in-Publication Data

Kaplan, Alice Yaeger.
    The collaborator: the trial and execution of Robert Brasillach / Alice
Kaplan.
        p.   cm.
    Includes bibliographical references and index.
    ISBN 0-226-42414-6 (cloth : alk. paper)
    1. Brasillach, Robert, 1909–1945—Political and social views.   2. World
War, 1939–1945—Collaborationists—France.   3. Fascism and literature—
France—History—20th century.   4. Fascism—France—History.   5. Trials
(Treason)—France—History.   6. Intellectuals—France—Political activity.
7. Authors, French—20th century—Biography. I. Title.
D802.F8 B6985   2000
848'.91209—dc21
    [B]   99-048291

CONTENTS

This book is for my mother,
Leonore Kaplan,
who taught me early on
that you could find out anything
with good research.

In the winter of 1944–1945, three months short of an Allied victory in Europe, a thirty-five-year-old journalist and man of letters named Robert Brasillach was put to death by the Liberation government of France. The charge against him was collaborationist treason with the Nazis. The Brasillach case was, and is still, a "cause célèbre" in France.

This book tells the story of Robert Brasillach's career, his dramatic trial, and his persistent legacy.

The world has changed radically since the end of World War II, yet we continue to debate today the issues raised by Brasillach's case: the accountability of writers and intellectuals, the power of words to do harm, the possibility of justice during wartime, and the dangers of revisionist history. With over fifty years' distance, the arguments around the Brasillach trial are as impassioned and as controversial as ever. We're still left wondering how the jury should decide.

Robert Brasillach's trial was both typical of postwar French Purge trials and absolutely unique. Typical because Brasillach was tried in a specially designed Court of Justice for treason, or "intelligence with the enemy" according to article 75 of the penal code, like any number of journalists before and after him. Unique in that the accused, in this one case, had a considerable reputation both as a writer and as an alumnus of the Ecole Normale Supérieure, that bastion of intellectual respectability and the training ground for the finest intellectuals of his generation. Brasillach was the only writer of any real distinction put to death during the Purge. For this reason, his death sentence has marked the intellectual climate of the postwar era.

My questions about this trial have focused on what we can know—and what we notice now—that couldn't have been known in 1944, in the heat of war's end. My research has taken me from the working-class suburbs of Paris, where the members of the Brasillach jury participated in local resistance movements; to the bar association of the Palais de Justice, where defense lawyer Jacques Isorni's papers are held; to Toulon, home of the family of Marcel Reboul, Brasillach's prosecutor; and finally, to Brasillach's own voluminous works—fiction, literary criticism, poetry and plays, political journalism.

Who was Robert Brasillach? A witty, nasty, or sentimental writer, depending upon the genre and the occasion, Brasillach appears at first glance far too talented to have been taken in by the Nazis. Yet despite his real gifts and the breadth of his literary culture, a strange combination of caustic cruelty and extreme sentimentality flawed his vision both as a novelist and as a critic. In the end, his rhetorical performance at his trial is more compelling than anything he ever wrote.

This trial remains one of the most vivid rhetorical representations we have of France coming to terms with the German Occupation, and one of the first extended public conversations about what happened in France from 1940 to 1944. Reboul for the prosecution, Isorni for the defense, and Brasillach the accused: each man was a rhetorical star in his own domain. Each had a month at the most to prepare for court. During that month, Brasillach practiced his lines in prison, with his friends. Reboul and Isorni were overwhelmed with other cases, yet they threw themselves into preparing for what they knew would be a highly visible event, attended by the intelligentsia of Paris. In the back and forth of the courtroom debates, the style and voice of each of these talented men is distinct, passionate. Almost in spite of itself, the published transcript of the hastily prepared Brasillach trial has all the tension and complexity of a great work of theater.

During the occupation of France, Brasillach was editor in chief of a newspaper called *Je Suis Partout*. The paper's line was hardcore pro-Nazi. Brasillach was not as fanatic as some of his colleagues at the newspaper. He could be sentimental and respectful about the conservative Vichy government of Marshal Pétain in the unoccupied zone of France. On the other hand, he was often critical, even disdainful, when he didn't think Pétain and the Vichy government had gone far enough in purging France of its Jewish and democratic elements. He wanted a fascist France, a national socialist France.

A highly visible figure on the intellectual scene of occupied Paris, Brasillach collaborated fully with Nazi propaganda efforts, and his denunciatory writing served as a source of information and an encouragement for many arrests. In his trial, his defense lawyer tried to recast Brasillach as a proponent of Vichy and Pétain, rather than as a pro-Nazi traitor; he further pointed out that both the prosecutor and the president of the court had worked for Vichy only months before, and charged them with hypocrisy. He portrayed Brasillach as a poet, not a propagandist. This has been the consistent strategy of all efforts to rehabilitate Brasillach, from 1945 all the way up to the National Front of the 1990s.

_____

The execution of Brasillach in February 1945 was the high point of the government purge of collaborators. His case was all the more striking because he was condemned for ideological crime, not for greed or corruption. A year later, the saying goes, he would certainly have drawn a lesser charge. He might even have received a presidential "grâce," or pardon.

One of the central motivating factors for my research has been the fact that, with the exception of one excellent book, attorney Michel Laval's *La Trahison du clerc,* studies of the Brasillach trial are apologetic, contributing to rather than questioning the Brasillach myth. Accounts of the trial have shown paltry interest in anyone who appeared in that courtroom the afternoon of January 19, 1945, other than Brasillach himself.

Brasillach is the main character in this history but not the only one. Marcel Reboul, his prosecutor, and Jacques Isorni, his defense lawyer, are each remarkable personalities with great verbal gifts and fascinating war stories of their own. The members of the jury, four men from the working-class suburbs of Paris, remain mysterious, but the outlines of their story are intriguing. The journalists who covered the Purge trials and the writers who analyzed them also appear throughout my book, members of a kind of chorus on the Brasillach condemnation, and on Liberation-era Paris.

_____

This book is a reconstruction of a January 1945 trial but it also measures the enormous changes in perspective on the events of the Occupation since 1945. We're taken aback today to see that Brasillach's anti-Semitism was really only mentioned in passing in his trial. This was not an oversight. The immediate postwar French Purge trials did not focus on questions of genocide, complicity in the deportation of Jews from France, or anti-Semitic ideology; they focused on treason. In 1964, when French parliament incorporated the 1945 London agreement on crimes against humanity into internal French law, it specified that there was no statute of limitations for these crimes. Only then could the French government begin procedures that led in the 1980s and 1990s to the prosecution of Klaus Barbie, the head of the Gestapo in Lyon; Paul Touvier, a leader in the Vichy militia; and Maurice Papon, a Bordeaux civil servant in charge of Jewish affairs, for their complicity in the deportation of Jews from France. This second wave of trials relating to the Nazi Occupation, which has sharpened public interest in the Occupation, has made it all the more necessary to look back at the first wave.

In the recent Maurice Papon trial for crimes against humanity, Papon's defense lawyer, Jean-Marc Varaut, cited Brasillach's case in his final statement. He used the Brasillach trial to argue that the Jewish question had already been examined in the immediate postwar era. It was a clever move, and a distortion. Varaut quoted, out of context, from an essay that historian Henry Rousso wrote to demonstrate the opposite. In his prosecution speech, Reboul had assailed Brasillach's anti-Semitic language passionately, but he had also specified that Brasillach was on trial for his treason against the nation, not for his racial intolerance or his fascist opinions.

In what follows, I want to restore for the record the full range of Brasillach's actions, attitudes, and motives—those that were considered criminal in 1945 as well as those that were passed over quickly or ignored at the trial. The focus and intensity of his anti-Semitism is of course central to this study. But there is also the metaphoric charge, made by the prosecution, that Brasillach's attraction to Germany was homosexual in nature—and this charge, one of the most contentious in today's context, is perhaps the most difficult one to analyze. Though many aspects of Brasillach's trial may appear dated, even caricatural, from today's perspective, what happened to this writer over fifty years ago commands our attention now for a reason that goes beyond simple historical curiosity: Brasillach, by virtue of his execution by a firing squad in 1945 and by virtue of his enormous productivity as a writer, has become a martyr for the extreme right, and worse, a hero for Holocaust revisionists. How did that happen, and why are people willing to go to so much trouble turning Brasillach into a hero?

———

In 1995, on the occasion of a commemoration day for the Rafle du Vél d'Hiv—the infamous roundup, by French police, of over 13,000 foreign and foreign-born Jews from Paris in July 1942—French President Jacques Chirac marked an official change in the government posture toward Vichy established by de Gaulle in 1944. He acknowledged French responsibility for Vichy, and he put the accent on the very episode that the Purge trials of the 1940s had overlooked: the deportation of 76,000 Jews from France. Chirac's statement was obviously spurred on by the recent crimes against humanity trials in France, most especially the trial, then in preparation, of Maurice Papon, who was eventually sentenced to ten years in prison.

Two years after Chirac's speech, Prime Minister Lionel Jospin went one better by offering to open the World War II archives to all researchers. Many of them have so far been available only by special permission.

There has been an intense polemic in France over access to World War II archives. My experience, before the change in policy, was that with expert assistance, patience, and paperwork, the documents I needed were available. In 1994, when I started my research on the Brasillach trial, certain files from the period were still closed by law, but access to them could be obtained by applying for an exceptional permission, or "dérogation." I met with archivists in the Contemporary Section of the National Archives, to find out which documents would be useful to reconstruct Brasillach's career, trial, and sentencing. Then I began the long process of obtaining dérogations, writing letters to the National Archives for permission to see a range of documents—on Brasillach's education, his arrest and trial, and on other journalists tried during the Purge. The archivists then forwarded my requests to the relevant ministries—the Ministry of Education for material pertaining to Brasillach's schooling; the Ministry of Justice for material about the Purge trials and juries; the Ministry of the Interior for police archives. In every case but one, the ministries gave me permission to study the files, as long as the people involved were no longer alive. These requests took from three months to a year to come through. Each time I received a dérogation, I was asked to sign a form saying I would not use any information from the documents that risked harming living people or damaging state security. While my research was underway, the National Archives published an exhaustive guide, giving the references to every archive, national and local, pertaining to World War II and the Occupation years. This guide allowed me to locate still more documents.

One of the first things I learned, thanks to Michel Laval's work before me, is that the Brasillach archives are incomplete. The "dossier d'instruction," the file assembled by the examining magistrate in preparation for the court case, is missing from the National Archives. There is an empty folder, with a note that the file was borrowed by two magistrates in the 1960s and never returned. I knew what a typical journalist's dossier d'instruction looked like from studying similar Purge cases, and I was able to reconstruct the contents of that file from a host of sources:

microfilmed copies of *Je Suis Partout,* including the articles quoted by
the prosecution; defense lawyer Jacques Isorni's papers, kept in the Paris
Bar Association; the papers of prosecutor Marcel Reboul, kept by his
daughter, Bernadette Reboul Bertone; Brasillach's police interviews,
kept at the archives of the Prefecture de Police in Paris. Fortunately,
Brasillach's pardon file, separate from the dossier d'instruction, was not
lost. It had been locked in a safe in the National Archives in 1965 by an
official in the Justice Department; no one had looked at it since. When
I asked for it, in the winter of 1998, it was made available to me quickly.

As a result of Jospin's 1997 policy statement, the dérogations I
needed for my work will soon no longer be necessary. The archives
surrounding the war years will be open. Perhaps someday, Brasillach's
missing dossier d'instruction will show up, in the attic of a magistrate's
grandchild, or in an unopened box in the stacks of an archive.

––––––

History is not only the accumulation of facts, the recovery of documents;
it is also the understanding of passions. To uncover what I could about
this fifty-three-year-old trial, I sought out everyone I could find who
had been in that courtroom on January 19, or who had been a player
in the Purge. In several instances I was able to interview the surviving
relatives of long-deceased participants in the trial. I purposefully did not
work with Maurice and Suzanne Bardèche, Brasillach's surviving family
members (Maurice Bardèche died in July 1998), even though it is they
who hold Brasillach's papers. I had interviewed Maurice Bardèche in
1981 for an earlier book, *Reproductions of Banality* (1986), and I learned
what I could from him then. His polemical stake in his brother-in-
law's legacy was so overwhelming, he has played such a controlling
role in research on Brasillach, as guardian of the archives, editor of the
complete works, and defender of his brother-in-law's fascist beliefs, that
it was crucial to find sources that did not come from him. Hence the
importance, in my study, of government documents and interviews.
Often, I refer to original Brasillach publications from the 1930s and
1940s, rather than to the *Oeuvres complètes* edited by Bardèche in the
1960s. I uncover and juxtapose Brasillach's original writings with those
presented as "complete," analyzing the places where they have been
sanitized and distorted. I hope in this way not only to call attention to
one remarkable case of ideological distortion, but to provide a more
general model for understanding how revisionism around a literary
figure works.

––––––

One of the people who has been most helpful to me in my research is the daughter of the man who sought the death penalty against Brasillach, the prosecutor named Marcel Reboul. Bernadette Reboul is a conservative woman with a law degree, proud of her father's role in history. She sides with French journalist Henri Amouroux in thinking that the recent trial of Maurice Papon for crimes against humanity was a dangerous business for France. As she sees it, justice was done in 1945; the painful chapter of the Occupation years should not be opened up again in the courts. There are many distinguished bureaucrats—including police and judges—in her family, and she is loathe to think that the French bureaucracy bears any responsibility for the Holocaust. She feels protective of her country. "I only ask one thing of you," she said to me in a January 1987 phone conversation: "in your book about the Brasillach trial, do not sully France!"

What does it mean to sully France, or any country? What is the difference between critique and condemnation? That was the question of the Brasillach trial, too.

Legal culture is different in France than it is in the United States, and the national elements in this trial are instructive. It is likely that an American court would not have condemned Brasillach to death in a similar trial because of our traditional commitment to free speech. In making comparisons, one needs to remember that the Brasillach trial took place after four years of foreign occupation, during wartime. And that even in peacetime, our First Amendment has an exception. "Fighting words"—hate speech, language that does harm—is actionable under American law. In the case of Brasillach, fighting words came, not from a marginal or crazy man, but from someone who had enjoyed the best education France had to offer, a man of vast culture and enormous charm, capable of great loyalty and friendship, who was caught and destroyed in a series of escalating polemics and their violent consequences. Education only made his language carry further. For anyone who makes their living reading and writing, that is one of the most riveting aspects of this cautionary tale.

Language is at stake in the Brasillach trial, the capacity of language to do real evil. But there is more. Brasillach's story shows, to a horrifying extent, how the power conferred by talent and wit can be misused. During his lifetime, Brasillach put his pen in the service of a distorted notion of reality. Since his death, the way his own reality has been reconstructed is as clear an example I've ever seen of how painful histories—personal, political, national—are revised, to ease the pain of the survivors.

My search to provide missing information about Brasillach's trial, to restore its original context, is matched throughout this book by an attention to the way Brasillach's texts have been reshaped and misrepresented so that his history can be rewritten for political reasons. I have worked with a sense of urgency, knowing there are fewer and fewer readers alive today who still remember the violence of those original Brasillach articles in *Je Suis Partout*.

During this long labor of tracking and uncovering, many people have asked what was driving me. What was fueling my insatiable curiosity about this event, these characters? Again and again, an image from childhood came into my head. In 1963, when I was eight, I opened the bottom drawer of my father's desk and found a gray cardboard box filled with black-and-white photographs of the Nazi death camps. They had been used as evidence at the Nuremberg war crimes trials, where my father had served as a prosecutor in 1945. He had been dead for less than a year when I opened that drawer. Since that day, I have thought often about those photos and what they represent. As I traced the itinerary of Robert Brasillach, a writer who believed that Nazism was poetry, I felt the shock of those photos more intensely than ever.

Alice Kaplan
Chapel Hill
January 1999

ONE THE MAKING OF A FASCIST WRITER

In the last week of August 1944, Robert Brasillach was hiding in a tiny maid's room on the rue de Tournon. All around him was the joy of liberation and the violence of the final battles, as the Germans left Paris and the people of the city expended their energy in the construction of homemade barricades, blocking the last Nazi tanks that were trying to make their way along the city streets. Brasillach did not share in that popular joy. Like thousands of other men and women who believed that the previous four years of German occupation had been good for France, Brasillach now understood the Liberation as his own undoing. Many of these collaborators were tried in the months that followed. In hundreds of Purge trials, government officials, political assassins, radio broadcasters, fascist party hacks, and journalists all attempted to defend themselves against the charge that they had betrayed France for the German cause. No other defendant spoke as eloquently, appeared as dignified or as proud of his past actions, as Robert Brasillach. After it was all over, after Brasillach was executed by the Liberation government, he remained, in the public mind, the symbol of the collaborator for generations to come.

How did Robert Brasillach, a writer, come to play that singular and shameful role?

He was born on March 31, 1909, in Perpignan, France, near the Spanish border, where the wine is dark and pungent, the heat is dry, the landscape dotted with cliffs and sandy beaches. His father was a military man, a graduate of the Ecole St. Cyr, France's West Point. Lieutenant Arthémile Brasillach served in the regiment of Marshal Louis Lyautey, a colorful figure in French colonial history, and he was absent for most of Brasillach's early childhood, stationed at one colonial outpost or another. Family legend tells how Brasillach's mother, Marguerite Redo Brasillach, tiring of the long separation from her husband, finally succeeded in taking her family to Rabat, Morocco, to join him, despite an official military policy that forbade the presence of women and children with the colonial army. Thanks to his mother's determination, Brasillach's earliest, most romantic memory was of a charmed orientalist life in the exotic Moroccan landscape. The family idyll was cut short

by World War I. Brasillach's mother took her two children back to
Perpignan; Lieutenant Brasillach stayed stationed with Lyautey's army,
preoccupied with fighting rebellious indigenous tribes.

In 1914, Arthémile Brasillach was killed in Morocco in the Kénifra
skirmish. His son was not yet six. When the young boy was nine, his
widowed mother, still a beautiful woman at thirty-three, became engaged to a doctor stationed at Perpignan, Paul Maugis. When Brasillach
learned of the engagement, he sent his future stepfather a letter full of
insults. It was a good beginning for a polemicist.

Brasillach's letter did not prevent his mother from marrying Dr. Paul
Maugis and moving the family to his hometown of Sens. The north-
ernmost city in Burgundy, in the shadow of the Parisian capital, Sens
was a huge leap, geographically and culturally, from the warm south—
colder, wetter, and more sophisticated. It was in Sens that Brasillach and
his sister Suzanne, one year his junior, grew up and went to school,
returning to the beaches near Perpignan for their summers. A half sister,
Geneviève, was born in 1921. Brasillach and Suzanne were inseparable,
and delighted at putting on plays with Suzanne's dolls in the attic of
their multistory house. Brother-sister relationships, deeply affectionate,
protective, asexual, appear in much of his fiction.

Sens has been a walled city since Roman times. Today, its boulevard
du Mail still circles the town like a rampart. The eighteen-room house of
the Maugis-Brasillach family stood right on the boulevard. In immediate
range were the places common to all French towns that could influence a
boy growing up in the twilight of the Third Republic, and that certainly
influenced young Robert: the ugly wedding-cake city hall representing
the Republic he would come to hate; the imposing twelfth-century
Gothic Sens Cathedral with its famous relics; and on the boulevard itself,
an elaborate classical monument to the First World War dead, where the
names of hundreds of men from the generation of Brasillach's father were
inscribed in marble. Across from that monument was a glamorous art
deco movie house, the Rex. What a welcome relief it must have been
from the municipal architecture that surrounded it! Down the boulevard
from the Rex, right across the street from Brasillach's house, was a huge
square lycée that looked like a prison.

It was a comfortable, bourgeois childhood. Brasillach's stepfather
had a lucrative practice. At age sixteen, young Brasillach left the lycée
at Sens for Paris, to attend two years of classes at the Lycée Louis-le-
Grand, in preparation for the competitive exam that would guarantee
his entrance to France's most prestigious intellectual institution.

The first real sense we have of Brasillach as a young intellectual comes from his two years at Louis-le-Grand. There he met a group of boys who would become, in their different ways, significant intellectuals—teachers, writers, journalists. A classmate named Maurice Bardèche stood and watched one fateful day as Brasillach and a theatrical young man named Roger Vailland stood on chairs and recited verses of poetry at one another. At Louis-le-Grand, Vailland, who later became a flamboyant communist, already identified himself as a left-wing anarchist; Bardèche was already a young man of the right. In the coming months, Bardèche managed to coax Brasillach out of Vailland's orbit and into his own, though in his memoirs Bardèche claimed it was Brasillach who chose him.

Brasillach described Bardèche in his own writing about their youth as a tough fellow who "wore a black jacket cinched with a belt." He was, in Brasillach's words, "quick, enraged, subtle and stubborn." Bardèche taught Brasillach how to work, had him read Proust and Barrès, took him to *bistrots,* to parks, and to working-class neighborhoods. They walked through the city by day and night.

Bardèche described Brasillach: "He was very brown-skinned and brown-haired, not very tall, his cheeks less full than later on; he wore a sort of violet jerkin decorated with an owl that I never managed to convince him was hideous, and ugly metal glasses behind which his eyes, somber and sweet, cast a sympathetic glance at everything." Their favorite teacher at Louis-le-Grand, André Bellessort, was a passionate intellectual in the tradition of Charles Maurras who lectured on classical Mediterranean culture and inducted Brasillach, along with his friend Maurice, into right-wing royalism.

Brasillach was admitted number 26 to the literature section of the Ecole Normale, in the class that entered in 1928. Low in rank—26 out of 28, but he made it in, along with Maurice Bardèche and Thierry Maulnier from the Louis-le-Grand gang.

The Ecole Normale Supérieure in Paris was and is still, though to much a lesser extent than in the 1930s, the elite training ground for France's best students in literature, philosophy, and science. The Ecole was designed to prepare young intellectuals for a teaching career in the secondary schools and universities of France, but graduates of the school often went on to glorious careers as ministers and presidents of the Republic, as well as writers and public intellectuals. The Ecole Normale Supérieure of the late 1920s produced Jean-Paul Sartre, future French president Georges Pompidou, and philosophers Maurice

Merleau-Ponty and Simone Weil. Samuel Beckett came on a fellowship from Ireland in Brasillach's first year, 1928, and acted as an English-language tutor. Like similar institutions reserved for a young intellectual elite—Harvard, Oxford, and Cambridge—the Ecole was known for its freedom and for the relative laziness of its students. It was very hard to get in, but once you were in, you were "in." You could do what you wanted.

Normaliens practiced a certain style of practical joke or hoax for which the school was famous, known in a slang unique to the school as "canulars." The novelist Jules Romains, a generation older than Brasillach, had fictionalized the spirit of the Ecole in his novel *Les Copains* [The chums—1913], which Brasillach claimed to know practically by heart. Brasillach later said about Romains that, for him, the entire world was like a vast high school in whose halls you could wander as an eternal adolescent trickster. Brasillach liked to think of himself as a lighthearted trickster in the Romains tradition. At the same time, this was not any high school, and these were not ordinary tricks. The literary *normaliens* were imbued with a long erudite tradition, with a sense of their own high culture references, their own place in a tradition. The pressure of excelling at oral exams made them born intellectual performers from the time they were eighteen. In front of the Ecole Normale, there's a sight line down the rue d'Ulm straight to the Pantheon, where France buries her heroes: Voltaire, Rousseau, Hugo, Marie Curie. Busts of great men line the rooftops on the second floor of the Ecole Normale building, and on a warm spring day students love to crawl out along the statuary. The school lends itself to childlike games and Pantheon-like ambitions.

In Brasillach's records from the Ecole, kept in the National Archives along with all the other *normaliens'* files (a mark of the centralized French system, and the care taken to record the careers of the elite), his file is stamped "pupil of the nation." As the son of a man who died for his country, he qualified for a full scholarship. One of his teachers in his second year (1929) lauded his class report on a Baudelaire poem and referred to his qualities as "essentially literary." As the 1930s advanced, along with Brasillach's career, different qualities emerged: Brasillach became a pungent critic, capable of the perfectly pointed insult, and he became the editor of a weekly newspaper that dreamed of a fascist future for France.

———

Robert Brasillach was a short round man with tiny shoulders. In some of his photos he looks like Charlie Chaplin in *Modern Times.* He wore the huge black-rimmed glasses that were standard at the time, which made his olive skin look paler than it was. He bore no resemblance to our stereotypical image of a black-shirted fascist tough guy. He looked harmless, a slightly chubby bookworm. It's very difficult today to get any reliable sense of his personality at age twenty, age thirty. The accounts that do exist are retrospective, clearly influenced by his later career as a fascist, or by his retrospective aura as a man condemned to death. A book published in the 1990s on the history of the Ecole Normale, playing to any number of clichés, suggests that Brasillach was a boy who liked to be bullied by meaner boys, who liked to give in. Apologetic accounts by friends describe him in exactly the opposite vein, as a charismatic leader whose charm and spirited love of literature drew people to him.

Along with Jules Romains's *Les Copains,* Brasillach's literary ideal was Alain-Fournier's 1913 novel *Le Grand Meaulnes,* the "Catcher in the Rye" of turn-of-the-century French adolescence. The plot is baroque, involving two young men, Auguste Meaulnes and Frantz de Galais, and their intersecting love affairs. Meaulnes loves Frantz's sister, Yvonne, and eventually marries her. But his loyalty to Frantz comes first, and so he loses Yvonne again. The early scenes of the novel are set in a magic castle hidden in the woods, where Meaulnes and Yvonne first meet. The writing is poetic, mystical; the male characters are innocent and masochistic, the women have either fallen from grace, or they are pure and unobtainable. Alain-Fournier's friendship with Jacques Rivière, who married Alain-Fournier's sister, provided one inspiration for the novel, and Alain-Fournier's story became Brasillach's own ideal: "I, too, wanted to write 'in tight, voluptuous little paragraphs' a story that might have been my own." He was attracted to a sensual writing style, and to a life that would lend itself to prose.

Politically, Brasillach was drawn from his earliest student days to the Action Française. The Action Française was at once a political party—the cradle of the French right wing in this century—a daily newspaper, and a way of thinking. The Action Française stood for anti-Semitic nationalism, royalism and Catholicism, and for hatred of foreigners—Germans as much as Jews. Its leader, Charles Maurras, took himself for a modern-day Socrates and promoted the cultural myth of a true French genius, "Mediterranean" or "Latin." Victor Hugo, paterfamilias of nineteenth-century literature and of Third Republic politics, was Maurras's nemesis. A militant offshoot of the Action Française called the "Camelots du Roi" fought on the street in its name, but there was always something abstract and almost unreal about the movement. It was, despite its Catholic, royalist pretensions, fundamentally oppositional—it was condemned at various times both by the Pope and the Count of Paris. Although Maurras was already a deaf old man by the time Brasillach first heard him speak, the movement still benefited, in the young man's eyes, from a revolutionary spirit. In Brasillach and Bardèche's milieu, the Action Française had the counterculture flavor of a "society for creative anachronism."

At a time when his friends were pairing off and marrying, there were no significant romantic figures in Brasillach's own life, but there are many allusions in his memoirs about the 1920s and 1930s to gracious young women who served as a kind of gentle décor for a charmed life. Claude Roy described Brasillach, pointedly, as a man who kept people at a "magic lantern's distance," who loved books close up but could only love women from afar.

Then one of his deepest literary wishes, his own *Grand Meaulnes,* came true. His best friend, Maurice Bardèche, became involved with his sister, Suzanne. Brasillach had introduced them at the Ecole Normale, when Suzanne, also a student in Paris, came to work in their rooms. In 1932 Brasillach wrote Bardèche, grilling him about his intentions towards Suzanne. Brasillach's desires and his sister's are so tightly linked in this letter that it reads like a marriage proposal for three:

> You talk about staying with us or going off to the Far East. And all that is a very big salad, dear and strange Nice. Do you see, there are two little points that you neglect in all you're telling me, and these two points are extremely important and the most important: it's that Suzanne loves you. First of all. And next that you love her and that you are jealous like a ferocious Siamese. A veritable Turk. Don't believe, in spite of all that I've told you, that I would want to separate from her—or from you—our way of life is something to be seen according to circumstances; but you can be very certain that I want, as much as possible, to live with the two of you.

When Bardèche and Suzanne went on their honeymoon, Brasillach went with them. From 1933 until the Liberation forced Brasillach into hiding, the three formed a household, first in the Vaugirard neighborhood, then on the rue Rataud, behind their dear Ecole Normale.

———

Brasillach's sexuality has been the subject of much speculation and little analysis. His principal biographers, Pierre Pellissier and Anne Brassié, present him as an eternal boy with discreet romances on the side; neither of them mentions homosexuality. Both go to great pains to describe his relationships with women, but the descriptions feel forced. In the absence of direct evidence in the form of interviews or letters, it's impossible to speak definitively about Brasillach's lived sexual life. It is significant, nonetheless, that he was perceived by several of his contemporaries, and by any number of commentators since, as a homosexual. Homoeroticism colors his work as early as a 1931 essay on Virgil. From the 1930s until his death, his writing is filled with references to the power and beauty of friendships among men.

The particular current of Nazi masculinity in Brasillach's writing suggests that his fascism may have been sparked and nourished by homoerotic feeling. His contemporaries—Louis-Ferdinand Céline and Pierre Drieu la Rochelle on the right, notably—refer to him repeatedly as a homosexual, but their remarks appear in private diaries and correspondence, in the form of insults. In a postwar essay, schoolmate Etiemble famously dubbed Brasillach and Bardèche "brasillèche et bardache" (lèche in French means "lick" and bardache means "a boy lover or young male prostitute). Because of the homophobia and sarcasm of these references, it is tempting to ignore the entire issue.

"Sociological problem: Why so many pederasts among the collaborators?" asks Jean Guéhenno in his Occupation diary in June 1941, at the beginning of a passage in which he mentions Brasillach by name. He perceives a link between fascism and homosexuality, but he doesn't have an answer to his question. It is a question that arouses suspicion today, in a society less threatened by sexual nonconformism. A critic of our own generation might be more likely to ask how many homosexuals were drawn to the resistance out of disgust with Vichy's family values.

In the specific case of Brasillach, what is historically significant is that the *accusation* of homosexuality haunts him, up to and especially during his trial. From what little we know about his life—his worshipful attitude towards powerful men, the central role of male friendship in his life, and, concurrently, the fragile dream-like quality of his relations with women—his attraction to fascist ritual seems to have been his way of living out a certain kind of homoerotic longing. When historians of fascist culture talk about the homoerotic pull of fascist culture, Brasillach's writing on the appeal of Nazi Germany certainly presents itself as a strong primary source.

Novelist Jean-Louis Bory, interviewed for the documentary film *Chantons sous l'occupation* (1976), acknowledged the existence of a homosexual collaborationist milieu in occupied Paris, and speculated on the attraction of gay collaborators to a Nazi esthetic. Brasillach is his case in point:

> As for the presence of the German army in Paris, there was a fascination that could play on homosexuals, the fascination that plays on the myth of virility, when virility is confused with force and with a sort of courage . . . a taste for boots, leather, metal, and the famous Nuremberg masses in which, obviously, homosexuals—I am thinking specifically of someone like Brasillach—could find the exaltation of a humanity to their liking. This is accurate. But it is not a reason for the attraction towards the military to teach you to collaborate with Nazism. That is a different problem.

Whatever the reality of his sexual life, Brasillach's writing suggests a homoerotic attraction to the rituals of fascism. Yet it would be far too easy to call on a trumped-up diagnosis of Brasillach as a homosexual, in a facile homophobic mode, to explain away this attraction. How many other fatherless sons were there among fascists? How many children of men killed in the First World War? And among them, how many only sons? Even if we had the answer to these questions, they could not account for the strange and disturbing specificity of Robert Brasillach's political trajectory.

His twenty-first year, 1931, marked Brasillach's coming of age as a critic. It was his third year at the Ecole Normale, and he was writing regular criticism for the *Revue Française,* the *Revue Universelle,* and the *Action Française.* He had already scored his first critical coup in 1930, in the *Revue Française.* It was a mock obituary for André Gide, who wasn't in the least dead. Gide was sixty years old, a monument of Parisian literary life and a maverick politically and personally—a former adept of the Action Française who had migrated towards communism; a Protestant who ended up a fervent atheist; a dry, ascetic personality who nonetheless argued, in *L'Immoraliste,* for bodily pleasure through homosexual love. Brasillach, in his pseudo-obituary, announced that Gide, once a profound influence on him, was now a washed up old man who had nothing more to say. He might as well be dead, so why not bury him? In the 1944 volume where he gathered this article along with the rest of his criticism, Brasillach said in a proud footnote that this article had earned him a mention in Gide's famous diary. In fact, Gide hadn't dignified the article by mentioning Brasillach by name, but he did refer to the title of the article: "Funeral Oration for M. Gide."

Brasillach's first critical success was, significantly, a death sentence. He discovered that he could make a name for himself by being clever—viciously clever—in print.

There was no better place to be viciously clever than the *Action Française*. Léon Daudet, in his regular column, as well as the old master Charles Maurras, were known, in the political and esthetic realm, for the bite and wit of their attacks, both ad hominem and doctrinaire, against anything left wing, democratic, Jewish, cosmopolitan, parliamentarian. In a writer like Daudet, these attacks had a rambling, hallucinatory quality; his rhetorical pleasure, his humor, often seemed to supersede the content of his critique. The Action Française, more than the Ecole Normale, schooled Brasillach in an approach, as well as a doctrine.

In June of 1931, Brasillach published his first book, *Présence de Virgile*. It was derivative of his teacher André Bellessort's book and lectures on Virgil, but Brasillach's strengths and weaknesses as a critic were already apparent in this first effort: a wide-eyed sensual style, a clear sense of chronology, a traditional assumption of a direct relationship between a writer's life and work, a right-wing emphasis on native geography, and, especially, an unapologetic projection of his own desires that gave the story life and verve, but made it finally more Brasillach's story than Virgil's.

The choice of Virgil was a political as well as a cultural one: every self-respecting Action Française intellectual could quote pages of the Latin poet by heart. *Présence de Virgile* is also Brasillach's most open apology, if not for homosexuality, than for the joys of love between men:

> He [Virgil] loved to surround himself with young people. A perfectly beautiful boy named Cebetès, who wrote poems and sang them, accompanying himself on his flute, lived in his house in Naples. And Virgil was often taken by the ambiguous charm of his peers. These are things we must not judge as Frenchmen of 1930 with our Christian heritage. Not only did everyone around him find this way of loving or this form of pleasure natural, but even more, in Virgil, it existed along with a voluptuousness that his friends recognized in him with a smile, it existed along with this desire to find his lost youth, even alongside the worry, the sorrow, the suspicion, the desolate nights, the jealousy.

In defending Virgil's love for boys as natural and charming, Brasillach was also presenting the Latin poet as an emblem of the "Mediterranean genius" endorsed by Maurras; his habits, his geography, his sensuality were all part of this genius, transcending the limits of the nineteenth-century image of the writer as paterfamilias against which the Action Française was in revolt.

The timing of this first book publication had a decisive effect on Brasillach's career. It clearly announced his affinities with the Action Française, and it distanced him decisively from the academic world, not so much because of its content, but because he chose to write and publish *Présence de Virgile* during the period when he was supposed to be preparing the *agrégation,* the national competition or "concours" that most students at the Ecole Normale take at the end of their third year at the school. Success in the agrégation guarantees entry into the French civil service as part of the national teaching corps. Maurice Bardèche took this route and eventually became a university professor. Brasillach failed the agrégation twice, in 1930 and 1931, and never took it again. He was doubtless too distracted by the excitement of literary journalism and by his first book project to concentrate on mastering the reading list for the agrégation, a task to which most successful candidates devote a year of intense study. Moreover, his writerly personality didn't lend itself to success in this most scholarly of French exercises, involving rigorous study of a discrete set of literary texts, disciplined answers in the French Cartesian style, references to an obligatory set of critics, and the thorough rehearsal of well-known arguments and positions. It was just the kind of exercise at which he liked to thumb his nose: spitting back wasn't his style. Without the agrégation, an academic career was closed to Brasillach. *Présence de Virgile* cinched his career as a full-time journalist and freelance writer.

In September 1931, Brasillach made another decisive transition: from literary critic to cultural critic and right-wing pundit, with decadence as his target. He conducted a series of interviews in *Candide,* a widely read cultural paper, asking well-known writers to comment on "the end of the postwar [period]." The First World War had destroyed an entire generation of French youth and had left the survivors in varying states of physical and psychological trauma. It also deeply inflected both French and German literary expression. In his series for *Candide,* Brasillach gathered together statements by royalist Action Française writers, conservative members of the Académie Française— France's traditionalist academy of letters—and writers associated with the highly intellectual *Nouvelle Revue Française* group. Gide and the surrealists came under particular attack. In response to the voices of his contemporaries, Brasillach condemned the decadence, the madness, the drug use apparent in so much writing by survivors of the Great War. He concluded his survey with a plea to move on to a healthier literature. It was an important statement for the young critic to make, because it established him as an expert not just on literature but on *moeurs* and on "eras," on the combination of event and mood that distinguishes one cultural moment from another. The "end of the postwar" survey was another Brasillach "coup," reported and quoted angrily by several newspapers to the left of *Candide,* giving the twenty-two-year-old critic further visibility.

1931 was also the year that Brasillach was put in charge of the literary page for the *Action Française* newspaper. At twenty-one, he was the youngest critic ever to write for that paper. *Action Française* was the newspaper of the royalist right, but it was more than that. It had a reputation as the indispensable newspaper for people who were interested in literature, whatever their politics. During the 1930s, if you were a young person with literary ambitions, anywhere in France, you bought both *L'Humanité,* the newspaper of the Communist Party, and the *Action Française,* for the book reviews. Thanks to his role at the paper, Brasillach became, if not a household name, a critic known to every amateur of literature, right and left. Even Walter Benjamin read the *Action Française* daily. Léautaud, an avid diarist in the 1930s, describes Brasillach's beginnings at the paper: he was impressive, at first, precisely because he didn't seem to have swallowed the cranky newspaper's party line and he wrote whatever he felt like. His articles were self-assured, cheeky, and memorable.

"Indefatigable" is the word that comes to mind in tracing Brasillach's beginnings as a man of letters. In 1931 alone he published the book on Virgil and a fictionalized transcript of the trial of Joan of Arc, and he became the regular critic for the *Action Française.* After he consolidated his position at Maurras's paper, he began to contribute literary and cultural articles to a second newspaper, *Je Suis Partout,* a "political and literary" international weekly, affiliated with the Action Française but younger in spirit and ambition, focusing on the world beyond France.

———

Between 1932 and 1939, Brasillach distanced himself from the classic Action Française line and moved squarely into the camp of French fascists at *Je Suis Partout.* There was nothing automatic about this evolution. Someone who started out on the nationalist, royalist right, so suspicious of all foreign influence, was not destined to become an apologist for the Nazis.

One single event, on February 6, 1934, was decisive in this evolution. On that day, nationalist groups protesting the corruption of parliamentary democracy marched down the Champs Elysées and fought with the Republican Guards in front of the Chamber of Deputies. Among them were the Camelots du Roi from the Action Française, and the Croix de Feu, a veteran's group. At a key moment, the Croix de Feu refused to charge on parliament and the event fizzled. Still, there were casualties, and consequences. Fifteen rioters died, 1,500 people were wounded, and the left-leaning government in power immediately resigned. Brasillach, who, characteristically, was out at the theater rather than on the streets that night, barely mentioned the riots in his literary columns but returned to the site each subsequent year with a bouquet of violets. February 6 became much more important for him retrospectively than in the moment. It came to represent the dashed hopes of a fascist takeover of France—the fantasized equivalent of Hitler's abortive beer hall putsch of 1923. After 1934, Brasillach would refer to the martyrs of February 6, struck down in the joy of their spontaneous demonstration by the men who guarded the symbol of Republican democracy—the Chamber of Deputies. February 6 furnished the extreme right with a spectacle and a narrative of revolt. The riots were also a warning to the left that if they didn't organize, fascism was a possibility in France. Henceforth, two camps were in place: there were fascists and antifascists in France. They even had their opposing salutes: the French fascists pointed their arms straight forward, as if about to show the Nazi "Heil!"; the Popular Front antifascists raised their arms upward and clenched their hands in a power fist.

Over the next two years, Robert Brasillach emerged on the public scene as the cultural spokesperson for a French fascism. 1936 was the point of no return. That year, Léon Blum, a Jew and a socialist, become head of the French government—part of an antifascist, socially progressive, worker-oriented Popular Front government that had gained power two years after the left's February 6, 1934, defeat. Brasillach reacted to the victory of the left in classic extreme right style, by accusing the traditional right wing of impotence, of being cuckolded. In the pages of *Je Suis Partout,* he became familiar to French readers as the author of a column, "Letters to a Provincial" (the reference is to Pascal's "The Provincials"), where he made fun of the Paris scene. Roasting the left-wing Popular Front was a constant theme. He was now a regular at *Je Suis Partout,* not just an occasional contributor. In 1936, too, he visited the Belgian Léon Degrelle, head of the fascist Rex Party, and wrote a romantic portrait of Degrelle's "Rex-Appeal."

Social life combined with political life to move the young writer towards fascist activism. Brasillach became involved in 1936 in a group called the "Rive Gauche Society," organized by a man named Henri Jamet and his wife, the petite, nervous young Annie Jamet, a militant right-winger and mother of six. Brasillach called her "the bird"; they spoke on the phone for hours, traveled together with groups of friends, planned events for the group's lecture series. In November of that year, Brasillach gave a series of lectures for Annie Jamet's "Rive Gauche" group on the topic "Will Europe Be Fascist?" He positioned himself, paradoxically and provocatively, as an Action Française variety fascist. The concept of "national socialism," he argued, was a term that had been invented by Charles Maurras—not Hitler. Nazism had a French birthright. Brasillach outlined burgeoning fascist movements in Italy, Rumania, Spain, Portugal, and Belgium. He suggested that the entire political world could be classified into destructive antifascists and constructive nationalists or fascists. France needed to choose sides. He mentioned that "the Jewish element" was an obstacle to the expansion of fascism, for (and here he had no argument, merely a definition): "fascism is anti-Semitic." Hitler, he continued, was a poet, a mythmaker, a Wagnerian orchestra conductor. The French should use Germany as a role model and "abandon their skepticism" towards fascism: "the reform that is needed in France must be social and national. To succeed, the French must find their poetry, their myths, their French images, as well as confidence in themselves and in a national ideal." He was asking the French to believe in a fascism that would be all their own, to invest their very imaginations in the fascist cause.

The scandal of Brasillach's concept of fascism is that he relied on the reference points and vocabulary of a literary critic—images, poetry, myths—with barely a reference to politics, economics, or ethics. He had no French leader in mind to bring about this social and national reform, nor did his brand of fascist reform revolve around a specific social or economic program. His fascism, from all appearances, was founded on esthetics and on racism, which together were supposed to restore national self-confidence and fortify a myth of the nation. All fascist movements throughout Europe were a source of wonderment to Brasillach, but he betrayed no concern about how these warring nationalisms might coexist. He did not ask, in his 1936 lecture, whether Hitler's "Wagnerian orchestration" had dangerous consequences for the

French. One might consider his "Will Europe Be Fascist?" lecture laughably naive. To the extent that it avoided the tough questions of economics and politics, it was also clever, designed to entertain a bourgeois audience for whom the political process was as chimerical as a good novel.

In 1937, Robert Brasillach became *Je Suis Partout*'s editor in chief. Although he was moderate in his tone and temperament compared to others on the paper—the rabid anti-Semite Lucien Rebatet or Pierre Antoine Cousteau, a specialist in Anglo-American conspiracy theory—Brasillach was nonetheless in charge. The atmosphere at *Je Suis Partout* was lively, polemical, and chummy, in the style to which Brasillach had become accustomed at the Ecole. Enthusiasts of Italian and German fascism, enemies of communism and of the Jews, they jokingly called their editorial team the "Soviet."

In 1937, Brasillach traveled to the Nuremberg Party Congress with Annie Jamet. Under the spell of that visit, he wrote his essay about the seduction of Nazism, "100 Hours with Hitler," published in the *Revue Universelle* in October 1937. The *Revue Universelle* was an Action Française publication; Brasillach was writing for the not-yet-converted.

In "100 Hours with Hitler," Brasillach continued to express the excitement over Nazism that had characterized his 1936 Rive Gauche lecture, only here he was obliged to punctuate his prose with notes of skepticism, to mollify the readers of the *Revue Universelle,* with their strong Action Française loyalties and traditional Germanophobia. He explained Hitler's Germany entirely on the basis of images, as though Nazism were purely spectacle, rather than a political reality. Brasillach exclaimed and worried about fascist ritual, about Hitler's power to move crowds with his voice, about his use of techniques from cinema and theater, about the beauty of flags and parades, and about the strangeness of all this from a French perspective. He found Nazi Germany so foreign as to be "oriental":

> And this is what is so alarming. Faced with this serious, delicious décor of an erstwhile romanticism, faced with this immense flowering of flags, faced with these crosses from the Orient [a reference to the swastika], I asked myself . . . if anything goes. . . . I don't know what the Germany of old was like. Today it is a great, strange country, further from us than India and China.

One has no sense that there is a critical edge to Brasillach's worry. What is clear is that is he is titillated, and fascinated, by what bothers him.

On the subject of anti-Semitism, Brasillach described a sign he saw
at the entrance to several villages and several inns: "Jews are not *desired*
here," admiring it for its "contained politeness." Only a single phrase
in the essay—"flowers don't prevent other more menacing realities"—
suggests that Nazi Germany may have been more than theater and image.
But Brasillach does not pursue the "menacing realities." "Everything
here is founded on a doctrine," he remarked, but he doesn't discuss
the doctrine.

Brasillach describes Hitler himself, with a touch of realism designed
to set up the magical contrast, as a "small, sad, vegetarian civil servant"
transformed by the power of Nazism into a god, an archangel descended
onto earth, even an archangel of death, capable of destroying his oldest
and dearest companions. Here Brasillach was referring to the 1934 Night
of the Long Knives, where Hitler had radical elements of the Nazi Party
(Röhm and his followers in the SA) murdered. Brasillach turns Hitler's
betrayal into a frightening but heroic, superhuman gesture. For Brasillach
to qualify Hitler as the "archangel of death" shows strikingly how
ready he was to romanticize even the most odious political infighting
and treachery.

In the place of infighting and treachery, Brasillach substituted the
camaraderie of the Hitlerjugend in their work camps: their joy and their
discipline, and their singing about "the seriousness, the virility, the hard
and powerful love of the country, the total devotion, all expressed in this
language of songs and in the chorus which is the true maternal language
of Germany." The spectacle of young men working together for mother
Nazi Germany is the utopian element that, for Brasillach, crowned and
exemplified the fascist achievement.

The fact that Brasillach was a film critic might lead one to conclude
that he saw Germany as a film. For another kind of critic, it might have
been a horror film, but for him it was an epic borrowed almost straight
from *Triumph of the Will*, Leni Riefenstahl's propaganda documentary.
Brasillach staked out in Nazi Germany a territory that was, in his words,
"a magic fortress." Hitler's Germany came to represent for him, after 100
brief hours, the space of a fairy tale, terrifying but also exciting.

A year after he traveled to Germany with Annie Jamet, the young
woman died suddenly. Brasillach worked feverishly to turn a second
series of Rive Gauche lectures on the classical tragedian Pierre Corneille
into a book dedicated to her memory. Corneille's theatrical characters,
were, in his imagination, recognizable contemporary figures: Polyeucte
was Charlie Chaplin, Horace was a young blond Nazi. Brasillach tried

to make Corneille's famous "will" into the same thing as Hitlerian will, as exemplified by Riefenstahl's documentary. *Corneille* was evidence that Brasillach couldn't stop dreaming about fascism, even—especially— when he was writing about the most traditional of French writers, the writer whose verses were memorized by every French school child. *Je Suis Partout* ran this ad for his Corneille lectures in 1938:

> Did you know that Corneille was: novelistic? ironic? antiparliamentarian? a precursor of fascism? Come listen to Robert Brasillach's four lectures. And see the staging of unknown, forgotten plays (*Clitandre, Théodore, Attila, Suréna*) that will reveal the true face of Corneille.

His writing was becoming more and more polarized; his journalism about France more and more bitter and pointed, denunciatory; his writing about fascism, in Italy, Germany, Belgium, and Spain, even in Corneille's theater—more and more heroic, romantic and soft focus, like the magic castle in his favorite novel, *Le Grand Meaulnes,* like one of his beloved films, or like one of his own novels at their most sentimental. Why this need to romanticize? It is as though for this writer, all versions of the world must be charming and seductive, or else totally corrupt. Germany, at a distance, was exotic, unknown, skillful at projecting its own propaganda, and therefore perfectly equipped to play the magic role in Brasillach's polarized narrative. The evil, corrupt world was located at home, represented by the Republic, by the Popular Front, by democracy.

As a consequence of this point of view, Brasillach's literary criticism was becoming increasingly politicized, and cruel. In 1937, he published this jab at François Mauriac: "Dostoyevsky, Gide, Proust, are reflected with ease in Mauriac's little novels, like high cliffs in a hand mirror." It was a funny and a nasty way of saying that Mauriac was derivative of great writers, but could only render them in a tiny domesticated way. Brasillach accused François Mauriac of lack of originality, lack of virility, of petit-bourgeois mediocrity, of idiocy. He accused him of being interested in left-wing politics. He even accused him of growing old. In 1938, he described Julien Benda, a regular contributor to the *Nouvelle Revue Française* and author of an influential essay, *The Treason of the Clercs,* as a "circumcised diplodocus." In a review of *Portraits,* Brasillach's first published collection of literary criticism, his teacher, André Bellessort, wrote: "Mr. Brasillach will perhaps remain more faithful to his antipathies, which are certainly justified, than to all his admiration. . . . He is a master of the attack."

The master of the attack remained at both *Je Suis Partout* and the *Action Française* until 1939, but his political identity was squarely with the group at *Je Suis Partout,* who were staking out an international fascist politics at a considerable distance from Maurras. Their old mentor was sentenced to an eight-month jail sentence in 1937 for calling for the murder of Léon Blum in the pages of his newspaper. Maurras was a violent verbal opponent of left Republicanism and a vicious anti-Semite. The difference between what he was preaching at *Action Française* and what *Je Suis Partout* was preaching in its pages is a matter of degree and focus. The younger generation at *Je Suis Partout* wanted to go beyond violent oppositionalism; they were suggesting a positive solution to France's ills through a French brand of fascism allied with the movements that already existed in Belgium, Italy, Germany, Portugal, and Spain. They had moved from right-wing nationalism to fascist internationalism.

Brasillach's political and literary heyday was cut short in 1939, when he was drafted into the French army. This was the start of the *drôle de guerre,* or "phony war," the period from 1939 to 1940, before the combat began, when the French sent its officers out on alert. During the previous eight years, the period from 1931–1939, he had evolved from Action Française nationalist to European fascist. He had found the time, in addition to his intense work as a reviewer and critic of contemporary literature and as a newspaper editor, to publish a book on Virgil, an adaptation of the trial transcript of Joan of Arc, a critical study of Corneille, two volumes on the Spanish Civil War coauthored with Maurice Bardèche, a book on the Belgian fascist Léon Degrelle, a major history of film, also coauthored with Maurice Bardèche, a collection of his literary criticism, an essay on contemporary theater, and five novels. He had visited Spain, Germany, Belgium, Italy, and North Africa. At thirty years old, he was a sparkling, feared critic, a controversial political pundit, and a cultural celebrity of the extreme right.

———

We know almost nothing about Brasillach's private life during this period of extraordinary literary production. It is not clear he had much of one. After Annie Jamet's death, he wrote, in an uncharacteristically confessional tone, "For me, who perhaps hasn't had a true friendship, of the kind I want to call virile, for any other woman but her, I still can't believe today that she no longer exists." A biographer refers to his letters to a woman from Sens who was in love with him, but they consisted mostly of apologies for dates canceled or rescheduled. Eventually, he hired her as his typist. What is certain is that he worked constantly, and that he took enormous pleasure in his work.

To the mystery of Brasillach's private life we can add a second mystery—his famous "double personality" as a writer. He was a powerful, witty critic, and a maudlin, sentimental novelist. As a critic, he mocked the kind of whimpering sentiment he himself indulged in his own fiction. This is not only a double personality, but a personality where one half—the critic—disapproves of the other half—the writer. This paradox or duplicity is worth examining.

Was Brasillach really, in the public mind of 1931–1939, the future of French literature, as his defenders would later say? Or was he a mediocre novelist, who hadn't made the transition from criticism to fiction? We can assess the novels and the criticism on their own merit, and we can get an idea from reviews of the period of the way Brasillach was perceived by his contemporaries, long before his death sentence cast its retrospective aura on his work.

Brasillach's career as a novelist began in 1932 with *Le Voleur d'étincelles* [The star stealer]. He constructed this first novel around a typical nationalist theme—the young Parisian student who returns to his roots in the south. As in much of Brasillach's future fiction, it's a magical world full of charming eccentric characters, observed by a clever narrator who is enamored of all he sees, but who remains, at the same time, distant, only experiencing life through the experiences of others. The most remarkable scene of the book, in terms of the author's psychology, comes at the end, where the young narrator is about to kiss an older woman on the beach. Their tender moment is interrupted by the woman's little boy, who has an accident. The narrator never gets his kiss. The kiss unrealized is the emblem of that distance.

His next two novels, *L'Enfant de la nuit* (1934) [Child of the night], and *Le Marchand d'oiseaux* (1936) [The bird peddler] don't deviate from the initial formula: eccentric characters; a charming but distant and quizzical narrator; picturesque settings, involving long, thick descriptions of offbeat surroundings. In *L'Enfant de la nuit* that setting is the Vaugirard neighborhood of Paris, among a sentimentalized lower middle class. As in *Le Voleur d'étincelles,* the scene is dominated by women, chief among whom is a fortuneteller and her homely but endearing niece. The narrator watches as the unfortunate girl falls in love with a gangster who is only interested in using her to commit a crime. Ultimately, the narrator and his friends succeed in rescuing the girl when she tries to drown herself. In telling this story, the narrator invokes nostalgia for his own lost youth, but whatever emotional connection he has to this poor homely girl is less apparent than his titillation by the low-life gangster who threatens her.

In *Le Marchand d'oiseaux,* Brasillach develops the penchant already apparent in *L'Enfant de la nuit* for violence and crime underneath a gentle surface. A lonely, aging woman adopts a pair of urchins, who murder another old lady to get her money. Brasillach plays on our expectations, contrasting the loneliness of the old women with the reckless violence of the children. It is powerful and disturbing material for fiction, but the novel is marred, once again, by a hapless narrator who observes these events from too far. His tepid love for a student named Isabelle, who ends up marrying one of his friends, adds nothing to the book. Brasillach is caught in the classic problem of the narrator-witness: he never succeeds in involving his narrator in the events he observes and, consequently, the reader is kept at arm's length from the novel.

Reviews of Brasillach's early novels aren't uniform, but one word that does appear repeatedly is "féerique"—fairy-like, magical, charming. One early critic warns that he's in danger of becoming formulaic, insipid. Even his friend, Thierry Maulnier, who referred in the *Action Française* to Brasillach's "destiny as a novelist," still complained in his review of *L'Enfant de la nuit* that Brasillach gave the reader too much consolation for the evil in his novel and that his work as a whole "lacked cruelty"— a judgment that would have been astonishing to anyone familiar with Brasillach's sting as a critic.

Today, Brasillach is dated; his writing looks precious and juvenile. What the *London Times* and the *Action Française* once considered "magic realism" has nothing in common with the bold fantastic magic realism so admired since the 1970s in Latin American fiction. Brasillach is naive and simplistic, almost Victorian by comparison. A letter he wrote to a fan in the late '30s shows that he, too, was dissatisfied with his own progress as a novelist, even though he was producing steadily. He wondered if he'd ever make it.

He wouldn't, or would at best halfway. His good maternal figures, his storytellers who observe more than they live, a surfeit of charming and minute description and a fairy-tale atmosphere, don't add up to entirely successful books. Brasillach's novels fail, as we shall see, partly because the relationships between men and women aren't plausible in his work. His narrators are too distanced and uninvolved; everything happens by proxy. The style itself is uneven. The critic for the *Nouvelle Revue Française* throws up his hands in consternation after reading *Le Voleur d'étincelles:* "Sometimes there are admirable pages, analyses, and descriptions done with great talent. Mixed with this is an ineffable naïveté."

———

There was one genre where Brasillach's strength as a critic and his talent for thick description came together, and that was in film criticism—the perfect genre for someone who, in Claude Roy's phrase, kept the world at a "magic lantern's distance." *Histoire du cinéma,* written by Brasillach with Maurice Bardèche in 1935, is more charming and genuinely interesting than any of Brasillach's novels. *Histoire du cinéma* was probably the first general history of cinema written in France, if not the world. One might go as far as to say that the French conception of the director as an artistic creator, as opposed to a studio hack, originated here, rather than with the New Wave critics of the 1950s to whom the phrase "cinéma d'auteur" is usually attributed. *Histoire du cinéma* told the story of cinema's birth and the traumatic transition from silent to talking films; it categorized and described films in a straightforward manner by national origin and by director. Bardèche's more directive, academic skills doubtless gave the writing a shape and direction that Brasillach would have lacked on his own. Brasillach and Bardèche were looking at cinema with their literary training, yet they respected the genre for what was unique in it. They didn't want cinema to be merely theater on the screen. Hence their preference for the "mystery" of artistic silent film, and their regret at the success of talkies. Their history was thorough, at a time when there was as yet no global assessment of cinema as an art. It was not merely encyclopedic; it was written with grace and charm. Even today, many descriptions of classic films, and actors, still hold up, such as this description of Chaplin's genius:

> Then gradually, [Chaplin] evolved an individual comic style based on the conflict between this little figure and a world ruled by somewhat analogous but radically different laws. What better moment to invoke Henri Bergson and his theory that laughter is produced by the imposition of the mechanical onto the living. Chaplin gets into trouble because he imitates the habits and the customs of real human beings. He imitates and he doesn't understand. He is a hero who dismays other heroes, a benefactor who profoundly shocks other benefactors. In its detail, his comedy arises most frequently from an extraordinary application of familiar gestures and reactions—he sows

wheat as a child makes mud pies, opens a clock as a person opens a can, sucks the nails in the soles of his shoes as if they were chicken bones and swallows boot laces as though they were spaghetti. In every case he has imitated, with the most scrupulous attention to detail, the behavior proper to quite a different set of circumstances.

With this book, lively and informative, Brasillach and Bardèche reached a whole generation enamored of the movies, who wanted to know, as passionately as they did, what the new form was amounting to. It was reedited many times and translated into many languages, notably by Iris Barry, for the New York Museum of Modern Art, in 1938. The book forever identified Brasillach with film culture and film criticism, and it gave Brasillach a wider readership for his other books. In later editions, during the war, the authors added anti-Semitic quips, to make their political commitment more explicit and to please the Germans. It is sad to measure the changes they made to correspond with their views: Leni Riefenstahl's *Triumph of the Will* is "monotonous and occasionally magnificent" in 1935, when their politics didn't yet mark indelibly everything they wrote; by 1942 Riefenstahl is "the greatest artist of the Third Reich," in a cinema desperately fighting off Jewish corruption and domination.

———

In 1937, the year he visited Nuremberg, Brasillach published *Comme le temps passe* [How time passes]. It was his best-selling novel. Here Brasillach used his love for the movies to good advantage, setting part of the story in the world of silent cinema. His main characters are two childhood sweethearts who marry. It was his first novel in which the description of a love affair was at the center of the plot.

Comme le temps passe contains the longest, most explicit sex scene in Brasillach's fiction. It is rendered in a slow motion that makes it excruciating to read. The joining of Florence and René, one moonlit night, is punctuated by references to their shared childhood—to their still-childish bodies and faces, and to a sadistic animal self-consciousness on the part of René:

> He lifted himself up onto his heels, contemplated it [her body] below him like a dead or submissive little animal, perceived himself in the shadow, his back turned to the moon, a young man's body, upright before his prey . . . a child who still remembers having been a child and yet who is already a man who has obtained his desire and his companion.

The writing doesn't ever get more explicit than that, but on and on it goes, towards a sweaty orgasm, six pages later. At least one of his contemporaries admired the scene for its sexual precision, but compared to the eroticism of Proust or even to the Gide of *The Immoralist,* still burning for today's readers, *Comme le temps passe* has aged badly.

The novel flirts with homosexual themes, but the flirtation remains parenthetical, and never succeeds in guiding the story in any significant way. René spies his young wife Florence embracing a military man. This military man, we learn, is still recovering from a passion he developed for a fellow schoolboy, whose image he has sought out in every woman he has met since. René, seeing them kiss, abandons his wife and their child and leaves for the Great War, where he enjoys the "union of man to man." There, a comrade named Jacques de Sur confesses to René on his deathbed that his life was shaped by his extreme love for his mother, a love he considers almost inhuman. "I thought later that a love and excessive respect (if you can say that) for one's mother can throw a man, in his amorous life, into disdain for other women, into deviations," René concludes. That is all we learn about this character's theory that homosexuality is a result of loving one's mother too much.

When he returns to civilian life, René meets Florence by accident at the theater and the couple comes together again. René gives no explanation for his departure; Florence expresses no anger. It's an implausible plot, made of equal parts of romance, abandonment, and chance. As in all of Brasillach's fiction, the novel is entirely invested— with the exception of the rather implausible and grittier war scenes—in turn-of-the-century charm and in a childlike "joie de vivre."

Comme le temps passe was translated into German, and in May 1939, it was one of ten books sent to Hitler on his birthday by the Reich's literary propaganda service, the Amt Schrifften. It was good, light reading for the Führer.

———

It is a strange profile emerging, of a writer who is sometimes naive and wide-eyed, other times vicious, depending on his literary genre. He does seem at first to be one or the other, without gray areas, as though he invests in a certain style—soft-focus novelist or hard-edged sarcastic critic—and sticks with it. But if you look closely, you can see the wells of perversity and violence surfacing from the soft focus of his plots, and you begin to see, as the decade continues, fictional naïveté emerging in much of his writing about politics. In neither persona, vicious or sentimental, is he entirely reliable. There emerges, in biographies as in memoirs of the period, the portrait of a young man with boundless energy and ambition and talent and loyalty to his friends, not much sense of difficulty, not much awareness of the long-term consequences of his writing, not much sense of the pain of making choices. One imagines him writing and writing and writing, looking to see if he can succeed in this or that genre, and trying them all: criticism, theater, poetry, novel, travel journalism.

Still, the question remains: could a writer capable of such brutal criticism of others really be, as the critic from the *Nouvelle Revue Française* put it, "ineffably naive" in his own novels? Wasn't there rather a kind of dissociative sentimentality behind his fascism? That question is basic to all the debates about his life and work, including the debates within his trial. Examining his political writing alongside his criticism and fiction only complicates matters.

There are always political gestures within a discourse on literature, and one can measure, as early as 1930, Brasillach's affinity for anti-Republican, right-wing nationalism of the Action Française variety. Can we identify a moment when Brasillach's writing became denunciatory, rather than simply polemical? One often has the feeling reading French accounts of Brasillach that some basic innocence was "contaminated" by the meaner, cruder men at *Je Suis Partout;* that these men ruined him. Although from the time he was twenty-two, when he wrote his fake obituary of André Gide, he was a critic who liked to play tricks and who didn't mind skewering his opponents. The crucial change seems to have come when his attention turned from literature to politics, especially the politics of race, which preoccupied him as of the victory of the Popular Front in 1936. This was when he consolidated the so-called "split" in his style, not only between political writing and literary writing, but within his political writing as well. Republican France, "home," was a ruinous place, the site of corrupt decadence, described in violent, angry prose. Nazi Germany, the exotic and unknown neighbor, was the locus of soft-focus fantasy, the site of an imagined purity.

By 1938, the year after he published *Comme le temps passe,* Brasillach had staked out what he considered a "moderate" position in the anti-Semitic diatribes filling the pages of *Je Suis Partout,* which was now the leading proponent of fascism and anti-Semitism in France.

This is what his moderation sounded like: "We don't want to kill anyone, we don't want to organize any pogrom. But we think also that the best way to hinder the always unpredictable actions of instinctual anti-Semitism, is to organize a reasonable anti-Semitism." This was cruelty clothed in the rhetoric of moderation, the same kind of false moderation he used in the 1937 essay on Nazi Germany, when he lauded the "Jews are not desired" signs for their politeness and reticence.

In June of that year, in his "Letter to a Provincial" column, Brasillach called specifically for racial laws against the Jews. In February 1939, in a second special issue of *Je Suis Partout* organized around the theme "The Jews and France," Brasillach argued that everyone knew Jews were foreign to France: "let's take away citizenship from every Jew, half Jew, fourth Jew. It's a simple measure, fair, with nothing offensive about it: the Jewish people is a nation." It was a twisted maneuver typical of anti-Semitic nationalism—the threatening idea of a virtual Jewish nation was a reason to strip Jews of their own French nationality. Brasillach felt constrained to make an exception for the 1,700 Jews who had given their lives for France in the First World War, for whom he envisaged a special category of "honorary Aryan." Similarly, he continued, "we grant ourselves permission to applaud Charlie Chaplin, a half Jew, at the movies; to admire Proust, a half Jew; to applaud Yehudi Menuhin, a Jew; and the voice of Hitler is carried over radio waves [les ondes hertziennes] named after the Jew Hertz." This writer willing to label artists as "Jews" or "half Jews" and to celebrate the invention of the radio because it carried Hitler's voice was no longer a literary critic: he had become a political hack.

A month later, debate raged in France around a proposed legislation called the Loi Marchandeau, designed to forbid the use of racial hate language in the French press. It was the government's tough response to denunciations in the French press, their attempt to curb inflammatory writing in a period of unrest. The law, aimed specifically at the far right, brought out the cruelest strain of Brasillach's sense of humor. He wrote his weekly "Letter to a Provincial" column on the subject "The Monkey Question," calling for "a reasonable state anti-simietism" (the pun works in English and in French). Everywhere in the article where the word "Jew" would normally occur, he substituted the word "monkey":

> What tribunal would dare to condemn us . . . if we denounced the extraordinary invasion of Paris and of France by monkeys? Doubtless you've remarked that in the old days, monkeys were restricted to certain regions, that is to certain zoos. Today you see them everywhere . . . we must acknowledge that there has developed in the public a rather strong anti-monkey complex. Are you going

to the theater? The audience is full of monkeys, they're hanging everywhere, in the balconies, on stage. In the bus, in the metro? Monkeys. And if I sit down innocently in the cafe? On my right, on my left, two or three monkeys take their places. . . . Their cleverness in imitating the gestures of men means that sometimes we don't recognize them right away. . . . What we are calling anti-simietism (please read this carefully), is becoming a more serious necessity every day.

The theme of Jew as monkey is commonplace in Nazi anti-Semitic poster art, but the linguistic pun is Brasillach's own contribution to the hideous genre. This was the writer at his most obnoxious: hyped up by his own brilliance, using his taste for wordplay with a schoolboy glee. All the while, through the humor, the message comes through clearly. Jews should not be citizens; they are animals, not men.

One has the impression, faced with the radical disjunction of his two styles—nostalgic and cruel, sentimental and dehumanizing—that, on the one hand, he wasn't able to channel anger and criticism into the world of his fiction, and, on the other, he wasn't able to nuance his critical judgment in the world of journalism. Both kinds of writing ended up lacking the kind of depth and maturity that comes from being able to move back and forth between toughness and kindness, criticism and generosity. The sentimental writing was distant and flat—Brasillach's wistful, smiling characters weren't believable. The racist writing had shock and humor to strengthen it, but ultimately, racism only took Brasillach further away from the reality of individuals and politics, and deeper into stereotypes and set ideas. These problems are much deeper than literary problems: what both his sentimental prose and his racist diatribe lacked was a sense of reality.

By the time Brasillach published *Les Sept couleurs* [The seven colors] on the eve of wartime, he had expanded his range technically, as a novelist, but he had not advanced emotionally. In *Les Sept couleurs* he portrays a young French fascist, disappointed in love, and his friendship for a German soldier. The plot of the book is fairly simple, involving a love triangle between Patrice, Catherine, and François. The settings move between France, Germany, and civil war–torn Spain, giving the writer ample opportunity to indulge his penchant for local color. The innovation of *Les Sept couleurs* is that each chapter of the book is written in a different literary genre: story, letters, diary, reflections, dialogue, documents, speech. The "colors" referred to in the book's title are these genres. Brasillach had become a more conscious manipulator of his own literary form—he was striving for modernism.

The other innovation in *Les Sept couleurs* is that here, for the first time, Brasillach found a way to integrate his political writing into his plot. There are entire pages in the chapter on fascism lifted directly from "100 heures chez Hitler," the article Brasillach published in the *Revue Universelle* after travelling to the Nuremberg rallies with Annie Jamet. These pages appear in a section of the novel called "diary," narrated by a Frenchman living in Nuremberg whose best friend and protector is a strapping Nazi named Siegfried, and whose mistress is a sweet young blonde named Lisbeth who doesn't get in his way. "I'm getting to know Germany," writes the Frenchman, "which may be useful in the future, when her eternal nature will pit her against us."

———

The original French edition of *Les Sept couleurs* was reviewed almost immediately by *The New York Times,* though the novel would never be published in English translation. The *Times* remarked that "Brasillach's sympathy with nascent fascism and Nazism, before they had turned to hatred and land grabbing, pulses with something like religious ecstasy." But this was giving him the benefit of the doubt. Hatred and land grabbing simply didn't concern him. The sentimental quality that had marked his fiction from the beginning was now marshaled for political arguments within his fiction. Fascism itself was sentimental, and it was virile:

> The young fascist, involved with his race and his nation, proud of his
> vigorous body, his lucid spirit, disdaining the goods of this world,
> the young fascist in his camp, amidst the comrades of peace who can
> become comrades of war, the young fascist who sings, who marches,
> who works, who dreams, is above all a joyous being.

Les Sept couleurs appeared on the list for the Goncourt Prize, France's top literary award, a year after *Comme le temps passe* had been nominated for a Prix Femina by a jury of women. The fact of these two nominations alone indicates that Brasillach was a novelist whose work counted on the Parisian literary scene. Yet it is almost inconceivable that the Goncourt would have awarded their prize to a book that took such a romantic attitude toward Nazism, as war with Germany was already underway. When the results of the 1939 Goncourt were announced, Brasillach had already been called up for military duty. In a letter to Bardèche, he joked about the fact that Léon Daudet, the

Action Française member of the prize committee, had voted for a Jew, Madame Simone. Anti-Semitism was by now an automatic response, a comfortable tic, for a man who, in his editorial columns, was blaming the Jews, not the Nazis, for the start of war.

As France was about to lose that war and be split in two, Brasillach bridged two parts of his writerly persona, the political and the aesthetic, by calling on his most sentimental, eroticized feelings about fascism. In *Les Sept couleurs,* his two main characters go to war as a consequence of their failure to love the same woman. The message: make war, not love. Brasillach, a fascist journalist who wrote quirky, sentimental novels, was now a fascist novelist.

TWO BRASILLACH'S WAR

The Fall

When France fell to the Germans in June 1940, the country was divided into two zones: the zone occupied and administered by the Germans, located on the Atlantic coast and in the north (including Paris), and a nonoccupied zone in the south and on the Mediterranean coast. Pétain and the defeated French government had fled Paris when the war started, and now they set up headquarters in the nonoccupied zone, in Vichy, a spa town 150 miles to the southeast of Paris, which even today is a three-hour trip by train. There were plenty of hotels there to house the ministries. A town where people had once gone to drink the waters for their health now furnished the backdrop for Marshal Pétain's right-wing "National Revolution," the supposed cure for what had ailed France during the 1930s: parliamentary democracy, political instability (whether of the Popular Front or weak right-wing variety), cosmopolitanism, rampant freemasonry, and Jewish influence. The National Assembly had voted Pétain "full powers" in July 1940, shortly after the signing of the armistice. Given a virtual free hand, he stopped assembling parliament and dissolved the previous constitution. Pétain flooded the country with paternalistic propaganda, substituting for the Republican slogan *liberté, egalité, fraternité,* the new motto *travail, famille, patrie* [work, family, fatherland], which people took to calling mockingly, "trafapa."

In the middle of this chaos, a little-known brigadier general named Charles de Gaulle set up a fledgling resistance movement in London. Among Pétain's first acts was to condemn de Gaulle to death for his treasonous flight. Next, Pétain sought to punish the Popular Front government of the 1930s for its responsibility in France's defeat. He jailed the former ministers and assembled a special Supreme Court at Riom to try them on charges of treason.

Despite Pétain's best efforts, testimony at Riom backfired, revealing that the defeat of France was the fault of the Army high command—not the ministers. Pétain, embarrassed, called off the proceedings. Brasillach was among the disappointed Parisian fascists who criticized Vichy for giving up their vendetta against the Popular Front. In his columns for *Je Suis Partout* in 1941 and 1942, he constantly fantasized vengeance against the Riom defendants. Sometimes it was

Blum and Reynaud, other times Mandel and Reynaud, that he imagined murdered:

> Who would ever have wanted to die for Reynaud or for Blum?
> We'll let them croak without batting an eyelid, be assured. But this
> is urgent.

> Ah! Certainly, if, among the nation's enemies, and if—for some
> absurd reason—we were obliged to remove the lot of them to
> some island in the Pacific, where we could choose just two for
> annihilation, I don't think we would hesitate: Mandel and Reynaud
> must be hung first. . . . Under these conditions, why wait?

Though he remained respectful, even sentimental, towards Pétain,
he complained regularly that the National Revolution was not going
far enough in its fight against the parliamentarian, Republican, Jewish,
and democratic forces in France.

In the beginning, Pétain promised to provide France with a shield
against the occupant, even though he governed almost entirely at the
Germans' sufferance: "I make to France the gift of my person . . . to
attenuate her suffering," he had promised in his avuncular way during
a first radio speech after the fall. But he failed even at that. With
Prime Minister Pierre Laval as his chief negotiator and henchman,
he made deal after deal with the Nazis. In 1942, after the Allies had
landed in North Africa, the Germans feared an Allied invasion of
Europe and crossed over the demarcation line dividing the two zones,
occupying all of the country. Again, Brasillach approved. The crossing
of the demarcation line meant to him a unified France, where Anglo-
Saxons and Jews could no longer sap morale in the unoccupied zone;
it meant an end to the hypocrisy of a "pseudo-National Revolution"
where Pétain's and Laval's orders were regularly ignored; it also meant
that France was part of a unified Europe, at one with Germany. His
headline in *Je Suis Partout* read: "So that France may live. France and
Germany desire the unity of our countries and the unity of the West;
we must want these conditions for ourselves." The column coincided
with the twenty-eighth anniversary of his father's death in Morocco in
the Kénifra skirmish on November 13, 1914. In a rare autobiographical
aside, Brasillach noted that the Americans had landed in North Africa at
Port Lyautey, were there was a street named for his father, and that the
town probably had stars and stripes flying by now. It was as though, in
his mind, the Americans represented the return of the rebels who had
killed his father.

After 1942, once the Germans had crossed the demarcation line, Vichy was nothing more than a puppet government, Pétain a rubber stamp for the Nazis.

————

In the beginning, in 1940, the sudden splitting of the country into two parts had been dramatic. Not only had France fallen; she was shattered in two. Mail from one zone to another was limited to "fill in the blank" postcards. It was illegal to travel without a pass. There were hundreds of everyday details that could serve as emblems of this world arbitrarily divided, this world turned upside down. One of them was the fact that Pétain, in Vichy, appointed a "general delegate of the French Government in occupied territories"—a de facto ambassador— to the Germans in Paris. A Vichy ambassador to Paris was the equivalent of Williamsburg sending an ambassador to Washington, D.C. It was a theatrical fiction that Vichy was its own power, yet in the occupied zone, it was also a myth that the Germans took total control. The reality was far more complex.

The German presence in France consisted of the Wehrmacht soldiers, the SS, the Gestapo, the military leaders in charge of the administration of occupied France, and their diplomatic and cultural representatives. In 1941 there was a military command in France numbering around 22,000 officers and staff; the number of German troops stationed in France during the Occupation ranged from 100,000 in December 1941 to nearly one million in early 1944. Germany made the big decisions, but even with considerable manpower, it wasn't practical for them to run everything. In both the occupied and unoccupied zones, the French administration from the prewar years continued to operate much as before: a system with prefects and subprefects, a government-regulated school system with its rectors and instructors, a national post office with its government employees, a national judicial system with its appointed judges assigned to different courts throughout the country. This infrastructure, nominally controlled by Vichy, stayed in place throughout the war; even in the occupied zone, high-ranking civil servants—prefects, officers, and magistrates—pledged an oath of loyalty to Pétain.

For both the people who lived in the occupied zone and those who lived in the unoccupied zones of France, but especially for those in the zone first occupied by the Germans, there were hundreds of large and small decisions to make about how to behave among the Germans. Was simple politeness an act of cowardice? Was putting one's foot out to trip a soldier on his way out of the metro an act of resistance? All over France, housing was requisitioned for officers stationed in one town or another. The first great novella of the resistance, Vercors's *The Silence of the Sea,* is about a family where a German officer is billeted, and about the tension of not speaking to him. The officer ends up in a pathetic soliloquy for days at a time.

For women, at a time when hundreds of thousands of men were gone in work camps or in prisoner-of-war camps, could a relationship with a German soldier remain a private affair, or was it an act of collaboration? Was the personal always political? On the question of food, could one give in to black market cooperation with Germans in order to eat? Or was black marketeering an act of resistance against the system? On the question of entertainment, one could find oneself easily in a night club or theater sitting next to German officers. Was laughing at the same jokes, crying at the same movie, enjoying the same dancing girls an act of collaboration? In every town in France there were stories of betrayal, accommodation, sacrifice, sainthood, and evil; there was not always agreement on which was which.

———

Life in occupied France was treacherous for everybody. For Jews, both foreign Jews and French Jews, it was an escalating nightmare. The relative administrative continuity of Vichy with Republican France had one important exception, and it involved French Jews: Anti-Jewish legislation of 1940 and 1941, decided upon by Vichy independently from the Nazis, stripped newly naturalized Jews of their citizenship, forbade to Jews the practice of medicine or law, removed Jews from the teaching corps and the army and the government. This anti-Jewish legislation was the lynchpin of Vichy's plan for national renewal, and a source of complicity with the Nazis.

The situation for Jews was worse in the occupied zone, and worst of all in Paris, where the Nazis concentrated their surveillance. There are horror stories about Jewish families who were called upon to register with the Commission for Jewish Questions. Some went willingly, because they assumed they'd be treated with good will by their own government. People operated according to their normal logic, but they were not operating in a logical world. In the occupied zone, Jews were required to sew a yellow star on their jackets as part of a process of identification. The information that was gathered on Jewish residents was used to organize roundups, internment, and deportation: German initiatives carried out with French police cooperation. From the time of the publication of the first anti-Jewish laws in 1940, Jews hid and changed their names in order to protect themselves and their families from arrest and deportation.

Je Suis Partout published a column each week entitled "Partout et ailleurs" [Everywhere and elsewhere], revealing the identities and locations of those who were trying to save themselves. In a scandalized tone, Brasillach's newspaper reported infractions against Vichy's Jewish law, Jewish doctors who were still daring to practice, journalists who were writing under false names, families who had moved to small towns in the south in the hope of avoiding arrest. The changing of proper names, one of the classic paranoid foci of traditional anti-Semitic propaganda, was a favorite theme in the unsigned column:

> We remember the warmongering Jew Charles Ruff, known as Lussy, former socialist deputy, leading light of his party, a mayor who has been removed from his post. Article 5, paragraph 2, of the law of June 2, 1941, prohibits any Jew from being the editor of a newspaper. Under the pseudonym of Jean Lubert, Lussy is nonetheless writing articles on Avignon and the Comtat in a regional daily. Is this because his ancestors had a ghetto in the city of the popes?

> The Jew David Rubiné, naturalized French at the dawning of the Popular Front, went by the name of Davidovici Ruben before May 1, 1936. He set up medical practice in Conches, in 1935, before he was given French nationality. Now that a decree of the Marshal Pétain takes away the benefit of that nationality from him, the Jew Davidovici plays dumb. He continues to practice. Perhaps it will be enough to point out this very curious anomaly to the Prefect of the Eure, responsible for carrying out the law?

Jews were not the only targets of these sarcastic notices in "Partout et ailleurs." *Je Suis Partout* skewered political leaders of the Popular Front, intellectuals in exile, and, as the war progressed, members of the resistance and Gaullists. These people were not simply criticized: their hiding places and pseudonyms were announced. Often their exact addresses were given.

We can measure the gravity of these denunciations against hard statistics: 76,000 Jews were deported from France during the Occupation, mostly foreign Jews who had sought refuge there in the early 1930s. Of these, fewer than 3,000 returned. 65,000 others were arrested and sent to camps as hostages, as common-law prisoners, or for their actions in the resistance.

———

In such a heightened and treacherous atmosphere, all aspects of daily life were politicized. The written word had a new status, a new power to do evil and good. Writers and intellectuals, whether they liked it or not, were read politically. Every decision they made about writing was political: what to publish, where to publish, and whether to publish.

A few writers, such as René Char and Jean Guéhenno, made the conscious decision not to publish a single line during the Occupation. Others—most famously Jean Bruller, whose pen name was Vercors—published with clandestine presses.

Others accommodated. Lucien Febvre, the *Annales*-school historian, so wanted his *Annales* to continue to appear in Paris that he asked his Jewish colleague, Marc Bloch, co-owner of the journal, to publish under a pseudonym. Bloch suggested that the journal might move to the unoccupied zone, but Febvre fought him, arguing that Paris was the center of intellectual life. Bloch went along with the decision reluctantly, and soon switched his energies to resistance work. As a member of the resistance, he was captured and executed by the Germans. After the war, students from the Ecole Normale booed Febvre in his Sorbonne classes.

Many writers and intellectuals preferred to set up shop in the unoccupied zone, where publication was less compromised. Roger Leenhardt, in his memoirs, describes a radio program at Vichy called *Vichy Jeunesse* that gathered together any number of writers who eventually joined the resistance: Leenhardt, Claude Roy, Pierre Schaeffer.

One of the strangest trajectories of all the resistance writers was that of Claude Roy, who started out as a close friend of Brasillach's. Their friendship dated back to the Lycée Louis-le-Grand, and until the war, they were part of the same Action Française intellectual milieu. Like Brasillach, Claude Roy wrote literary criticism for *Action Française* and *Je Suis Partout;* he published alongside his friend in *Combat,* the nonconformist magazine of the right where you could read articles by Thierry Maulnier and Maurice Blanchot. After the fall of France, Brasillach and Roy were held prisoner-of-war in different camps; Brasillach was released, and Roy escaped. Roy continued to write for *Action Française,* which had moved from Paris to Lyon, in the unoccupied zone. He also wrote for *Candide,* another right-wing paper. He worked for the Vichy radio station, Vichy Jeunesse. In Lyon he became linked to Louis Aragon, who introduced him into the milieu of resistance poets.

This association changed the course of Roy's life and his politics. He began publishing in publications known for their affiliation with the literary resistance: *Confluences, Messages,* and *Poésie 43,* where, by 1943, he was making fun of fascist writers. It is hard to know what could account for such an abrupt change of heart. He later told a Brasillach biographer that he had pleaded with Brasillach not to remain at *Je Suis Partout.* He had tried to convince him of the horror of Vichy's anti-Semitic legislation, using his affection for his Jewish wife as a way of bringing the issue home to Brasillach, who responded, Roy remembers, "with tears in his eyes." In 1945, Claude Roy emerged from the war a communist. After Brasillach was sentenced to death, Roy hesitated but finally declined to sign a petition recommending that his former friend be pardoned.

There were writers who didn't actively collaborate but whose actions were embarrassing to those around them. Jean Cocteau, who loved the glittery social world of Paris, attended the opening of a sculpture exhibit by Paris's most visible Nazi artist-in-residence, Arno Breker, who was showing off his epic sculptures of Nazi men at the Orangerie. The entire A list of the collaboration was there. Eluard wrote Cocteau a letter reprimanding him. It was the kind of gesture that was remembered after the war, when writers were called to account for even less.

A famous anecdote tells how Otto Abetz, the putative German ambassador in Paris, announced to his aides that there were three major nonmilitary targets the Nazis needed to bring under their control: the Communist Party, the Bank of France, and the *Nouvelle Revue Française*—the literary magazine of the Editions Gallimard, France's most important publisher. At the *Nouvelle Revue Française,* editor Jean Paulhan played a perverse game. He gave the administration of the journal over to Drieu la Rochelle, a major figure on the French fascist intellectual scene, but he continued to feed him articles on the side. Meanwhile, he worked actively for the resistance. When Paulhan was arrested by the Gestapo, Drieu got him released.

These are examples of the many courses that different intellectuals chose under the Occupation. Some of their trajectories were ambiguous, some were confusing. Many intellectuals shifted their positions radically during the Occupation. Brasillach didn't. From the beginning to the end of the Occupation, he was a fervent supporter of National Revolution and an apologist for the German presence.

Prisoner of War

Son of a career officer who died for France in 1914, Brasillach took his own military training in Lyon in the summer of 1932. He himself was not a career military man as his father had been, but as a draftee with student status he was given the lowest officer's rank, sous-lieutenant, and a desk job. He was called up for duty in September 1938 and promoted to the rank of lieutenant. The French military was on alert for a war against Germany, an alert canceled upon the diplomatic agreement reached at Munich by the British, the French, and the Germans. After Munich, Brasillach was sent home.

His first tour of duty over, Brasillach wrote his history of the Spanish Civil War with Bardèche, celebrating Franco's "Catholic fascist" victory. In September 1939, he was called up a second time, during the "phony war." On June 6, 1940, a soldier on the Maginot line, Brasillach learned that *Je Suis Partout* was accused by the government of weakening the national fabric and inciting the enemy. Brasillach was called to Paris police headquarters to testify. Charles Lesca, the major stockholder in the paper, was arrested and interned with another colleague in a camp at Gurs, but Brasillach returned to his garrison with only a small fine. *Je Suis Partout* was not published during the chaos that followed France's defeat. When the newspaper reappeared in Paris in February 1941, much was made of this prewar event. The headline in the first Occupation-era issue of *Je Suis Partout* read: "Attack by the Jew Mandel [Minister of the Interior] against *Je Suis Partout*." The interrogation of Brasillach and the detention of his colleagues at *Je Suis Partout* became the cornerstone in a mythic construction of an evil Third Republic France that was to blame for starting the war and for persecuting innocent men. *Je Suis Partout,* in turn, announced that these evildoers needed to be crushed by Vichy.

France had capitulated on June 19, 1940, after only six weeks of fighting. The rate of casualties rivaled the great slaughter at Verdun, in World War I. When they were taken prisoners, Brasillach's unit had been marching aimlessly through the forests and towns of the Lorraine. They hadn't seen combat. Their general hoped that the signing of an armistice would guarantee their freedom, but it didn't. Brasillach was taken prisoner on June 25 along with nearly two million other Frenchmen. He spent ten months in two different Oflags, prisoner-of-war camps reserved for French officers. In his writing about the fall, Brasillach describes corrupt, indifferent officers drinking champagne the day of France's defeat. We never have the sense in reading him that he was a treasonous officer who hoped the Germans would triumph. Rather, Brasillach saw himself as a tried and true Frenchman, and he blamed democratic, parliamentary France for his country's defeat at the hands of the Germans.

As in many aspects of the Brasillach story, there are two opposing versions of his activities in prison camp. In one version of the story, Brasillach was a patriotic Frenchman, a loyal comrade. In the other, Brasillach denounced fellow officers as Jews and Gaullists. These versions emerged in the years after his execution, sparked by interviews, by documentaries, by biographies and memoirs. In trying to understand what happened, one is constantly in a position of wading through edited material, polemic, memory.

It is important to go to what Brasillach actually wrote about his experience in the POW camps. We can start by looking at just one aspect of his prison-camp behavior, his anti-Semitism. In the 1930s, Brasillach himself claimed to be a moderate, rational anti-Semite who was primarily concerned about the intrusion of foreign Jews into French life. He even acknowledged Jewish heroism and, as we have seen, imagined the creation of a special category—"honorary Aryan"—for the Jews who had died fighting for France in the First World War. By the time the Second World War broke out, the category of "honorary Aryan" had disappeared in his mind: the Jew had become the completely unambiguous enemy of France. This intensified anti-Semitism inflected his writing in and about the prisoner-of-war camp: in the letters he wrote to his family members, in the stories about camp life he published in *Je Suis Partout,* and in the literary texts he wrote while a prisoner, such as the play *Bérénice.*

Writing to his sister and Maurice Bardèche on July 29, 1940— one of his earliest letters home from the camp—Brasillach joked, "I'm with seven officers. . . . For distraction there is church service . . . the expulsion of Jews, inaccurate news reports, and the theater." Whatever we already know about his anti-Semitism, it is still jolting to see Brasillach, in the intimacy of correspondence with his best friend and his sister, suggest that the expulsion of Jews from his camp was a form of entertainment for him.

Even writing to his mother, his treatment of Jews in the camp is a subject of mirth and an occasion to show off literary knowledge: "I created a scandal by publicly forbidding a Jew to speak—but he will speak no longer (just like in Act I of Cyrano de Bergerac). It was very funny." This is the snappy voice of the critic writing home from the camp. Brasillach is referring here to the opening of Edmond de Rostand's *Cyrano,* where the swashbuckling nonconformist hero, the large-nosed Cyrano, ridicules the turgid actor Montfleury, that "bloated nincompoop," and orders him off the stage for a month. Cyrano wants the theater cured. Brasillach, in 1940, sees himself as a daring nonconformist, and the Jews as the essence of all that is corrupt, official, and diseased in his own defeated nation.

———

Aside from these comments in private letters, Brasillach wrote about Jewish prisoners in several articles in *Je Suis Partout*. When most scholars discuss his wartime writing, they look to Brasillach's complete works [*Oeuvres complètes*], published in the 1960s, where the *Je Suis Partout* articles are reprinted. What they find there is a sanitized version of what he actually wrote. Before looking at the comments he made about the Jewish prisoners of war in *Je Suis Partout,* a word is necessary about how Brasillach's writings were edited for these posthumous complete works.

Before Brasillach died, he left instructions that his more descriptive, memoir-style writing about the Occupation years—including reflections on the prison camp published in *Je Suis Partout*—be assembled in a volume to be entitled *Journal d'un homme occupé,* which means "Diary of an occupied man," but also, by way of a clever pun, "Diary of a *busy* man." These memoirs would be a sequel to *Notre avant-guerre,* his memoir of the 1930s. It was a knowing pun: Brasillach was indeed busy and thriving during the Occupation. The POW period, in particular, was a good time for him, a period he looked back on with great nostalgia. "Naturally, you should cut what is no longer of value," Brasillach wrote in his last instructions to Bardèche. He trusted his closest friend to determine, in the years that were to follow the war, what would be "no longer of value." Bardèche cut every mention of the Jewish prisoners of war from the *Je Suis Partout* pieces. To understand Brasillach's attitude, we must turn to the original articles.

The first of these appears in late May 1941, a month after his release. In "Les Universités des camps" [Universities in the camps], published on page one of *Je Suis Partout,* below his regular front-page editorial, Brasillach describes the educational programs set up in the camps. Officers who in civil life were professors or intellectuals lectured on the subjects of their expertise; colonial officers described their faraway posts. Brasillach, a lover of Spain, gave a talk on Gibraltar and another one on the history of literature. Officers tutored simple soldiers in math and in languages "in the most touching manner." On the subject of Jews:

> We won't surprise the readers of *Je Suis Partout* when we explain that although some Jewish orators gave literary lectures before our arrival—however infrequently—this regrettable fact didn't repeat it-

self thereafter. My God, I will admit that I had nothing to do with this directly, but we must believe that the presence of fervent nationalists in and of itself was enough to "crystallize" certain opinions and to prevent certain errors being committed according to the liberalism that is sometimes in fashion. But as of seven months ago, in my camp at least, this is no longer happening.

The absence of agency here is suspicious. Brasillach acts as if the Jewish speakers were silenced by magic. There is a coyness in his remarks that keeps Brasillach innocent, but that at the same time gestures to the ability of his loyal readers to understand that he is boasting: After he arrived, no more Jewish officers gave lectures in the camp.

The article ends with a nostalgic view of camp life, continuing the theme of Brasillach's most popular novel, *Comme le temps passe:*

> In these great agglomerations of men that resemble colleges, one rediscovers—some discover for the first time—culture that is disinterested, with a youthfulness of spirit which is that of adolescence. And youth regained permits us, precisely, to forget the time that passes, the absences, and the exile.

Camp life, the bonding of men, was deeply satisfying for him, so much so that one feels in what he wrote about it afterward that he was never again so happy in civilian life.

In the reproduction of Brasillach's *Je Suis Partout* articles in his complete works, this 1941 column has been omitted in its entirety. Bardèche's editor's note mentions the column but explains that it was not reproduced because it contained "mostly practical information on the prison camps." On the contrary, "Universités des camps" is one of Brasillach's most stylized, characteristic pieces of writing, where we can clearly observe his two writerly tones: clever insult giving way to gauzy nostalgia.

Again in 1943, Brasillach returned to the subject of the Jewish prisoners in an article called "National Revolution and Romantic Captivity." In reproducing the article, Bardèche cut only one paragraph. That paragraph reads:

> One was asked to point out the Jews. There were a few Jews in the camps whom we saw wandering sadly, bent over their noses [*le nez penché*]. Were they going to be put in a special camp? A rumor circulated. The official records bore the trace of very few Jews, for all of them had miraculously become Christians. There were even

those who went to look for a Catholic or Protestant chaplain, to
get themselves baptized *in extremis.* . . . Others, taking advantage of
the loss of their ID papers (sometimes they had just burned them),
transformed their names. We laughed for three days over a Dreyfus,
suddenly named Trépied. Besides, one had to notice from what
followed that all these fears were vain, and that the Jews were mixed
with the French in the camps, and treated exactly like them.

First Brasillach says the Jews were going to be transferred. Then he makes
fun of them for changing their names so they wouldn't be transferred.
Then he mocks them again because they weren't in fact transferred.
Which part of this garbled mass of prejudices should we believe?

There is little specific information available in the scholarly literature
about what happened to French Jewish soldiers taken prisoner-of-war
by the Nazis—factual information against which one might measure
Brasillach's mocking prose. At least one historian of the French captivity,
Yves Durand, has written that Jewish officers were better off inside the
camps than they would have been in Germany. They were not deported
to Nazi death camps. Yet, as prisoners of war, they were isolated and
discriminated against, forced to wear yellow stars. In one POW camp,
Jewish doctors were forced to treat typhoid patients unprotected. About
so-called "reprisal camps" such as Lübeck, where Jewish prisoners of war
were said to have been isolated, we have even less information.

Brasillach's passages on Jewish prisoners were cut from the complete
works in spite of the fact that their editor, Bardèche, makes a point
of insisting that the articles from *Je Suis Partout* have been reproduced
"in order to represent the dossier held against Brasillach in 1945 at
the moment of his trial." Bardèche also insists in his 1955 editor's
notes to the *Journal d'un homme occupé* that, in reconstituting Brasillach's
wartime memoirs, he decided to leave in even allegations about the
conduct of war that turned out to be false, in order to remain faithful
to Brasillach's worldview.

Why cut these specific passages, when even the two revolting letters
home are included in the complete works?

These passages, in particular, do damage to the myth of Brasillach
as a French officer who stood by his fellow officers, who fought against
the Germans and suffered imprisonment by the Germans as a French
patriot. More important, we see the mark in this writing of an actual
public denunciation. Denunciation does not consist merely in saying,
"He is a Jew"; it consists in saying "He is a Jew" in the knowledge that

such a statement will result in a punishment, whether it be stigmatization or isolation or expulsion. Denunciation, in these circumstances, is not opinion; it is language that goes beyond opinion and ideology, to action. And according to the penal code used in the 1945 Purge courts, denunciation was a treasonous crime.

––––––

Brasillach's May 26, 1941, *Je Suis Partout* article begs the question by insisting too much: "My God, I'll admit I had nothing to do with it directly." The first sentence of the 1943 passage is also oddly without agency: "On demanda aussi de désigner les Juifs" ["One was asked to designate the Jews"]; not, "They asked us to designate the Jews." It is a fudge, a syllable away from a confession that he, Brasillach, did, when asked, designate the Jews in his camp. Certainly someone was asked. Someone—was it Brasillach?—denounced fellow French officers who had fought and fallen prisoner for their country.

When Brasillach was sentenced to death in 1945, comrades from the prison camp wrote in large numbers to de Gaulle to defend him. They described his camaraderie, his charm, his willingness to give lectures on literary subjects to distract and instruct the men of the camp. One man described the way he sat and wrote, in their presence, beautiful novels "with no cross outs." His loyalty to certain of these men was exemplary: there was Jacques Tournant, who wrote to de Gaulle that his brother, arrested by the Gestapo as a suspected resistant, was saved only by a gesture on the part of Brasillach. Ridicule and exclusion of a Jewish enemy went along for Brasillach with intense loyalty to a chosen few, to his schoolmates, his fellow Aryan officers, to his family, for whom he would do anything.

––––––

While he was at Oflag VI A in Warburg, Brasillach wrote a play, *Bérénice.* On at least two festive occasions, fellow officers read the play out loud, part of evening entertainment at the camp. As we shall see, anti-Semitism was not a particular focus of Brasillach's trial, nor did the question of Jewish prisoners of war emerge at the trial. These questions only surfaced in 1957, when Brasillach's play was staged at the Théâtre des Arts in Paris to violent public protest. The performances of *Bérénice,* retitled *La Reine de Césarée,* were greeted with picketing, leafletting, and angry demonstrations by former resistance groups. A third performance was interrupted by demonstrators who smashed props on stage and shouted down the cast. Police evacuated the theater. The next day, the Paris City Council voted to close down the play, although the national

government—the Ministry of the Interior and Prefecture of Police—
did not second them. All this time, a polemic raged in the press. Was
anti-Semitism vital to the play? Did the laundering of the play save it?
Was the context in which it was written, and Brasillach's legacy as a
fascist who believed in Vichy, enough to condemn the play? Should the
play be judged on its own merits, independent from Brasillach's life?

Bérénice is about the demise of a love affair between Bérénice, Queen
of the Jews, and Titus, Emperor of the Romans. Brasillach chose a
theme treated famously by both Corneille and Racine, the pillars of
French classicism, and by numerous Roman authors before them. As
in the sources, Bérénice is an older Jewish woman, who has sacrificed
her own queenly duties to serve as young Titus's courtesan. Titus must
now abandon her in order to rule over Rome. Critics have compared
Brasillach's treatment of the classic story to Colette's *Chéri,* the novel
about the young dandy called "Chéri" who takes up with Léa, an aging
demi-mondaine, then leaves her. In Brasillach's rendering, however, the
courtesan is pointedly an overly perfumed *Jewish* courtesan.

Most of the anti-Semitic commentary in Brasillach's play comes
from the mouth of Paulin, the Emperor's adviser. In attitude and
rhetoric, Paulin bears a striking resemblance to a columnist in *Je Suis
Partout.* Out of Paulin's mouth come the following lines:

> I imagine that this woman must have been beautiful; but the Ori-
> entals fade quickly. After age twenty-five, they're nothing but a soft
> package of grease on which a few jewels are floating, like balls of fat
> on bouillon.

> There are fat Jewesses and thin Jewesses, two types of vermin.

> With her heady perfumes, her pimp's behavior, the tears in her
> dresses disguised by fake jewels, her dyed hair, her painted nails, her
> blouses stained with grease and henna, she is that which all the men
> and all the women of my race instinctively hate the most.

Brasillach drew on Paulin's descriptions of Queen Bérénice when, in
1942, he described the French Republic itself as "an old syphilitic
whore, stinking of patchouli and yeast infection." Brasillach was a good
enough playwright to make Paulin a distinct and obnoxious character,
to distinguish his disdain from Titus's affection for Bérénice, and to give
Bérénice her own dignity. He was capable of making human distinctions
for literary reasons that he could not or would not make in his political
writing back in Paris, a year later.

In addition to *Bérénice,* Brasillach drafted a novel in the POW camp. It wasn't published during the war, but three hundred pages were published posthumously, in the form of a finished draft. It was to be a long fascist bildungsroman called *Les Captifs* [The captives]. The hero of his novel was the son of a Third Republic representative to French parliament. The book describes his rebellion from his father and his coming of age as a fascist orator. Although unfinished, it is probably Brasillach's best, least sentimental fiction—more realist, more bitter than Brasillach's prewar work. Like so many of Brasillach's heroes, this one has troubled or muted relationships with women; the only sexual relationship that does seem successful in the novel takes place between an older woman and a younger man—the same theme pursued in *Bérénice.* The description by the main female character of her young male lover's body is the first erotically effective description in Brasillach's *oeuvre. Les Captifs* also tells about the pleasure of public speaking. After he has finished addressing a crowd, Gilbert Caillé, the hero of *Les Captifs,* feels as though he had just made love. Brasillach wrote the passage during a period when he was taking great pleasure in his own role as political orator in the camps—as orator and as censor of Jewish orators. His time in the POW camp was, as he would label it two years later, a romantic captivity for him.

———

In March 1941, a month after *Je Suis Partout* resumed publication in occupied Paris, Brasillach, still in his POW camp, sent the paper his first article since the German invasion. In it, he celebrated the Vichy regime, which had had ten months to establish itself. He supported Pétain's handshake with Hitler in the famous meeting at Montoire. He reiterated *Je Suis Partout's* prewar demands for anti-Jewish legislation and demanded that the nation acknowledge that Third Republic socialism had brought the country to its knees.

A month later he was released. At Brasillach's trial, the prosecution would argue that his article had resulted directly in his April release. The defense had an entirely different story. They would quote a letter from a minister at Vichy, who claimed that the Vichy government had requested Brasillach's release from prison as early as June 1940, so he could become Commissioner of Cinema. According to their account, and according to several Brasillach biographers, Brasillach did begin work as Commissioner after his release, but quit due to German interference.

The records show that in September 1941, someone else was in fact named as Commissioner of Cinema. Brasillach was indeed nominated for the job, but he was not chosen. On the reasons for his release, both the prosecution and the defense at his trial were wrong. He was released by official request of the German Embassy in Paris, who established a list, as early as October 1940, of French ideologues who could help the Nazi cause. By the time Brasillach published his article in *Je Suis Partout* in 1941, the request for his release was nearly six months old. It had made the official German rounds. The article in *Je Suis Partout* was the proof of what the Germans expected from the young writer, not the cause of his release. Whether or not he knew this is another matter. But the fact is, the Germans were counting on him.

Paris

Brasillach returned to Paris as a liberated prisoner of war, as the returning editor in chief of *Je Suis Partout,* and as the author of a memoir published in his absence: *Notre avant-guerre* [Our prewar]. He had finished the book in 1939 but its publication had been delayed by the war itself. *Notre avant-guerre* is narrated entirely in the first-person plural, with Brasillach speaking for his whole entourage, his comrades—the Action Française boys who had met at Louis-le-Grand and gone on to the Ecole Normale and to *Je Suis Partout*. With its 1930s Paris landscapes, its reminiscences about art and culture and the Ecole Normale, its portrait of famous writers encountered, its enthusiastic account of plays and movies enjoyed and its whimsical descriptions of the rise of fascist regimes throughout Europe, *Notre avant-guerre* continued to do what Brasillach knew how to do best: describe an era as it was about to end. For in *Notre avant-guerre,* Brasillach developed a concept of cultural history that he had launched in *Candide* in September 1931 with his survey on "la fin de l'après-guerre," the end of the post–World War I era. Now he was telling France what life had been like in the 1930s, excitedly recounting the rise of European fascism, evoking the Popular Front decadence that had led up to the fall. For a population whose everyday life had gone up in smoke, whose country had virtually disappeared, the reconstruction of a "before" was as valuable a commodity as coffee and chocolate.

Bardèche had gotten *Notre avant-guerre* through the German censors while Brasillach was still in his POW camp. The book contained various pieces of Brasillach's prewar journalism, such as "100 heures chez Hitler," the slightly worried report on the Nazi rallies at Nuremberg from Brasillach's 1937 trip. Bardèche easily cut the article's occasional hesitations about Nazism, so that what remained was positive, enthusiastic. *Notre avant-guerre* sailed through the censors. In fact, the German Propaganda-

Staffel in Paris put it on one of their early lists of books thought to serve their cause.

Not all of Brasillach's friends endorsed the German presence, but enough did so that collaboration felt like a family affair. Brasillach's beloved Annie of the "Rive Gauche Society," who had died in 1938, was survived by her husband Henri Jamet. Jamet now founded the Librairie Rive-Gauche in conjunction with a German bookseller, with support from the occupying authorities. The bookstore and cultural center on the boulevard Saint-Michel was designed to promote Franco-German intellectual and literary ties. Then Jamet was named to head up a publishing house that had been taken over from its Jewish owners. Vichy legislation forbade Jews to own businesses, under its policy of "Aryaniza-tion." The government confiscated the publishing house Calmann-Lévy, renamed it "Editions Balzac," and put Jamet in charge. Brasillach's half sister, Geneviève Maugis, worked at the Editions Balzac as a typist. With Jamet busy, Maurice Bardèche's brother, Henri Bardèche, took over as administrator of the Librairie Rive-Gauche and Brasillach joined the board. Maurice Bardèche was preoccupied with his academic career, but he published a literary piece from time to time in *Je Suis Partout*. A 1941 interview with Bardèche in *Jeunesse*, a weekly collaborationist newspaper aimed at youth, presents him as the academic star of the collaboration, "speaking in his own name, independently," but with "direct frankness." In *Jeunesse*, Bardèche advocates a macho Pétainism with fascist overtones, consistent with Brasillach's *Je Suis Partout* line:

> We have to give to youth the cult of the hero, the virtues of force, courage, enthusiasm, responsibility, sacrifice, a taste for brutality and energy. . . . It is important [for youth] to adapt a revolutionary attitude without reticence and distance themselves from certain elements which, in the nonoccupied zone, have worked in a way which has not been what the Maréchal desires and which has served as an instrument for the Judeo-Gaullist opposition. . . . The time has come for a unified youth, an extension of the single party; this is an essential condition to fulfill if we want to speak on the same ideological basis as the other European powers and reintegrate with Europe.

Eight months later, when Brasillach spoke at a huge *Je Suis Partout* rally on the importance of a fascist France, Maurice Bardèche, always his steady supporter, sat on the stage behind him under the giant photo of Marshal Pétain.

They were the fervent collaborationists. Occasionally, their colleagues in the mainstream of intellectual life appeared ready to meet them more than halfway. A sign of the times: Brasillach's *Trial of Joan of Arc,* first published in 1931 by Alexis Rédier, the editor of *La Revue Française,* was reissued in a condensed version in 1941 by Editions Gallimard. Gallimard's flagship literary magazine, the *Nouvelle Revue Française,* was now under the editorship of fascist intellectual Drieu la Rochelle. The *Nouvelle Revue Française* was uneven. Depending on who was writing, it was sometimes a mouthpiece for the Révolution Nationale and for fascist intellectual values, sometimes as rarefied and esthetic as before, and blind to the political situation. In September 1941 the *Nouvelle Revue Française* reviewed Brasillach's *Trial of Joan of Arc* in a highly ideological spirit, arguing that France needed the myth of Joan to recover from the decadence of the prewar period. "We must leave behind the sterile verbosity of dead ideologies and return to the fundamental values of our genius," it began. Joan had long been a model for the right: a prisoner of the English, a mystic Catholic, she fed the pro-Vichy, anti-English sentiment of the moment and provided a heroic model in a time of national crisis.

The Nazis' intellectual occupation of Paris was organized around several German cultural institutions in the city: the German Institute, created in the fall of 1940 to promote intellectual exchange; the Propaganda-Staffel, which kept its eye on the Parisian press, allotted paper, and monitored newly published books; the Rive-Gauche bookstore; and the German Embassy. Brasillach developed literary, social, and political relationships with men in each of these places. In June 1941, Brasillach and his closest collaborator at *Je Suis Partout,* Henri Poulain, met with Lieutenant Heller, in charge of the literary division of the Propaganda-Staffel in Paris. Heller noted in his administrative diary that Brasillach had promised to launch an attack against the writers who were hostile to the Franco-German collaboration. He mentioned in particular François Mauriac, whose new novel, *La Pharisienne,* had just been published.

At the German Institute, Brasillach formed a friendship with the associate director, Karl Heinz Bremer, a handsome blond who had taught German briefly at the Sorbonne and the Ecole Normale before the war. Bremer was popular with Parisian intellectuals because of his intense love of France and deep knowledge of French culture. Between deadlines at *Je Suis Partout,* Brasillach might be seen lunching at the Institute—famous for its good meals in a time of shortages—or attending a reception at the Rive-Gauche bookstore, surrounded by Nazis in uniform. He was, as the title of his memoir of the period signals, an "homme occupé"—a busy man and an occupied man. It was a good life for him.

It wasn't a good life for France. By 1941, the situation in Paris was already bad, the resistance sparse and unorganized. Vichy's anti-Jewish legislation was in effect, along with massive anti-Allied propaganda. Food shortages had begun. In April of that year, the headline of the front-page column of *Je Suis Partout,* signed "l'Ubiquiste" ["Mr. Every-where"] was "The War of the Rats." The rats who were threatened with extinction, *Je Suis Partout* reported, were swearing that they were really cats, exotic cats from places like Siam and Persia, and therefore unrecognizable. They dared present their papers, proving they had cat mothers, cat fathers, cat grandparents. The column concluded, "In a Paris eaten away, sucked dry, devoured by rats, you can't meet a single rat once you start to look for them. I don't know why this makes me think of a Jewish story." It was the cat version of Brasillach's 1939 article on "The Monkey Question." Only the stakes were higher—rats had replaced monkeys; extermination was the subtext. As of 1942, Jews in the occupied zone were required to use one of their precious ration tickets for cloth to purchase the required yellow star—a combination of indignities that baffles the imagination. In July 1942 came the Vél d'Hiv roundup.

The Germans began executing hostages in reprisal for the first resistance actions in August 1941. It was a clever strategy to execute civilians in response to the resistance, sending a message to the French public that any resistance to the German presence was going to endanger French lives. In 1943, when things became desperate, Vichy itself got into the act. One of Pétain's right-hand men, Darnand, formed the *Milice,* a terrorist police force or militia, to combat armed resistance. The Allies had begun bombing Paris in the spring of 1942; the casualties were great, and the bombings themselves provided Vichy with opportunities for anti-Allied propaganda. By 1944, the last year of the Occupation, the resistance was better organized, but so were the Germans. They had sapped French resources, French manpower, French morale. The French were killing the French. None of this conflict and degradation emerges in Brasillach's version of the Occupation, or it emerges in such a twisted way that it appears that the Germans were France's saviors, the Jews and resistors the power-mongers and terrorists.

The occupied France we see depicted in Brasillach's writing is about male bonding in POW camps, about the inspirational German soldier, the Franco-German alliance. It's about the "practice and poetry of fascism," a largely imaginary affair, and about the evil forces—the Jews, the communists, the Third Republicans—stopping fascism from blossoming. There were nuances in the resistance as in every other political group, but only someone who was very comfortable with the occupation of his country by Germany could have dismissed its goals as terrorist.

In looking back on this era and on Brasillach's role, it is important to remember that Brasillach was one of the most famous and despised figures of the collaboration. He was a symbol. Jean Grenier, in a 1941 entry in his occupation diary, remarks in passing that Brasillach had been released from his prisoner-of-war camp to serve German propaganda interests. This was the public perception. That same fall, professor and writer Jean Guéhenno, who kept a diary later published under the title *Le Journal des années noires* [Diary of the black years] was preparing his students at the Lycée Henri IV to take the entrance exam for the Ecole Normale. He was haunted by the fear he might be training men whose very glibness and ability to manipulate the "logos," would lead them astray. He described the type:

> those whose lack of character, whose excess grandiosity, whose impatience, or even whose excess of cleverness turn into the new sophists serving the established powers, the ignoble servants of those who are more powerful than they.

He specified: "Other masterpieces of the Ecole and the *logos:* Déat, Brasillach, etc. . . ."

Brasillach did not consider his activities to be lacking in character. He was an eager, articulate spokesman for collaboration. He thought of his position as "collaboration standing up"—as opposed to collaboration lying down, of which he was later so pointedly accused. Brasillach had no impression of giving in. If anything, he felt that his active pursuit of relationships with the German occupiers was courageous and daring, a way of helping the French soldiers who remained in POW camps, a slap in the face to the socialists and democrats who, in his conception, had led his country to ruin. He was still playing Cyrano de Bergerac, Act I.

Brasillach's Ecole Normale, like every institution in France, was deeply affected by the Occupation. The anti-Jewish legislation of 1941 meant that Jewish students could still take the entry exam for the Ecole but wouldn't be admitted even if they passed it. The school's prewar director, Jérôme Carcopino, a conservative historian of imperial Rome, was appointed Minister of Education by Pétain and signed the anti-Jewish legislation that affected his school. During the war, the student body as a whole identified with the resistance. The wartime directors were Georges Bruhat and Jean Baillou, resistance intellectuals who did their work in a scientific laboratory.

One day in July 1942, Robert Brasillach went to study at the Ecole Normale library with his brother-in-law Maurice Bardèche. Bardèche and Brasillach lived directly behind the school, on the rue Rataud, and its library had one of the best literary collections in the city. It happened to be the day that prospective students came to the school to learn the results of the entrance exam, posted on lists in the hallway. Students were poised along the second floor rooftop terraces waiting to water balloon the hopeful candidates for admission, as they did every year. Everyone at the school knew that the despised Brasillach was a former *normalien* (or "archicube," according to the school slang) and that he lived around the corner. Students used to boo him regularly from out of the windows of their rooms. Now was a chance to release their water bombs on Paris's most notorious literary collaborator and his brother-in-law; Brasillach and Bardèche were too good a target to miss. Shortly after the incident, an anonymous letter on Sorbonne stationery—doubtless written by Brasillach and Bardèche themselves—was sent to the rector of the university. The letter claimed that the *normalien* students had injured old people with their balloons and demanded an explanation. The rector of the Paris universities, in turn, wrote to Bruhat, asking him to explain the incident. Bruhat replied to the rector that throwing water balloons at candidates for admission to the school was an old *normalien* tradition, that no aged person had been harmed, and that the letter itself was probably a fake.

Farce was a luxury in those years, with tragedy close behind. Bruhat had plenty else on his mind. Between February and August 1944, there were four raids on the Ecole by the Gestapo. In August 1944 Bruhat was deported for his political activity in the resistance. He died at Buchenwald.

Travel
Six months after his liberation from POW camp, in October 1941, Brasillach traveled to a writer's conference in Weimar with other notables of the collaboration, accompanied by Karl-Heinz Bremer, the charming

associate director of the German Institute in Paris. The Embassy funded the trip. Among the specific treason charges against Brasillach at his trial was the fact that he had traveled in the interests of German propaganda.

Brasillach's friendship with Bremer, the former German lecturer at the Ecole, was an important part of his wartime experience. Bremer, according to one historian of the period, was the heartthrob of the collaborationist homosexual milieu and an object of hero worship for Brasillach. After the trip to Weimar, after one glittering year at the Institut Allemand full of cultural activity and plans, Karl-Heinz Bremer was sent to the Russian front. His transfer was rumored to be a punishment for an excess of Francophilia. He was killed in combat. Brasillach's heartbroken obituary in *Je Suis Partout* shows that he understood their friendship as a kind of Franco-German alliance expressed in miniature:

> Dear Karl Heinz, we had made plans together; once peace came, we wanted to go walking, go camping, find twin landscapes, fraternal cities of our two countries.

According to Brasillach, Bremer never renounced being German but he knew all about France, her literature, her poetry, her jokes. Brasillach, in turn, wanted to love Germany the way Bremer had loved France: devoting himself to the other, yet remaining himself. But it seems Bremer got sent to the Eastern front for loving France too much. If anything could have convinced Brasillach of Nazi Germany's brutality and intolerance, it was this treatment of his friend. When Bremer died, Brasillach's own dream of a perfect collaboration died with him, but without in the least awaking his critical perception of Nazism. He took the death personally.

There is a back-and-forth pattern in Brasillach's occupation journalism. A brutal denunciatory column is often followed by a nostalgic one, or, when his nostalgia is disappointed, a denunciation will come on its heels. Following the tender, even sentimental obituary for Bremer, we see Brasillach's snide nasty side come into full flower. Bremer's death was clearly the fault of a Nazi policy that shipped officers off to die on the Eastern front, but Brasillach directed his violent anger at his own country. "Les Sept Internationales contre la patrie," the column he wrote the day after the Bremer obituary, was as severe and aggressive an article as he had ever penned. In it he classified the enemies of France into seven categories, in this order: the communists, the socialists, the Jews, the Catholics, the Protestants, the freemasons, the financial world. In this article, in the section on the Jews, was the line where Brasillach spoke of the need to "separate from the Jews *en bloc* and not keep any little ones," suggesting that Jewish children be deported with their parents. The phrase, as we shall see, returned to haunt him at his trial.

It was in part out of a sense of loss and mourning for Bremer that Brasillach made his second trip under German auspices, this time to the Eastern front, where Bremer had lost his life. In July 1943, he accompanied the representative of the French government in Paris, Fernand de Brinon, on a trip that culminated in Katyn, Poland. The Soviets had executed 21,857 Polish officers there in 1940, and the Nazis were using the discovery of the mass grave as an anti-Soviet propaganda tool on the eve of their defeat at the Russian front. In France, the Nazi reputation for brutality was so great, many people believed that the massacres could only have been the Nazis' doing. On a rare tape recording of a radio broadcast from the Occupation era, "The Voice of the Reich," we can hear Brasillach's voice for a mere ten seconds. It is a serious but boyish tenor. This is all we hear: "Do you have any thoughts about what you've seen?" the reporter asks. "I don't have much to add to what his excellence the ambassador de Brinon said before me. The incredulous need to come see for themselves."

Later, at his trial, he said he had traveled to Katyn solely as an investigative reporter. On the tape, he sounds like a lackey.

The Break with *Je Suis Partout*

In the dog days of 1943 a dispute took place that would break up the editorial team at *Je Suis Partout,* that would lead Brasillach to tender his resignation as editor in chief and force him to sever all relations with the paper. The issues were money and politics. Brasillach lost.

Je Suis Partout, still France's leading fascist newspaper, was the most widely read newspaper in the occupied zone: 150,000 copies per issue were printed in 1941; 250,000 copies in 1942; 300,000 in 1944. From April 25, 1941, until August 13, 1943, Brasillach's name had appeared on the upper left-hand corner of the *Je Suis Partout* masthead as the weekly paper's editor in chief. The themes of his regular page-one columns were consistent: loyalty to the cause of the prisoners of war, the perfidious treachery of Third Republic democracy, the dream of a fascism custom-made for France. Like every fascist in occupied France, Brasillach was caught in a fundamental contradiction: how to live out his dream of a fascist nationalism with the reality of Nazi domination; how to make Nazism and French fascism rhyme. On this issue and others, Brasillach had often played the moderate to colleague Lucien Rebatet. Rebatet was another young Action Française writer who had turned to fascism and whose anti-Semitism was even more extreme and pointed than Brasillach's. Rebatet, not Brasillach, had appeared as special editor of the two prewar issues of *Je Suis Partout* devoted to anti-Semitism.

In 1942, Rebatet's *Les Décombres,* an indictment of prewar France, had become a national bestseller, making him the most visible political satirist in France. It included a hilarious parody of the old men who produced the *Action Française* newspaper, portraits of their incompetence and senility. Rebatet did not forgive Maurras for supporting France's war effort against Germany in 1939. Brasillach's review of *Les Décombres* was typical of the way he positioned himself on the paper. He agreed with Rebatet in essence: for him, Maurras was the man who gave up on his antiwar stance, who was old (Brasillach accuses everyone of being old: Gide, Mauriac, now Maurras), and whose admirable anti-Semitic, antidemocratic passion had faded. But characteristically, Brasillach remained nostalgic about the Action Française:

> All that was left for this strange [political] house was to harbor genius under dust, courage under conformism, love of country under illusion. . . . You can't take away the fact that it has been the only political school of the twentieth century. Today, now that its history is finished, we must bear witness to that without fear and with friendship.

Although he says it sweetly, what he means in this 1942 review is that the Action Française movement was finished, dead for him. He maintained that what France needed instead was a distinctly French brand of fascism: "It is not about transporting the German way of life here," he insisted as late as 1943, "it's about giving birth to a French national socialism, in the same way that Falangism is Spanish and fascism is Italian." Brasillach was caught, as were his peers, in a contradiction that taxed his rhetorical skills: how does one collaborate with the Nazi occupiers yet remain a fervent proponent of the authoritarian French state? He maintained a filial Pétainist tone in many of his articles, as though he were following the politics of Vichy, but his actual beliefs were compatible with Rebatet's.

That compatibility would dissolve in 1943, the turning point for *Je Suis Partout,* and for the collaboration in general. That year, Mussolini's fascist government collapsed; Germany was being massively bombed and losing the war. An Allied victory was looking more and more certain. In this atmosphere, both Vichy collaborators and Parisian pro-Nazis were shaken; once the Nazis appeared to be on the verge of defeat, there were many defections from the ranks of the collaboration.

At this moment of crisis, one faction at *Je Suis Partout,* close to the major stockholder Lesca, wanted to go further in the direction of pro-German politics. This group of writers, including Lesca, Cousteau, and Rebatet—the so-called "hard-liners"—actively supported Jacques Doriot's fascist political party, the Parti Populaire Français, and cheered the actions of the Vichy Milice.

Brasillach led the other, so-called "soft" faction, allied with Henri Poulain and Georges Blond. Since Germany was clearly going to lose the war, Brasillach wanted the paper to stop talking about German victory. He wanted to orient the paper's line toward literary questions—as if such a move would be possible after all that *Je Suis Partout* had said and done to promote fascism, especially German fascism.

One single article makes clear how much Brasillach was trying to revise *Je Suis Partout*'s direction in the eleventh hour. On August 6, a day when the readers of *Je Suis Partout* awaited Brasillach's analysis of Mussolini's arrest, they found instead a book review by Brasillach of Anatole de Monzie's *La Saison des juges* [The season of the judges]. De Monzie, a lawyer and former minister during the Third Republic, can be classified neither as a resistance intellectual nor as a collaborator. He was a highly conciliatory intellectual—considered by many a kind of liberal of the collaboration. *La Saison des juges* criticized the "accusatory mania" so rampant in France, both in everyday life, in the Vichy courts, and in newspapers like *Je Suis Partout*. De Monzie ridiculed the surfeit of new laws, and both private and public denunciations that had befallen the country since the Occupation. The Vichy magistrature came under special attack—for the Riom debacle, for the Special Tribunals, for the exaggerated verdicts of the black-market courts, and for caving in to German interference. De Monzie recommended blanket political amnesty to safeguard individual liberty in a period of crisis.

In his review of *La Saison des juges,* Brasillach took de Monzie's accusation personally. He insisted, in so many words, that *Je Suis Partout*'s political attacks on ministers like Reynaud and Mandel were of a different order—braver and more just—than what the French were doing when they denounced their neighbors anonymously and falsely to their local Kommandanturen. A revolutionary like himself, Brasillach argued, could not give up on the idea of social justice.

Brasillach was untruthful here. *Je Suis Partout*'s very identity was tied to the act of finger pointing, from the relative safety of the printed page, with the intention of promoting direct, violent results. In *Je Suis Partout*'s "Partout and ailleurs" column, Jews, Gaullists, and resistance activists had been denounced, their names and addresses printed, while imprisoned political figures of the Third Republic had been attacked regularly in signed columns calling for murder, for the previous three years. Insolence and cruel humor, part of *Je Suis Partout*'s trademark, were inseparable from the power of its accusations: Brasillach himself had set the tone before the war with articles like "The Monkey Question." Oddly, Brasillach's disagreement with de Monzie, polite and respectful, was suddenly that of a good student, as though he wanted to hide the fact that he himself was the very example of the "attack dog" or "tape-dur" [hard-hitter] de Monzie considered among the most dangerous "judges" of the era.

The respectful tone of Brasillach's review, as well as its timing, were a clear provocation to his colleagues. The factions were already in place, but this article brought the editorial staff into open conflict. Lesca, the head of the hard-liners, challenged Brasillach. The public had wanted an article on the Italian crisis. Why was Brasillach wasting his column on de Monzie, that liberal? A series of meetings, an exchange of bitter letters ensued between Brasillach and Lesca's fellow "hard-liners," Cousteau and Rebatet. For Lesca, the ideological argument may well have been a pretext for further consolidating his financial control of the *Je Suis Partout* stock. As a result of this battle, the *Je Suis Partout* "soviet" split in two: Blond and Poulain left the paper with Brasillach; the hard-liners stayed on with Lesca. Brasillach said in his interview with the examining magistrate before his trial that *Je Suis Partout*'s net profits for 1943, at the time of his departure, were four and a half million francs. He made a bonus of 120,000 francs for his work that year. It was a nice nest egg, but he was leaving a gold mine. Reading the accounts of the break, we conclude that Brasillach engineered his own departure from *Je Suis Partout*. He may well have had no choice in the matter.

On August 13, 1943, the *Je Suis Partout* masthead appeared for the first time without Robert Brasillach's name as editor in chief. On August 27, Brasillach published his discreet adieu. In a brief appendix to his last regular column, he explained that several trips, especially the one to the Eastern front with Ambassador Brinon, had kept him far from *Je Suis Partout*. Now, various work was preventing him from applying the intense focus that an editorship demanded. "I cease my functions as editor in chief," he wrote. "Pierre-A. Cousteau will take care of the paper."

From the time of his release from the POW camp, to the end of the
Occupation, Brasillach serialized two novels in the collaborationist press.
La Conquérante [The woman conqueror], his fantasy about the French
colonization of Morocco, appeared in *Je Suis Partout* from April to
August 1942. With its celebration of French colonial power, it offered
good escape for beleaguered, defeated readers. *Six heures à perdre* [Six
hours to kill] appeared in *Révolution Nationale* from March to June 1944.
Even the crisis at *Je Suis Partout* hadn't slowed his pace.

Six heures à perdre, like so much of Brasillach's writing from this
period, was inspired by his nostalgia for life in the POW camp. The
narrator, a newly released prisoner of war, has one day in Paris between
trains home and goes to see his best friend's girlfriend. He reflects on
the intimacy that links prisoners of war, even stronger than the ties
between lovers: "I don't think there are many prisoners who haven't
one day told a comrade what they could never say to their nearest and
dearest in peacetime." The book is ostensibly a detective novel about his
friend's girl and her troubled life, but the narrator's nightly confidences
with Bruno in the camp, followed by their tearful farewell scene at the
gates of the camp, are the emotional highlights of the story. The loss
of his gang at *Je Suis Partout* is obviously present between the lines of
this novel.

Brasillach's skewed view of daily life under the Occupation emerges
in *Six heures à perdre,* as well. Resistants are referred to in the novel just
as they were in Vichy propaganda as "terrorists" or "dissidents." They
were to blame for the German murder of hostages, for the sacrifices
demanded of the French people.

The real terrorists in France were on the side of Vichy, in Darnand's
Milice. By the end of the Occupation, this militia, armed and subsidized
and government trained, had become a death squad. The Milice assassinated many of the men targeted in the columns of *Je Suis Partout* in 1944:
Jean Zay, former Minister of Education imprisoned by Vichy, was taken
out of his prison cell and shot in a grotto. Georges Mandel, Minister
of the Interior in the Reynaud government and the man responsible
for the arrest and interrogation of the *Je Suis Partout* team in 1939, was
gunned down in the forest at Fontainebleau in reprisal for the resistance's
execution of fascist radio star and Minister of Information Philippe
Henriot. Victor Basch, eighty-one-year-old founder of the League of
the Rights of Man, was led out onto a road with his wife and shot in
the back. These were murders of Frenchmen by Frenchmen. Blum and

Reynaud, the other principal targets of *Je Suis Partout,* were deported to political detention camps.

Brasillach knew people in the resistance. He was sought out by fellow *normaliens,* by prisoners of war, to intervene in favor of family members who had been arrested, and, when there was a personal tie, he seems to have tried to intervene. But in public, in his writing, Brasillach remained hostile to the resistance, indifferent in particular to the risks taken by intellectuals. Marc Bloch, Jacques Ducour, Georges Politzer were among the distinguished intellectuals shot by the Germans for their acts of resistance against the occupier. Writers arrested simply for their race, such as poet Max Jacob, perished in transit or in extermination camps.

Je Suis Partout, more than any other newspaper, any other instrument of propaganda in occupied France, was identified with these deaths. Brasillach claimed at his trial that he hadn't been an enthusiast of the Milice. Perhaps he wasn't, but it made no difference. From March 1941 to August 1943, on the front page of the largest-circulation newspaper in occupied France, Brasillach had asked for vengeance, had demanded the destruction of his political enemies. The Milice had come along, funded and organized by Vichy, to make his dreams a reality. Although he had quit the paper a year before the liberation of Paris, Brasillach had been the editor in chief of *Je Suis Partout,* and his name, talent, and identity as a writer and intellectual were forever linked to language so hateful, it seemed to have been transmuted directly into thousands upon thousands of murderous acts.

———

After Brasillach left *Je Suis Partout,* the remaining team at the newspaper wrote about holding firm, sticking to the fascist program. They organized an inspirational political meeting at the Salle Wagram, a Paris convention center, under the slogan "Nous ne sommes pas des dégonflés" [We are not deflated]—a not-so-indirect cut on Brasillach's defection.

From our perspective, it is easy to imagine Brasillach in 1943 as a man who was finally waking up to the political reality of treasonous collaboration. To the men who stayed at *Je Suis Partout,* he was a rat deserting a ship he had decided was going to sink. "Fidelity to National Socialism" was the title of one of Rebatet's last editorials. Behind the headline was Brasillach, the infidel. In a private letter to Rebatet at the moment of their rupture, Brasillach sounded as French as he could: "I am Germanophile and French. French more than national socialist, really," he wrote; and, "In case of danger, one must stick with the nation: only she does not betray"; and "I don't want to be more German than the Germans"; though he added a sentence that his apologists have never quoted: "In a word, I have confidence in the Wehrmacht and in Adolf's patriotism." It was typical of him to take refuge in a sentimental nationalism, leaving aside the implications of his collaboration with the occupier, at the same time as he sounded lightheartedly supportive of the German army, with no sense of a contradiction. Nonetheless, his letter was a first effort at self-defense, as though he could already anticipate having to justify his behavior.

Brasillach may well have hoped that the departure from *Je Suis Partout* would protect him if he was called to account for his actions after a German defeat. Any collaborator in Paris who had any sense at all had plenty of reason to be frightened by 1943.

What appears foolhardy—if in fact he did begin to sense he was in danger of being arrested at the Allied victory—is that Brasillach did not convert to an exclusive French patriotism after he broke with *Je Suis Partout*. He continued his collaborationist writing in a series of editorials for *Révolution Nationale*, Lucien Combelle's newspaper, whose title referred to Pétain's grand design for Vichy, and whose major columnist was the fascist literary figure Drieu la Rochelle. He showed no signs of a change of heart. If anything, Brasillach's rhetoric at *Révolution Nationale* became more pro-German than ever. What he changed was his tone. He was less political and more sentimental in his approach to political subjects.

What was really motivating this rhetoric is a point of contention. Brasillach's apologists like to present his departure from *Je Suis Partout* as an act of courage and independence. Anne Brassié, his biographer, reports that Brasillach thought that Rebatet had denounced him to the Germans; she contends that Brasillach thought his mail was being opened, and that he feared that he might be arrested by the Gestapo for having abandoned his post at *Je Suis Partout*. The idea is preposterous, although Brasillach himself cultivated something close to this story when he was interrogated in preparation for his trial. He told a police inspector that the German propaganda office had reported on his departure from *Je Suis Partout*, and that a clandestine resistance journal had reported on the Germans' report. It's as though he wanted the Liberation government to believe he had undergone a conversion experience, that he was hated by the Germans for leaving the paper, and that he had become, after 1943, a subject of interest to the resistance—almost one of them.

His story is belied in the report published by the German propaganda office in Paris in October 1943. Here is how the Nazis analyzed

Brasillach's departure from *Je Suis Partout* and his move to *Révolution Nationale:*

> Brasillach, editor of the courageous political weekly *Je Suis Partout*
> . . . suggested to the editorial board of his paper that they should
> retreat from coverage of current political issues and in the future
> offer only literature—this under the influence of Mussolini's 'res-
> ignation.' . . . Brasillach's proposal to flee politics was rejected by
> a majority. Brasillach left the editorship. As if they needed to be
> forgiven, the remaining editors redoubled their political credo. . . .
> The number of courageous articles, signed personally, increased.
> Brasillach, motivated by a sort of shame, published an article in
> *Révolution Nationale* on the collaboration of hearts between Ger-
> many and France. Encouraged by his entourage, he has resumed his
> valuable political work.

In other words, his loyalty to Germany had been tested, and he was as useful to the Nazis at one collaborationist newspaper as at another.

If this report is any indication of the political situation, Brasillach's fear of retaliation from the Germans was either misguided or disingenuous. The Germans themselves spelled it out in the text of their report: he had more to fear from the resistance than from them. He was obviously better off sending freelance articles to *Révolution Nationale* than working full-time as editor at *Je Suis Partout,* whose editorial office on the rue de Rivoli must have been one of the most tempting targets for resistance bombs in Paris. The German Propaganda-Staffel report had also commented that various "friends of Germany" were becoming targets for the resistance: "the question of personal protection becomes more and more urgent." They were probably referring to the execution of Belgian journalist Paul Colin, a fascist greatly admired by Brasillach. The Nazi propaganda bureau in Paris, in raising the issue of personal protection for the collaborationist journalists in their report on Brasillach, seemed to be saying that they approved of his withdrawal from the *Je Suis Partout* editorship to a more discreet role.

What remains more difficult to explain, if he did indeed leave *Je Suis Partout* both to protect his personal safety and in anticipation of a treason trial, are his last articles with their loving references to Germany. These, as we will see, would serve in his trial as the rhetorical nails in Brasillach's coffin.

In a September 4, 1943, article in *Révolution Nationale,* Brasillach described meeting a friend on the street who told him of his sudden change of heart, his sudden rush of sympathy for the German occupier, at the moment when Germany was being bombed at home and beaten on the Russian front. The fiction of a man on the street allows Brasillach to express affection for the Germans, and pretend at the same time that he's just an observer. (The nuance would be lost on his prosecutor.) "I love the Germans," the fictional friend tells the reporter Brasillach, and continues:

> When I see German soldiers, on the street or in the countryside, these soldiers against whom I waged war, as my own people have done for three generations, I want to talk to them, to shake their hands for no particular reason, as though they were our own boys. It must be since they've received some bad blows that no one can deny. . . . I tell myself that they are courageous beyond what we even know, I tell myself that they're strong, and especially, I tell myself that they are *ours*. . . . I want to shake them by the arm, talk to them and give them moral support, explain our misunderstandings to them frankly, tell them, as if I were speaking to my brothers, that they've made mistakes, errors, but that, so what! We're still side by side, and friends of the same race [*copains du même sang*]. To sum it up, I was once a collaborationist out of logic; I've become a collaborationist of the heart.

Who is this narrator? It was someone who allowed Brasillach, the reporter, to say what he could not say directly—that his identification and his affections were with the German soldiers occupying Paris, not with the resistance, not with the Allies who had landed in North Africa. There was nothing in the article to distinguish Brasillach's own point of view from that of this mysterious friend on the street, and so the reader had to conclude that the friend on the street was he, Brasillach.

On February 19, 1944, six months before the Allies marched into Paris, Brasillach wrote an article which we might consider his swan song as a collaborator. He deploys here his famous sense of an ending, his penchant for nostalgic description of adventures that are about to come to an end. Here, he is no longer hiding behind the fictional friend:

> It seems to me that I've contracted a liaison with German genius, one that I will never forget. Whether we like it or not, we will have lived together. Frenchmen given to reflection, during these years, will have more or less slept with Germany—not without quarrels— and the memory of it will remain sweet for them.

"We will have lived together" [*Nous aurons cohabité ensemble*]: it's a strange nostalgic verb tense, this future perfect—a future that anticipates the past. Of all Brasillach's metaphors, of all the images in his fiction, of all his clever phrases, this is the one for which he will be remembered the longest.

In one interpretation of the famous line, Brasillach is responding to attacks by his former friends who accused him of abandoning the collaborationist cause, of being "deflated" [*dégonflé*]. In French, the word *dégonflé* means "wimped out"; it is also a metaphor for impotence, detumescence. Not only had Brasillach stuck by Germany, was his answer, he had slept with her. He wasn't limp. In another possible reading of the same passage, he is still writing in the presence of the German occupier, protecting his reputation as a cooperative Frenchman. It is quite possible he was doing both.

After the Allies invaded the coast of Normandy in June 1944, the Germans knew that their days in Paris were numbered. They prepared to retreat from the capital, while to the north, the D-day forces hesitated about their own military strategy. Shouldn't they bypass Paris, whose liberation was an expensive and time-consuming proposition, and march directly towards Alsace-Lorraine? De Gaulle lobbied Eisenhower to order a French-led battalion into France's capital. He argued that the French themselves needed to play a key role in expelling the German occupiers from their headquarters and in striking down the collaborationist Milice. De Gaulle's deeper concern was to ward off potential threats to national unity, and to his own sovereignty. He feared an American occupation of France almost as much as he feared a communist takeover.

It is a famous story. Eisenhower finally gave in to French lobbying and allowed the French division under his command to enter the capital, bolstered by large numbers of Americans. The divisional commander was General Philippe Leclerc. On the evening of the 24th of August, 1944, the first men in Leclerc's division crossed the city limits. Paris had been in the throes of a communist-inspired insurrection against the Nazis since August 19.

———

Bernadette Reboul, whose father, Marcel Reboul, sought the death sentence for Brasillach, tells about the week of August 19 as though there were a novel in her head. The Rebouls lived on the rue Geoffroy St. Hilaire, which ran alongside the Jardin des Plantes. Two days before the insurrection, the curator of the Jardin des Plantes put the *tricolore* French flag up on the gate marking the entrance to the gardens. Everyone in the neighborhood gathered beneath the flag, to sing the Marseillaise. It was the first national anthem they had sung since Paris had been occupied, and little Bernadette's first, ever. Marcel Reboul, renowned for his speaking voice in the courtroom, sang completely off key. Bernadette's mother sang and cried as she tried to hold her daughter in her arms. Jacques Isorni, their neighbor across the hall, their landlord and their friend, was with them. He was a successful lawyer in the Paris bar, who, by a quirk of fate and circumstance, was going to play opposite

Reboul six months later, as Brasillach's defense lawyer. Isorni said to Madame Reboul, "You can't sing, cry, and hold the little one at the same time—I'll take her." Perhaps all Bernadette Reboul remembers, in her mind's eye, is the view of the trees from Jacques Isorni's arms, but by now, the scene at the Jardin des Plantes is a family legend, with all its details and lines of dialogue intact. Today, she laughs at the idea that her first Marseillaise was in the arms of the man who defended Brasillach and Pétain against the French state.

At the garden, she says, the Reboul family heard the sound of gunfire coming from the rooftops. The snipers were collaborationists, members of Darnand's militia. The FFI, the Forces Françaises de l'Intérieur, who had established themselves as the armed forces of the Liberation, came to the Jardin des Plantes and announced to the people who had gathered, "It's too early, don't come out yet. It's dangerous. Go back home."

It was indeed dangerous to be walking in the streets of Paris that week, but Bernadette's mother, a handsome forty-year-old with shining black eyes and gray hair, wanted to see what was happening. On August 18, she stopped on the street for conversation with a judge's son, complimenting him on the *tricolore* rosette—a symbol of the French nation—that graced his lapel. He told Madame Reboul that there was a man selling the rosettes in the metro, out of an upside down umbrella. The merchant had a friend keeping an eye out for him, because if German soldiers saw him, he would be arrested. The next day, the day of insurrection, Madame Reboul found the rosette merchant; he was making a fortune in the entrance to the Maubert Mutualité metro station. She bought a rosette and put it proudly on her blouse. She walked down the rue des Ecoles, on her way to the boulevard Saint-Michel. At the Ecole Polytechnique, she saw a German officer coming at her in the other direction. He looked at her and stopped in his tracks. Mrs. Reboul froze. He pulled out his gun and cocked it. There was a moment when nothing happened, when she trembled. Slowly, almost reluctantly, the soldier put his gun back in his holster and walked the other way. When she stopped shaking, she remembered the *tricolore* symbol on her blouse. How could she have forgotten it! She put it quickly into her purse and continued on her way, her legs like jelly. She made it home alive.

The residents of 51, rue Geoffroy St. Hilaire, had become intimate friends during the Occupation, because of the hours spent hovering together in the basement, during the bombing raid *alertes*. During the insurrection, neighbors Marcel Reboul and Jacques Isorni went out

into the street together to turn sacks of sand, cobblestones, and old
bed frames from their basement into barricades. Tanks couldn't be
stopped by sandbags, so the barricades didn't make much logistical
sense anymore, but they were a Parisian custom, Bernadette Reboul
explains, a revolutionary ritual. Isorni and Reboul had never been
on the same side judicially, with Isorni at the bar and Reboul at the
bench. They had already participated on opposites sides of the same
trial during the Occupation in a black-market case—Isorni defended
the black marketeer, Reboul prosecuted for the Pétainist state. But
they were colleagues, part of the same legal community. The Brasillach
trial would change that relationship forever, take them beyond their
neighborhood, beyond their legal community and into a larger world
of political contention. In August 1944 they were still comrades in arms.

Marcel Reboul did not belong to any official resistance network.
He had signed an oath of loyalty to Pétain, along with every member of
the magistrature, save one. But he identified fully with the Liberation
forces. On August 23, the day before Leclerc's division arrived in the city,
Reboul was with members of the resistance who had taken possession
of the Palais de Justice when the insurrection began.

On the afternoon of August 24, Madame Reboul made her way to
the Palais to get her husband; a friend was dying, and it was time to go
to his bedside. The Rebouls took their familiar route home, crossing the
Ile de la Cité towards the river. On the Pont Neuf, a working-class man,
who seemed to recognize Reboul, stopped them. "Go to the balcony
and open your window at dawn tomorrow morning, and you'll see the
French flag floating atop the Hôtel de Ville." He knew that General
Leclerc and his tanks were approaching Paris.

Nearly a week had passed since Isorni and the Rebouls had sung the
Marseillaise at the Jardin des Plantes. That night of the 24th, Bernadette
Reboul's parents were at the bedside of their dying friend. Paris was
nearly silent. Suddenly Bernadette heard a noise on the street. The little
girl peeked through the curtains out her living room window and saw
an enormous tank coming up from the Cuvier Fountain on the other
side of the street. A machine gun sticking out of its turret was scoping
the rooftops.

"Is it more Germans?" she said to her grandmother.

"No dear," she remembers her grandmother answering, "this time
it's the Americans and we're free."

There were apartments on one side of the rue Geoffroy St. Hilaire;
the other side was the wall of the public gardens. The apartments were

bourgeois, with decorative wrought-iron balconies and tall, narrow windows. The night of the 24th, if you walked along that street, you would have seen every window thrown open wide. Inside the apartment houses, every household opened its doors to receive people. The hosts went into their cellars, where for four years they had gone regularly during the air raid alerts, to dig out their last bottles of champagne or their last bottle of good wine to drink with the liberators.

Bernadette remembers that her parents came home and took her out onto the rue Geoffroy St. Hilaire, hours past her bedtime. One of the French boys asked permission to kiss her mother. He had been in Chad, he said, had crossed the desert, had come to Paris with Leclerc and was going on to take Alsace. He hadn't seen his family in two years. "Of course my mother kissed him," Bernadette remembers. The Americans were distributing chocolate, oranges, chewing gum, bananas. She had never seen a banana, and she bit into one without peeling it. "Of course I had never seen an orange, either." Everything had been requisitioned by the Germans.

That first night, the neighbors housed the Allied officers in apartments along their street. The enlisted men, the GIs, slept in tents under the beautifully sculpted trees inside the Jardin des Plantes. Thus Bernadette's tale of Liberation begins and ends in a mythical space, a garden of liberation.

―――

That summer, a young man from the southwest named Roger Grenier was living in Paris, managing the distribution of flasks, glasses, and bottles for a government agency called the OCRPI. He was also a member of the resistance. As the Liberation approached, he decided to keep track of events in the city, day by day, in notes he could share later with his fiancée in Clermont-Ferrand. His modest journal describes how the Liberation made him a reporter, one of the new generation who would replace the Robert Brasillachs of France.

On August 16 he wrote, "There's no more metro now. Yet I'm supposed to go to the office. It's odd, I still don't write everything down. The habit of suspicion is tenacious." That evening he continued taking notes, and what came out on the page were terse headlines: "The gas is cut. They're going to close the restaurants. . . . The police strike continues."

"These brief news items," he added with a young writer's self-consciousness, "remind me of one of the techniques that Malraux uses to explain a situation."

August 17: "In the morning, around 6:30, I'm awakened by the angry voices of people standing in line at the bakery. I try to go back to sleep, but we're very nervous right now. You hear detonations in the distance." The food shortages were at their worst, and people were willing to get up with the sun for the dark-brown, unrefined, tasteless doorstops that counted as bread. What Grenier was hearing were the sounds of the Allied troops at Dreux, a few hours west of Paris:

> They say that the Germans will leave today and that the Americans will come. I ate at Solange's bistro, everyone was talking about it. It's idiotic, because the Americans still have the Germans right in front of them and the Germans, too, will have to go somewhere. When I look at Paris, I try to take its pulse, not from people's faces, but from the avenues and intersections. What kinds of faces are the houses making, tonight? The ones at the corner of the Gobelins don't look like they're expecting an important event to happen. . . . There are no more German vehicles on the boulevard. Perhaps that's a sign.

By Friday, the 18th, the distress of the departing German soldiers was palpable: "It seems that they fire on the crowd at any provocation—over nothing [*pour un rien*]. They're leaving for good this time, in haste." It was in this tense setting that a soldier would almost gun down Madame Reboul for wearing a rosette on her lapel. Crowds were rushing to scavenge buildings as quickly as the Germans abandoned them, looking for food and coal. "Resistance posters are calling for insurrection," Grenier noted. "The printers are on strike, the hospitals are on strike. There are no newspapers. Last night's explosions were gasoline supplies being detonated by the Germans." His last comment for the day: "I get scarcely a tiny dribble of water from my faucet."

He announced the insurrection on August 19: "Tricolor flags at the Hôtel de Ville, the Palais de Justice, Notre-Dame. Germans pass by in their cars and look surprised." Going to work was inconceivable. Grenier walked through what he called the "nerve centers" of the city, with his jacket slung over his shoulders to hide his camera, a Voigtlander. He was planning to take pictures.

At the center of the battle, boulevard Saint-German and boulevard Saint-Michel, the Germans were making people cross the street with their hands in the air. At a calmer intersection, rue de Bellechasse and the boulevard Saint-Germain, a soldier stopped him, searched him, put a machine gun under his nose. He tried to show his work papers from the OCRPI; the soldier ignored them. Instead, he seized Grenier's camera and threw it into the gun turret of one of the German tanks. Grenier tried to protest: "Photo . . . expensive," but the soldier simply barked, "Go!"

Another search twenty meters later was a different story. The German soldiers stopped him and ordered him to put his hands in the air. He felt another machine gun pushed into his back. They searched him. No one looked in his vest pocket, where he had put a tricolor rosette that he, like Madame Reboul, had purchased from a street merchant. It was a good thing he'd forgotten about it, he would have been even more frightened. The soldier pushed him, asked him to advance and turn around more completely.

"I was certain it was all over," Grenier wrote in his diary. "Although I remained quite attentive, I was thinking deep inside that I hadn't accomplished anything yet in my life; 'already?' I said to myself, and I was furious."

A couple of old people who could speak German emerged from the doorway of their apartment building down the street and started talking to the Germans, distracting them. Finally the soldier made a sign. "I didn't understand very well that I could go. In my doubt, I told myself that at the point where I was, I couldn't risk anything worse. The German in charge repeated his sign. I took one step, then another, and I left timidly, turning my head around to see if they weren't calling me back."

The boulevards were jammed, so Grenier took a circuitous route home to his apartment at the Gobelins. "I stopped in a café to drink water with mint syrup [*menthes à l'eau*]," he wrote. "My thirst was inextinguishable."

That afternoon he finally made contact with his comrades in the CDLR—the resistance group known as "Ceux de la Résistance" [those of the resistance]. At dawn they were going to occupy the Hôtel de Ville, the big wedding cake of a building on the right bank of the Seine and the headquarters of Paris's administrative prefect. Grenier joined them early in the morning of August 20. He spent the rest of the week occupying the prefect's office, as the organizer of the liberation movement's press dispatches. The taking back of the Hôtel de Ville, the arrest of the collaborator prefect, was one of the high moments of Liberation week. Grenier's adjunct duty, the same week, was to serve as CDLR representative for the eighteenth arrondissement, in Montmartre. He had never before set foot in the eighteenth, but there weren't enough members of the CDLR to go around. Each

arrondissement, or district, of Paris had its own city hall, and each
city hall was liberated by a "Committee of Liberation," composed of
representatives from the major resistance groups. Under the umbrella of
de Gaulle's provisional government, the local Committees of Liberation
took power the week of August 19, replacing the collaborationist mayors
and city council members. Veritable mosaics of the resistance, the
Committees of Liberation furnished the mayors, the adjunct mayors,
the members of the city council in every arrondissement and suburb of
Paris after the war. In the heady months of fall 1944, the Committees
of Liberation purged the collaborators in their own communities and
served as official advisers to the justice system, helping compose lists of
potential jurors. That was how the members of the jury for the Brasillach
trial were chosen.

In the thick of the fighting between the free French and the
remaining Germans, Roger Grenier ran back and forth from the Hôtel
de Ville to the eighteenth arrondissement, due north. He stopped from
time to time to take shelter in the entryways of apartment buildings
along his way. There were bodies in the streets, blood everywhere; and
wherever he went, he had to be on the lookout for stray bullets. Along
the quais, he witnessed an attack on a German truck: two men killed,
six prisoners taken. He dragged one of the dead to the Hôtel de Ville
entrance: "He was heavy and I had to run. This morning, I had been
home to put on a light-colored suit jacket and a new tie to receive some
of the big shots with dignity. A great idea, since I then had to crawl from
office to office [avoiding bullets] after dragging this dead man who was
pissing blood."

On the 22nd of August, he wonders, "When will we see the Allies?
We've held out for four days, most often thanks to a bluff, with a few
arms taken from the enemy. Still, it pains me to think about the moment
when the battle will stop. You have to imagine the luxurious office
of the prefect: wood paneling, mirrors, gilded surfaces, and precious
antiques. I eat a sandwich next to an FFI shooting from the windows,
important fellows are carrying on conversations underneath tables. My
friend André Brane, in a corner, looks for jazz on the radio, a cameraman
is filming nonstop. That's the usual ambiance."

"They're here," he announces on Thursday, August 24, in a passage
marked "10:30 P.M.":

Everyone ran out screaming in joy. On the square the first of
Leclerc's cars arrived, and light tanks. We shot all that was left of

our ammunition in the air, and flares, too. I climbed on the tanks, tanks manned by Frenchmen. A collective delirium. . . . I phoned up all the newspapers. The bells are ringing, ringing in all of Paris.

On August 25, dazed and exhausted, but satisfied, Grenier writes:

I played the American reporter. . . . Today I organized the press service. I am happy with my exclusive on the arrival of the French troops and on the broadcast of the interview with the lieutenant that Lerclerc's avant-garde left behind, along with two tanks. Actually, the situation is very confused. There are tank battles all over Paris. I have to sleep a little. My friends under attack at the Palais Berlitz don't answer the phone anymore. I hope they were able to evacuate. Victory.

From this point on, for another five pages, what he writes has the feel of an epilogue. Paris is liberated.

———

For Arlette Grebel, the arrival of Leclerc and his tanks was an "immense rumor that crossed Paris and made the entire city shudder . . . the cry of a young boy running in the streets, 'They're at the Hôtel de Ville!' . . . the clacking of a thousand shutters and windows that popped out like corks on every facade . . ." Citizens of occupied Paris had been painting their windowpanes navy blue so that no glimmer of light could get out to guide the Allied airplanes in their nightly raids. Now the windows were opening. Fifty years later, recalling the events of August, Grebel refers to a description of liberated Paris she has never forgotten, an evocation of the buzzing noise coming from inside the Tuileries gardens. The gardens were teeming with people making love. "How can I describe it. We had overthrown Nazism; we had our whole future in front of us and we were going to build a new world."

In August 1944, Arlette Grebel was twenty years old, a recent graduate of a journalism school on the rue Notre-Dame des Champs in Paris. There she had attended lectures by Georges Montandon, the racial anthropologist and friend of Céline's who was a member of the school's conseil d'administration. Another of the school's administrators was Alphonse de Chateaubriant, the editor of the anti-Semitic newspaper *La Gerbe,* a white-haired, bushy-bearded ideologue who would finish out his days as a hermit in the Black Forest, escaping a French death sentence for treason. Grebel despised him. The faculty of her school also included a priest in the resistance who rounded out his lectures with courageous anti–Nazi remarks. In this confused ideological atmosphere, Grebel graduated first in her class, knowing something about how a newspaper functioned.

Like Bernadette Reboul, Arlette Grebel was alone with her grandmother, on the rue Danton in suburban Levallois-Perret, the night the Allied tanks arrived. Her brother, a member of the resistance who had spent the last months of the war in hiding, appeared at the house with a suitcase full of bottles of champagne that he had seized from the abandoned quarters of a German officer. When they opened the windows, they saw the other open windows and the Allied flags flying— Russian, American, and British flags. The neighbors had pieced them together from precious scraps of fabric.

On June 22, 1944, De Gaulle's provisional government declared the collaborationist press illegal and ordered its assets seized. The anarchist diarist Jean Galtier-Boissière baptized Brasillach's former newspaper "Je suis parti" [I'm out of here!]. The abandoned headquarters of *Je Suis Partout* on the rue de Rivoli were immediately ransacked. A new press corps had organized itself out of the various resistance movements—by August, once clandestine papers were ready to go public. They took the names, and the moral guarantee, of resistance groups: *Franc-Tireur, Combat, Libération, France-Libre.* This was the world that Arlette Grebel longed to join.

The week of August 25, these papers were so newly "above ground" that their addresses were still unknown. Arlette Grebel's brother, now a member of the Forces Françaises de l'Interieur in Paris, discovered where *France-Libre* had set up shop and brought her a freshly printed paper on its first day of publication. (*France-Libre*'s printing presses were taken over from *La Gerbe.*) Dressed in her only decent outfit, white bobby socks and a scout skirt, Arlette presented herself at the *France-Libre* editorial office. The editor on the scene was overwhelmed by the events in the city and the challenge of reporting them. "I'm not so great at reporting, but I'm excellent at writing columns," she announced boldly. She didn't have a day of newspaper experience in her life. He was charmed by her innocence, and besides, he was short of reporters. "There's a lot happening, go out in the street, find a story, write it up, and we'll see." He added, "Don't get yourself killed."

She spotted George Steven, the famous American news photographer, taking photos from a jeep. She jumped up into the jeep, shook his hand, and introduced herself for the first time in her life as a colleague: "I'm with *France-Libre*." With her bobby socks and scout skirt and the results of the Occupation diet, she was afraid she looked fifteen, rather than twenty.

She took her story back to her editor, who gave her suggestions and told her to go out again the next day. It was the day of de Gaulle's immortal speech at the Hôtel de Ville, the speech where the brilliant strategist of the Free French had seized the symbolic meaning of the insurrection, claiming that Paris had "liberated itself," thus giving a sense of healing power and control to the people who had been defeated and humiliated for four years:

> Paris brisé, Paris martyrisé, mais Paris libéré! libéré par lui-même!
> [Paris has been broken, Paris has been martyred, but Paris has been liberated, by herself!]

At the Hôtel de Ville, members of the Milice started shooting from their hiding places on the rooftops; a young soldier sheltered Arlette behind a tank.

An older, experienced reporter turned in his own version of those events. He got the by-line. But Aymé-Guerrin, the editor at *France-Libre,* liked Arlette's prose. He took choice phrases from the article she turned in and inserted them in the text signed by the seasoned reporter:

The Joy of Paris
Oh yes, look at us, in our own home now! People are going up to one another and they're hugging one another and they're kissing one another, men, women, children, in this incredible fervor . . .

Four months later, Arlette Grebel became a regular staff reporter for *France-Libre.* As the newspaper's special correspondent in Lyon, she covered the trial of Charles Maurras, beginning January 25, 1945, only ten days after Brasillach was condemned to death by the Paris Court of Justice. The Maurras trial was her chance to make a name for herself at *France-Libre.* Arlette was so green that her editor had had to explain to her who Charles Maurras was: the founder of the royalist Action Française, the most important right-wing polemicist of the century, but also, a notorious anti-Semite and collaborator. "Don't think of him as Charles Maurras, the great writer," Aymé-Guerrin advised her, "think of him as a man on trial for treason." The Maurras trial was an incongruous spectacle where, in response to the charges against him, the great polemicist of the Action Française responded with an eight-hour lecture defending his entire intellectual and political career. In her article of January 29, Grebel explained: "It isn't the politician we are judging, but the man who, during the Occupation, encouraged the repression of patriots, denounced many communists and Gaullists, stirred up persecutions of the Jews."

The staff at *France-Libre* clamored to read Arlette's daily dispatches, to see if anyone so young could possibly do the story justice. The old royalist escaped a death sentence with life in prison, prompting Brasillach to hope for his own pardon: "It seems to me a good thing in and of itself, and good for me," he wrote to Maurice Bardèche from his cell: "It's an argument, the master and the disciple, etc."

After the Maurras trial, Arlette Grebel, now a proven court reporter, was part of a lively scene of Liberation journalists, and she recalls with particular fondness her visits to *Combat,* where Roger Grenier, too, was starting out as a reporter. The seven-story building at 100, rue Réaumur, housed the major resistance dailies: *Franc-Tireur, Défense de la France,* and *Combat*—each on a separate floor, sharing a common printing press and typesetting stone. They had taken over the space from the *Pariser Zeitung,* the daily German-language newspaper of occupied Paris. With its three cramped offices and big pressroom, *Combat,* more than any paper in liberated Paris, had the feel of a collective. Grebel was inspired by the paper's sense of adventure and high purpose, and by the intense friendship among its staff. Whenever she arrived at *Combat,* she remembers, the office boy who sat at the front desk used to cry out, "France-Libre is here!—which one of you is waiting for France-Libre?"

———

While his colleagues were on trains heading towards Germany, escaping certain arrest and perhaps death sentences; while Arlette Grebel, Roger Grenier, and the Reboul family were anxiously awaiting the arrival of the Allies in Paris, the former *Je Suis Partout* editor was enjoying a last dinner at the German Institute, the Nazi-sponsored cultural center. It was a warm August night. Dinner was served in the gardens, under the trees. Brasillach sensed all around him the ghostly presence of his beloved Karl-Heinz Bremer; he was almost happy his friend wasn't alive to see their common dream of a Franco-German collaboration going down to defeat. Brasillach had already refused several chances to flee to Germany. Jean Luchaire, the collaborationist editor of *Les Nouveaux Temps* and head of the syndicate of the press, suggested it first. Brasillach's position was: he hadn't emigrated during the Occupation and he certainly wasn't going to leave his country now! By this stage of the war, he took a nationalist line whenever he talked to the "ultras"— the die-hard collaborationists. His former comrades from *Je Suis Partout* did leave with Luchaire. Now Karl Epting, the head of the German Institute, tried to convince him to join them, and he said no again. In the course of their long dinner, Brasillach performed his French patriotism for Epting and Heller, who reciprocated with nostalgic regrets about leaving France. "We stayed chatting in the garden for a long time, evoking what had been, what might have been," Brasillach wrote in his *Journal d'un homme occupé;* " . . . there were still delicious moments, and wakes have their charm. Tomorrow, the Institute would close: but why not get together again after the war?" Did he have any idea that his life was in danger? In August, could he even imagine the possibility of a treason trial, and did he think he was exempt from punishment?

On August 17, Brasillach went with his brother-in-law to the theater, the last night of theater in Paris, before the real theater of the insurrection began. The title of the play was perfect in a way they couldn't have appreciated: Sartre's *No Exit.* On August 18, Brasillach, like Roger Grenier, read the posters calling for insurrection. He was on his way to the Bibliothèque Nationale to put the finishing touches on his anthology of Greek poetry.

On August 19, Brasillach packed his bags and moved to a hiding place in a converted maid's quarters on the top floor of 16, rue de Tournon, down the street from the Luxembourg Gardens and the Senate building, where the Germans had governed. Marguerite Cravoisier, a friend from Sens, had prepared the hideaway for him. She had been in love with him for years despite his lack of response, and had worked for him intermittently as a secretary-typist.

"Jews have lived in cupboards for nearly four years. Why not imitate them?" he quipped in his diary.

Meanwhile, Sens, Brasillach's hometown in the north of Burgundy, was aflame with Liberation fever. The Forces Françaises de l'Intérieur, assisted by an enthusiastic and vengeful mob, arrested 2,000 citizens during the ten-day period from the 21st to the 30th of August. On the 21st, they rounded up a large crowd of women suspected of what came to be known as "horizontal collaboration"—sleeping with German soldiers. The women's heads were shaved bald, and they were paraded nude through the town. Général Leclerc took up brief residence that week in the Hôtel Paris et Poste, the best hotel in town.

On August 21, the Forces Françaises de L'Intérieur paid a call to Brasillach's mother and stepfather in their bourgeois mansion on the boulevard du Mail and arrested both of them, because they were his parents. His mother went to a prison reserved for common-law criminals, largely prostitutes. His stepfather was released and later arrested a second time.

On August 25, still ignorant of his mother's arrest, Brasillach heard the bells of Notre-Dame singing out the liberation of Paris, like everyone else. Stuck in his maid's room on the hot top floor of the apartment building, he was overwhelmed by fatigue. He slept nearly all day. In the week to come, when he wasn't sleeping, he was reading. Friends brought him copies of the new resistance newspapers, and he writes, "I learned to read this surprising press, born of the Liberation":

> I discovered the smug accounts of German atrocities, the tortures by the "French Gestapo." At the same time, among the hundred books that furnished my retreat, I read an account by Andrée Viollis on Indochina, with a preface by André Malraux, where they enumerated the French police atrocities in 1931, during the incidents at Yen-Bay. The two stories seemed like copies of one another, with tortures by electricity, massacred villages, sexual orgies, and they did not inspire a vivid love of the police in me, wherever they might come from.

This was Brasillach's reasoning: It was the police, finally, who were responsible for the evil done to men. He read the communist poet Aragon, now a spokesperson for the resistance, bitterly noting the contradictions between the antiwar poetry of his youth and the "inflamed patriotic poems" he had written during the Occupation. As for current events, "the papers taught me that the Liberation of Paris was a glorious taking of arms, shared by all, but they hid from me the assassinations, the personal vengeance, the abominable crimes committed that week . . ." In his diary, Brasillach was intent on building analogies, and in his prose, the German atrocities, the orgies of Indochina, and the excesses of the Liberation melted into one generalized crime, which had nothing to do with him.

On September 1, Maurice Bardèche was arrested and taken to Drancy. The housing project that had served as the transit camp for Jews awaiting deportation was now being used as a holding tank for collaborators. Brasillach, certain that Bardèche had been arrested because he, Brasillach, was nowhere to be found, was tempted to turn himself in. His friends convinced him to stay put.

After three weeks in the common-law prison, Brasillach's mother was transferred to detention in a boy's school, Lycée Mallarmé, with the political prisoners and so-called "horizontal collaborators." A friend came to the hideaway on the rue de Tournon to inform Brasillach, who was stunned by the news. Brasillach's mother's arrest decided him and sealed his fate. A letter to her he had begun in his hiding place on September 6 ended on September 14 with his decision. In the course of the letter, he gave her his sense of the Liberation:

> I did what I thought was right for four years, and besides, they'll have to grant us that it was right, since it permitted others to live. These past weeks, when there has been so much brutality and horrible things, show what the Occupation might have been like for four years if there hadn't have been calm, collaborationists, a Vichy government.

For Brasillach, collaboration with the Germans had meant a calm and safe France; liberation was a defeat, an invitation to the forces of anarchy and brutality.

After a month in the maid's room, Robert Brasillach walked from the rue de Tournon to the river. He crossed the bridge to the Préfecture de Police, now securely in the hands of the established Liberation government, and he turned himself in for arrest. The man at police headquarters who received him happened to be a fellow student from the Ecole Normale. They had both been in the class of 1928; Brasillach in the literature section of the school, the man who arrested him in science. As Brasillach tells it, the man deeply regretted having to take a fellow alumnus into custody. "Not I," Brasillach reassured him. "I find it rather funny." In his diary, the incongruous scene is yet another occasion for a wisecrack.

Brasillach's letter to his mother, announcing that he was turning himself in, arrived in Sens a few days later. His sister, Suzanne, read it to the man in charge of political prisoners, a leader in the Sens resistance named Lieutenant Germain. Once Germain had verified that Brasillach was safely under lock and key, he went immediately to the Lycée to release Brasillach's mother. The government's attack on the sanctity of his family would be foremost on Brasillach's mind as he prepared his defense.

———

The week Robert Brasillach got himself locked up was, for France, an unprecedented opening.

Roger Grenier, who had been employed in a lowly job distributing bottles, organized the press corps at the Hôtel de Ville and joined Camus's team at *Combat* a few months later. In 1947, Camus published

Grenier's first book of essays on the justice system, *Le Rôle d'accusé,* in his series at Gallimard. Grenier's career as a writer had begun. Arlette Grebel went from journalism school to reporting the most important event of the century by waltzing into the newspaper headquarters in her scout skirt. There was no interview, no test, no competition; she had simply seized the moment. The Liberation was a window of opportunity that, if only for a brief moment, seemed to supersede family, education, all the traditional patterns of influence and privilege in France.

The new press itself was, as Brasillach himself put it, "born of the Liberation." Whether they were communists or Gaullists, whether they wanted a tough purge or a gentle one, the journalists of the postwar era used the punishment of the collaborators to mark the moment, to delimit a before and after, a corrupt France of collaboration, and a new France, *France-Libre.* In one of his first open editorials in *Combat,* Camus had called the Occupation-era journalists—the Brasillachs of France—"the shame of this country." He vowed to lead the Liberation press in undoing that shame.

The purge of collaborators gave both Roger Grenier and Arlette Grebel their start as writers. Though neither of them would be present at the Brasillach trial itself, many of the journalists who did sit in the press box that day in January 1945 were as new to the trade as they were. Simone de Beauvoir, ten years older than Grebel and Grenier—and who did cover Brasillach's trial—described this new generation with envy: "To be twenty or twenty-five in September of '44 seemed the most fantastic piece of luck: all roads lay open. Journalists, writers, budding film makers, were all arguing, planning, passionately deciding, as if their future depended on no one but themselves."

As if their future only depended on no one but themselves. What the myth of liberation gave to all of France, finally, was the sense that the country was young and starting over, rather than defeated and humiliated—the sense that the future was theirs to control. In this atmosphere, Robert Brasillach went on trial for his life.

FOUR JAIL

Brasillach was in prison for five months, first at Noisy, then at Fresnes. It is horrifying to say it, but to judge from his writing, the energy and concentration evident in it, this was arguably the most creative, joyous period of his life. It was also a period he spent vigorously shoring up his own sense of unreality, about the war, about fascism, and about his own role, preparing it as a legacy for others.

Whether he was comparing himself to André Chénier during the Terror or contrasting the preparations for his trial with a series of "gags," he was constantly constructing analogies to glorify his situation, give it echoes across history. He tried new genres: he wrote plays and essays, translated Shakespeare, imagined the posthumous publication of his work. A comment in his diary, in the beginning, shows his excitement about the opportunity of incarceration: "This time, I was going to learn about prison, real prison, the one people talk about in books." Was reality for him only what people talked about in books? Judging from his sense of what had gone on in France for the previous four years, his grasp of political reality was distorted beyond all recognition.

His company in prison was the motley crew of collaborators who hadn't fled the country in the early August days of 1944, militiamen, publicists, and petty politicians. In Brasillach's own cell was a twenty-year-old named Claude Maubourguet from the staff at *Je Suis Partout;* an obscure Catholic writer named Paul Bazin; Maurice Levillain, a city councilman; and later Henri Bardèche, Maurice's brother.

Finding himself in the same cell with Maubourguet was a drama in itself. The nephew by marriage of Charles Lesca, the major stockholder at *Je Suis Partout,* young Maubourguet had been squarely in Lesca's camp of "hard-liners" when Brasillach broke with the paper in 1943. Maubourguet had joined the Milice in the eleventh hour. Now he, too, was to be tried for treason, his life also at stake. Prison reconciled the two men, all the more so when Brasillach and young Maubourguet learned they would both be prosecuted by Marcel Reboul. The two men's fates would be even more closely linked by prosecution speeches that referred to one another. They spent several months together in cell

#344, until Maubourguet was sentenced to life in prison and transferred to solitary confinement.

To hear Brasillach tell it in his diary, his letters, and his essays, the prisons were full of writers, high-minded intellectuals, just as they had been during the French Revolution, during the Terror. But right there in his cell was Maurice Levillain, the crass politician. Manager of a garage before the war who joined up with the fascist party of neosocialist Marcel Déat and represented the city council for the Charonne district— a working-class artisanal neighborhood of Paris—Levillain was described in his court file as a man who had dreamed of becoming the head of the police in Paris under the Nazis. The judge in charge of investigating his case concluded that he had collaborated both from ideological conviction and out of personal ambition. For Brasillach, who saw himself as a pure, high-minded literary and ideological collaborator, Levillain was a slightly ridiculous Philistine who talked too much about his political campaigns. He was a distasteful reminder of the banality of collaboration.

Brasillach had literary clout, even with the prison officials; one of them, a fan of *L'Histoire du cinéma,* got him moved into a cell with Maurice Bardèche's brother Henri. Henri Bardèche had been arrested in his bookstore during Liberation week by the FFI, the resistance militia, for "notorious collaboration." The FFI proceeded to occupy the Librairie Rive-Gauche themselves. Brasillach's official support of Henri's Franco-German bookstore (the fact that he had been on the board of directors) was part of the treason charge being leveled against him by the French state.

First with Bazin and Maubourguet, then with Henri Bardèche, Brasillach prepared the interrogation that would take place at the beginning of his trial, imagining the worst accusations that the president of the court could make: "You wanted France to take lessons from a foreign power, by becoming 'fascist' "; or, "You were delighted by the defeat of France"; or, "The Germans had committed atrocities and yet you wrote that you considered them 'buddies' or 'brothers.' " In that way he turned his cell into the kind of atmosphere he had loved when he was a student at Louis-le-Grand, preparing for the competitive exam that got him admitted to the Ecole Normale. "Like the accused of 1793," he wrote Isorni, "we put on sessions of the revolutionary tribunal in the evenings. We ask each other the most insidious, meanest questions to accustom ourselves to the future climate. It is both amusing and useful. I feel as though I'm preparing the oral part of an exam." Just like school days, only now he was defending his life. His strategy was never to apologize, never to express regret, never to take back anything he had said or done. Dignity first. It was a dangerous strategy that would garner him the sympathy of his existentialist enemies but wouldn't do a thing to save his life.

He was visited regularly by Mireille Noël and Jacques Isorni. On October 28, he was taken to see the examining magistrate, M. Raoult, who questioned him about the major issues in the case. As Reboul and Isorni prepared their respective arguments for the prosecution and defense, one of the decisions they both faced was whether or not to call witnesses; they discussed the possibilities at length, together, and Isorni discussed the issue with his client. Brasillach wrote to Bardèche in December, "I mistrust witnesses terribly. People have a pale terror of showing up, and their lawyers, whom I can't blame, encourage them to hide." For the defense, Isorni thought of using Jacques Tournant, a fellow prisoner of war whose brother Brasillach had helped to liberate from the clutches of the Gestapo. For the prosecution, Reboul counter-proposed Alexis Zousman, an examining magistrate for the Court of Justice (he would later be in charge of the case of Céline). Zousman was prepared to testify that he was one of the Jews whom Brasillach had forbidden to speak in the POW camp. One gathers from Brasillach's correspondence, and from what Bernadette Reboul learned from her father, that Reboul and Isorni decided their two witnesses canceled out each other's effects. "Finally, I'll have no witness, which is just as well," Brasillach wrote Maurice Bardèche four days before his trial. "There was supposed to be Jacques Tournant, but he was 'traded in' for Zousman, the witness that the prosecution wanted. I certainly won in the exchange. And besides, I don't like witnesses." There would be no Zousman, no Tournant, only Reboul and Isorni, face to face—which made Brasillach's own performance during the interrogation all the more important.

When Brasillach wasn't practicing for his trial, he wrote. He manufactured a pen holder for himself by shoving his pen into the stem of a pipe. Judging from the amount he produced, he must have written all day long. Literary texts and letters—to Maurice Bardèche, also imprisoned, to his sister Suzanne, to his half sister Geneviève, to his mother. He was a mythical figure for all the men around him. His cell at Fresnes, much like the dorm room at the Ecole Normale in 1928–1930, and the German prisoner-of-war camp in 1940–1941, became a center of intense literary productivity and a locus of intense camaraderie with other men.

In June 1944, de Gaulle's Free French Resistance Council in Algiers published a set of decrees establishing a provisional government for a liberated France. These included the establishment of new jurisdictions for the punishment of collaborators. The Purge jurisdictions had been in the planning since 1942, the result of long reflection by two resistance groups, a Comité Général d'Etudes and a Comité National Judiciaire. The legal experts who planned the Purge were conscious that Vichy had made a travesty of French jurisprudence by imposing a series of circumstantial special courts and passing laws that were to be applied retroactively. In planning the judgment of collaborators, they looked carefully to the legal codes of the prewar Republic to guide them. To punish the most important acts of collaboration, they settled on articles 75–86 of the penal code, recently revised in 1939. Article 75 specified a death penalty for "any Frenchman who, in wartime, undertook intelligence with a foreign power or its agents, with a view towards favoring the enterprises of this power against France." This was the crucial charge of treason under which Brasillach would be tried. Article 77 punished espionage; articles 79–86 addressed various threats to the external security of the nation; article 83, for example, punished "acts of a nature to threaten the national defense." As we saw above, the 1939 penal code was revised, in 1944, to include the act of denunciation during the Occupation as a treasonous crime, now punishable under article 84. In an additional change that proved more controversial, the Liberation government defined a new crime called "national indignity," which could either accompany the more serious charges or be used in minor cases of collaboration. National indignity was punished by "national degradation," which meant the loss of basic civil rights, including the right to vote or to hold public office, the right to own a company.

The courts would operate at several levels. A High Court of Justice, whose function was already described by the constitution of the Third Republic, would oversee the punishment of members of the Vichy government. Courts of Justice were established throughout France to judge important acts of collaboration by French citizens who weren't part of the government. These courts, operating in the twenty jurisdictions of the French Court of Appeals, were entitled to give a range of punishments for acts of collaboration, from simple confiscation of property and loss of civil rights (national degradation), to life in prison, to the death sentence. Robert Brasillach would be judged by the Court of Justice of the Seine. Finally, a "civic chamber" judged more mundane acts of collaboration according to "national indignity"—the newly defined category that was neither misdemeanor nor crime. Civic chambers could decide either for the acquittal or the national degradation of a collaborator.

Trial by the Court of Justice resembled a criminal trial, with a state prosecutor, a defense lawyer, a court president or judge. The jury, which in the regular French court system was composed of nine members, was reduced to four. The prosecutors in the Courts of Justice were called "Commissaires du Gouvernement," or government prosecutors. They could be chosen within the realm of professional magistrates, as in the regular court system, or they could be chosen among anyone holding a law degree.

The Courts of Justice operated in France from October 1944 until January 31, 1951. They condemned 6,763 people to death, of whom 1,500 were actually executed. Another 2,702 were sentenced to forced labor in perpetuity, and 10,637 to lighter sentences of forced labor. 24,927 were sentenced to imprisonment, and another 3,578 people to national degradation. The Courts of Justice acquitted 6,724 people.

In evaluating all these figures, one has to remember that virtually everyone who escaped the death sentence in the late 1940s was amnestied by 1955, and that no one was left in jail on charges of collaboration by 1964. The Purge was a severe but short-lived manifestation of justice. Lest the Purge seem gratuitous, it is crucial to compare these Purge statistics to the statistics concerning the number of people who were arrested during the Occupation, often by French police, with no due process, for acts of resistance or simply because they were Jews. It is crucial to take into account the fact that many of these trials, including the Brasillach trial, took place before the Second World War ended in May 1945. They were acts of war in a country only partially liberated.

When the Court of Justice began trying journalists in October 1944, many of the leading figures of the collaboration had yet to be brought back into French jurisdiction. Brasillach's colleagues from *Je Suis Partout* had fled France in August and taken up residence in the castle at Sigmaringen, along with Pétain and Laval and other Vichy ministers, who had been taken there—more or less—by force. Pétain and Laval weren't brought back to France and tried until the summer and fall of 1945. That meant that there was nearly a year before the High Court began its judgments of the top of the heap, the high government officials responsible for the collaboration. In the meantime, the lower Court of Justice went to work. The first wave of public trials in the

Paris Court of Justice, la Cour de Justice de la Seine on the Ile de la Cité, involved media personalities, gangsters, and assassins. The number of media personalities in this first wave is one reason why people like to say that Frenchmen were judged more severely for collaborationist propaganda than for collaborationist action. The first Court of Justice trials in Paris targeted journalist Georges Suarez (October 23); the murderers of prewar minister Georges Mandel (October 25); Lucien Felgines, a broadcaster for Nazi-controlled Radio Paris (October 27); the journalist Stéphane Lauzanne (October 30); and an author of anti-Semitic tracts known as the Comte de Puységur (October 31).

———

Georges Suarez, editor of the collaborationist newspaper *Aujourd'hui,* was tried for treason by the Cour de Justice de la Seine in its first official sitting on October 23, 1944, three months before Brasillach. Suarez was a well-known political writer, but with none of Brasillach's literary pretensions. He was charged—much as Brasillach would be—with attacking the Allies, with applauding the German execution of hostages, and with denouncing resisters. He had recommended in his editorials that Jews and Anglo-Saxons be taken hostage, in order to stop the Allied bombings. He had been among a group of hard-line collaborators who had complained to the German ambassador in Paris that Vichy was lukewarm. Suarez was condemned to death and executed by a firing squad.

Writers were easy to try. Their files, crumbling now, are rather thin: clippings of their articles from the collaborationist press, underlined in red and blue ink with an occasional commentary; a report by the prefecture of police outlining their political affiliations and behavior during the Occupation; a list of witnesses called by the defense and the prosecution; interviews of the accused, before the trial, going over the charges against him; letters from friends—and enemies—sent to the judge before the trial. It was easier to organize a case against a journalist than a case against a common-law criminal or a financial collaborator. The bulk of the evidence was in newspaper clippings, quickly compiled. This facility was especially important during the period from the Suarez trial in October 1944 to the Brasillach trial in January 1945—the busiest period of the legal purge.

In the wake of Suarez's condemnation, it became clear to the other collaborationist journalists awaiting their own trials at Fresnes that the Court of Justice was mainly relying on press clippings, rather than on witnesses or police investigations. In addition to answering general challenges about his attitudes, Brasillach could be sure that specific sentences he had written were going be quoted against him. He needed to imagine specific responses. For a literary critic who was himself so adept at quotation, it must have been a brutally self-conscious moment.

Brasillach's most repulsive sentences, at least in terms of metaphoric register, were undoubtedly the ones he had leveled at the Third Republic in *Je Suis Partout* in February 1942, in an article called "La Conjuration anti-fasciste au service du Juif" [The anti-fascist conspiracy in the service of the Jew]. Brasillach linked the Republican regime of the 1930s with the presence of Jews ruining the country and decried the survival of Republican attitudes during the Pétain years. The Republic was

> an old syphilitic whore, stinking of patchouli and yeast infection, still exhaling her bad odors, still standing on her sidewalk. In spite of her canker sores and her gonorrhea, she had taken so many bills into her garters that her clients didn't have the heart to abandon her.

This was no longer the "moderate" Brasillach, arguing for a "reasonable" anti-Semitism, in contrast to his more violent colleagues at the paper; this was the editor in chief of the newspaper, stretching his polemical range, reaching to sexual registers for the utmost provocative effect. The specific enemies named in his article were the Popular Front ministers, especially Léon Blum. Blum, in February '42, was on trial in Riom, accused by the Vichy government of responsibility for France's defeat. Brasillach was thus attacking a man awaiting official condemnation. The second part of his article involved an attack by hearsay. Brasillach launched into an anecdote he had heard about a mayor of an unnamed town in the Hérault district who had dared to organize a local Bastille Day celebration, in spite of Pétain's orders to the contrary. During the festivities, a young man had gotten up and made a speech ridiculing Pétain's voice. The young man wore a badge on his arm reading "sold out." The mayor had applauded him. In spite of an investigation by the Légion des Combattants, Brasillach reported, the mayor had kept his job, due to what Brasillach considered some absurd Republican legalism. In fascist Italy, circa 1922, he pointed out, there would have been a punitive expedition against the village by the fascist youth.

The fascist youth of that unnamed town in the Hérault, part of the unoccupied zone, could not have read his article—the Parisian press was unavailable to them—but the Vichy police in the unoccupied zone would have had access to *Je Suis Partout*. By insinuation, by reported anecdote, Brasillach was practicing denunciatory journalism, fanning the flames of anti-Semitic, anti-Republican sentiment. In his memorandum in prison he claimed he had never supported the fascist militia—the Milice—organized by Darnand in 1943, that he had broken with the rest of *Je Suis Partout* over this point. That was when the war was clearly lost. Before 1942, when German victory still looked imminent, he was practically suggesting a fascist raid on the town—exactly the style that would become the trademark of the Milice in its antiresistance actions. When we think of Brasillach's own verbal playfulness, his love of practical jokes, it is surprising that he was incapable of appreciating a mockery of Pétain—even one from the left. After all, his own colleagues at *Je Suis Partout* mocked Pétain regularly.

There was worse. A single sentence of Brasillach's political career, written in *Je Suis Partout* at the height of the deportation of Jews from France, is considered the most damaging phrase he ever wrote: "We must separate from the Jews *en bloc* and not keep any little ones."

He wrote this sentence in September 1942, two months after the Vél d'Hiv roundup. Just what exactly did Brasillach mean? He was echoing the official policy of Vichy Prime Minister Laval, which was to deport Jewish children along with their parents. We know the figures: during the year 1942, 1,032 children under the age of six, and 2,557 children between six and twelve, and 2,464 adolescents between thirteen and seventeen were sent to Auschwitz. Laval was under pressure to "produce" a certain number of Jews for the Nazis' deportation effort. His stated policy was to sacrifice foreign Jews—recent immigrants—in order to save the lives of Jews who were citizens. He decided to deport their children as well. Although the extermination of all the Jews of France was one of the Nazis' objectives, they didn't yet think that either Vichy or French public opinion was ready for such a radical step. Laval urged the children upon them. One sees through Laval's decision how Vichy's politics of accommodation could result in anticipating the Nazis in their barbarism.

Historians Michael Marrus and Robert Paxton, in trying to explain the horrible logic of Laval's policy, surmise in their *Vichy France and the Jews* that the deportation of children allowed Laval to meet his deportation quota with the Nazis. And perhaps, they add, he preferred to see the children go to a certain death than to have thousands of orphans on his hands in France's unoccupied zone. Vichy propaganda included much talk of "family values." Children left without their parents due to an action of the state wouldn't look good—even if they were merely

Jewish children. "Incredibly," Marrus and Paxton remark, "Laval seems to have believed that deporting children to Auschwitz would improve his image."

Sometimes entire families were deported together, including babies. Sometimes families were separated: Parents were deported immediately; children were sent to French internment camps and deported later. By the summer of 1942, the summer of massive arrests, both in Paris and the south, the deportations were public knowledge. Public protest was vigorous, especially among the clergy. The Archbishop Saliège of Toulouse was the first to make his attack on the government public, in a pastoral letter that was widely distributed:

> That children, women, men, fathers and mothers are being treated like a vile flock, that members of the same family are being separated from one another and sent off to an unknown destination, is a sorry spectacle reserved for our era. Why does the right of asylum no longer exist in our churches? . . . Father, have pity on us. . . . In our diocese, touching scenes have taken place in the camps at Noé and Recebedou. Jews are men. Jews are women. Foreigners are men, foreigners are women. All is not permitted against them, against these men, against these women, against these fathers and mothers of families. They are part of humankind. They are our brothers like so many others. A Christian cannot forget it.

It was precisely this courageous statement that Brasillach was attacking in his September 1942 article. The Archbishop, he wrote, was wrongheaded. The brutal separation of Jewish children from their parents, he claimed, was the fault of provocative policemen who were trying to foster reactions of pity towards the Jews among the French Aryans.

Although anti-Semitism was not a central feature of the charges that would be leveled against Brasillach—he was on trial under article 75 of the penal code, for treason, rather than for his beliefs—Reboul would comment at length on the sentence about deporting the Jews *en bloc*, and more particularly on the detail of Brasillach blaming the police for the separations.

It is difficult to believe that someone could be deluded enough to imagine that the French police were *agents provocateurs,* striking out against Jewish families in a twisted propaganda maneuver against Vichy. In fact, members of the Paris police, under the command of René Bousquet, were put in charge of arresting over 13,000 Jews of Paris in

the "Vél d'Hiv" roundups of July 1942. Brasillach might well have seen
the buses, crammed full of stunned men and women, heading towards
the indoor bicycle stadium in the early hours of July 16 and 17.

Now, anticipating his trial from his prison cell in 1944, there were
plenty of reasons for the phrase "we must separate from the Jews *en
bloc* and not keep any little ones" to come back and haunt him. The
first reason was that the subject of children and separation from their
parents, deportation and the loss of home and property, was now his
own family's problem. He had turned himself in for arrest in the first
place because of the arrest and imprisonment of his mother in Sens.
His brother-in-law Maurice had also been arrested. Their apartment
on the rue Rataud was confiscated and requisitioned by the Liberation
government for another family.

In a memorandum in his own defense, given to the examining
magistrate in October 1944, a month after his incarceration, Brasillach
protested that his sister Suzanne hadn't even been able to go back to
the apartment to get winter clothes for her children—if there were any
clothes left, for the apartment had been pillaged. The memorandum,
written in a sober, factual style, begins with Brasillach's indictment of
the treatment of his family by the resistance, proceeds to defend the
legitimacy of Vichy, and includes as well a defense of Brasillach's own
anti-Semitism:

> Like many Frenchmen of all tendencies, including Gide and Gi-
> raudoux, I showed my desire well before the war to diminish the
> power of foreign elements, particularly Jews, but I never asked for
> any brutal persecution against them, I spoke much less about the
> Jewish question during the Occupation than before it, and I even
> *wrote that women must not be separated from children and that we must
> arrive at a human solution to the problem.*

In the imaginary interrogation he prepared with his cellmates, he repeated this argument: "I approve of no physical violence, I found it
deplorable and inhumane that, in certain cases, Jewish women were
separated from their children."

Children were on his mind—not the fate of the Jews. In November,
two months before his trial, he drafted an essay, "Lettre à un soldat
de la classe '60" [Letter to a soldier who will be drafted in the year
1960], dedicated to his four-year-old nephew, Maurice and Suzanne's
son Jacques. This was a boy who, in Brasillach's words, had never seen a
banana or an orange or a chocolate éclair because of the food scarcities

of wartime, and who would be twenty in the year 1960. Writing to this nephew who was still just a small child, suspecting already, perhaps, that he wouldn't live to see him grow up, Brasillach tried to justify his fascism and anti-Semitism for his descendants—or rather, since he had no children of his own, his sister and brother-in-law's descendants.

His November 1944 "Lettre à un soldat de la classe '60" is full of mystifications, backwards logic, and denial, but Brasillach was perfectly direct in acknowledging one topic he has long been supposed, by his supporters, to know nothing about—the politics of extermination:

> I am an anti-Semite, history has taught me the horrors of the Jewish dictatorship, but that families have so often been separated, children cast aside, deportations organized that could only have been legitimate if they hadn't had as their goal—hidden from us— death, pure and simple, strikes me, and has always struck me, as unacceptable. This is not how we'll solve the Jewish problem. I should add that if these methods have added to the passionate discredit of Germany in France, anti-Semitism will remain anchored from now on in the French people, and the return of the Jews will certainly not be seen with a friendly eye.

The extreme convolution of his prose makes a closer look at this passage necessary. Brasillach makes several claims here. First, he argues that deportation would have been fine if its goal had not been death. Did he imagine a "benign" deportation of the Jews to an island somewhere, as in the Nazi's 1940–41 Madagascar plan? He doesn't say. But he does manage, in this bizarre context of attacking death and promoting the principle of deportation, to repeat his knee-jerk defense of family values. A further twist of delusion is that he believed deportations were bad for Germany's reputation in France, but not bad for the reputation of anti-Semitism itself.

In other words, in his prison cell, facing death, Brasillach was still committed to anti-Semitism as part of the bedrock of a French belief system. Even Germany's actions, he explains in this passage of "Lettre à un soldat de la classe '60," weren't capable of giving anti-Semitism a bad name.

The passage is important for another reason. It is a commonplace among conservative historians such as Henri Amouroux to say that, until the spring of 1945, no one knew about the death camps. And yet, Brasillach *did* write, in a text dated November 6, 1944, that deportation had actually had as its goal "death, pure and simple." Did Brasillach have

enough contacts in the German community in Paris, who would have
been privy to policy, to know?

The day of the Vélodrome d'Hiver roundup, conducted in the early
hours of the morning, *Je Suis Partout* published this note in its "Partout
et Ailleurs" column:

The Expiation Is Starting

The new measures eliminating Jews from national life and preventing
them, notably, from access to restaurants, theaters, pools, etc. . . . are
certainly rigorous.

Much less rigorous still than the measures the Jews would take
if they won the war.

We saw the Jews at work in Hungary and in Russia. As soon as
they are king, they hurry to exterminate the Aryans, or, as they did
in France under the Blum government, to eliminate them totally
from administrative positions.

In addition, as long as this war lasts, the only solution to the
Jewish problem remains the one we have advocated: making Jews
into prisoners of war and making massive use of their manpower to
undertake work projects for the benefit of the public.

In a projective mechanism typical of anti-Semitic writing from the
period, it's the Jews themselves who are accused of exclusion and extermination, of Aryans. The enormous Vél d'Hiv arrest operation goes
unmentioned; only Vichy anti-Jewish laws are openly acknowledged.
At the same time, the paper is openly supportive of the idea that Jews be
taken as prisoners of war. Only the subtitle, "The Expiation Is Starting,"
implies that something has happened to make this policy idea a reality. It's
a wink of the eye to the deportations, an open fantasy of forced labor but
not of extermination. Later, in 1943, the newspaper will note in passing
that the Jews in Vichy, who had once thought they were safe in the
unoccupied zone, were starting to "run in all directions like poisoned
rats." The line between fantasy and actual knowledge of extermination
policy is hard to draw.

If he didn't know about the death camps during the war, did
Brasillach learn about them in prison, between September 1944 when he
turned himself in for arrest and February 6, 1945, when he went before
the firing squad? True, most of the press reports on the camps didn't
appear until after Brasillach's death, in April and May of 1945, with the
liberation of Auschwitz. But reports on the camps were trickling in to

Paris in the fall and winter of 1944. As early as September 7 a headline in
Combat had announced, "Auschwitz, Extermination Camp." Brasillach's
former schoolmate Roger Vailland, now a member of the Communist
Party, sent a dispatch to the communist newspaper *Action* on December
15, 1944, from the camp of Struthof, in newly liberated Alsace; an article
on the liberation of Maïdanek was published in *Ce Soir* on January 10,
1945. Brasillach might well have seen articles like these in prison—his
letters refer to much reading of the press. He referred specifically in
his letters to the fact that he was reading the debates on the purge of
collaborators taking place that fall in the French Assembly, and published
in the *Journal Officiel de la République*. In those debates, a member of de
Gaulle's first national assembly referred as early as December 6, 1944,
to "death camps" and to the death of Frenchmen in gas chambers in
Poland. "We all know," he said.

What Brasillach knew about the death camps when he finished
"Lettre à un soldat" is impossible to know except through his own
words and his own context, which tell us he knew a great deal. What is
most shocking is that even having admitted that deportation amounted
to "death pure and simple," Brasillach was still perfectly comfortable
defending his fascism, his anti-Semitism, and the politics of deportation.
He was still willing to claim, to his examining magistrate, to his cellmates,
and to his young nephew, in a document written for posterity, that
arguing for the deportation of children with their parents had been a
humanitarian act.

———

Brasillach saw their names inscribed on his cell. Throughout his imprisonment, he looked at the graffiti on the walls at Fresnes and imagined
the members of the resistance who had been imprisoned there only
months before him. He wrote a poem about it called "The Names
on the Walls," which Isorni would read out loud at his trial, hoping
to soften the resistance jurors and convince the court that prison had
turned Brasillach into a poet:

The Names on the Walls
Others have come through these halls
Whose names on the moldy walls
Already are peeling and faded:
They have suffered and waited,
And sometimes their hope came true;
It tricked these walls for a few.

Come from near, come from far,
We hadn't the same heart,
They told us. Why should they be right?
What does it matter what we were!
Our faces foggy in the blur
Look alike in the dark night.

It's you, brothers never known,
On whom I think, at night alone:
O fraternal adversaries!
Yesterday is so close to today.
In spite of ourselves, united we stay
In our hope and in our misery.

I think of you, you who dreamed;
I think of you, you who suffered.
To me your place has been conferred
If tomorrow my life is spared.
The names on the walls that are spread
Will they be our password?

The men of the resistance were his "fraternal adversaries," the ones
he thought of alone at night. The psychological similarity of this poetic gesture towards the resistance with his sentimental writing about
German soldiers in 1943 is striking. In both cases, the expression of
intimacy with enemies is self-serving. In the case of the resistance, it
is also hypocritical, representing a violent about-face, a denial of his
previous positions.

Poetry, more than any other genre of writing, was the medium that
had distinguished the literary resistance. It had been the most appropriate
genre for a period of censorship: poems were short, elliptical, and easy
to distribute in mimeograph, clandestinely, in a time of paper shortages.
Poetry that sang the resistance elliptically could be published openly in
the unoccupied zone in magazines such as *Poésie 42–43, Confluences,*
and *Messages,* and in *Fontaine,* in Algiers.

Immediately after the Liberation, poetry was consecrated along
with the resistance movement itself. Poems by Eluard ("Liberté") and
Aragon ("La Rose et le réséda") set the tone for the heroic postwar
commemorations of resistance martyrs. For Brasillach to write prison
poetry in 1944–1945 was to work in a medium that was identified with

the resistance—to compete with it, as it were. Poetry symbolized the literary accomplishment of the Occupation years.

Brasillach's prison poem implies brotherhood with his adversaries in the resistance, with "you who suffered." Yet who had contributed to that suffering? In "A travers Lyon dans les brumes de l'attentisme," a February, 28, 1942, article for *Je Suis Partout* on life in the unoccupied zone, Brasillach denounced *Confluences* and *Fontaine* for "indulging in sneaky Gaullist propaganda" under the cover of literature and surrealism. He applauded the arrest of Emmanuel Mounier, the former director of *Esprit:* "Well done." He strongly recommended supporting efforts to purge the literary world: "All it would take would be ten suppressions, ten arrests to restore everything to order. . . . Patiently, the work of purging [the anti-Vichy elements] is being accomplished. But we have to help it along."

Brasillach sharpened his campaign against the literary resistance in the summer of 1942, in a July 31 article entitled "Is There a Renewal of Poetry?":

> The young poets aren't worth much more [than Aragon]. They use all the tricks, images without grammatical links, an absence of rhythm, purely sensual unorganized evocations of everything, anarchy without music—scratched on the lovely cheeks of a poetry that we're supposed to take for a [political] battleground! Ah! no, they won't get this poor girl pregnant, with their teasing and wimpy caresses!

He concludes this article on a note that echoes a standard Nazi cliché about modern art:

> The false surrealism of 1942 is comparable to a simple degenerateness.

Brasillach's February 28, 1942, article calling for the arrest of writers is reprinted in the complete works as part of the posthumously reconstructed wartime memoir, *Journal d'un homme occupé.* Every sentence encouraging the arrest of writers has been cut. Bardèche omits Brasillach's 1942 "Is there a renewal of poetry?" entirely from his edition of the wartime *Je Suis Partout* articles. At the same time, he claims in his editor's notes to be including the wartime *Je Suis Partout* articles in their entirety, because not to do so would be, in his words, to go against "all the rules of criticism and even, we think, honesty." "Literary article, which we omit," reads a note on this missing article. Why? Nowhere are Brasillach's Occupation-era politics more obvious than here, in these attacks on resistance writers. The attacks were omitted because they do too much damage to the image of Brasillach in prison reaching out to his brothers in the resistance through a common genre, poetry; the image of Brasillach's poetic affection for his "fraternal adversaries."

Brasillach gathered his Fresnes poems, that winter of 1945, and, with his irrepressible taste for gags, he bound them together for his lawyer, Jacques Isorni, writing "Editions de Minuit et demi" [Editions Midnight and a half, or Editions 12:30 A.M.] on the cover page. It was a play on the Editions de Minuit, the underground resistance press that had published Vercors, Mauriac, and many poets, and which in 1944 published an anthology of resistance poetry called *L'Honneur des poètes* as one of its first "above ground" books.

If, on the one hand, he was competing—in parody, but whole-heartedly—with the genre of resistance poetry, Brasillach elided that competition in "The Names on the Walls" by basing his poem his favorite theme from Corneillean tragedy: love among enemy brothers. On the same theme, he wrote a tragic dialogue in prison called "Enemy Brothers," a conversation between Polynices and Eteocles, Oedipus's warring children. In Brasillach's version, the enemy brothers confess in private that they actually love one another. The public version of their quarrel remains unchanged.

Wishful thinking! The theme of "The Names on the Walls" is empathy, but empathy directed in Brasillach's favor. If he thought kindly upon the resistance, if he hid his previous disdain and began to identify with their struggle, perhaps now the resistance—which was putting him on trial—would identify with his condition as well. In preparation for his trial, Brasillach tried to furnish the defense with the names of people in the resistance whom he had helped. He had actively sought to help a fellow student from the Ecole Normale, Daniel Gallois, who was arrested for acts of resistance ("espionage") and imprisoned in Fresnes in August 1944, the month of the Liberation. Before Brasillach's gesture could have an effect, Gallois was freed on the 16th, by prison guards who fearfully evacuated the prison upon the news of an Allied advance on Paris. Gallois wrote a letter in favor of Brasillach, but Reboul and Isorni's decision against calling witnesses kept him from testifying at the trial. According to one biographer, Brasillach made gestures in favor of several other people linked to him through school ties and friendship. Disinterested acts, rather than acts of personal kindness to friends, were the kind of moral equivalency that might have helped his defense. The men and women of the resistance did not forget that he had not raised his voice publicly to save the lives of the best-known resistance intellectuals executed by the Germans: Politzer and Ducour, shot for resistance in 1942; nor for Max Jacob, Cocteau's great friend, arrested in 1944 and who died in Drancy transport camp on March 5; nor for Robert Desnos, deported in 1944, who died of typhus when his camp was liberated. Over and over again, in *Je Suis Partout,* Brasillach had called for the death of any number of Vichy's enemies—Jews, Republicans, Gaullists, resistance fighters, and dissident writers. One letter from a school chum was not going to save him.

FIVE MARCEL REBOUL: GOVERNMENT PROSECUTOR

In the Purge trials that followed the liberation of France, defense lawyers trying to save their collaborator clients frequently attempted to assail the men sitting on the bench—members of the French magistrature, prosecutors, and presidents of the court—for their role during Vichy, as if they had all collaborated and therefore had no moral standing to try collaborators themselves. There's a famous moment when the High Court of Justice (the court empowered to pass judgment on the Vichy Government) tried Pierre Laval, the Prime Minister under Pétain, and by 1945 the most hated man in France. Laval himself accuses his accusers: "You were all under the [Vichy] government's orders, even you, Mr. Prosecutor General!" The prosecutor in the Laval trial, André Mornet, had been chosen among a generation of elders, already part of the judiciary during the First World War. He had served under Vichy as the president of a commission that studied the denaturalization of Jews and other foreigners threatened with deportation. Not an appealing credential, but one that didn't prevent him from participating in the purge of Vichy's Prime Minister. Claude Roy, covering Laval's treason trial for *Les Lettres Françaises,* remarked that Laval was being judged not by France, but by his own accomplices, by a prosecutor and a court president who had spent their whole lives saying "yes" to whatever regime they were in. Roger Grenier, covering the same trial for *Combat,* wrote bitterly about the old men who were judging the collaboration in the High Court of Justice. He wondered why collaborators couldn't be judged by a popular tribunal without any professional magistrates. Laval was condemned to death and executed, but the procedure of his trial was so bungled, so fraught, that even his enemies were disgusted by it.

On the eve of the Brasillach trial, which was acknowledged by all to be among the most dignified moments of the Purge, the communist resistance fighter Pascal Copeau (son of the great theater director Jacques Copeau, who signed the petition to save Brasillach), wrote in the communist newspaper *Action* that Marcel Reboul, Brasillach's prosecutor, had been in charge of the repression of terrorism under Vichy. The communists were suspicious of the Purge because they were suspicious of the Gaullists, suspicious of the continuity of power between Pétain and de Gaulle—men from the same military class who were close enough so that it was long rumored that de Gaulle's son, Philippe, had been named after Philippe Pétain.

At the first Purge trial held by the Cour de Justice de la Seine in October 1944, that of the journalist Georges Suarez, the defense lawyer, Maître Boiteau, started his plea by quoting Talleyrand: "Treason is a matter of dates." Then he played on the phrase "national sentiments," since de Gaulle had decreed that only men and women who had shown "proof of national sentiment" could pass judgment on collaborators. Members of the Committees of Liberation, whose "national sentiment" was unquestioned, had assisted the magistrates in identifying the people in their community who were politically fit to serve on the juries of the Purge trials; these people now sat before him:

> Yesterday, members of the jury, president of the court, you were hounded for your national sentiments, those sentiments that you weren't afraid of exhibiting in daylight, and today, those same national sentiments make you worthy of the honor of sitting in this court, and make me worthy of pleading before you. You have been called here to judge, to do the work of justice, and of justice alone. And my brief experience of the political process permits me to tell you how happy I am to have before me a jurisdiction which bears no similarity to those tribunals called "Special Courts" or "Sections Spéciales" that I knew during four years of occupation.

Boiteau, like many lawyers in the Purge courts, is playing directly to the jury, invoking his own resistance credentials along with theirs. He is young, like them, and like them, he suffered under Vichy—he implies that he had to argue before a Special Section, where men and women like them were sentenced to death for acts of resistance. A lawyer named Maître Ribera, who defended Lucien Felgines, one of the first collaborators to broadcast Nazi propaganda in France, also assailed the justice system under Vichy and made himself out to be a fellow traveler of the resistance, for having bravely and publicly contested Vichy justice: "I argued behind this bar during the Occupation; I argued for two years before the Special Tribunals that you remember. And each time, I marked my disapproval of their methods of justice."

To listen to these lawyers, one could get the impression that the magistrature went from Vichy to the Liberation unchanged. This is not entirely true. As we saw in the last chapter, in the early summer months of 1944, during the planning stage of the liberation in Algiers, de Gaulle organized the new set of jurisdictions that was to punish collaborators in French courts. Prosecutor Maurice Rolland, a magistrate who had served as an intelligence agent for the resistance and then gone into hiding during the later part of the Occupation, played a key role in the Algiers task force. He was instrumental in drafting the Purge laws and designing the new courts. It was he in particular who defined the notion of "national indignity."

Before the work of those new jurisdictions could begin, the magistrature undertook a purge of collaborators within its own ranks, reviewing the presiding judges and prosecutors and the examining magistrates assigned to courtrooms throughout France. The magistrature was like many other institutions—the press, the world of film, the literary world—and it was like every ministry of the government, in that it conducted its own intraprofessional purge during the first months after the Liberation. Vichy was now illegal, but it wasn't realistic or feasible to replace every civil servant who had signed a loyalty oath to Pétain. France needed trained judges and prosecutors. Nonetheless, individual magistrates who had committed truly reprehensible acts of collaboration during the Occupation were in no position, morally or politically, to judge collaborators. A "clean" magistrature was needed, and it was needed quickly, with the work of the ambitious new Purge courts underway as early as October 1944.

The Purge commissions charged with examining France's magistrates included members from the resistance and members of the judiciary: Prosecutor Mornet was in charge, along with a number of judges, resistance militants—including widows of men tortured and executed by the Gestapo, among them the widow of martyred judge René Parodi—and several prominent communist lawyers who had been part of the organized legal resistance movement, the Front National Judiciaire. Out of 3,000 magistrates, 370 were examined; of these, 165 were removed from the magistrature, 100 others were sanctioned. Just as in the Purge trials themselves, acts of treason towards the nation, such as sentencing a resistance fighter, were much more severely sanctioned than acts of anti-Semitism or ideological attitudes.

Judges who had condemned resistance fighters to death were the first to be relieved of their duties. Other sins of the magistrature, such as the harsh penalties for abortionists (including the death penalty), did not exclude a person from the postwar magistrature. Nor was the application of the anti-Jewish laws systematic grounds for purge. The judges who had served in the shameful Paris Special Section were all examined by the commission during the period November 16–23, 1944. In June 1945 they would be tried in a criminal trial in the Salle des Assises, the room were Brasillach was tried five months earlier.

Once the purge of the magistrature was underway, judges could be tapped from the surviving magistrates within the system to serve in the special courts dealing with the punishment of collaborators. Any magistrate who was chosen would have to be approved by the "Comités de Libération," those groups under the jurisdiction of the new provisional government who represented a confederacy of the resistance movements in every town and county of postwar France, and who were instrumental in reshaping civic life in the chaotic months after the disappearance of the Vichy apparatus. Their judgment was being sought in the choice of jurors for the Courts of Justice, and in the choice of presiding judges and prosecutors. The opinion of the communist-oriented Front National Judiciaire was also an important factor. Marcel Reboul was immediately tapped to serve as prosecutor in the important Paris branch of the newly designed Court of Justice. The man who designated him in this role was his great friend Maurice Rolland. They had taken the exam to enter the magistrature in the same year; they were both thirty-nine years old, and, oddly enough, they both suffered from a bad hip as a result of similar childhood illnesses.

His voice, his oratory, his sense of justice: for all these talents Reboul was recognized by his peers, both under Vichy and under the Republic, as a man capable of taking on the most sensational cases. The judicial hierarchy selected him for its most important functions. His success, both under Vichy and during the Purge, underlines a point made repeatedly by legal historian Alain Bancaud: that there was significant continuity between Vichy and the Liberation. Even with all the measures taken to cleanse the magistrature, the Liberation courts were essentially Vichy courts; the Vichy courts had been essentially Third Republic courts. Brasillach's trial and death sentence was a heavily symbolic moment, marking a rupture between occupied France and liberated France, but the presence of Reboul, the presence of Vichy judges in that courtroom, points to a deeper continuity in the French system.

Had Reboul in fact resisted the Nazis during the Occupation? He was not part of any organized resistance network under Vichy, but placed as he was in the judiciary, as a representative of the French state, he had a certain amount of discretionary power. No judge could have had a real power of resistance in the Vichy courts—there were simply too many constraints built into the system. What resistance there was, is impossible to prove, because it had to be clandestine. Bernadette Reboul explains that her father made certain papers disappear; he helped Jews get to the *zone libre;* he modulated his presentation of the government's case to save a life; men who were in flight came to the house to get their fake papers and IDs. There are no documents to prove it, perhaps because this resistance was so often about making documents disappear.

We can try to reconstruct Reboul's actions from his daughter's stories, from the archives, from what we know about the period, but such a reconstruction is inevitably based on a hunch about what's right. Marcel Reboul signed the oath of loyalty to Pétain, as expected. He discovered, as the war went on, that he could use his powers in small but effective ways against German rule and French injustice. He was respected by his colleagues in the Third Republic courts of the 1930s, the Vichy courts of the 1940s, and at the Liberation. He was handpicked by de Gaulle's right-hand man, Rolland, to serve in the most visible Purge cases. If there had been any stain on his record, any moral ambiguity, he wouldn't have been an appropriate choice. He had the respect of the resistance, and he had merit.

———

What emerges most often in accounts of this magistrate is the power of his voice.

While Marcel Reboul was still a law student, at the University of Aix, he enrolled in the drama school, the Conservatoire. They "placed his voice"—taught him to find the most effective register, to make his words carry across a room, to use intonation to carry his thoughts. His success as a magistrate wasn't due to voice alone but to a rhetorical genius that gave people the impression they were listening to the sound of justice. *Combat* reported that in the trial of the French Gestapo, "His words fell, like the blades of a guillotine . . . ," and described the room vibrating to his voice and to his eloquence in the turn-of-the-century mode, à la Mounet-Sully, an actor from the era of Sarah Bernhardt.

Arguing against the famous French Gestapo gang of the rue Lauriston in December 1944, a month before the Brasillach trial, Reboul was "tall, black-haired, bony, tensing his thick lips to chew his words like bullets" and "painting a hallucinatory fresco with his grave and powerful voice." "M. Reboul roars," read the headline in *Libres-soir:* "The sonorous and ample voice of M. Reboul, his magnificent oratorical talent, his clearheaded and willfully ironic intelligence, make him one of the most appealing personalities at the Palais de Justice." A caricature drawn of Marcel Reboul in December 1945 represents him in his robes, his head forward, but especially his lips pointed outwards.

Angular and thin, in family photos he is enormously handsome, relaxed, radiating Provençal charm and warmth. In his administrative photos his black hair is slicked back, his suit sits squarely on his torso, his ears stick out. You see where the caricature came from: full lips contrasting with boniness and a tight jaw. His youngest grandson, Vincent Reboul, today a twenty-nine-year-old graduate of the law school at Toulon, is his grandfather's spitting image: olive skinned, bone thin, and handsome, with startling cavernous eyes. A glance that could work magic with a jury.

Marcel Reboul was descended from the solid French military bourgeoisie—therefore from the political right. His father, Charles, was one of those thickset, broad-mustached military men we associate with the French nineteenth century. After serving as a doctor for the colonial troops, Reboul père, Major-Doctor of the Colonial Infantry, retired to a superb house in bourgeois Toulon, on the Mediterranean Sea. He ran his household like an officer, raising his children in military style. His rigidity was probably exacerbated by the premature death of his wife at age forty-four, when Marcel was only fifteen. Major Dr. Reboul never recovered from this loss, and maintained the household in a permanent state of mourning. Marcel left home at age twenty-two, to marry. He adored his father but didn't like living in his shadow. His sister, Marguerite, didn't fare as well; she remained in the grief-stricken home, taking care of her father for the rest of his life. In England, it would have been a classic Victorian story.

His bad hip—the result of childhood coxalgia—kept Marcel Reboul from escaping home in the family military tradition, by going into the navy. Instead he finished law school and started practicing in Toulon. A constant theme in his conversations with his father was the Dreyfus Affair; Reboul père was sure that Dreyfus was guilty, because the French military, who had court-martialed him, couldn't be wrong. Marcel disagreed vehemently, and eventually got his father to acknowledge the evidence of Dreyfus's innocence. If the young man had wanted to become a defense lawyer, winning that argument with his father would have been an auspicious beginning. But his situation in Toulon was far from independent. All of his father's friends expected free legal counsel, and soon young Marcel realized that he would never earn a decent living as a local lawyer. If he stayed on his father's territory he would remain a son, and a helper. That's why he chose the magistrature. It was an institution, like the army or navy, with ranks, robes, and a system of values all its own.

———

As a young man of twenty-five, having ranked third in his class in the magistrate's exam, Reboul argued before the court as an "attaché titulaire" at the Ministry of Justice in Paris. The elder magistrate evaluating him wrote in his file that Reboul had set the level of argument at such a high level, he never thought the young man could maintain his tone through to the end. He had spoken without using any written notes, in his warm, low-pitched voice, with perfect, discreet gestures. You had the feeling Reboul was improvising, but a peer could recognize that every effect was perfectly prepared. This was a magistrate who knew how to impose himself. He was ready, at age twenty-five, to serve as an examining magistrate.

———

A French magistrate can be either "sitting" or "standing." Among the sitting judges in the French system are the examining magistrates, or *juges d'instruction,* who prepare the indictment, or the *instruction,* in their studies, basing their views on information they've been given by the police. They decide whether or not the case should come to trial. Examining magistrates are often at the beginning of their careers. Later, they might accede to a role as presiding judge—another sitting function—or they might change tracks and take on a standing function on the *parquet,* or floor, as a prosecutor arguing for the state. Standing and sitting judges are trained within the same system, but their roles and their relationship to the cases they try are completely different. Marcel Reboul served as an examining magistrate—part of the *siège*—for three years. His reports were praised for their polished sobriety. But his talents as an orator were so clear, as was his desire to exercise those talents, that in 1938 he asked to be transferred to the *parquet,* in order to argue his cases standing.

From the beginning, Marcel Reboul was recognized as someone who could argue the most delicate cases.

Under the Third Republic, Reboul was described in his administrative file as someone loyal to Republican principles. Under Vichy, he was described in the same file as someone loyal to Pétain's New Order. These political remarks (including the phrase "political correctness") are pro forma in a magistrate's administrative file. In France, a magistrate is not allowed to belong to a political party or to make his opinions known—that's what it means, in the judiciary, to be politically reliable. Reboul was not a chameleon. He was an effective prosecutor, admired by his superiors. The words "political" in a judge or a prosecutor's career file refer to the politics of the profession; or perhaps to the fact that the magistrate is not political in any offensive way. The drama of occupied France is that the magistrature under Vichy was, in essence, the same organization as the Republican magistrature, the same personnel having passed the same magistrate's exam and operating according to the same codes of conduct and performance. A good judge in one system would be recognized as a good judge in the other. Only the laws were different, changed by Vichy and by a more and more intrusive German occupant. There is very little trace, in an administrative dossier, of the real drama, the real moral choices, which had to do with a magistrate's response to those laws. But the precise response of French magistrates to Vichy's laws would be the decisive factor in their survival in the court system after the war.

Just as one would expect, Reboul's administrative file gives only the pro forma remarks about his political views. Reboul's daughter, Bernadette, provides a different perspective. She remembers her father as a political moderate, a bourgeois liberal. He had applauded the improvement in the lives of workers during the Popular Front, she says, but he badly mistrusted the communists. Like many Frenchmen, Reboul believed in Pétain, in the beginning—at least until October 1940, when the old war hero shook Hitler's hand at Montoire and agreed to a politics of collaboration. Then he realized that Vichy was not a protection against Nazi Germany, but a disaster. After the war he became a loyal Gaullist. Bernadette, summing up his views, says, "He detested extremes."

1940: Vichy France. Marcel Reboul is now thirty-five years old. Like every magistrate in the French system, with the exception of a man named Paul Didier, who was immediately relieved of his functions, he will sign the standard oath of loyalty to Marshal Pétain.

———

When France fell to the Germans, Marcel Reboul was living with his wife, Marcelle, and his daughter Bernadette in an apartment at number 47, boulevard Saint-Michel, at the corner of the boulevard and the Place de la Sorbonne, where the great university of Paris stands. By a quirk of fate, number 47 happened to be the building that housed the Librairie Rive-Gauche, that landmark of the intellectual collaboration where Brasillach would serve on the board of directors. More than once, Marcel Reboul walked home from the Palais de Justice, exhausted after a day in court where, according to Reboul family legend, he would have manipulated to spare the life or reduce the sentence of a resistance fighter. He looked in the window of the bookstore and saw Brasillach happily engaged in conversation with German officers. ("Plastronnant"—swaggering—is the word used by Reboul's daughter in recalling her father's description of Brasillach.)

As early as 1941, the resistance marked the location of the Rive-Gauche bookstore as a target. They started planting bombs to go off near the building. All the residents of 47, boulevard Saint-Michel, were frightened by the explosions. Marcel Reboul set out to find another apartment. Through his relations with Jacques Isorni, a lawyer and member of the Paris bar, he ended up renting an apartment in the building owned by Isorni at 51, rue Geoffroy St. Hilaire. The lease is dated April 1, 1942.

That is how Marcel Reboul, Brasillach's prosecutor, became the tenant and the neighbor of Jacques Isorni, Brasillach's defense lawyer. The two men often took the bus to the Palais de Justice together, gossiping about the courts; their wives became close friends. In fact, the whole building became very close, because they would meet in the basement in the middle of the night during the air raids. After the Liberation, Reboul and Isorni joined forces to get one of their neighbors from 51, rue Geoffroy St. Hilaire, a movie actor, released from Fresnes.

During the Occupation, as a member of the Vichy magistrature, Reboul served as public prosecutor in a court charged with pursuing economic violations—primarily violations of commerce, instances of black marketeering. You can read some of his cases in the law digests of the period. He was prosecutor in the government's case against the president and director of the Societé des Messageries Nationales (National Company of Messengers), who appeared in court for having raised the price of renting out his little messenger trucks, his "hippomobiles," to the pharmaceutical cooperative of Melun, without state authorization.

Reboul's charge was to defend the nation against the corruptions of the black market that were so pervasive during the era of incredible restrictions, when every meter of cloth, every ounce of meat, was doled out in ration tickets according to your age and sex. He prosecuted people who bought and resold huge quantities of cheese at unfair prices; people who hoarded vast quantities of chocolate and sardines in order to profit by selling to their neighbors; people who sold used sewing machines, in 1942, for more than their 1939 purchase price. Most of the cases took place in a court presided over by Maurice Vidal, who would become, in 1945, presiding judge in the court that tried Brasillach. "You can imagine what it was like having a father who argued cases against the black market," said Bernadette Reboul. "We operated strictly on the basis of ration tickets, strictly by the rules. There was no possibility of getting anything on the sly. We were hungry!" she says in mock horror, but with pride.

In addition to the economic court, Marcel Reboul was tapped to serve as a prosecutor in a "Special Tribunal," a court specially designated by Vichy and one of several "exceptional tribunals" created during the Occupation. This "Special Tribunal" of the Seine district was created in early 1941 to deal with "agressions nocturnes"—night actions. The cases dealt with arms and explosives, and were usually linked to actions by members of the resistance. Vichy is famous for a variety of "exceptional tribunals," the most notorious of which were the explicitly political Special Sections, set up under pressure from the Germans to punish communists, anarchists, and terrorists. In one of the infamous chapters of the Occupation, the Germans told the French magistrates that if they didn't choose six jailed resistance fighters to be condemned to death by the Paris Special Section, the Germans would proceed to the execution of fifty hostages. Three men were indeed sentenced to death by the French judges and guillotined on August 28, 1941. The court continued its work throughout the war; Jacques Isorni regularly defended men brought up before the Paris Special Section. Marcel Reboul was not a prosecutor in the Special Section, and the special court where Reboul did serve, the Special Tribunal in the Seine district, was gentle enough in its verdicts so that the Germans complained. After 1942, when Reboul started prosecuting there, the punishments were especially lenient.

The most recent research on the magistrature under Vichy, based on a study of the court files, shows that when the French police made arrests, the prefect of the police or the court asked the German military courts if they wished to handle the case or not. If the Germans decided it was worth their while, the case was taken out of the hands of French justice. Very few cases were handled with autonomy by the French police and French courts. In the cases that did come their way, it was a Vichy judge's responsibility to determine the fine line between a criminal act and a political act. By 1944, after several resistance magistrates were murdered by the Germans, resistance among the magistrature grew. You start seeing cases in the archives where charges were clearly diminished—from murder to attempted murder, for example. But in spite of their growing distance from Vichy, the magistrature did not question the legitimacy of Vichy law. For example, the word "terrorism" is used consistently in court files, for all cases of armed resistance. The magistrature, by training and temperament, is a body that respects order and the letter of the law. A magistrate's charge is, as historians Alain Bancaud and Henry Rousso argue, "to loyally serve the regime in place." Understandably, magistrates did not find it easy to accept certain acts of resistance, especially when they involved attacks on the police.

Reboul may have had more room to maneuver in his economic court than in the Special Tribunal, since in black market cases, the Germans protected the people who worked in the black market with them. By punishing black market violations, he was often punishing the German occupiers—not the resistance. Although suppressing the black market was also one of Vichy's goals. After the Occupation was over, the gang from the rue Lauriston known as the "French Gestapo" were up to their ears in sensational black market extortions—Reboul would send them to their deaths in 1944.

Bernadette Reboul remembers one of her father's favorite war stories:

Marcel Reboul was in his study at the Palais de Justice with his court secretary, "cleaning" a dossier. Two SS officers arrived. He received them in his office. Their French was very good. "We would like to know," they began, "why the files that are leaving the Kommandantur full of papers are returned to us by you nearly empty, with a pathetic set of interview notes and two or three other pieces of paper." (The Kommandantur, she explains, transmitted the file to the Special Tribunal, which was supposed to pass it on to the Gestapo.) Reboul, as he used to tell it, would add: "I felt the cold breeze of defeat. If I blow this one, I thought, I'm good for the firing squad." So he said the first thing that came into his head: "Well you know, we hate paperwork in France, especially in wartime, things need to work smoothly. We like to eliminate any excess." It was an especially idiotic explanation, Bernadette adds, for anyone who knows anything about the French.

The SS officers left, didn't insist. In Bernadette's memory, the story ends with them complaining that Reboul was gumming up the works, and Reboul was transferred from the Special Tribunal to the economic court. I did not find any record of such a move in his career file, and his black market decisions go back to October 1940.

Marcel Reboul loved telling the story and loved his punch line: "Si je loupe mon coup, je suis bon pour le peloton" [If I blow this one, I'm good for the firing squad].

A family story doesn't have the veracity of a document in the archives, but this story has a meaning, even if it's a wishful one. How much autonomy did the French courts have from the Germans? That's the question Reboul's anecdote sets in place. Reboul told his family that he had had responsibility, along with the capacity to do good, and that his choices put him in danger. There is no evidence, sitting in a file, that will indicate exactly how Marcel Reboul furnished this or that Jewish magistrate with the false papers that allowed him to flee the country, or demonstrate how he cleaned a dossier of an arrested member of the resistance, saving his life. The archives themselves are no guarantee: what's in them, what's missing, has its own story. In this instance, there is only testimony, one generation removed. I like to imagine that Marcel Reboul was more decent than the structure allowed, that he was principled in an unprincipled time. Maybe here I am indulging too much in the American tendency to think about this period in terms of "good guys" and "bad guys": either I pin a medal on him, or I suspect his resistance stories. The only real proof we have of his behavior under Vichy comes after the fact: Maurice Rolland appointed Marcel Reboul to have a major prosecutorial role in the purge of collaborators. He was the best speaker in the Palais de Justice, and he was untainted. It is easy to imagine the way he told the story of the SS men to his daughter, the way he shaped it, with his booming voice, his rhetorical skills.

Marcel Reboul was only thirty-nine years old at war's end when he was asked to take on the two great trials of his career: the trial of the thirteen men known as the French Gestapo, and the trial of Robert Brasillach. The case against the French Gestapo, who were headquartered on the rue Lauriston in the sixteenth arrondissement, was cut and dried. They were revolting opportunists and murderers—political criminals and common-law criminals. Eight of them were executed.

The Brasillach case was a different story. It involved political treason in writing, rather than in action. Reboul would have to decide, in his own conscience, nothing less than whether there was such a thing as "intellectual crime." Intensifying the case was the fact that it involved a figure in French cultural and literary circles, a former student of the prestigious Ecole Normale. The trial would take place at a moment when the four-month-old Court of Justice was still seeking legitimation. The fact that the defense counsel was Reboul's friend and landlord, Isorni, had its advantages, and its disadvantages. They consulted one another on the complexities of the case. They made decisions, including the one not to call witnesses—either for the defense or the prosecution. In a way this made the trial even more dramatic: it would be the three principals—Brasillach, Reboul, and Isorni—and no mediation. Isorni's job would be to define Brasillach as a poet, a man of letters, a French national treasure whose life could not be extinguished without irreparable damage to the nation. Reboul's job would be to counter that definition: Brasillach was not a poet, he was a propagandist for the enemy, a turncoat. Whether Brasillach was acquitted or condemned, it would be difficult for a prosecutor in such a case to make peace with the consequences of his act. Either he would be remembered as the man who had spared the life of France's most prominent Nazi intellectual, or as the man who had sentenced a writer to death.

The decision about whether or not to take on the prosecution of Brasillach was probably the most difficult of Reboul's career, and he took several months to make it. As he was hesitating, André Boissarie, Procureur Général, and Germain Laurent, Premier Commissaire du Gouvernement, came to see him in his apartment on the rue Geoffroy St. Hilaire. They spoke of his duty as a Frenchman and of the honor of the magistrature. They reminded him that he came from a long line of military men and told him he would be serving his country by wearing his robe, just as his ancestors had served in uniform. They even told him that to shirk his duty any longer would be an act of cowardice. They had known him for many years and they knew what arguments to use. He said yes. As his daughter puts it, "From that moment on, he knew what a dangerous path he had chosen and what thorny problems he was transmitting to his family. He did it out of duty and out of obligation, but at no moment was he crazy enough to ask for that fearsome honor himself."

In understanding the judgment of Brasillach, it's important to remember that it took place after the liberation of Paris from Nazi occupation in August 1944, but before the official end of the war in May 1945. There was a moment during the cold winter of 1944–45 when the Germans took the offensive in the Ardennes; it looked like the Allies were in danger of losing everything. Brasillach's colleagues from *Je Suis Partout* had fled to Sigmaringen, in Germany, along with ministers of Vichy. There they set up a radio station from which they continued to broadcast declarations of their loyalty to a French fascism. Reboul family legend tells how the men in Sigmaringen, pumped up with last-minute hope for their cause, read over the radio a list of personalities of the resistance whom they would have shot if the

Nazis came back to power, with Marcel Reboul at the top of the list. Madame Reboul pleaded with her husband to quit the Court of Justice. He said to her, "Look, I could have been in the dry goods business like my grandfather—we would have been rich and worry free. But I'm a judge, this is my duty, and I will go all the way in defense of that duty." During the entire period of the trials, the apartment at 51, rue Geoffroy St. Hilaire, was guarded. Marcel Reboul had a bodyguard. Every morning, at breakfast, the concierge delivered the mail; each day the mail included a little red coffin, sent by his enemies. For years he saved a coffin as a souvenir, but it disappeared in one of their moves.

———

There was enough public uneasiness about the role of judges under Vichy that an attack on the moral standing of the magistrature was readily available to the defense lawyers for collaborators. The young men and women in the press box—the Arlette Grebels and Roger Greniers— were also suspicious of the courts, who represented the status quo, law and order, and all that this had implied under Vichy.

Reboul was not in a position to speak to the press about his support of the resistance or about the lives he had saved—if he had saved lives—or to distinguish between the Special Sections and the more lenient Special Tribunal where he had served. Nor could he defend his punishment of black market profiteers. Justice was mute outside the chambers. Reboul could make no public statement, but once within the courtroom he became the voice of the state, the voice of justice. He was allowed to defend himself, allegorically, within the rhetorical space of his prosecution. When we read his courtroom speeches today, far removed from the political drama of 1945, their language sounds brilliant, but pompous to our casual contemporary ears.

"Justice," recalled Frédéric Pottecher, the great theatrical court reporter for French radio and television in the 1950s and 1960s who used to imitate the voices of defense and prosecutor on the airwaves— "Justice is god, but you're not allowed to say so, so you say that it's destiny." [*La Justice, c'est dieu, mais il ne faut pas le dire—c'est plutôt le destin.*] In all of Reboul's prosecution speeches—and he wrote them at an incredible rate, with enormous skill, during the period 1944–1946— you feel the pressure he was applying to the events, a constant defense of the magistrature in grand, almost Greek tragic tones, a response, between the lines, to all those who dared to doubt the moral standing of the French court.

The hostility—among defense lawyers, among reporters, among
the public at large—towards a court system that had survived Vichy did
not prevent Marcel Reboul from using his own experience as a Vichy
government prosecutor in his speeches to the Purge juries. When, in
November 1944, he prosecuted Brasillach's *Je Suis Partout* colleague
Claude Maubourguet for his role in the Milice, he referred to the black
market and to the punishment of "night actions"—in other words, to
both of his tasks within the system at Vichy. But he referred to them
with the consciousness of someone who had protected people from the
police state:

> While, from an economic point of view, Germany was bleeding our
> nation white, the weight of its police state grew heavier each day.
> Remember: this was a time when the possession of a rifle qualified
> you for a death sentence and when staying late on the street after
> the curfew risked increasing by one the next day's list of hostages.

Marcel Reboul, in other words, was thinking about the ethics of the
situation in which he found himself in 1944. He himself had served as
a prosecutor under Vichy, and now he was being asked to punish Vichy
personnel. Nothing in his speeches indicates that he was crippled by
guilt or bad faith, that he felt he had anything to hide. On the contrary,
he called on his own experiences under Vichy as a point of reference
for the jurors.

———

One night during the period of intense preparation for the trial, Jacques
Isorni delivered a package to the Reboul apartment. It was a copy of
Brasillach's collected literary criticism, *Les Quatre jeudis,* inscribed to
Madame Reboul by Brasillach. The wife of the prosecutor found it a
very strange gesture. In his letters, Brasillach was bitterly sarcastic towards
his future prosecutor. "I take him for a grotesque character in the style
of Joseph Prudhomme," he wrote to Maurice Bardèche, referring to
the comic bourgeois character of nineteenth-century French theater, a
famously sententious ninny. "He's what is called a man of talent." He
asked his defense lawyer to let him make fun of Reboul during the trial:

> If only Isorni would let me say two or three funny things in my trial.
> But he won't. He wants me to be serious, it's no fun. I'd still like to
> have one on Reboul, tell him, for example, that the cashier at the
> Rive-Gauche bookstore is named Reboul (which is true). I'd be a
> big success.

Brasillach quoted to Maurice one of Reboul's remarks in the French Gestapo trial. He must have seen it in the press. Reboul had addressed his remarks to one of the members of the gang whose criminal activities were confined to paperwork. He warned him that he couldn't save himself by pleading he had done nothing but sit in an office. "You believed that your leather seat cushion would be your life preserver," Reboul told him, "it will be your shackles." Brasillach mocked the metaphor. "If he lets out a line like that about me," he wrote Bardèche, "I won't be able to keep a straight face."

SIX JACQUES ISORNI: COUNSEL FOR THE DEFENSE

The Brasillach trial was a show of three competing verbal personalities, three distinct rhetorical geniuses: Brasillach, the *normalien* writer and critic, still a boy at thirty-five, whose impertinent style dated back to his days as a critic for the *Action Française;* Marcel Reboul the state prosecutor, just shy of forty years old, with his deep voice and *Provençal* passion; and finally, defense lawyer Jacques Isorni, age thirty-four, Franco-Italian Parisian, precocious verbal star of the Paris bar. You might say that these three extroverts overshadowed the other players in the courtroom—Vidal, president of the court, and the four jurors. Brasillach, Isorni, and Reboul performed the most brilliant verbal tricks in the trial.

———

Magistrates, unlike lawyers, take an oath of discretion. They are not supposed to speak about their decisions. What we know about Reboul's attitude towards the Purge comes almost completely from statements he made within his prosecution speeches, and from interviews with his daughter.

The case of Jacques Isorni couldn't be more different. The nickname for a lawyer in nineteenth-century French is "le Bavard"—the blabbermouth. Isorni, an elegant witty *bavard,* wrote again and again about the Brasillach trial, and about his even more famous client, Pétain, in a whole series of books about his work, including a memoir in three volumes. The Brasillach trial launched Isorni on a career in politics, and in writing about himself. It is thanks to Isorni that the transcript of the Brasillach trial was published in 1946. In 1951, still a brilliant young lawyer, riding on his notoriety in the Brasillach and Pétain cases, he published *Je suis avocat,* a confession of his love for the law, and a personal philosophy about his practice. In 1984, at age seventy-three, he published the first volume of his memoirs. In this installment, covering the period through 1945, he recounted his childhood, his early years in law practice, the Occupation, and the Purge, devoting the most dramatic chapters to his defense of Brasillach and of Pétain. Our sense of Isorni's education, his actions, his attitudes during the trial, during the Occupation, and during the Purge, come directly from him. Memoirs such as his are a problematic source for any history, but also an appealing one, since the story they tell is the story of the author's personality, passion, and point of view. The challenge in reading Jacques Isorni's account of how he came to defend Robert Brasillach is to try and distinguish the events themselves from the extraordinary force of his personality, which shaped everything he wrote.

———

Jacques Isorni was born in 1911. His father, Antoine, was an Italian who immigrated to Paris from Locarno. First a painter, then a commercial artist specializing in fashion drawings, Antoine Isorni became the biggest supplier of fashion drawings to Paris department stores. Isorni's mother, born Marguerite Feine, was a Left Bank Parisian from a bourgeois Catholic family. The touchstone of Isorni's self-conception as a dyed-in-the-wool nonconformist, even more than a man of the right, involves his mother's fervent Republicanism and support of Captain Dreyfus, a position that made her an oddity for someone of her origins. Family legend told how, at age twenty-two, Marguerite had rejected a beloved fiancé when she saw his signature on a list of anti-Dreyfusards. She sacrificed love for her sense of justice! Isorni cherished the story. Ten years later, at age thirty-one, Marguerite married Antoine Isorni after a three-week whirlwind courtship. As Isorni tells it, his grandmother never recovered from the scandalous union of her daughter with a foreigner.

Jacques Isorni was raised in relative affluence in a series of apartments in the seventh arrondissement of Paris, the aristocratic Faubourg St. Germain. He attended the prestigious Protestant Ecole Alsacienne. He was an angelic-looking little boy with fine features and a mass of dark curls. At twelve, his favorite activity was to go to the Chamber of Deputies with his father and listen to the debates. He heard the greatest political orators of his day: the pacifist Aristide Briand; lawyer and right-wing man of state Raymond Poincaré; radical party leader Edouard Herriot; and Léon Daudet, the *Action Française* journalist who served a four-year stint as a *député*.

Certainly the French men and women of his generation were nowhere near as attuned to their ethnic identity as their American counterparts in our immigrant society. Nonetheless, being half Italian counted enormously for Jacques Isorni. In his first school, a Catholic grade school in his neighborhood full of young aristocrats, the students laughed out loud when he pronounced his name, "Isorni." They called him "macaroni" and "gnocchi." He retaliated against their teasing by kicking a few selected schoolmates in the balls. That is how he gained their respect, he remembers proudly. He was, from earliest boyhood, a smart aleck, a stubborn nonconformist, someone who took the most provocative positions and who, at the same time, was painfully sensitive to the least slight. As a lawyer, he became a lifelong champion of lost causes.

———

Isorni's father was conservative, and his mother was Republican in the French sense of that word, a champion of the secular parliamentary government that had replaced the Kings and the Bonapartes. His father's side won out for the most part, although there was in all of Jacques Isorni's political views that touch of rebellious nonconformism. Friends at the Ecole Alsacienne first converted him to the Action Française. He joined an association called "Circle of Students and Lycéens for the Action Française." It was there that he heard a speech by Charles Maurras, whom he described later as "Socrates teaching his disciples." He read the *Action Française* daily. When a conflict between Action Française writer Léon Daudet and the Republican police ended peacefully, he threw himself on his bed and wept in disappointment. He dreamed of right-wing revolution, but it was an intellectual dream. He wouldn't have considered taking to the streets himself.

After his baccalaureate, Isorni pursued a joint degree in law and literature at the University of Paris. He received a standing ovation in the amphitheater of the Sorbonne for his exposé on Rousseau's *Les Rêveries du promeneur solitaire:* "I understood what the strength of a successful oration was all about, the effect it had on the emotions." As he tells it, literature excited him far more than the law. His curls were gone by now, he was thin and handsome, much appreciated by the women in his class. By the time he graduated from law school, he was writing regular columns for right-wing student papers. "My adolescence," he wrote, "was devoured by the need to get excited by speaking and writing."

When Isorni took his oath as a lawyer in 1931, he became the youngest lawyer in practice in all of France. He entered the most prestigious competition for young lawyers in the Paris bar, the exercise in oratory skills that conferred the title "Secrétaire de la Conférence du Stage," an event that took place annually at the Paris Bar Association, L'Ordre des Avocats, housed in the Palace of Justice. Twelve were chosen annually for the honor. They became the elite of the bar. The first year he competed, Isorni had to treat the following question: "Is it legal for the head of the police to arrest people for preventative purposes before a demonstration?" He claims he was eliminated in part because of the way he had dressed. He had only buttoned his lawyer's robes by the top button, so that the rest of the gown hung inelegantly around him. He looked like a raven with its wings flapping, he said. During his speech, he had cried out, "Gentleman, let us elevate the debate!" A senior colleague explained afterwards that discussion in a court of law was by definition always at the highest level—it was an insult to the court for a lawyer to suggest elevating it. Isorni had made a terrible faux pas. The second year, he was asked to speak about the following situation: "A tutor is put in charge of the education of a young blind man. He tells him of the marvels of the world. When the blind man regains his sight, he realizes the tutor tricked him. Can he file suit, asking for reparations?" Isorni was told to argue in favor of reparations. His clever maneuver, during his speech, was to look intently at the exit door of the courtroom while he spoke. His audience had the illusion that Isorni was looking at the poor blind man who had just regained his sight on the spot. Isorni's performance received an ovation. The prestige of being "premier secrétaire de la conférence" stayed with him for the rest of his career. He had learned that a gaze, and a story, can work magic in a courtroom.

But even at the moment of his glory, he felt bitterness and resentment. For the banquet where he was to speak to an assembly of the previous *secrétaires de la conférence,* Isorni planned an audacious speech, full of worries and complaints instead of the expected compliments and congratulations. He submitted the speech to his elders in advance, and they refrained from suggesting he might stick to the convention, or even warning him that what he planned would probably embarrass him. At the banquet, his speech was greeted with a scandalous silence. His own conclusion was that his elders in the *conférence* had coldly set him up to fail.

The next year, Isorni recounts proudly, when it was time to choose the twelve secretaries for the *conférence,* he and his comrades chose five Jews. This exceeded the traditional quota. Isorni brags that he was fiercely attacked in *L'Insurgé,* a paper edited by Brasillach's friend Thierry Maulnier, for "Jewifying" the bar. It is useful to go back to the source here. Isorni doesn't give a reference for the article, but it is not impossible to find, since *L'Insurgé,* a weekly newspaper of the nonconformist, racist right, only existed for one year, from 1936 to 1937. *L'Insurgé* was obsessed with a single target—the Popular Front, and a single cause—anti-Semitism. The article that targets Isorni, "Israël chez les avocats," dated May 3, 1937, gives a good sense of the repulsive quality of anti-Semitic feeling during the 1930s. It is similar to the sort of article Robert

Brasillach was writing at the same time in *Je Suis Partout*. In fact, the editors of *L'Insurgé*, Jean-Pierre Maxence and Thierry Maulnier, were *Je Suis Partout* fellow travelers, with the same political roots in the Action Française. "Israël chez les avocats" was signed "Ellie," who may have been either Maxence or Thierry Maulnier, or a combination of writers:

> If a good French peasant should find himself in the Palais de Justice at the start of the afternoon, the time when lawyers are crowding the halls, he must feel a profound malaise. All these banana noses, hooked fingers, cunning and fleeting gazes he crosses at every step give him the impression of feeling very far from Paris. . . . Few professions have been as massively invaded by the Semites as that of lawyers. . . . A remarkable example of this invasion is furnished by an institution called the "*Conférence du Stage*," which is supposed to represent, among the young lawyers, the twelve best of each year. For a long time, there has been a custom: they only took one Jew as secretary. But this year, thanks to the cowardice of a few young lawyers who wanted to be forgiven for their "right wing" ideas, and in the front row of whom we have to place the previous first secretary, M. Isorni, this proportion has been multiplied by six. . . . Six Jews! Truly good work, Maître Isorni and consorts.

Isorni was already known in Paris as a man of the right. Here, *L'Insurgé* accuses him of wanting to compensate for his right-wing ideas by a liberal gesture. The paper also inflated the number of Jewish *secrétaires* from the five that Isorni claimed to have admitted, up to six. Other anti-Semites, Isorni remembers in his memoirs, accused him of secretly being a Jew from Florence.

Why should he insist on this story? In 1984, there is a self-defense written between the lines: that the defender of Brasillach, the defender of Pétain, was never, all expectations to the contrary, an anti-Semite. On the contrary, he is demonstrating, he was a champion of Jewish colleagues at the very beginning of his career. Both before and after the war, Isorni appears to have been above all a champion of the excluded, who loved the opportunity to buck the system, whatever the system. He was a cowboy. By his account, he and his colleagues in the *conférence* did succeed in imposing their choice of Jewish "secrétaires de la conférence" to a solidly anti-Semitic bar.

The anecdote had further punch for him, because Thierry Maulnier, the editor of *L'Insurgé*, was a schoolmate and great friend of Brasillach's. *L'Insurgé* was close in its political affinities to *Je Suis Partout;*

in fact, being attacked by *L'Insurgé* in the 1930s amounted to pretty much the same thing as being attacked by *Je Suis Partout*—by Brasillach's kind. Telling the story was Isorni's way of bragging that Brasillach's kind had attacked him for his philo-Semitism, but that he had defended him after the war anyway. A further irony for Isorni was that Maulnier eventually become his tenant on the rue Geoffroy St. Hilaire. Maulnier and his wife moved into the Reboul apartment after the prosecutor left Paris for Aix. As Isorni remembers it, neither he nor Maulnier ever mentioned the article. For Maulnier, who had maintained political distance from his fascist friends at *Je Suis Partout* as soon as France fell, it would have been an embarrassment.

Isorni may not have spoken about the article to Maulnier, but he never forgot it. His memoirs show, again and again, that he was exquisitely sensitive to the memory of a slight and, at the same time, that being attacked excited him. Nor was he above crowing over the idea that another man's views—in this case Thierry Maulnier's—were more reactionary than his own. Isorni's politics are paradoxical but profoundly consistent. He was as proud of being criticized by protofascists for having defended the inclusion of Jews in the bar as he would be for defending an anti-Semitic fascist during the Purge. In defending these men, he retained an image of himself as a brave, beleaguered outsider.

The function of a lawyer, in Isorni's view, was to defend the outsider, to speak from one's own position outside the realm of power. In 1951, in his first autobiographical book, *Je suis avocat* (I am a lawyer), he writes as follows:

> Being a lawyer in order to remain a free man who neither asks nor owes anything to any person; this remains a certainty for today and for tomorrow, a reason to be proud. Independence, too! Never hoping for anything from power, not even a decoration. Attack power if it deserves it, speak to it from on high, whether or not it lends an ear, and, once back under one's own tent, know that power regrets having let us speak. Expect nothing, in a word, except from yourself! These are great joys!

Along with this independence must come a strident anti-institution-alism, directed at the legal system itself:

> Sometimes I feel profoundly revolted by the completely insensitive mechanism we called Justice and which, from the police to the penitentiary administration, by way of the prosecutor's office, the

tribunals, and the courts, seizes the guilty party in its cogs and doesn't let him go.

Lawyers cannot always choose their causes, and these grand attitudes on the part of Isorni did not always insure him the grandest cases. As a new member of the Paris bar, Isorni's first clients were Monsieur Alfred, a civil servant who embezzled funds in order to seduce young male bicyclists, Monsieur Fauveau, a citizen of Lyons accused of poisoning his wife, and Monsieur Robert, who was caught dressing up as a woman in order to take an exam his wife was afraid of failing. Even in the oddest cases, Isorni acquired a reputation for the stunning victory, for pulling the judicial rabbit out of the hat.

When France fell, Jacques Isorni was drafted into an army medical service. Later, in remembering the defeat, he was bitter about the neutral position taken by Roosevelt, which he believed had left France helpless. As he tells it, after a short-lived enthusiasm for de Gaulle, he came to see Pétain as the man who had stayed with his country, who was protecting France; de Gaulle, fleeing to London, was the deserter. The full powers voted to Pétain were "the beginning of hope." By the time he wrote this story, in the mid-1980s, Isorni had been arguing for forty years that Pétain had shielded France from harm. In describing Pétain's accession to power, he uses the same language that is usually used to describe the relief people felt when they first heard de Gaulle on the BBC.

In fact, Pétain did not represent the beginning of hope for Isorni. On the contrary, he nearly cost the young lawyer his livelihood. In early fall 1940, Isorni returned to occupied Paris, and to the practice of law. But on September 10, a new Vichy law passed by Pétain's government declared that in order to practice law or medicine, or to be part of the civil service, one had to be born of a French father: Isorni's father had only been naturalized after his children were adults. Isorni was therefore stripped of his vocation. He claims that there were thirty other members of the Paris bar revoked along with him. The national figure was 203.

His Italian-sounding surname continued to make him an easy target. According to his own retrospective account, Charles Maurras, his idol, had already referred to him during the 1930s in the *Action Française*—his own paper of predilection—as one of the "métèques"—the half-breeds—of the bar. Now Vichy was taking his job away. "To tell the truth, I felt like a Jew and wondered if they were going to point me out." It's an experience that might have led another man to detest Vichy, to strike out against its laws, or even to leave the country. This was far from Isorni's reaction. The day he received word of his exclusion, he purchased a house in the country, on the banks of the Marne. His thinking was defensive: A man with land of his own surely had the right to be a lawyer! Instead of lashing out against the regime, Isorni was relieved to find that the law affecting him included special dispensations for "exceptional" men.

The lawyer he hired to help him—a future leader of the Palais de Justice resistance named André de Chauveron, submitted a report to the Ministry of Justice, invoking Isorni's distinguished siblings, all French citizens, and emphasizing Isorni's own extraordinary talent. A *premier secrétaire de la conférence* was someone who should be maintained in the bar association. Isorni was quickly restored.

In his 1984 memoirs, Isorni acknowledges this experience as a victim of Vichy legislation, and he acknowledges its powerful effect on his psyche. Yet it remained for him a personal slight, with little obvious effect on his sense of the larger political scene. In October, when Vichy published its first "Jewish statute," forbidding to Jews, among other things, the right to practice law or medicine, Isorni convinced himself, bizarrely, that this was a measure to protect the Jews of France. He doesn't elaborate, but one gathers from the cryptic remarks in his memoirs that he believed removing Jews from professional life would "shield them from the terror" being visited upon France by the Nazis. Many of his friends and colleagues died in deportation, and he remembers them in his book of memoirs with great sorrow. And yet this sorrow had no effect on his political views, since in his mind, Vichy was a shield against deportations.

Memoirs tell us only how a person understood events many years after the fact. We can't know exactly what his attitude was during the 1940s, but when he looked back at the Occupation in the 1980s, Isorni described it as an era of hostages. For him, the trouble had started when the communists began striking out against the German occupier and the German military responded by arresting Frenchmen and executing them. The violence, in his view, was the fault of the communists.

Which leads us to yet another twist of contradiction in this contradictory character. His deeply held anticommunism did not prevent Isorni from defending communists. On the contrary. His work defending the men who went before the Paris Special Section was for him a source of great pride, which he pointed to in subsequent years as his "titre de noblesse," his own version of resistance.

The inaugural session of the Paris Special Section has gone down in French history as one of the horror stories of the Occupation. On August 14, 1941, a new Vichy law enabled the government to prosecute politically motivated acts of resistance in specially designated courts called Special Sections, which existed in both the unoccupied and occupied zones of France. The communist resistance was their target. The Nazis called for six death sentences during the first week of the Paris Special Section. They threatened massive acts of retaliatory violence, including the execution of fifty elite hostages, if the French courts didn't respond to their demands. The judiciary did comply, and in August 1941, three (rather than six) communists were condemned to death and guillotined for failing to obey the 1939 ban on the French Communist Party. The legal fault of the special sections was flagrant: men who had already been charged with other acts were now being charged a second time, and judged according to a retroactive law.

In his memoirs, Jacques Isorni tells how he met with the magistrates at the Palais de Justice during the Special Section crisis. They told him that, should he agree to represent any of the men called before the Special Section, his role would be essentially symbolic. He would be a "presence" for these poor communists, a companion to escort them towards their deaths. He would not be able to defend them truly, he would rarely be able to save their lives, but he would help them die with dignity. He adds proudly that his first client, a communist, got off with forced labor for life.

In his account of ongoing participation in the Special Section, Isorni describes a horrible ritual, where, in the best of cases, lawyers met secretly with the Presiding Judges before the trial, to figure out if there was any way a death penalty could be avoided. German officials sat in the audience and observed the proceedings. Isorni tells of magistrates in the Special Section who, after the war, didn't hesitate to punish collaborators in the Purge courts who had done less harm during the Occupation than they. His story is doubtful and certainly exaggerated, since it is a matter of historical record that prosecutors and presiding judges who sought the death penalty against resistance fighters in the Paris Special Section were among the most severely sanctioned by the postwar Purge commission. One senses, as in all of Isorni's stories, a bitterness, a desire to insist on injustice and moral hypocrisy in others.

The power of rhetoric to fight the system is another theme of his Vichy defense stories. Isorni took great pleasure in recounting a single case during the Occupation in which he believes his turn of phrase alone made all the difference. A communist resistance demonstration in front of a grocery store on the rue de Buci in May 1942 had resulted in the death of three policemen. Thirty people were arrested and brought before the Vichy Tribunal d'Etat, or State Tribunal. They were all threatened with death sentences. Isorni was to defend a twenty-year-old communist from Orgerus, one of the group of thirty. For some reason, the name "Orgerus" and the boy himself—big and strong as an oak— brought to his mind a picture of forests and of woodsmen. Since he was looking for a way to distinguish his own client from all the others on trial, he seized upon his own image and started referring to the boy as "The Woodsman of Orgerus." "Remember," he said to the court, every time he finished a point in his argument, "this is the woodsman from the forest of Orgerus!" It became the refrain of his speech, repeated ten times over. The boy was spared the guillotine. Thus, he concludes, he was able to save his client by the sheer poetry of his defense speech, which distinguished that one boy from the many others on trial. No one in the courtroom seemed to know, or to care, that there was no forest in Orgerus. At least that is how Isorni understood what he had done. He would embroider the story of the woodsman even further during his defense speech for Brasillach.

One aspect, at least, of Isorni's view of occupied France is born out in histories of the period: he saw occupied France as a hostage nation. He saw to what extent the courts, in particular, were manipulated by the Germans. But his vision of history was passive. He did not focus on the responsibility of Vichy for what had gone wrong, nor on the margin of freedom that certain individuals had to manipulate against the Germans within that system. As he understands the situation in the 1980s, the Vichy courts were total dupes, practically tantamount to the enemy. There is a stunning paradox, a contradiction, in Isorni's attitude. The man on top, the man who incarnated the laws and courts of that hostage nation, the man who took the moral responsibility for caving in to the Nazis was the Marshal Pétain. For mysterious reasons, when it was all over and Pétain was held accountable for what had happened in France, Isorni declared that Pétain had been the only guarantee against total defeat. France was passive, German-controlled, but Pétain had been a hero. Isorni invested his heart and soul in Pétain's defense and his rehabilitation.

Jacques Isorni lived in the building he owned on the rue Geoffroy St. Hilaire, where during the final two and a half years of the Occupation, he rented the apartment across the hall from his own flat to Marcel

Reboul, who became his friend. Isorni does not say, in his memoirs, exactly how many cases brought him into the courtroom to defend a client prosecuted by Reboul, representing the Vichy state. He does describe one specific case, where he defended a man imprisoned for black market sugar traffic. Isorni stood for the defense, Reboul for the prosecution, and the presiding judge in the black market court was Vidal.

Isorni pretended that Laval, Prime Minister of the Vichy government, had set up this client to take a fall in a case concerning huge payments for sugar supplies. Isorni, in his classic maverick devil-may-care way, had written a harsh note to the judiciary, accusing Laval of being involved in the affair. His colleagues in the Palace of Justice warned him he might lose his job, even be arrested over the incident, when Laval learned of his accusation.

According to Isorni's account of events, Reboul wanted to ask for the maximum punishment. But when Laval received word of Isorni's charge, Reboul suddenly attenuated his prosecution—as though he had gotten an order from on high, from Laval, frightened by Isorni's note—and Isorni's client was let off with the minimum punishment. We can read this tale for what it tells us about Isorni's attitude. Isorni told the story of the sugar case to show his own independence from official powers. He considered his actions part of his own "resistance" to Vichy. He also used the story to contrast his behavior with that of Reboul and Vidal, the "government men," whose decisions, in his view, were dependent on the whims of government officials. Without the documents, and because of the highly partisan way Isorni tells the story, it is very difficult to know what really happened. There is no transcript of the trial, no file available to show what might have happened in and out of the courtroom. The original actions of the sugar merchant are foggy, and the story is confusingly told. But the intended moral of Isorni's tale is that Reboul was a servant of Vichy, while Isorni was a man of daring and courage who wouldn't let Vichy push him around.

Because Isorni was not marked publicly under Vichy as someone sympathetic to the resistance, he was in a good position to defend resistance fighters. We do not have access to his war case files, but he writes that he returned often to defend communist resistance fighters before the Paris Special Section. His waiting room became a gathering place for clandestine resistance fighters; he helped people who had been tortured file civil suits. As soon as the Liberation occurred, his activities as a defense lawyer would change radically, along with the population in his waiting room. He was a champion of underdogs, and suddenly, in 1945, there was a new class of men and women who considered themselves underdogs and victims—the men and women arrested for collaboration with the Nazis, many of them detained in great haste, with little evidence against them other than word of mouth. Everyone's behavior during the Occupation was suspect in the immediate postwar period, so a reputation for having defended resistance fighters under Vichy, or for having belonged to the resistance oneself, was practically an unspoken requirement for a lawyer defending collaborators in courts marked by passionate proresistance sentiment.

As a lawyer who had been excluded, however briefly, from the bar under Vichy and who had defended communists in the Paris Special Section, Isorni had exactly the right profile, despite his allegiances to the Action Française, to Pétain, and to the right. He was overwhelmed with requests to defend people on trial for collaborationist treason, people in the arts, in literature, in journalism, in the professions. He specialized in society cases: an opera singer, a composer, the automobile magnate Louis Renault, as well as Brasillach and Pétain himself.

The Purge hardened his sense that men were hypocrites, that injustice was the norm in the world he lived in. Isorni considered de Gaulle's law declaring Vichy illegal to be an act of terrorism, an act which put France on the course toward civil war. "Do not compare the sufferings of the Purge with those of people who were deported during the war!" He believed that what the collaborators endured after the war was far worse than what the deportees had endured during the Occupation. He writes in his 1984 memoirs: "Most of the deportees died because of what the enemy did to them, in wartime, and not because of what their fellow citizens did, once the enemy had left." Despite his own experience under Vichy, Jacques Isorni did not see, did not want to see, that the deportations from France took place with the complicity of his fellow citizens. For him, deportation was always a lesser evil than the arrests and punishments of the Purge. His work defending those accused of collaboration embittered him in all his opinions, pitted his vast rhetorical talent squarely against the Gaullist state—responsible, in his view, both for the excesses of the Occupation and those of peacetime—and completed the evolution of this right-wing nonconformist into a dedicated reactionary. "Article 75," he wrote, "was ravaging France."

It was Isorni's legal associate, Jean-Paul Amiel, related by marriage to a friend of Brasillach's from the Lycée Louis-le-Grand, who suggested

he might defend the writer Brasillach. Suzanne Bardèche visited Isorni
personally and asked him to take on her brother's defense. True to so
many aspects of Brasillach's life, it was the old school network that had
gotten him a lawyer.

When Vidal was designated as president of the court, and Reboul
as prosecutor, Isorni was astonished. Not only would he be defending
Brasillach against his tenant and his neighbor, he'd be in the courtroom
with Reboul under Presiding Judge Vidal—exactly the same personalities as in the black market sugar case. He and Reboul spent hours talking
about the case—on their way to the Palais on the city bus, over dinners,
late evenings on the rue Geoffroy St. Hilaire. As for Vidal, Isorni went
to pay him a courtesy call before the trial. The judge was also struck
by the coincidence and said to him, "So! We'll be meeting up again,
all three!" Isorni reported the conversation to Brasillach in one of his
visits to Fresnes. The clever writer burst out laughing and retorted, "Yes,
you'll all be meeting up again, and I'll be playing dead."

This reunion of the familiar threesome only added spice to the
situation. Robert Brasillach was an ideal client for the young lawyer:
"The one whose name shines in the artistic or intellectual or scientific
scene of the moment, the one who hires a lawyer for a trial known as
'literary' is a choice client who lends a glittering aura to any practice.
For the trial he brings against another or submits to himself will have
his particular mark. It will inspire the interest of the judges. It will allow
him to fight around a principle or an idea." This, at any rate, was how
Isorni described the privilege of defending celebrities in "literary" trials
six years after he had lost Brasillach's case.

In 1945, Isorni's intention had been to defend Brasillach's ideas
along with Brasillach no matter what the consequences. This was a
matter of principle. In *Je suis avocat,* he describes in general terms his
belief that a political defendant's system of thought must be respected,
revealing much of the philosophy that lay behind his defense strategy in
the Brasillach case:

> If the man exists who is ready to sacrifice his ideas in the hopes
> of saving himself, there also exists the man who refuses to betray
> his ideas, who persists in seeing in these ideas the justification
> for his actions. The task is simpler in the first case, although it
> lacks grandeur. It is always easy, or less difficult, to argue confused
> thinking, the responsibility of a third party, mental weakness, the
> pardon for "faults" or the role of destiny. For the second kind of

man, even if the defender is not obliged to make the political concept his own, at least he is required not to diminish it. The man who is tried for his ideas or for acts that are the consequence of his ideas always feels that he is the victim of power. This feeling of persecution helps him tolerate misfortune. . . . To detach him from his ideas, to provoke a renunciation in the hopes of an uncertain success, would be to weaken him in advance and, to my mind, prepare him badly for the ordeal whose ending one never knows. Unlike in civil law, the lawyer who argues a political case has made his own commitment.

It is easier to claim your client is foolish or wrong, and to excuse him for his mistake, but this method "lacks grandeur." Everything in Isorni's education, everything about his personality, his philosophy of law, and his vision of life, led him to seek grandeur instead.

SEVEN MISSING PERSONS: BRASILLACH'S SUBURBAN JURY

The legal designers of the new Courts of Justice wanted jurors who would represent the people of France, and who would execute the people's justice. In part this was a reaction to what Vichy had done to French courts of law during the previous four years. In many courtrooms, Vichy had eliminated the role of juries altogether, showing the same kind of contempt for representative government that had resulted in the abolition of the National Assembly. Vichy's "exceptional courts," which included Special Sections, Special Tribunals, and a State Tribunal, had meted out justice by passing laws that could be applied retroactively, thus violating a sacred principle of French law. Due process had been abandoned under Vichy. In restoring power to jurors in the Purge trials, the Liberation government aimed to revitalize the democratic process.

On a practical level, the jurors for the Courts of Justice were chosen in the following manner. They had to be French citizens at least twenty-five years of age. They could be of either sex. Four names were to be drawn for each case from a list of twenty on which would appear only those citizens "who had not ceased to show proof of national sentiments," meaning citizens who had proved their patriotism. Who, in postwar France, was qualified to identify citizens who had shown proof of national sentiments? Jury lists were established by magistrates in cooperation with representatives from the Committees of Liberation that had formed in every department, county, town, and district of France. As we have seen, these committees, composed of representatives from the major resistance movements, were set in motion during the dramatic week of liberation. In Champigny-sur-Marne, for example, the local Committee of Liberation included representatives from the trade unions, from a youth movement, from the communist resistance movement, the Socialist Party, the resistance group known as "Liberation," from a women's group, a war widows' group, and a former prisoner-of-war group. In many townships, the Committee of Liberation appointed a special "Purge commission" to insure that local collaborators were brought to justice. The power given to these Committees of Liberation to suggest jurors for the Purge courts, and thus to enter into the supposedly impartial system of justice, was one of the most controversial aspects of the Purge.

The involvement of the Committees of Liberation in jury selection lasted for approximately a year. In November 1945, the French lawyers' association launched a strong critique and the law was amended in December. What remained intact, even after December 1945, was the proviso that members of the jury needed to have shown "proof of national sentiments" during the Nazi occupation.

The phrase "national sentiments" is one heard over and over again in the speeches made within the Purge courtroom, both by the defense and the prosecution. National sentiments, national feeling: how interesting that it was a state of mind, an emotion, rather than any specific action or membership in a specific party, that described the requirement for political correctness. "National sentiments" became a judicial shorthand, a badge of good behavior. The phrase is key for understanding the period.

For over a year, from the trial of Georges Suarez in October 1944 until the trial of the anti-Jewish administrator Xavier Vallat in December 1945, departmental Committees of Liberation had a huge role in determining who would serve on the Purge juries for the Courts of Justice. From his prison cell at Fresnes, where rumors and information mixed, Brasillach himself had a gangster-like vision of the constitution of the juries: "The jurists were drawn at large from a list of the resistance established quite simply and quite officially by the communist Midol." The name Midol appears on membership lists for the Paris Committee of Liberation during these early months, and there was a famous Midol family in the resistance: Lucien Midol, a Communist Party union leader, and his two sons. In a discussion about the purge that took place in the Consultative Assembly, the Minister of Justice had indeed explained that a "M. Midol, union representative," was the representative from the Paris Committee of Liberation who helped establish juror lists for the Paris Court of Justice. Isorni had brought the published minutes of that discussion for Brasillach to read in prison. Perhaps it was reassuring to think that a single enemy, a communist, was responsible for the constitution of the Purge juries. Certainly the idea that the Purge was being conducted "on the orders of Moscow," as former *Je Suis Partout* writer Pierre-Antoine Cousteau said in one of his radio broadcasts from Sigmaringen, was appealing to the collaborationists. In fact, what the jurors in Brasillach's trial had in common wasn't political so much as geographic. Only one of the four men who judged Brasillach was a member of the Communist Party, but all of them were from the Parisian suburbs. That geography, we shall see, has its own significance.

The Purge victims and the right wing were not the only ones to criticize the process by which the jurors were chosen. In 1952, Jean Paulhan published his critique of the Purge from within the literary world, *Lettre aux directeurs de la Résistance*. Paulhan, a resistant and pillar of the Editions Gallimard, had helped to found the Conseil National des Ecrivains, a group of writers who conducted their own informal purge from within the literary profession. Immediately after the liberation of Paris, the CNE published a list of writers tainted by the collaboration, asking that they not be published alongside them. The group was tied to the Communist Party, to Aragon and Eluard, from the outset, and became more closely identified with the communists as the months passed. After Paulhan resigned from the CNE in 1946, he took the whole system of the Purge—both legal and intraprofessional—to task.

The Courts of Justice, Paulhan argued vehemently in *Lettre aux directeurs de la Résistance,* had appointed juries of "specialists," men and women who had personally experienced the collaboration as its victims. You ask a specialist to fix a clock, he said, but you don't need a specialist to tell you what time it is. A jury should be composed of someone ignorant of the crimes in question, not a former victim, nor a supporter of the criminals. Someone who has no investment: that's what democracy is. But how to find such a person in postwar France? Emile Garçon put it mildly in his 1952 analysis of the French legal code: "It was surprising to see individuals accused of acts of collaboration judged by those same people who had suffered bodily harm and damage to their property, because of the collaboration." Paulhan went a step further than Garçon in his critique, in turning the word "collaboration" on its head. The jurors out to punish the collaborators were themselves collaborating with the communists. Paulhan articulated a critique of the Purge that would become a right-wing theme in postwar France: the Purge as "terror," as repetition of the Terror of the French Revolution:

> I've seen some of them, some of those jury members! They were beautiful to behold. They moved in columns. Often the most honest people in the world, the straightest arrows. But still, they knew they were there to condemn. The [Communist] Party had told them. The Republic seemed to be repeating it. And they condemned. With all their might. They were inflexible. Were they just?

The myth of Purge juries composed uniquely of communists, operating under the orders of their party, was solidified by Paulhan. But was it just?

One important aspect of the Purge juries is surprisingly little commented on in accounts of the press, for reasons that may become clear below. For the first time in French history, women were authorized to serve on the juries of the Courts of Justice. This doesn't affect the Brasillach trial per se. There were no women on Brasillach's jury, nor, oddly, on the list of twenty from which his jury of four was chosen. Although women did not participate in Brasillach's jury, misogyny and masculinity were important factors in the rhetoric of the Brasillach trial. Masculinity was bandied about in 1945 as an aspect of resistance heroism; accusations of femininity were a weapon used against the collaborators.

French women had finally received the right to vote from de Gaulle by an April 1944 decree of his provisional government; the right to serve on a jury came along with the right to vote. De Gaulle's gesture was considered a "prize" to the women of France for their acts of heroism in the resistance, rather than a response to a massive suffrage movement, as in the U.S. or England. It was a strange, disturbing moment in French history, in that the granting of the right to vote to women coincided with the brutal "shaving" [la tonte] and parading through the streets of women punished for "horizontal collaboration" with German occupants. Honored with the vote and scapegoated for their sexuality, both in connection with the Occupation: one might say that women were the first French citizens to be symbolically "recognized," positively and negatively, for their behavior during those difficult four years.

The Suarez Court of Justice trial in October was thus the first time in French history that women could serve on a jury. Alex Ancel announced the event in Le Parisien Libéré: "For the first time in the judicial annals of France, women have been admitted to sit on the jury bench. Along with other patriots chosen among the heroes of the resistance, they will be asked to make pronouncements in the name of society." It so happened that of the twenty people on the original list for the Suarez trial, of which there were four women, no women made it to the final four. "Members of the jury, two office workers, a hospital attendant, a doctor," Madeleine Jacob reported neutrally. Jacob, Jewish and left wing, a sharp-penned and brilliant legal correspondent for the Liberation-era daily Franc-Tireur, didn't even mention the presence of women on the initial list of twenty. Something vital had happened in French society, but one has the impression reading the press reports of these first trials that the presence of women was a rather minor event. It was as though women had been absent from official political life for so long that it

was unnatural to notice their sudden presence. Only with several years'
retrospective can one find speculation on the role of women jurors. An
article in *Esprit* from 1947 acknowledges their importance, then falls
into the worst stereotypes:

> Women, full partners in the jury, came to court untamed. One
> would have expected them to be rigid, instead they were merely
> nervous. The verdicts they rendered did not acknowledge the av-
> erage virtues. Then, after some contact with reality, their sensibility
> awakened and their profound instincts as well. They became women
> again, and they could be seen, their faces tense, on the verge of
> tears, listening to pleas by the defense. Others never relaxed, for
> they carried the memory of their dead. They have the right to
> our respect.

When you study the official lists of jury members for the Purge you can
feel the purposeful reaction against Vichy in their composition. If not
communists, many suburban jurors were from the working class. On
the list of twenty for the Suarez trial, the women gave their occupations
as housewife, office workers, and ironer [*repasseuse*]; the men called
themselves booksellers, office workers, railroad workers, artisans, tool
sharpeners, as well as "industrialist" and medical doctor. Five people
on the list lived within the city limits of Paris. The other fifteen were
from the outlying suburbs, most of which, in 1944–45, were still either
heavily rural or served as headquarters for the factories and the factory
workers who, since 1870, had been pushed out of the city limits towards
the north, the south, the east of Paris. The myth of Paris's "red suburbs"
that had existed since the 1920s was more than a myth: in the first
elections after the Liberation, the Communist Party took control of
sixty out of the eighty townships in the Seine region around Paris; fifty
of these towns elected a communist mayor. Very few suburbs of Paris,
in 1945, could be called affluent or bourgeois.

   At the moment when French women got the vote, the Paris suburbs
also came of age. The Purge trials were a way of recognizing the
participation of Paris's suburbs in the resistance against the Nazis and
in the liberation of the city. The trials, in their own way, announced
the importance of the outlying zones for the city's future. In 1945,
Paris was part of one "département," or district, called "La Seine";
around it was another vast district called "La Seine et Oise." In the
postwar years the Paris suburbs would explode; the Seine district would

disappear and be combined with the Seine et Oise into four large administrative units. Aubervilliers and Villetaneuse are now in Seine-Saint-Denis; Champigny and Saint Maur in Val-de-Marne. In postwar cinema, too, the suburb would no longer be a vague countryside, it would be represented as a zone of proletarian heroism (Lotar and Prévert, *Aubervilliers*); of Americanization (Tati, *Mon Oncle*); of reconstruction (Gabin, *Rue des Prairies*). The everyman of the French 1950s was no longer confined to the *grands boulevards.*

———

Albert Camus, writing about his impoverished family in his last, auto-biographical novel, *The First Man,* describes the difference between a rich, layered bourgeois memory and the memory of the poor:

> . . . poor people's memory is less nourished than that of the rich;
> it has fewer landmarks in space because they seldom leave the place
> where they live, and fewer reference points in time throughout lives
> that are gray and featureless. . . . Remembrance of things past is just
> for the rich. For the poor it only marks the faint traces along the
> path to death.

The same might be said of our capacity for remembering people who aren't rich or privileged. When it comes to what one might call the ordinary person, how few traces a life leaves! The higher someone's social class, the easier it is to learn something about them fifty, sixty, or seventy years after their death.

In 1986, Jean Maitron published the fourth volume of his massive *Dictionnaire biographique du mouvement ouvrier français,* with biographical sketches of union leaders and other prominent members of the working class, covering the period 1914–1939. Lucien Midol is there—the Communist Party union leader whom Isorni and Brasillach suspected was "masterminding" the jury selection. But the *braves gens* who served as jury members in the Brasillach trial are not in Maitron's dictionary. The hundreds of men and women, most of them working class, chosen to be jurors in the Purge trials, among them the four men who voted the death sentence for Robert Brasillach, are all but invisible in the histories of the Purge. Their invisibility is a question of sources. When it comes to the Purge, it's easiest to trace the collaborators themselves: there are court files. It's easier still to learn about the elite writers put on trial—Brasillach, Henri Béraud, Maurras. There are stenographic records of their trials, there is their writing itself, and there are often bitter memoirs of the Purge years written by them, by members of their family, or by their supporters. For the magistrates who served in the Purge courts—Reboul, Didier, Lindon—there are professional files, now open to historians by special request or *dérogation,* and there is the history of the institution of the magistrature. The magistrates during Vichy and the postwar era have been studied in great detail by Henry Rousso and Alain Bancaud, among others. The trials of individual writers have been described at length in books like Pierre Assouline's *L'Epuration des intellectuels.* The jurors of 1945 were, by definition, "common people"— de Gaulle wanted what he called a "jury populaire." And for them, there are only scraps.

———

René Desvillettes, André Van der Beken, Emile Jean-Marcel Riou, Lucien Grisonnet: what is there to learn about the four jurors who condemned Brasillach to death? Finding them became my quest in writing this book. What I had to start out with were the alphabetical lists of jury members for different sessions of the Cours de Justice, kept in a dusty box in the contemporary section of the National Archives. The lists gave the name of each juror summoned, their place and date of birth, their profession, and their address. For Brasillach's trial, as for the others, there was an initial list of twenty. A separate book of court records told me which four of these men had been picked to serve.

    With nothing but name, address, profession, and a birth date to start out with, I went as far as I could. For Lucien Grisonnet, a printer from Aubervilliers, I could add the vague memories of the men in the local historical society. The posters he printed in the postwar years are kept in the Aubervilliers municipal archives, an extremely well-organized and well-documented place, proud to catalog and conserve traces of the town's rich history. André Van der Beken, a middle-class engineer from bourgeois St. Maur, was easier to learn about than the others because I was able to locate his children, a pastor, and a psychiatrist. They remember his serving on the Brasillach jury. René Desvillettes, the youngest member of the jury, the one juror I hoped would still be alive today, died a violent death in the early 1950s. I know something about him through the testimony of a man who knew him in the Champigny Communist Party. The press accounts of his death told me nothing about his work on the Brasillach jury. The fourth juror, Emile Riou, is almost a shadow. I found a niece, who told me his sister had died six months earlier. I was able to read the wartime archives from his suburb, Villetaneuse, and infer from them something about what his life was like during the Occupation.

Lucien Albert Grisonnet

Born in Aubervilliers, April 5, 1888. Printer.

Lives at 70, rue du Moutier, in Aubervilliers.

Lucien Grisonnet's name doesn't appear in the official histories of the Aubervilliers resistance; his part was small. He was fifty-six years old in 1945 when he served on the Brasillach jury, a printer from Aubervilliers. The contrast with Brasillach is obvious: an artisan in a heavily communist suburb passing judgment on a graduate of the Ecole Normale, a member of Paris's literary elite.

Printers such as Grisonnet play a big role in our imagination of the resistance. Vercors's *The Silence of the Sea,* the legendary underground novel that launched the Editions de Minuit in 1942, was typeset by a man named Oudeville, whose regular job was to print death announcements. Printers during the Occupation made fake IDs, fake food coupons; they published underground newspapers, produced transport passes that allowed people to move from the occupied zone across the demarcation line to Vichy France. Unlike the Maquisards, who were in hiding, printers in the resistance worked out of their own homes. They were especially vulnerable to denunciation and arrest. The printers of the resistance had their martyrs: Eugène Pons in Lyons and Henri Lion in Toulouse were caught, arrested, and deported to camps.

Printing presses play a role in the documented resistance stories of Aubervilliers: in December 1940, five young men printed the first issue of the underground newspaper *Résistance* in the local branch of the aeronautics club for the famous "Musée de l'Homme" group. In 1943, on the rue Goutte d'Or in Aubervilliers, an underground press was installed in the Larbodière factory for the resistance movement "Défense de la France." It functioned until January 1944.

Lucien Grisonnet was born in the northeastern working-class suburb of Aubervilliers on April 5, 1888, in his parents' house at 2, rue Heurtault. His origins couldn't be more typical of a "gars d'Auber," a "guy from Auber": His father was a lockkeeper on the Canal de l'Ourq, which traverses Pantin to the south of Aubervilliers and empties into the basin of La Villette, which housed the city's vast slaughterhouses. Animal fat, bones, and blood, waste products from the meat treated at La Villette, were sent by canal to Aubervillier's chemical factories, where they were turned into perfume, soap, margarine. Grisonnet's mother is listed on his birth certificate as "frangeuse"—a fringe-maker. The *Grand Robert* dictionary lists a masculine and feminine version of this strange specialty, and a variant, "frangère," as though making decorative fringes for cloth was once a standard occupation.

Aubervilliers—Auber, to its citizens—was the toxic dumpsite of Paris. In addition to its factories for waste products, Aubervilliers was famous for its scavengers who worked the garbage for food and scrap metal. People lived in shacks, on "the zone," the periphery of the city, once the site of its military fortifications; people lived along the canal in wood-slat barges, and in crates that had held automobiles. In 1945, Aubervilliers was immortalized in a documentary by Eli Lotar, with lyrics by Jacques Prévert. The film, called simply *Aubervilliers,* shows rows and rows of substandard housing, children playing in garbage. Then a chemical worker is shown dipping his hands into vats of acid chemicals. The close-up of his hands reveals that they are peeling, ravaged, and a voice-over says, "The hands are nothing; imagine what is going on inside."

Aubervilliers was the land of rag pickers and rats. There were so many rats in the slaughterhouses of Aubervilliers, that an enterprising man named Monsieur Gustave organized races, where enormous rats were pursued by dogs.

Today, the rue Heurtault, where Lucien Grisonnet grew up, is one of the most run-down streets in Aubervilliers, where immigrants from Mali live in terrible conditions. This new wave of immigrants replaced the Spanish Republicans of the 1930s, who had replaced the Italians of the 1920s, who had replaced the French who had migrated from the Auvergne region at the turn of the century, who had replaced the Alsatians of 1870. In 1944, part of the street was hit by an Allied bomb, aimed at a railroad line north of the capital. By then, Lucien Grisonnet was grown and established as a printer, with his own shop on the rue du Moutier.

Lucien Grisonnet was a fixture on the rue du Moutier from the 1920s until the 1960s. It helps to imagine where he lived. Walking down his street today there's only the shadow of the old artisan's neighborhood: there's an appliance repair shop, small boutiques, a few bars. The street runs in a spoke behind the town square, off the church and the city hall. It's the oldest street in the town. Just as on the rue Heurtault, many of the houses, including Grisonnet's, have archway entrances and inner courtyards paved in stone, remnants of the farms that had been there at the start of the last century, transformed into workshops.

In 1929, Grisonnet was affluent enough to apply to the city of Aubervilliers for a construction permit to enlarge his house from one to two stories. His addition was designed by an architect, in sober art deco style with a slight flourish: the letter "G," in wrought iron, was mounted like a printer's logo on the door to Grisonnet's shop. In 1932 a more modest renovation gave him an extra room. In census and tax records he is listed as a printer-typographer with no employees. In 1945, the rue du Moutier was a street of artisans and tradesmen. Compared to most people in Aubervilliers, Grisonnet and his neighbors were well off.

––––––

During the Occupation, Grisonnet belonged to a local resistance movement composed of the small shopkeepers who lived around city hall—the baker, Lavie, was their founder, and the florist, Dufour, their treasurer. They called themselves "Libération." Dufour lived on the rue du Moutier, too. Lavie, a huge man favoring linen suits and berets, had a bakery on the other side of the Place de la Mairie from the rue du Moutier, on the rue Achille Domart. A cowboy-maverick, he had been arrested by the Germans for his resistance activities but had managed to escape from the train leading him east. The group was linked to the leading resistance hero of Aubervilliers, the Belgian Henri Manigart (code name: "Papa") of "Ceux de la Résistance." Manigart was commander of the vast CDLR sector in the northern suburbs, with over 3,000 men under his control, including 832 in Aubervilliers alone. At the Liberation, he was in charge of the whole northern sector of the Forces Françaises de l'Intérieur (FFI)—the resistance militia. During the August 1944 insurrection, members of the Groupe Henri attacked the Germans; many were killed. The rue du Moutier was one of the trouble spots. Sacks of sand piled on the sidewalks sheltered the insurrectionists from the German convoys passing by. A twenty-six-year-old member of the Forces Françaises de l'Intérieur was killed on the street; two others lost their lives behind the city hall. Finally, the Leclerc Division passed by the Place de la Mairie. With it were the Americans in their combat uniforms, with tanks.

Much resistance history is based on testimony, because it was secret, undocumented work. Daniel Lancia, a member of the Aubervilliers historical society, describes Grisonnet in one conversation as "an active member of the resistance" and in another as "a leader of a resistance group." Retrospective oral history is as unstable a source as memory itself. In this case, Lancia had the only information available on Grisonnet's work in the resistance. He remembers going to Grisonnet's printing press on the rue du Moutier in August or September of 1944, right after the Liberation, needing some kind of official "attestation" and seeing him there in conversation with "Henri dit Papa." Lancia imagines that it was probably on his printing press at number 70 that Lucien Grisonnet produced the tracts that called the population of Aubervilliers to insurrection. Didn't he also print fake ID cards and ration tickets? Since printing done for the resistance was never signed, this is impossible to verify, but the posters produced by Grisonnet after the war are in the Aubervilliers archives today. For all of France, there is a problem in determining not only what a resistance action was, but who took part in the resistance, because the threat of arrest and torture made it essential to keep one's identity, and the identities of one's comrades, secret.

After Paris was liberated, many members of the resistance came out of the woodwork to claim their glory. So did some people who weren't in the resistance. A photo at the Aubervilliers historical society shows the group of Aubervilliers "résistants" standing on the steps of city hall that week. Natty and round, wearing a little black beret and a wry smile is the Belgian, Henri Manigart—"Henri dit Papa." Towering over Manigart is Armand Lavie in a white linen suit and loud plaid tie, a beret perched on his head, a cigarette in his hand. In 1944 he was dreaming of becoming mayor of Aubervilliers, but Charles Tillon, former communist *député* from Aubervilliers, head of the Francs-Tireurs Partisans resistance group for all of France and now minister to de Gaulle, came back to the municipality from his wartime hiding place, and swept the local elections. In the background, thin, wearing an Italian-style hat is Dufour, the florist. Is Lucien Grisonnet in this photo? No one knows.

———

Those smiling artisans from the Aubervilliers resistance need to be understood in light of the other legacy of the "red suburb," a legacy of collaboration and fascism. That city hall on whose steps they were standing so triumphantly in 1944 was from 1923 to 1944 the political seat of Pierre Laval. During the Occupation, Louis Pagès, one of Laval's men, served as adjunct mayor, and the town continued to operate with Laval's cachet, under Laval's spell.

Pierre Laval, a scrappy man from the Auvergne, in central France, never lost his country manner. He got his start as a populist-socialist lawyer, helping the working people of Aubervilliers—including many who had migrated from the Auvergne with him—in their causes. He worked his way up to city hall. Laval's transition from socialist man of the people to wily head of the government under the arch-conservative Maréchal Pétain is a story which has been recounted brilliantly—a story worthy of American Southern gothic—by Robert Paxton in his classic *Vichy France:*

> Laval was an ideal scapegoat, a man plausibly reputed to have invincible lobbying prowess, a symbol of evil incarnate by 1944, a man who was dead and could not cry "tu quoque." Black Peter [Pierre], the only French politician whose name spelled the same whether one moved from Left to Right or Right to Left, a cartoonist's godsend with his swarthy round face, his inevitable cigarette, and his white necktie . . . Laval can be understood only if one remembers that his political base in working-class Aubervilliers remained intact, nurtured by Laval's plebeian manners and his effectiveness in helping constituents. A nonparty man, pragmatic, nurturing ties with both Left and Right, basing everything upon personal contacts—that had become Laval's political style.

Laval became mayor of Aubervilliers in 1923, minister eleven times and four times Prime Minister from 1931 to 1944—including twice under Pétain. In 1945, Laval was Pétain's fall guy. Always compared unfavorably to the handsome, avuncular Philippe Pétain, Laval emerged as the unsavory politico willing to make a deal, until the deals involved the Nazis. Laval is the man who said that he "wished for the victory of Germany." It was he who insisted that Jewish children needed to be deported along with their parents. 10,700 children were deported from France to death camps.

The connection from Lucien Grisonnet to Brasillach is indirect, but implicit: the town of Aubervilliers nurtured Laval's political talent, and Laval's policy furnished Brasillach with his most noxious piece of prose. "We must separate from the Jews *en bloc* and not keep any little ones": this was Brasillach mouthing Laval. Grisonnet, the jurist, who had lived under Laval's shadow for many years, might have recognized the line when the prosecutor quoted it.

Laval was still in Germany in January 1945. He wouldn't go on trial for another nine months. Aubervilliers had a mayor to purge from its local psyche, and Lucien Grisonnet, who lived two blocks from Laval's city hall, was the representative of an Aubervilliers that hoped to free itself of Laval's taint.

André Raymond Victor Van der Beken

Born in Pré St Gervais, December 6, 1901. Engineer.
Lives at 56, avenue de la République, in St. Maur.

André Van der Beken breaks the mold of the Brasillach jury and of the Purge juries in general. He was from one of the few affluent suburbs, St. Maur. He wasn't wealthy, nor was he a worker or an artisan. He was an engineer trained, like Brasillach, at a Grande Ecole.

Physically he was the largest man on the jury: five foot ten, thick, balding in 1945, with a moustache. He had spent a lot of time outdoors, on construction sites, in boy scouting. He had worked hard from the beginning, making his way through the Ecole Centrale on a student loan plus a scholarship and working extra hours to pay back his "prêt d'honneur." He was a successful student, who knew both German and English. He had become a successful engineer, though he lived modestly. Even at the height of his career, he didn't own his house, he rented it.

Most of what I know about André Van der Beken, I learned from his children. He had an unusual name for a Frenchman, which made it easier to locate his family. His grandson, listed in the phone book, now goes to the same engineering school as he did, the Ecole Centrale. One of his sons is a pastor in Nice; a daughter is a psychiatrist in the Paris suburbs. His grandson knew nothing of his participation in the resistance, but his children proudly told me his story.

André Van der Beken was an engineer with COLAS in the public works at Bonneuil, across the river from residential Saint Maur. His wife, Yvonne Van der Beken, taught at L'Ecole d'Adamville, a girls' school. The couple had five children, born between 1927 and 1944. Their house has now been replaced by a fancy modern apartment building. But on the other side of the Avenue de la République, you can still see houses in its genre: multistory structures covered in a mix of brick and ceramic ornamentation, the French equivalent of Victorian architecture. Of the Van der Beken's house, all that's left is one of the oak trees on the edge of the property.

———

The quickest way to get a sense of St. Maur is to think of the street scene in Jacques Tati's 1958 film *Mon Oncle*. For a perfect send-up of provincial French village life, Tati chose for the location of his film an old part of St. Maur, where the fronts of boutiques seem to jut out over one another, providing the perfect picturesque setting for the *garçon de café*, the butcher and the baker, the cop on the beat. Locals worked as Tati's extras. St. Maur is still a timeless bourgeois town on the banks of the Marne river, the landscape that Pissarro and Segonzac liked to paint. Many streets are still lined with the late nineteenth-century homes of decorative brick and colored ceramic, known in French as *pavillons*. There is something whimsical, almost toy-like, about the town's attempts at luxury.

Van der Beken was part of the railroad resistance, a highly organized network whose job was to prevent the transport of goods aiding the war effort out of France to Germany. The railroad resistance was prime material for the heroic commemorations of 1945, mythologized in René Clément's film *La Bataille du Rail*. If you went to the movies in 1945 you could see Lotar's documentary *Aubervilliers,* as a short, followed by Clément's railroad resistance epic.

At his job in Bonneuil, Van der Beken supervised a factory that repaired roads and airstrips. He dealt with pebbles, tar, and other building materials. During the Occupation, the Germans delivered raw material to his factory; he treated it and sent it back to Germany so that the Germans themselves could make repairs to their own roads or airstrips. It was rare, after the war, that Van der Beken ever talked about his role in the resistance to his children, but he did like to tell the story about a shipment of uranium that arrived mysteriously in his factory in Bonneuil. No one but he recognized what it was. Was it part of the German effort to build a bomb in the last days of the war? He told the foreman it was waste material and ordered it mixed up with a shipment of concrete and sent by train to Germany.

He worked with the train station manager at Sucy en Brie, above Champigny-sur-Marne, to orchestrate the errors in shipments and to warn the resistance that a valuable shipment was coming through. One goal was to make sure certain shipments were destroyed; another was to insure that shipments arrived months and months late. When there were building materials to be sent in railroad cars to Germany, he regularly made shipments disappear, by sending them in the wrong direction. His role in the resistance might be described as "chaos manager."

During the week of the Liberation, Van der Beken continued to do his part, modestly and quietly. His son remembers going to the garage during the tumultuous days of August and seeing that there were no more wheels on the family's car. "I lent them to the FFI," his father told him. All the bridges of St. Maur, on a loop of the Marne River, were guarded by the resistance militia, the FFI. Van der Beken had to cross the bridges to go to his factory in Bonneuil, the COLAS public works.

The liberation of St. Maur was a remarkably calm affair, but the week of the insurrection, Janine Van der Beken Steenkiste, André Van der Beken's daughter, sixteen years old in 1944, remembers that so many young men came by the house she assumed they were boy scouts. Her father was a scout troop leader. After his death, his children found his FFI arm band and attestation. They never remember him wearing it in those days of August 1944, even to cross the bridge to his job in Bonneuil.

At forty-four, Van der Beken was the second oldest member of the Brasillach jury. Van der Beken had studied the law briefly, before engineering school, and his son, Jacques, speculated that he might have been chosen for jury duty in part because of this legal training. The son of a pastor, and a leader in the Protestant church of St. Maur, a scout leader, André Van der Beken was a deeply serious, conscientious man, bearing many of the traits that the French like to call the "Protestant personality."

Emile Jean-Marcel Riou

Born in Clichy, August 16, 1901. Employee C.P.D.E.
Lives at 10, avenue du Maroc, in Villetaneuse.

About Emile Jean-Marcel Riou, we know less. Born in 1901, he lived with his wife, a typist, and his mother-in-law, in a white stucco bungalow on the rue du Maroc, a street that used to be surrounded by fruit orchards and has kept its country feeling, although it now runs directly behind the modern University of Paris XIII.

His town, Villetaneuse, a far northern suburb of Paris, had only 826 inhabitants in 1901; by 1954 it had grown to 3,937. Villetaneuse was the smallest township in the Seine district when the German occupation ended. It was still largely rural, with fruit trees and tiny vegetable farms everywhere. In 1945, the township was only beginning to house Parisian factory workers. Riou's niece, Denise Altenbourger, his only surviving relative, remembers him as a small man; straight arrow, discreet, and kind. In 1936 the census lists him merely as "electrician." He worked in the city of Paris for the CPDE, the regional electricity company. He would take the train in to the Barbès-Rochechouart station, in the north of the city. He was "a nonpracticing Catholic with Breton roots, probably a socialist, in his ideas, but definitely not a communist," Denise Altenbourger says, though she adds that Emile Riou never spoke to her about politics. She had no idea he had ever served as a jury member in a Purge trial.

A few photographs owned by his niece show him in 1938, wearing a short-sleeved white shirt, a vest, and a tie, standing by a fruit tree in front of the bungalow on the rue du Maroc, square-bodied with carefully combed brown hair. In 1940 he wears a black beret and the uniform of a French reserve soldier.

Riou's job in Paris was reading meters. Electricity didn't come to Villetaneuse until 1927. We get a flavor of life in Villetaneuse during the Occupation from the reports on local morale and material conditions that the mayor was required to send to the Kreiskommandantur of Seine Saint-Denis. In October 1943, the mayor describes his township:

> This essentially working-class population is especially involved in the cultivation of little gardens, which are numerous in our township since they have currently reached the number of 828 for a population of 2,544 inhabitants at the present time.

As for the economic situation:

> Most of the population works outside the town in the factories and public utilities, either in Paris or in Saint-Denis and suburbs to the west. Some live off their salaries, others are farmers (landowners and agricultural workers), of whom many have truck farms.

As the Occupation continued into its most difficult months, the mayor of Villetaneuse reported a serious shortage of milk, the evacuation of children into different parts of the country, and the cultivation of gardens in response to food shortages. In March 1944 at 4:20 P.M., an American plane fell from the sky onto a group of buildings. No pilot was found in the wreckage. No one was hurt. All the goods from the plane were recouped and removed. On July 14, "The population continues to attend to its usual business, with no show of nervousness." On August 14, two weeks before liberation, "Every day is more difficult, especially in terms of milk for the children, which is arriving in smaller amounts, frequently soured."

Electricity happened to play a little part in the local resistance. In July 1943, a tricolor French flag, imprinted with a Lorraine cross— the symbol of the resistance—was hung on an electrical wire at the corner of the rue Saint-Leu and the Avenue de Saint-Denis, a half block from Riou's house on the Avenue du Maroc. Was Riou part of that stunt?

During the famous August days of 1944, Liberation week, escaped Russian prisoners fought at the sides of members of the FFI and attacked a German convoy. The township was liberated on August 26–27, without incident, thanks to the presence of the Leclerc division.

Riou's name appears in the Villetaneuse archives, number 116 on a list of members of the local FFI, dated 1942–1944.

René Emile Desvillettes

Born in Alfortville, September 6, 1912. Technician, Est-Lumière.
Lives at 63, blvd. A. Briand, in Champigny-sur-Marne.

René Desvillettes, at thirty-four, was the youngest man to serve on the Brasillach jury. He is the only juror who corresponds to the stereotype; the only active Communist Party member among the four. What I know about Desvillettes firsthand comes from André Mauny, former communist city council representative in Champigny-sur-Marne, where Desvillettes lived. Champigny was and is a communist stronghold, the home of George Marchais, longtime general secretary of the French Communist Party.

André Mauny and his wife, Madeleine, are eloquent in recalling the privations of the Occupation years: they recall that the delicatessen owner in neighboring Nogent was arrested for selling sausages made from dog meat. "It was like in 1870, when people ate rats," muses Madame Mauny, proudly invoking her great-grandfather, a member of the Paris Commune who served nine years doing hard labor overseas for his actions. During the Occupation, Madame Mauny worked for the Lumière brothers' camera factory in Joinville, across the river. Both she and her husband remember the bitter cold, how the forest in Coeuilly (a section of Champigny) was cut down for fuel. They used to wait in line at the marketplace at 4 A.M. to see if any food would arrive.

Desvillettes worked as a technician at Est-Lumière, the local electric company, before the nationalization. The severe deco-modern Est-Lumière building is still there today, empty now, in the center of Champigny off the rue Maxime Gorki. The street where Desvillettes lived has been completely renovated. It was once lined with comfortable, but smaller and more modest, houses than the one where the Van der Beken family lived in St. Maur. The main thoroughfare of Champigny today bears the names of political leaders victimized by the far right: Roger Salengro, Marx Dormoy, Jean Jaurès. Champigny is one of the rare French towns to have a rue Robespierre.

During the Occupation, there was a terrible shortage of coal and fuel. People were freezing cold, they used to fix their meters to cheat on their heating bill by blocking the counter. Desvillettes was in charge of catching them. He worked with another electrician, known for his pro-German sentiments; they went around together and made people pay fines.

Desvillettes should have let the cheating utilities customers off the hook, Mauny says—indeed it was his patriotic duty to do so—but he didn't. By the end of the war, Desvillettes had joined the resistance group known as "Libération." It wasn't an eleventh-hour switch, because Desvillettes had never been an active collaborator, but it was opportunistic.

Champigny was a town that had its genuine martyrs, where the Communist Party leaders had to go underground in 1940, when the party became illegal, and continued to fight in a clandestine manner. The history of the Champigny resistance is hard to trace, a recent book on the town's history explains, because members of the resistance were in secret cells and weren't allowed to know the other members of their "network." In Desvillettes's own factory, Est-Lumière, the head of the communist resistance, René Damous, was arrested in a reprisal roundup by the Germans following the assassination of two Nazis. Damous was shot at Mount Valérien with fifty other hostages in October 1943. In 1944, a street was named for him. Isorni, in the Brasillach trial, tried to pretend that Brasillach opposed the resistance because their actions created just this kind of reprisal. The people of Champigny would never have agreed.

André Mauny is bitter and disgusted when he talks about his former comrade Desvillettes and his rise through the party ranks. He recalls that Desvillettes's nickname in the resistance was "Lieutenant Curieuse," because he couldn't mind his own business. The feminine adjective—curieuse—was part of the insult to this dark, squat, tough-looking man. He made his start in local politics in Champigny as secretary of his section of the Communist Party, through Est-Lumière, in the late 1930s. It was an efficient about-face from his role catching people who cheated on their heating bills to his activity in the resistance. Two months after the Liberation his name appears in the minutes of the Champigny city council meetings. The tone of those early meetings is utopian. The municipality dreamed of seizing the energy and spirit of the resistance. On October 15, 1944, the president of the local Liberation committee gave a speech at the city council meeting, as part of the transition between the provisional Liberation government and the postwar city council:

> I wish to give homage to all the authors of our liberation, to those
> who hastened it, to our allies, to the USSR, who, acting alone for a

long time, stopped and destroyed a great part of the kraut force; to
Great Britain, who neutralized the enemy navy and disorganized the
German war machine; to the United States who have liberated the
greater part of French soil. . . . France was liberated with the aid of
the resistance, in particular the FFI. . . . We have the good fortune
of bringing together a majority of all those French people who
want a National Revolution. In order for this revolution to exist,
we need the unity of all those French who have shown that France
wasn't dead, must not be a myth. . . . The Charter of the Resistance
anticipates the suppression of monopolies, of all those who prefer
their particular interest to the interests of the country; this action
has begun. To bring it to term, we must all fight hand-in-hand. At
the heart of our government, unity exists in making an abstraction
of all political ideas, it must exist at the heart of the municipalities;
if not, instead of working for France, we will waste all that these
four years of suffering, of courage, of humiliation, permitted us to
achieve. In fact, it's under the most violent reigns of terror that the
most noble ideas, the most profound revolutions are born.

This is what the heroic communist rhetoric sounded like in the postwar
era. The city council members saw themselves as keepers of the flame
of resistance, remaking the world for the revolution. They were totally
committed to communism.

That was the rhetoric. The Communist Party was also a powerful
agent of socialization, of mobility, a vehicle for ambitions. Mauny
remembers being with Desvillettes in Communist Party cell meetings
and hearing him announce, "I want to be deputy"—the equivalent
of congressman. He remembers Desvillettes as a ladies' man, whose
personal life eventually got him into trouble. The rest is obscured.

———

This imperfect sketch of the four members of the jury is as clear a picture as we're ever going to have: Desvillettes, the Don Juan and ambitious
Communist Party hack; Riou, the straight-arrow electrician; Van der
Beken, solid scout leader and Protestant humanist; and Grisonnet, the
good printer, the artisan risen from the working class. One communist,
one man with socialist ideas, two men whose resistance had no special
party affiliation. All of them from the suburbs. These were four ordinary
men, not superheroes of the resistance, and yet in their hands fell the
power to adjudicate the moral authority of the postwar era in a highly
symbolic trial. French historians have ignored them so far.

Important work on the Purge is underway in places like the Institut d'Histoire du Temps Présent. So far it has concentrated on the "top," on institutional questions like the role of the magistrature, or the prefects, or on ideological questions such as the importance, or lack thereof, of anti-Semitism in the Purge trials. One model of history is the institutional model, where authority comes from the top down. This is tempting in France, where power is notoriously centralized, and where bureaucracies exercise enormous control over people's daily lives.

Yet the French are also known for their cultural histories of the micro-details of everyday life: the history of smell, the history of prostitution, the history of reading. In the case of the Occupation, institutional history is particularly important because of the role of bureaucracy in the deportation of Jews and the denial of civil rights under Vichy. Again, in the postwar period, de Gaulle's institutional maneuvers were crucial in remaking France.

What interests me both for the war years, and for the Liberation that follows, is the intersection of those top-down rules with individual destinies. Individual actions, celebrated and glamorized in countless resistance stories, can easily be forgotten in the equally dramatic legal and institutional realignments of the immediate postwar era. In studying an institution such as the Court of Justice, one forgets that individuals also made choices there, no matter how bound they were by rules.

Perhaps the men and women of the juries have been ignored because it is easy to be cynical about how much power they actually had. After all, when it came time for their deliberations, the president of the court went into the chambers with them, guiding them. Paulhan, as we have seen, thought the Communist Party had told them what to do in advance. I've heard historians say that the death sentence for Brasillach was a foregone conclusion, once the Minister of Justice had told Reboul what he wanted. And yet here they were, four free men, asked to make a decision. The prosecution and defense speeches were addressed to them—or were supposed to be addressed to them—according to the conventions of the court. They listened and wrestled with their consciences, according to their personalities, their own experience, their sense of justice. We have virtually no access to their subjectivity. What leads up to their decision is inaccessible.

———

Or almost inaccessible. We do know that on the 18th of January, the day before the Brasillach trial, the same jury sat in judgment on two other cases.

The first case involved a thirty-six-year-old prostitute, arrested by the FFI for having had "relations with the Gestapo." These "relations" amounted to the fact that she had denounced one of her clients to the Gestapo after he had robbed her at gunpoint.

Their second case also involved denunciation. An industrial drafts-man was arrested the week of the Liberation for having anonymously denounced two escaped prisoners of war in his apartment building. His concierge had written to the judge to say he was a member of the fascist RNP, the Rassemblement National Populaire, and that he received their newspaper. A veritable carnival of denunciation. Ten people testified in his defense.

Both the prostitute and the draftsman were accused on the same treason charge as Brasillach, Article 75 of the penal code. The jury found the prostitute innocent of treason but sentenced her to "national degradation"—the penalty that deprived her of the right to vote, hold public office, practice a profession or own a company. The draftsman, better equipped to rally his own defense—his concierge denounced him but at least he had a concierge!—was acquitted of all charges. How did these cases influence the jury on the Brasillach trial? Impossible to know.

After their week of jury duty, Grisonnet, Van der Beken, Desvil-lettes, and Riou never spoke or wrote publicly about any of their decisions. I would like to tell their story but finally I can only describe them, pointing to them as a cast of characters, locating them on a map of postwar suburban Paris that is largely unfamiliar, compared with the sacred historical ground of the Ile de la Cité.

The act that did get recorded and remains theirs alone was their signature on these three verdicts, the week of January 15 to January 20, 1945. Only one of their verdicts would migrate from the "livre des arrêts," the register of judgments delivered, into the larger history of France.

EIGHT COURT

January 19, 1945: Paris was liberated but the rest of France was still at war. The paradox is almost impossible to fathom: it was a time both of immense relief and anxious anticipation. The Germans were still holding various pockets along the Atlantic, as well as Colmar, in Alsace-Lorraine, the Eastern border region that had been passed back and forth between the French and Germans since 1870. Thirty-four days before the Brasillach trial, on December 16, 1944, Von Rundstedt's offensive nearly succeeded in recapturing Alsace-Lorraine for Germany and launching a new invasion whose goal would be to retake Paris. The liberated city wondered if its celebrations hadn't been premature.

The Germans, who'd kept more than an eagle eye on the Vichy justice system, had left the city during the bloody week of August. De Gaulle's provisional government now occupied the National Assembly, the city halls, and the courts. Vichy had disappeared.

The voice-over on the newsreel that played in the movie houses that week announced, "The cold continues its terrible offensive." It was the worst weather of the war, the canals and the Seine were frozen solid, the countryside "an immense icebox." The marketplace at Les Halles was empty and bakers had posted signs on their doors that read, "Bakery closed for lack of flour and lack of wood to fire the ovens." Because of paper shortages, the newspapers had reduced their formats to half-sized pages. An event like the arrival of concentrated milk made headlines.

"Existence in Paris is still abnormal with relief, with belief. The two together make for confusion," wrote *New Yorker* correspondent Janet Flanner in her "Letter from Paris": "Nourished by liberation, warmed by the country's return to active battle, France is still, physically, living largely on vegetables and mostly without heat."

———

Robert Brasillach's trial was scheduled to start at 1 P.M. on January 19, cutting the lunch hour short. A rationed hunk of cheese, thin soup, ersatz coffee—what else was there to eat in January 1945?

The jurors, Lucien Grisonnet, André Van der Beken, Emile Riou, and René Desvillettes, bolted down their meals, then made their long trek into Paris on the trains in from the suburbs, from Aubervilliers and

Villetaneuse, due north, and from Champigny and St. Maur, due west, then to the metro.

They each got off at the stop called "Cité." The Ile de la Cité is a bottle-shaped island in the center of Paris that houses the reigning institutions of France's old and new regimes—the Préfecture de Police, the Hôtel Dieu hospital, the Notre Dame Cathedral, and the Sainte Chapelle, with its deep blue stained-glass windows, standing in the center courtyard of the massive Palais de Justice, which housed France's Kings before the Louvre. Walking solemnly through a massive iron gate topped in gold, the jurors were suddenly aware that they represented the people, the very conscience of the resistance. Inside the building, they proceeded down the wide marble hall known as "the room of lost steps," reminiscent of the corridor in a train station. It led them to the Salle des Assises, the courtroom used for criminal cases. It was here that Robert Brasillach was going to be tried.

Brasillach himself took a long ride from his suburban prison. He was handcuffed and transferred from his cell at Fresnes to a prison van, which made its way in one straight line down the route d'Orléans, past the porte d'Orléans—the old gate of the city—continuing for a mile along the avenue d'Orléans, to the Luxembourg Gardens and the boulevard Saint-Michel. From there he was on familiar territory, passing through his beloved Latin Quarter until he reached the Seine. There was an entrance to the Palais along the quai de l'Horloge. Brasillach and his guard walked up a labyrinth of stairs and hallways, known as the *"souricière"*—the mousetrap—to a small room. There, he waited.

His defense lawyer, Jacques Isorni, left home earlier than usual, since he didn't want to take the bus to the Palais with Marcel Reboul, his neighbor and Brasillach's prosecutor.

Inside, the press corps was already bundled up against the cold cavernous space in their thick woolen jackets, known as *canadiennes*. With trials scheduled at a fierce pace morning and afternoon, day after day, the Palais had practically become a reporter's dorm. Specially accredited court reporters, who filed anonymous dispatches for the press agencies, had their own office in the building. Then there were the star reporters, with their recognizable by-lines, sent by the major papers to cover a specific trial. The press corps was preoccupied with the annoying paper shortages, which meant they'd have to limit severely the length of their stories on the trial.

The public entered the Palais de Justice in the same place as the jurors, through the big iron gates along the boulevard du Palais, facing away from the river bank. French law stipulates that trials are open to the public, and the Purge trials were enthusiastically attended—the great social theater of the Liberation era. In addition to a press box, there were seats for a hundred people in the back of the Salle des Assises, another twenty behind the prosecution, and there was standing room for twenty or thirty more. There wasn't a single empty seat that day. The crowd at Brasillach's trial looked like high society out for entertainment. The women were wearing gorgeous new hats, as though they were at a theater premiere. Wealthy people were there, free to leave their workplace or with no workplace at all. They had little in common with the working men of the jury.

Not that there weren't weighty thinkers in the courtroom. Representing postwar existentialist France were the philosopher Maurice Merleau-Ponty, two years ahead of Brasillach at the Ecole Normale, and Simone de Beauvoir. They were already in the planning stages of a magazine they would call *Les Temps Modernes,* to be directed by Jean-Paul Sartre. In the press box, to the left of the accused, were representatives of all the major resistance newspapers. Roger Grenier was away in the north of France, investigating the coal shortages that were making Paris suffer; wild-eyed Alexandre Astruc covered the trial for Camus's *Combat.* Women were well represented in the press: there was Madeleine Jacob for *Franc-Tireur,* whom Isorni had nicknamed "the hyena," and Francine Bonitzer for *L'Aurore.* Many of the journalists were in their twenties—the generation of Arlette Grebel and Roger Grenier—and were cutting their teeth on the Purge trials. The press corps was so changed by the Liberation that Edouard Helsey, for the conservative *Figaro,* was practically alone among them in having been a colleague of Brasillach's in the 1930s, when he was still the precocious critic for the *Action Française.*

France has what is called an "inquisitory" system of justice. Its trials are divided into distinct acts, like the parts of a play. First there is the indictment, read out loud by a *greffier,* or court secretary, which is like a prologue. It sets out the facts that the rest of the play will confirm, or unravel.

Act I is the interrogation, where the president of the court questions the accused at length. Here, in the interrogation, the accused has a chance to express him or herself, in dialogue with the president— the presiding judge. Jurors, prosecutor, or defense may ask their own questions of the accused. Next, witnesses for the defense and for the prosecution are called: this is considered a part of the interrogation

process. Judge, defense lawyer, and prosecutor may question the witnesses. Thus the interrogation, with its open dialogues, is tantamount
to the cross-examination that takes place in an American court.

After the interrogation comes Act II, the prosecutor's speech against
the accused, known as the "*réquisitoire.*"

Act III is the speech by the defense lawyer, the *plaidoirie,* or "pleading," for the accused.

With the exception of the interrogation, with its challenges both
to the accused and to the witnesses, each participant in a French trial
speaks in a controlled soliloquy.

At the end of the trial, after the defense lawyer's speech, the presiding
judge asks the accused if he or she has anything to add. The right
of the accused to a last word is a fundamental principle of French
justice. The members of the jury then leave the courtroom for their
deliberation. While an American jury is left alone, choosing a foreman
amongst themselves, the French jury retreats into chambers along with
the presiding judge, who assists them in their deliberations by explaining
the punishment that goes along with each possible decision. The court
comes back into session, and the verdict is read.

In the Brasillach trial, each act was to have a distinct mood, and vastly
different *dramatis personae.* The stark theatricality of the proceedings was
only heightened by the surprising absence of witnesses.

———

Prologue: The Indictment, 1 P.M.

The "door of the accused" opened. Brasillach entered the vast courtroom in the company of a single gendarme dressed in blue, a *képi* on his
head and a leather holster across his chest. "Like a bull leaving his pen,"
he said of himself in that singular moment. "A wild beast unleashed at
the circus," wrote Francine Bonitzer for *L'Aurore.*

Brasillach immediately took his place in another sort of pen, "*le
box des accusés*" [the box of the accused]—the French name given to
the boxed-in, oak paneled defendant's dock where Brasillach and his
guard would remain throughout the proceedings and from which he
now peered hopefully at the audience. Many of his friends were in
exile in Germany, in hiding in Paris, or, like his brother-in-law Maurice
Bardèche, in the same prison at Fresnes where Brasillach himself was
being held. Only a handful of close relatives and friends were there: his
sister Suzanne, cartoonist Jean Effel—sympathetic to the communists
but loyal to Brasillach—and Jacques Tournant, a fellow officer from the

POW camp who had been a potential witness on Brasillach's behalf. Tournant had served as Brasillach's go-between during the week of the Liberation, while he was hiding in the maid's room. Brasillach gave them all a shy little wave. Edouard Helsey thought he looked like a naughty schoolboy brought up before the principal.

It was Maurice Vidal who was playing the part of the principal that January afternoon. President of the court, Vidal was a bookish gray-haired man of fifty-two who seemed far older than his years and whose one bad eye gave him a distracted look. He was a modest man, a dignified judge, and, like Brasillach himself, a lifelong bachelor. "Deferential," "irreproachable," and especially "*courtois*"—courteous—are words that appear in his administrative file. He sat behind a long table at the front of the courtroom, his notes spread out before him. He announced that court was in session and asked Brasillach to rise: "Your name is Brasillach, Robert," he said, looking at the defendant crosswise. "You were born March 31, 1909, in Perpignan. You are a man of letters and a journalist. You live in Paris."

"Yes, Mr. President," Brasillach answered, trying to clear his voice, still hoarse from the freezing air outside. He could smell the vapors from the painting hanging over him, a huge blue fresco commissioned under Vichy that hadn't had time to dry in the first month of 1945. The fresco depicted the nine-year-old King Louis XIII taking his vows on that very same historic spot in 1610, in the company of the queen mother and a few heroic greyhounds. It was a bright and gaudy backdrop for the scene, and another reminder of the embarrassing continuity of Vichy and the Liberation courts.

The president of the court asked Brasillach to be seated, then added, according to the time-honored formula: "Brasillach, be attentive to what you are about to hear. Mr. Secretary, please read the indictment." Brasillach had time to look around. On the ceiling was artwork several hundred years older and that much more subdued than the Vichy fresco. There was a woman pleading for a male prisoner, a painting of Christ on a cross, two cherubs holding a tablet marked "lex"—the law, another woman holding a sword representing liberty, two more cherubs holding the scale of justice. Brasillach himself was looking something like a cherub, the press said, although he had lost much of his chubbiness by the end of the war and he was drowning in his big suit jacket. His face had gone pale and he accentuated that paleness by wearing a red wool tie against his white shirt. In preparing for this moment, he had been dreaming of Julien Sorel, the guillotined hero of *The Red and the Black*.

The courtroom was organized in three sections. In the front of the room, facing the audience, was the tribunal, a long elevated wooden bench. There sat Presiding Judge Vidal, and to his immediate right the jury of the people, dressed in their Sunday best: Lucien Grisonnet, the printer from Aubervilliers; Emile Riou from Villetaneuse and René Desvillettes from Champigny, the electricians; André Van der Beken, the engineer from St. Maur; and two alternates, a house painter from La Courneuve and a mechanic, also from the working-class suburbs. It was the third case they had sat on together that week, and they knew it was the one that counted. They were awed by the city, the court, the weightiness of their role.

To the left of the tribunal, along the left wall of the room, was Brasillach's box, at the same elevation as the tribunal. Isorni, for the defense, was positioned on a bench directly below Brasillach, along with his defense team—M. Amiel, Mlle Frère, M. Hubert, and Mlle Mireille Noël, the sweet-tempered woman with the big bouffant hairdo who had visited Brasillach almost daily at Fresnes. A few fellow members of the Paris bar were there for the show. Each lawyer wore a black robe and thick white jabot.

The press corps was squeezed onto three long benches next to Brasillach's box. Madeleine Jacob, in her astrakhan hat and matching coat, had the best spot, front left. Brasillach immediately recognized the infamous court reporter: "So ugly she's scary." From his elevated box, Brasillach could glance down and see the back of his lawyer's head. Isorni wore his hair long in the back, curling on the nape of his neck, like an artist. Debonair and elegant, he had the same fine, angelic features he had had since childhood, the same pale skin. He was ready to defend Brasillach as passionately as he would defend the Marshal Pétain seven months later. Pétain's Vichy legislation had removed him from the Paris bar in 1940, because his father wasn't French. He had only been reinstated by special dispensation. Now, in the name of Vichy's legitimacy, he was about to defend Brasillach, and defend him as a true Frenchman.

Directly across from Brasillach and Isorni's bench, along the right wall of the room, stood Isorni's friend and neighbor Marcel Reboul, the state prosecutor, with his bony, passionate face, his voice ready to boom. Reboul's perch was elevated, like Brasillach's, allowing for the maximum visual confrontation between the prosecutor and the accused.

In this setting, the play continued to unfold. The court secretary, or *greffier,* seated at a modest table of his own beneath the tribunal, began to read the lengthy indictment. Brasillach, according to his first words, was "a thirty-five-year-old publicist, held in Fresnes prison." "This former student at the Ecole Normale Supérieure," he continued, "is the author of several novels of an incontestable literary value." The prologue, like each part of this judicial drama, would begin with an obligatory reference to Brasillach as writer, as though both sides of the case—the state and the defense—needed to remind themselves this wasn't a mere journalist on trial. The court secretary went on to describe in detail how Brasillach had actively and willingly participated in advancing the themes of German propaganda, how he had entered into relationships with official enemy institutions. He was therefore being brought up on article 75 of the penal code, "intelligence with the enemy." Brasillach, anticipating his own performance, observed that the *greffier* stumbled over these sentences.

The minute the court secretary put down his text, the show was on. Isorni rose to make his first move: a request for a mistrial on political grounds. Pétain and Laval, the leaders of the Vichy regime, hadn't yet been brought to justice. Until they were tried and judged, Isorni argued, Brasillach could not be tried and judged. Brasillach, he said, was not a traitor; he had been a French patriot, following Vichy policy. His guilt or innocence depended on the guilt or innocence of the Vichy leaders; the state had no grounds for judging him before it judged them. Pétain, he reminded them, "had been invested with all powers, even constitutional powers, by the National Assembly on July 10, 1940 . . ."

But General de Gaulle had declared Vichy illegal in November 1944, and this illegality was at the very heart of the Purge trials. De Gaulle's famous decree stated that "the form of the French government was and remains the Republic. The Republic has never ceased to exist." De Gaulle was asking France nothing less than to rewrite its history: Free France, de Gaulle's resistant France, would henceforth be, in retrospect, the true government of the nation; Vichy was to be considered a parenthesis in French history, a legal sham.

And so when journalist Georges Suarez's lawyer had tried to argue for a mistrial in the first Purge trial held in the Court of Justice of the Seine in October, the court had rejected his move on the basis of de Gaulle's decree. Suarez had been condemned and shot.

In response to Isorni's motion, Reboul declared to the court that Brasillach's trial was independent from that of any Vichy officials and need not wait on any other legal decision: "It is a trial that suffices unto itself." He underlined the illegality of Vichy: "Besides which, the ordinances of the provisional government of the Republic, under whose aegis you judge, have proclaimed the nullity, in principle, of the acts of the government known as the Vichy government. All acts of collaboration have been declared illegal, and they cannot serve as a point of departure for any judicial thesis."

Vidal asked Brasillach if he had anything to add. "I have nothing to add, Mr. President." It was a formulaic question. There was nothing Brasillach could have contributed on these procedural grounds.

The judge and jury, known, in French parlance, as "the Court," left their table by a special door behind the tribunal to discuss Isorni's motion in their "deliberation chambers." They returned less than fifteen minutes later, having swiftly rejected Isorni's motion. The trial would go on.

Act I: The Interrogation, 1:45 P.M.

The interrogation marked the opening of the trial itself. It was the heart of the event, the moment Brasillach had prepared for in his cell for hours. It was his time to speak, and to shine. He couldn't let his attention wander, for his performance was all he had to convince the jury in his favor. Judge Vidal's job was to surface information gathered by the examining magistrate and bring all the accusations clearly to light, preparing the grounds for Reboul, the state prosecutor, who would follow up the interrogation with a speech demanding a guilty verdict. Vidal's role was not a flashy one; nor would he have been capable of flash. His charge was more scholarly and substantive than Reboul's—which suited his dutiful, deferential personality. Nonetheless, the pressure on him was intense. His task was double. He needed to prevent Brasillach from shining too much, and he needed to indicate every step at which his quick-witted adversary had willingly betrayed France. Vidal was a good man, a solid magistrate, and he was about to fail.

It was a long and almost unbearably polite exchange.

Vidal asked Brasillach to rise. The accused stood at the edge of his box, holding the railing with both hands. Vidal was gray and dignified behind his table; the jurors sat upright. As Brasillach positioned himself for the interrogation, the press corps scanned him carefully, looking for just the right physical detail to capture a thirty-five-year-old writer on trial for his life. "Short fingers," noted Francine Bonitzer; "tiny little hands barely sticking out from his sleeves," wrote Helsey, the elder statesman from *Le Figaro*.

Vidal launched his gambit: "You have a polemicist's temperament, a violent temperament besides. You did your first jousting at the newspaper *L'Intransigeant?*"

"I worked at *L'Intransigeant* for one month." A point for Brasillach: he had already caught the court in an exaggeration, practically a mistake.

Vidal tried to recover: "And it seems obvious that this paper did not have a political flavor well adapted to your temperament?"

Brasillach's response was modest and measured. "There are, in the indictment, a certain number of small errors of detail that are otherwise quite unimportant. It reports my collaboration at *L'Intransigeant,* which was completely ephemeral; it says that I worked at a newspaper called *L'Insurgé,* which is inexact, I never worked there; it says that I worked for the paper *Le Jour,* to which I contributed nothing but a single article on tourism; it says that my pen name was 'Midas,' which is false, since that is the name of the gossip columnist at *Je Suis Partout,* which I have never been. These are insignificant errors, but I prefer to rectify them in advance, so as not to have to speak of them again."

Brasillach corrected the errors in the indictment with the most extreme care and politeness, with a disinterestedness, like a good historian wanting to set the record straight. Beneath the perfect diction of the *normalien,* you could hear the shadow of an accent, the singsong of the Roussillon. More important, Brasillach's tone was gentle. That tone in itself belied the charge of "violent temperament" in Vidal's opening.

Vidal could only thank him: "You are right to rectify errors that might have slipped into the indictment, but in any case, you did work for a month at *L'Intransigeant* and you next took your pen to the *Action Française.*"

What a shock for Vidal to have prepared to interrogate the famously rude Brasillach, and find instead a meticulously kind and gentle respondent.

Brasillach's pose not only surprised Vidal, it intimidated him. From that first moment on, his interrogation lacked direction and focus. He broached Brasillach's editorship of *Je Suis Partout* next, but he jumped forward to the writer's break with the paper in 1943. He was starting at the end of Brasillach's career, instead of the beginning.

Brasillach, standing in his box, quickly sized up his adversary. "Very nondescript, but impartial, to be fair." He was encouraged in his strategy, which was to "push him out of the way and insert the longest possible speech." On the subject of his break with *Je Suis Partout,* Brasillach took control of the floor for nearly fifteen minutes. Beneath him, on the defense bench, Isorni was optimistic. So far, their plan was working far better than he had expected.

On his departure from *Je Suis Partout,* Brasillach argued that he had sacrificed economic gains out of high patriotic principle. He had left the newspaper at the height of its financial success when he thought the fascist cause was lost. Vidal managed to interject a brief word, suggesting it wasn't principle, but opportunism, since Brasillach knew in 1943 that his side was going to lose. In his own defense, Brasillach quoted well-chosen passages of a private letter he had sent to his colleague Rebatet at the time of his break. The letter had been seized at Rebatet's apartment for state's evidence: "I am French . . . more than national socialist," and, "In case of danger, one must stick with the nation: only she does not betray." It was a clever use of prose that was supposed to count against him.

When Vidal accused Brasillach of calling the Gaullists "traitors," Brasillach responded evenly, "Today I do not blame those who chose to fight for their country, against their native soil, but I ask that it be recognized that those who chose their native soil back then were acting in the direct line of a certain French tradition."

"But we are all very happy today that there existed those whom you called 'Gaullist traitors,' for I don't know otherwise where we would be today," Vidal countered.

"That is a question we can treat in a minute with respect to the articles," Brasillach replied. It was an astonishing retort. Brasillach was not only holding the floor, he was presuming to guide the direction of the debates. This was not a reassuring moment for Prosecutor Reboul.

A crucial question in determining the validity of the treason charge was whether or not the Germans had engineered Brasillach's release from his POW camp in Germany. Vidal was so awkward and so indirect in approaching this issue that it was difficult to understand what he was getting at.

Vidal: "I believe you made a request for liberation."

Brasillach: "I didn't make the request for liberation myself."

Vidal: "I thought you made a request for liberation."

Brasillach: "A request for liberation was made for me."

Vidal: "Well, after the publication of your article, a request for liberation was made for you, to the Armistice Commission in Wiesbaden, by the Vichy government."

"It had already been made," Reboul sang out from the prosecutor's bench. The valiant President Vidal was so flummoxed by Brasillach's sang-froid that he was forgetting the facts of the case. Reboul was clearly worried, and vigilant, ready to come to Vidal's rescue at any moment.

Brasillach calmly seconded Reboul's correction, "The request had already been made: it was dated July 1940." He must have resisted the temptation to grin over the fact that he and Reboul knew the case better than Vidal. But the audience missed no opportunity for merriment, and you could hear a few guffaws in the back of the room.

It was at this point that Isorni jumped in with a crucial piece of evidence—a letter saying that Brasillach had been released by Vichy to serve as French commissioner of cinema. The letter came from a high-ranking Vichy official, Jacques Benoist-Méchin, another inmate at Fresnes. Benoist-Méchin claimed that after several months as commissioner-designee, Brasillach realized he wouldn't have enough autonomy from the Germans, and resigned. Supposedly, the job then went to another man.

There were two holes in this evidence. First, it was implausible that Brasillach, editor of *Je Suis Partout,* the most pro-Nazi newspaper in occupied Paris, gave up a chance at a Vichy ministry because he resented German interference. Second, the letter came from someone who was also waiting trial for treason, and whose version of the war years was officially suspect.

Vidal let it all pass. He questioned neither the source of the evidence, nor its content.

Yet something had changed in his attitude, for when he introduced a new subject, he spoke in an angrier key. He attacked Brasillach for two propaganda trips he had made to Germany. On Brasillach's October 1941 visit to a colloquium in Weimar with six other writers who held pro-German beliefs, Vidal asked, "Do you think the moment was well chosen to go embrace German intellectuals? When, all the same, you knew very well that every day people were being deported, every day people were put in concentration camps. And you went to raise your glass to German intellectuals! Do you find that normal?"

"Mr. President," Brasillach responded, "I believe that in 1941 the German occupation was certainly much gentler that it was afterwards." Even in response to an angrier Vidal, Brasillach was unflappable. "France had to continue to live and the politics of the Occupation, the politics of collaboration was a politics that tried to allow Frenchmen to live, tried to permit them to put up a sort of curtain of collaborationism between the

occupier and the occupied, which was sometimes a very thin curtain."
Brasillach had embarked on yet another impassioned speech.

Vidal quipped, "One-way collaboration, which consisted in pillag-
ing the occupied country." He spoke from experience, as the presiding
judge in a court that had prosecuted black market violations under Vichy.

"Mr. President, the French collaborators were not those who pillaged the country. They were the ones who tried to prevent the country
from being pillaged, perhaps they . . ."

Here Vidal should have let Brasillach continue, for the defendant was
on thin ice, but he interrupted before Brasillach had time to incriminate
himself. "I believe that you did not succeed," the judge concluded dryly.

Next, when Vidal accused Brasillach of attending the German Institute, the cultural organization that served elegant lunches throughout
the hungry Occupation years, the writer quipped back, "I saw Duhamel,
Giraudoux, Gallimard there." Duhamel, a prolific writer, was a member
of the Académie Française, head of the Mercure de France publishing
house, and an unambiguous anti-Nazi; Giraudoux was a former ambassador, a distinguished playwright, and Minister of Information at the start
of the war; Gaston Gallimard was France's premier publisher. There was
more tittering and enthusiastic laughter when Brasillach named those
glittering names. Reboul, long and tense on his prosecutor's bench, now
understood how hostile the audience was to the magistrature. His work
was cut out for him.

I wasn't doing anything everyone else wasn't doing, Brasillach was
arguing in effect—so why am I in trouble? In the specific example of
the German Institute, he was right. Many intellectuals, including the
resistant François Mauriac, had lunched there. The difference between
Brasillach and the others was critical: while they might have been
shortsighted, or *arriviste,* or insensitive to the political meaning of their
behavior, they weren't pro-Nazi.

What about your links to Nazi propaganda outfits? Vidal asked
next. What about the Rive-Gauche bookstore, where you served on
the board?

That luxurious bookstore had beautiful window displays, reading
rooms, meeting space, and space for exhibits—pro-Nazi exhibits. In
1941, you could have seen a display there lauding the opportunity to
do work service for the Reich.

"Mr. President," Brasillach responded, "there is a profound error
here, for an extremely simple reason. Which is that I do not see
how a bookstore that sells essentially French books—since they sold

ten French books for every six German books . . ." As the charges
mounted up against him, Brasillach sustained his polite tone, his lack of
defensiveness. Astruc, for *Combat,* admired what he saw as Brasillach's
unflinching pride, his dignity, while Madeleine Jacob, more suspicious,
saw "a touch of insolence in his serenity." But everyone was struck by
his astonishing control.

"We reproach you with having sat on a German board of directors.
You don't deny it: we reproach you," said Vidal.

It was another one of those empty accusations that allowed Brasillach
to insert a speech, a good five minutes long this time, giving the history
of the Rive-Gauche bookstore and its mission: to furnish German troops
with reading material, to encourage translations and Franco-German
intellectual exchange. Brasillach leaned towards the tribunal, letting his
glasses slide down his nose:

> The bookstore was most concerned with selling the French classics
> in beautiful leather-bound Pléiade editions to libraries in German
> towns and universities that had been bombed by the Allies. We
> sold an incalculable number of works by Molière, Saint-Simon,
> Corneille, Racine. We sold, in particular, collections of Pléiade edi-
> tions in great quantity, to be sent to reconstitute French collections
> that were missing in German universities.

The writer was on home turf here, arguing about the value of literature.
Yet even his most literary defense gives a sharp insight into his politics.
For most Parisians, the Rive-Gauche bookstore had represented collaboration, fascism, and the presence of German soldiers on the streets of
Paris. For Brasillach the only tragedy was that German cities were being
bombed by the Allies, and that German citizens were being deprived of
great French literature.

Here is how Henri Jamet, its founder, described the bookstore's
mission in the *Cahiers Franco-Allemands,* the magazine of the collaboration, in 1941. Rive-Gauche, he said "was up against the tenacious
resistance of antifascist intellectuals and above all against the long-lasting
hatred by Jewish milieux, who have exercised a strong pressure on the
French editors."

Vidal made another leap in his questioning, from Brasillach's support
of the bookstore, to Brasillach's love for Germany in general. He referred
to one of Brasillach's articles from 1943, "La Naissance d'un sentiment"
[The birth of a feeling]. "You proclaimed your love, and these are your
terms: 'your love for the soldiers of the Feldgrau.' You want to 'shake

their hands for no particular reason as if they were our own boys.'" Vidal was finally advancing on the terrain where he believed Brasillach was most vulnerable.

But he had put his foot in his mouth again. Reboul, alert to the faux pas, rose immediately, hoping to save his colleague from embarrassment: "Mr. President, if you allow me, the first phrase was taken from Brasillach's interview with the examining magistrate M. Raoult. 'Love for the Feldgrau'—this is the exact term you used—does not appear in the article. Many other things, hélas!, do appear, but I have to say that, in truth, the words 'love for the Feldgrau' do not figure there and were not used."

Vidal should have moved on immediately, but he insisted on his own mistake: "You didn't write those lines?"

Brasillach responded charitably. "I believe there is an error, not a typo, but a slip of the pen. They put quotation marks in the wrong place. And 'your love for the Feldgrau' is M. Raoult's phrase."

Vidal could only add, "You did say that the Germans were 'friends of the same race'?" [*copains du même sang*].

Brasillach reassured him, "On the other hand, that phrase is mine."

"I won't quibble with you about the word 'Feldgrau.' It is in the same spirit," said Vidal.

But he just had quibbled, and wasted more precious time.

Brasillach gathered strength from the judge's error, and he took the floor at length again, beginning with a scholarly explanation of the phrase 'friends of the same race,' and verging into a defense of the Germans as a necessary protection against the communists. As far as German atrocities went, he claimed the French colonial atrocities in Indochina, circa 1930, were much worse. It was a rhetorical victory. He had managed to change the subject completely, from German crimes in France to French crimes in the colonies.

———

Vidal continued for another hour. He tried to weaken Brasillach's claim that he was a Vichy patriot, not a Nazi traitor. He began to quote from Brasillach's journalism: attacks against the Third Republic ministers, romantic references to fascism and Nazism, attacks on the Gaullist traitors, Brasillach's repeated desire for a "quick and prompt justice," "a repression without pity" against his political enemies, who were also the enemies of the Nazis. It is where he should have started, with the idea that Brasillach's attacks served the enemy. These written attacks—

not the Rive-Gauche bookstore, not the German Institute, not the trips to Germany—were the basis of the treason charge.

By now, Brasillach had been standing for two hours. He was still leaning against the railing of his box, his hands clasped together politely, very much the professor at his lectern. A thick strand of black hair had fallen on his brow. He responded: "What makes you think that the Germans ordered me to say what I said? They could care less what I said."

"The instant you understood that your writings served the Germans, you should have abstained from making those attacks," was Vidal's moralistic reply.

"I believed that my writing served my country above all," countered Brasillach. And he launched into a series of declarations, patiently outlining his attitudes one by one: toward the Republic, which he saw as responsible for the defeat; toward the Gaullists, whom he considered illegitimate; towards the internal resistance, which he considered contaminated by bandits and foreigners; towards the communists, whom he considered a danger for France. His anti-Semitism in particular, he said, was in place long before the war broke out, and it was part of a deeply French tradition, practiced by eminent writers such as Giraudoux and the Tharaud brothers. "I never approved any collective violence," he added. "I never approved, for example, that families be separated, that women be separated from their children."

Reboul, who knew the *Je Suis Partout* articles by heart, was outraged. Why wasn't Vidal challenging this distortion?

Whereas on the issue of tradition alone, no one could deny that there was more than a grain of truth in Brasillach's claim. Anti-Semitism had been a powerful strain in French thought at least since the Dreyfus Affair. With his focus clearly on defending himself against the treason charge, Brasillach insisted that his collaboration had been in the best interests of France. When confronted with the denunciatory language he used towards his own countrymen, Brasillach replied that his beliefs were French beliefs, his fascism was a French nationalist fascism, his anti-Semitism belonged to a French, not a German, tradition. In that way, he hoped to refocus the debate on his French identity, rather than on the content of his beliefs.

———

The next day, *Lettres Françaises* complained that Vidal was "lamentable." He had allowed Brasillach to deliver a lecture. The interrogation had seemed more like a reception at the Académie Française than a court-room proceeding.

Although the content of Brasillach's argument was weak, he had easily controlled the interrogation. The key to his success lies with his marshalling of one word, "responsibility." Six times during his interrogation, Brasillach claimed responsibility for his actions. His rhetoric deserves quoting in full, to show how he took the upper hand:

> I wasn't part of the Action Française, I was a literary contributor to the newspaper, solely literary. I say this out of respect for the historical truth, if I can express myself thus, and not at all to flee my *responsibilities,* but simply because that is how it was. . . .

> I was a collaborationist at work on the collaboration, but I wasn't the one who enacted a certain number of things that the ministers of the French government accepted in that moment. Once again, I don't say this in order to place my *responsibilities* on other shoulders: it's simply to express a fact. . . .

> I asked for exemplary measures against the communist leaders because I have always had the most vivid sentiment of the *responsibility* of the leader. It was those [in the resistance] who, rightly or wrongly, ordered attacks against German soldiers, who should have been pursued, and not the poor fellows who were arrested as hostages. . . . I have always had the most vivid sense of this *responsibility* of the leader, of this *responsibility* of those who might have led other men and it is even for this, I can tell you, Mr. President, that I am here and not elsewhere, in other foreign countries [*dans d'autres pays étrangers*]; because I did not want to abandon the people who might have believed in me. It is because I have had this sense of *responsibility* that we, on our side, can salute with respect the memory of a man we once attacked, Gabriel Péri, because Gabriel Péri, we now know, [after he was arrested and tortured] refused to disavow the attacks made against German soldiers; if he had disavowed them, he would have saved his life. . . .

> I will always salute with the greatest respect those who want to take *responsibility* for their troops, and I asked that the communist leaders accept their *responsibilities,* so that it not be only the troops who accepted them. . . .

Cardinal Suhard, who welcomed Marshal Pétain in the Notre Dame Cathedral of Paris in April, was ready to welcome General de Gaulle in August, if the resistance hadn't prevented him from doing so. I don't much like people who don't take *responsibility,* who play a double game. Perhaps I'm wrong, I excuse myself for this form of temperament.

To cap off this representation of himself as a man of responsibility, Brasillach ended his interrogation by describing how he refused to go to Germany, and had gone into hiding instead, in Paris. As he told the story, what happened next was a hostage situation in his own family:

> I discovered that my whole family had been arrested, my brother-in-law, my stepfather, my mother herself. When I learned that they had arrested my mother, I decided not to wait any longer and to turn myself in. My mother was arrested in the provinces, she stayed for three weeks in a filthy prison, thirty persons to a three-by-four-meter cell, with four straw mats for the thirty. As soon as the letter arrived in Sens announcing that I had turned myself in as a prisoner, she was liberated immediately.

Brasillach wanted the court to know that he had accepted responsibility where it most counted—in the bosom of his family. He glanced at the jurors sitting dutifully at Vidal's side. It was their right to ask questions during the interrogation, but they had remained silent. He thought they looked wooden. Unbeknownst to him, one of those blank-looking jurors, the big man with the mustache and the wind-burnt face named André Van der Beken, was horrified to learn that Brasillach's mother had been used as bait for his arrest.

Each time he raised the issue of responsibility, Brasillach attempted to move the discussion from an ideological representation of two opposing sides—collaboration and resistance, one wrong and one right—to a larger, nonideological moral vision where a good man could "take responsibility" on either side, be a hero either of the collaboration or the resistance, by sticking to his guns. A good man could be either a collaborator or a resister, depending on his strength of character.

It was the first time since the Court of Justice trials began in October that a collaborator had refused to apologize. Brasillach looked out at the crowded courtroom and in his cool tenor, capped the entire interrogation with a memorable final phrase:

"I can regret nothing of what I have been."

Act II: The Prosecution, 3:45 P.M.

Had this play ended with the interrogation, Brasillach might have been acquitted. But it was Marcel Reboul's—the prosecutor's—turn, and here, Brasillach would meet his match.

Reboul, dressed in a simple black robe, rose from his seat. He wasn't wearing the prosecutor's traditional red, for he was only ranked as a substitute. His colleagues had told him he ought to put on the red gown anyway—the occasion warranted it. But he was playing by the rules, and he knew he didn't need the color—his words flamed on their own.

He turned away from the audience and faced the tribunal from his elevated perch, not much bigger than Brasillach's. He was in his element, and there was much lost ground to regain.

He started with a solid five minutes of literary flattery:

> Brasillach presents himself before you armed with all the seductive powers of the writer, and now that I have heard him speak—since I did not know him before—I can also say, armed with all the seductive power of persuasive eloquence.

Reboul outlined Brasillach's status as a former student at the Ecole Normale, acknowledging his novels with their "endearing plots and precise psychology" and their "rich and colored language," granting the writer an "incontestable intellectual preeminence before he had even reached age thirty." He was not going to let Isorni have the first word in describing Brasillach's talent.

He saved his highest praise for Brasillach's work as a critic:

> Whether he is being tender with Péguy, fanatic with Maurras, impertinent with Gide, or reticent towards the audaciousness of Giono, Brasillach possesses to the highest degree a sense of the penetration of texts governed by his vast erudition and his perfect knowledge of classical rules. His critical authority is born from a particular talent he has for putting the reader in a spiritual intimacy with the author he is describing.

Reboul was warmed up now, his voice filling every corner of the room. His familiarity with Brasillach's writing impressed the intellectuals in the audience. Brasillach, for his part, was amused; he had signed a copy of his collected criticism, *Les Quatre jeudis,* for Madame Reboul, from prison. Isorni had delivered the book to the rue Geoffroy St. Hilaire on his behalf. It had obviously served its purpose.

Brasillach's self-satisfaction was short-lived, for Reboul moved deftly towards the wheel and turn that everyone in the courtroom was expecting:

> Why did this man, rich with so much talent, laden with so much success, and who, if he had remained on track with his first aspirations, could have become one of the most eminent writers of our country—why did this man abuse his gifts, his success, his authority, in order to try and lead youth, first towards a sterile politics, then towards the enemy?

The word "sterile" was the rhetorical key to what would follow.

Next, like a writer who has his subject clearly in hand, Marcel Reboul juxtaposed the two Brasillachs—the brilliant, sensitive critic and the rash, violent polemicist:

> Can we believe, for example, that the pen that dissected the complexities of Marcel Proust or the misogynistic insolence of M. de Montherlant, could trace these same lines, where talent seems to have flown off to make room for the verbosity of a shrew: "The Republic . . . that old syphilitic whore, stinking of patchouli and yeast infection . . . still standing on the sidewalk . . ."

Reboul was nailing Brasillach on the quality that had ruined his talent—meanness of character. He turned from the tribunal to the accused, and eyed him severely across the room: "Yet now you come to this Republic . . . with no memory of your insults, and appeal to its commitment to freedom of 'opinion.'"

One by one, Reboul listed the different groups and people that Brasillach had targeted with his mean prose: communists, freemasons, Third Republic government leaders, Jews, even the Sorbonne. Professing these anti-institutional beliefs in peacetime was one thing, Reboul argued, but doing so in a country occupied by a foreign power, with real lives threatened, was a different matter all together.

———

Suddenly, without a pause, Reboul shifted gears. He reminded the court that this was not a trial of opinion, but a treason trial:

> [The Republic] will not put you on trial for your tragic errors, for your deadly intolerance, for your subversive opinions, but she will, in the context of article 75 of the Penal Code, with all the evidence assembled, put you, the clerk who has betrayed, on trial for your treason.

How do you prove treason? How do you prove that a man like Brasillach was no longer a citizen of his own nation? For Reboul, the proof was not in Brasillach's phrase about the Republic as a whore, nor in his attacks on specific individuals or institutions. It was in the symbolic sentence that Brasillach had written in 1944, in his article for *Révolution Nationale* called "Letter to a Few Young People," at a time when it looked to him as though the adventure of collaboration was over. Reboul quoted Brasillach's own words to the court at length:

> If you want to know my entire opinion, I will say that I was not a Germanophile before the war, nor even at the beginning of the politics of collaboration: I was only seeking the interests of reason. Now, things have changed: It seems to me that I've contracted a liaison with German genius, one that I will never forget. Whether we like it or not, we will have lived together. Frenchmen given to reflection, during these years, will have more or less slept with Germany—not without quarrels—and the memory of it will remain sweet for them. The ordeals of Germany are not exactly our ordeals and the French nation has ordeals of its own, though I don't know why it is that these are more fraternal ordeals than those of another country. The feeling is there now, and if you want to know what I am about, you have to give it its due.

Reboul paused, looked at the jurors—at Van der Beken, Desvillettes, Grisonnet, and Riou, stiff and alert at their tribunal—and he glossed Brasillach's long and turgid paragraph in one sharp phrase: "This feeling that dare not say its name, and which is *love*!" In 1945 the phrase "this feeling that dare not say its name," the most celebrated line of one of the most famous trials of the last century, the Oscar Wilde trial, was a recognizable euphemism for homosexual desire. Most of the people in that courtroom recognized the reference, and if they didn't, they knew what it signified: Reboul was accusing Brasillach, in a symbolic register, of homosexual desire for Germany. The writer was, in print if not in deed, a "horizontal collaborator."

With a genius for extended metaphor, Reboul embarked on another long quotation, from Brasillach's "Naissance d'un sentiment." This was the September 1943 article that had just given Vidal so much trouble, where a supposed friend of Brasillach's confesses that he "loves the Germans." Reboul was playing on the sexual metaphor in Brasillach's writing, to argue that Brasillach's love for Germany was tantamount to an infidelity to France—and worse, a perverse infidelity. Brasillach was perverse, unproductive, un-French.

"It's only too easy to draw a convenient effect from these painful passages," Reboul admitted. "I won't do it, but I want to underline the outrage they must have represented, at the moment when they were written, for all the hostages, all those who were tortured, for all the martyrs, for all France's misery." He wouldn't draw a convenient effect, but he did.

He considered these articles as Brasillach's way of seeking favor with the German occupants, even as a form of flirtation:

> I ignore what smiles such platitudes might have won you in the salons of the Stülpnagels—even if you weren't there. I don't know what kind of intellectual popedom they led you to hope for at the German bookstore. But I know perfectly well that no one today could read a line of this diatribe in Oradour-sur-Glane without the dead rising up from their graves.

Reboul was referring to the horrendous massacre and destruction of the entire town of Oradour-sur-Glane by the SS on June 10, 1944. Six hundred villagers shot and burned alive. The Oradour massacre took place nearly a year after Brasillach published "Naissance d'un sentiment," with its loving portrayal of German soldiers. By the time Brasillach stood trial, the burned-out village was already the supreme symbol of France's wartime suffering. Reboul was not making a link between Brasillach's article and the horrible event, but he was using Oradour to introduce the standard trope of a prosecutor seeking the death penalty: the image of the dead in their graves, raging against the killer. Brasillach, in his box, was furious. He thought Reboul was fudging the dates, trying to make it look as though he had written about loving the Germans the day after the massacre. As if he wanted to believe that what had happened at Oradour was the only Nazi violence of its kind.

———

Although Reboul's sexual dig was provocative, it was not entirely gratuitous, given that Brasillach was a writer known for his homosexual leanings. Nothing like this extended rhetorical play on homosexuality exists in any other trial of the period. It wasn't a matter of one passing remark, either. Referring to Brasillach's liberation from the POW camp, Reboul embroidered the fault: "He sleeps with Germany, and the day after that fornication, they slip a return ticket in his palm." He proffered, repeated, intensified the metaphor of homosexuality with a metaphor of sodomy. "Any idea of resistance to penetration of the first [France] by the second [Germany] seems to you a monstrous act," he said. And he concluded his account of Brasillach's motivations with: "we understand better, after this psychological analysis, how your quasi-carnal love of brutal force could have pushed you to try and lead your country into the bed of such sweet memories." You could hear the rumblings of discontent from Brasillach's supporters in the courtroom.

It's a time-honored courtroom strategy to compound guilt by metaphor and association. Why is this particular metaphor so powerful—the high point, one might argue, of the prosecution? Reboul was drawing on the deepest rhetorical fears of everyone in the courtroom, the fears and loathing of an invaded nation. It's difficult to generalize about the psychology of an entire country—or even about a collective identity, though the phrase is used often—but one can imagine that when a country is defeated, each citizen feels a damage, suffers a wound; each citizen's narcissism suffers for the loss of national pride. A defeat, an invasion, an occupation—all these events have a powerful effect on individuals, and on a community, and they translate effectively into sexual terms. We were dominated, humiliated, we were forced into submission. We were buggered, Reboul is saying, and this man liked it.

To the extent that Brasillach's writings about Nazi Germany were metaphorically homoerotic, Reboul's metaphorical charge was true. He was giving an accurate reading of Brasillach. At the same time, his rhetoric played on the real fear and hatred of homosexuality that was alive in the culture, and used hatred of homosexuality to reinforce the hatred of Brasillach. Reboul's speech touched on a crisis of masculinity, targeted a nation of men who had felt defeated and powerless for four years, men who were now coming back into their own. Desvillettes might have been a ladies' man, Van der Beken a family man—but whatever their difference in personality or way of life, they had both lived with the defeat. Their Liberation was economic and political; it was also a state of desire. Reboul understood this, and he knew how to talk to the jury.

———

The metaphoric treason charge took up the middle part of Reboul's prosecution speech. For his conclusion, Reboul started in on another rhetorical strategy, echoing back Brasillach's words in their full, sinister meaning, drawing out their implications, making what was covert, overt. Reboul had scandalized the jurors. Now he would awe them with a sense of justice.

Reboul read from a letter that Brasillach's colleague Rebatet had received from Pierre Antoine Cousteau at the moment Brasillach had left *Je Suis Partout*, describing the exceptional cultural sway the paper had on the youth of France. "Without *Je Suis Partout*," Cousteau had written Rebatet, "we are nothing but poor little ninny journalists or writers without an audience, with no one to listen to us and no real influence. . . . People don't say, 'Brasillach is the author of [*Présence de*] *Virgile*'; they say, 'He's the editor of *Je Suis Partout*.' "

"There lies the explication of Brasillach's actions," Reboul concluded. "He seeks out an audience, he seeks a real and especially a political influence, and for that he went to the extreme limits of intellectual intelligence with the enemy" [*l'intelligence intellectuelle avec l'ennemi*]. To the French phrase "intelligence avec l'ennemi"—which means simply "treason"—Reboul added the adjective "intellectual." Brasillach was an intellectual traitor, a traitor of distinction.

Over and over in Brasillach's writing, Reboul found the expression of a desire for quick official vengeance. It came as early as the first article Brasillach sent to *Je Suis Partout* from his POW camp, where he argued there should be no extenuating circumstances for the Third Republic ministers, who were on trial at Riom for their responsibility in the defeat of France. Reynaud, Blum, and Mandel were special targets.

Again and again, Reboul quoted Brasillach's desire for vengeance, his desire to make his enemies suffer. "We'll let them croak without raising an eyebrow, but it's urgent"; "Why wait to execute the communist deputies?"; "It's without remorse, rather with immense hope, that we vow for these men to go to a concentration camp, if not to the firing squad." The men in question were Brasillach's countrymen, Third Republic deputies, resistance fighters, Gaullists, communists— men whose lives were threatened by the Nazis, men with whom the jury could identify fully. In the case of the Third Republic ministers on trial at Riom, Brasillach had written, "We don't want to hear about extenuating circumstances." Quoting him, Reboul quipped, "Really, you didn't?" He was enjoining the jury, turning Brasillach's own words against him. The next day, Brasillach wrote to Maurice Bardèche: "I find him ridiculous. Full of bad faith and ignorance. . . . All he does is read from articles that he has cleverly cut." What a moment for Brasillach, who had made his own glory as a critic through the nasty manipulation of well-placed quotes! Here he was deluding himself, for he knew full well that longer quotations would not have helped his case.

Among the sentences Reboul read to the jury were Brasillach's attacks against the Jews. Reboul isolated two of Brasillach's worst anti-Semitic phrases: "We must treat the Jewish problem without sentimentality," and "We must separate from the Jews *en bloc* and not keep any little ones." He contrasted these statements with Brasillach's claim, in his interrogation, that he had been a *humanitarian,* opposed to collective violence. Reboul was making up here for the ground that Vidal had lost. He wasn't a particularly dramatic gesturer, but he could carry an immense amount of anger and passion in his voice. He addressed his words to Brasillach, and Brasillach alone:

> And even when, seeing the excesses, you think it opportune and politic to shed a tear over those horrific separations imposed on Israelite mothers, torn from their children, when you sense what is atrocious about this martyrdom that begins for the Jews in Paris and ends in camps in Poland, exceptional in their severity, you say: "I disapprove of these separations," but rectifying immediately—and I quote your article "Les Sept Internationales contre la Patrie"—you specify, "We must not forget that these separations are the work of a few troublesome policemen," do you think this is serious? Do you think today that you can uphold the argument of pity after having written that sentence in bad faith: the separations, the work of a few troublesome policemen?

Reboul spoke of "camps in Poland, exceptional in their severity." The phrase "extermination camp" did not yet exist in January 1945, and the full extent of the Nazi final solution was not yet known. What was known were the yellow stars on the streets of Paris, the roundups and the disappearances. But the evidence of mass murder was growing. The BBC had begun to talk of extermination as early as 1943; many had listened. Struthof, on the Alsatian border, was liberated by American troops on November 23, 1944; Maïdanek, in Poland, had been liberated by the Red Army ten days before the Brasillach trial, and the headline in *Ce Soir* had read "Maïdanek, vision of horror." In evoking the martyrdom that led Jews from Paris to Poland, Reboul conjured up in that courtroom the memory of hundreds of Jewish friends and neighbors who had not returned, who would not return. He devastated Brasillach's so-called humanitarian defense, which had been, in reality, a defense of efficient deportations.

The essence of Brasillach's character, Reboul concluded, was that he was a denouncer. The accused had denounced the Sorbonne for harboring faculty in the resistance, he had denounced students at the Lycée Lakanal for tearing down a portrait of the Maréchal from a classroom wall, he had denounced a youth in the Hérault district who ridiculed Pétain in a Bastille Day speech. For everyone in that courtroom, the mere word "denunciation" brought forth images of the thousands of petty letters of denunciation that had poisoned daily life during the Occupation—neighbors denouncing neighbors, gentiles denouncing Jews, rival businessmen using denunciation to eliminate one another—all the furtive pettiness of the previous four years.

Reboul went one step further. He specified that Brasillach's was no ordinary kind of denunciation. He took pains to define it:

> Doubtless, you are not the denouncer who goes to the Gestapo for blood, but we can legitimately consider you today as another, broader type of denouncer, more schematic, an almost official denouncer, since your crime is crowned by the fact that we can't know with certainty whether or not the Gestapo, after reading your articles—and they did read them—paid a call to the Sorbonne or to that village in the Hérault or to the Lycée Lakanal.

Had the Gestapo arrested the mayor of the little town in the Hérault or deported the schoolboys who dared tamper with Pétain's portrait? The prosecutor left it as an open-ended question—which is exactly what it was for everyone in that courtroom.

An hour and a quarter into his prosecution speech, Reboul delivered this bullet directly to the accused: "Your work is bad [*votre oeuvre est mauvaise*], Brasillach, and it calls for a mathematical conclusion: that is the death penalty, and I am seeking it against you." If he didn't realize it before, Brasillach now understood that his life was in danger. From the press box, Helsey scanned him carefully. Brasillach didn't flinch, but the *Figaro* reporter thought he saw a little saliva forming at the corner of his mouth.

It could have been an ending, but Reboul had twenty minutes to go. For now, he pulled back and changed his focus. He lowered his gaze from Brasillach's box to Isorni's bench, as though aware of the defense lawyer's presence in the courtroom for the first time: "You'll tell me I haven't spoken of his defense. His defense? I'm not familiar with it. It will doubtless be beautiful. I haven't heard anything about it. I know Isorni's talent: it is very great." He proceeded to anticipate the exact tactic of Isorni's defense to come: "Will you, perhaps, attempt another trial?" He was anticipating, accurately, that Isorni was going to attack the magistrature for having collaborated with Vichy. He turned back to Brasillach and explained his insight: "I had that impression when I read what you, Brasillach, said to the examining magistrate, when he accused you of waging an ardent battle against the communists. You responded: 'I did what the magistrature did!'"

"Don't pull that! Oh no!" Reboul cried out, both to Jacques Isorni and to his client. He forthrightly defended his colleagues in the magistrature, using the occasion to underline Brasillach's vaunted sense of "responsibility." "Today's painful trials prove that in all areas of the State, there are a few who strayed." Reboul pointed at Brasillach, and continued:

> But these are men like you, who are responsible for their commit-
> ment, and you can't use them as an excuse. In any case, I insist
> on telling you that as far as we are concerned, the sacrifice of a
> Parodi, the sacrifice of this judge who coughed up his blood in the
> ungodly bathtub of the Gestapo, the sacrifice of tens of others, the
> obstinate resistance of hundreds of others working obscurely at their
> posts, has placed us far too high for that same magistrature, proud
> of its unflinching patriotism, to have lost the right to delegate a
> representative to face you and ask for your punishment.

Having claimed his own moral ground, with René Parodi, the great resistance martyr of the French judiciary, as his guarantor, Reboul was ready to deliver his penultimate blow. He had shown, rhetorically, that Brasillach had enjoyed being buggered by the Germans. Now he would turn the trope of domination in the other direction, and argue that Brasillach, dominated by the Germans, had in turn led younger Frenchmen astray. Not only was he seduced by the enemy—he was a seducer. Specifically, Reboul was referring to a case he had prosecuted three weeks earlier, the government's treason case against young Claude Maubourguet, *Je Suis Partout* journalist, nephew of Charles Lesca (the major stockholder in *Je Suis Partout*) and a Vichy Milice recruit. Reboul had sought the death penalty, but Maubourguet had gotten off with life in prison:

> . . . infected with this propaganda that you distilled at *Je Suis Partout,*
> he signed up for the Milice, he strapped on a rifle and went to fight
> against the Maquis resistance. His lawyer saved him. When I asked
> for his death with some reservation, because of his youth, [his lawyer]
> rushed into that breach I had introduced in my prosecution and he

said to the jury: "What will you do when those who are intellectually responsible for Maubourguet's crimes are here before you?"

Well, here he was, Reboul was arguing: if young Maubourguet had become a fascist, if he had joined the Vichy Milice, it was Brasillach's fault. In asking for the death penalty for Brasillach, Reboul claimed to be fulfilling a promise he had made to the jurors in the Maubourguet trial that the truly responsible man would be punished:

> The jury followed [Maubourguet's] lawyer. He had just unwittingly pronounced the most terrible prosecution against you, and the indulgent verdict of the jurors in the Maubourguet case does seem to commit me to precisely the merciless verdict I am seeking against you.

It was a brilliant rhetorical maneuver, for Reboul was effectively reminding the jury, one more time, that Brasillach was ready to take full responsibility for his ideological leadership.

In the last minutes of his speech, Reboul abandoned all his scorn, all his disdain. He looked across the room at Brasillach, and he modulated his booming voice into an intense whisper. He explained to Brasillach that he had searched his writings again and again for a reason not to ask for the death penalty. His tone was religious, and at the same time Reboul was turning Brasillach's responsibility and lack of regret fiercely against him. In the fading afternoon light, Reboul was a long black silhouette, the very image of human conscience:

> What I was looking for was just one word of pity. . . . That was what I wanted, that is what I was looking for and I found nothing because there was nothing. So I understood that you were alone, alone with your magnificent talent, which was useless because it wasn't merciful. I understood that I needed to rise up to do my duty, because if I didn't, too many voices beyond the grave could have whispered in my ear that terrible phrase you prepared for others: "Why wait?"

Brasillach had extracted vengeance against his enemy, the Republic. Now Reboul claimed vengeance for that Republic. It was an eye for an eye, the oldest form of justice. And there was something else. Reboul had made it clear that there was a perfect harmony between what Brasillach wanted—total responsibility for his actions—and what Reboul was offering him: death.

Act III: The Pleading, 5:20 P.M.

There was a fifteen-minute break in the proceedings after Reboul finished, a chance to stretch. The overcrowded room, minimally heated, was steaming from the weight of all the bodies, all the words. The blue gendarme escorted Brasillach to his holding room behind the door of the accused, where Isorni's assistant, Mireille Noël, brought him a cup of coffee to revive his spirits. By the time he was escorted back to the Salle des Assises, the sun had set.

Jacques Isorni stood up for the defense. He stood directly in front of his client, a kind of verbal bodyguard. Brasillach remained seated demurely in the box of the accused.

———

Isorni began his pleading with a saga:

> Sometimes, in the destiny of a family, there are strange coinci-
> dences. . . . In January 1915, Madame Brasillach, Robert Brasillach's
> mother, who had been without news of her officer husband for
> weeks and weeks, learned that he had perished in the battles at
> Kénifra, that he had given his life for his country. Thirty years
> later, almost to the day, in the name of that same country, you are
> being asked to take the life of her son. Lieutenant Brasillach was
> thirty-five years old, the age Robert Brasillach is today. Lieutenant
> Brasillach took to his grave the finest hopes of the French army.
> Robert Brasillach is the finest promise of contemporary letters—a
> promise kept.

It was a smooth transition from the ill-fated father to his son, the writer. Isorni's challenge was to take the ugly picture painted by Reboul and substitute a romantic portrait.

"When I listened just now to the government prosecutor quoting so many violent texts, I couldn't help but think about the complexity of Brasillach's nature, and I asked myself how an author whose pen was so acid and an author who wrote so many tender, delicate things could be the same man . . ." Like Reboul, Isorni insisted on Brasillach's talent; like Reboul, he deployed the argument of the double personality. The difference was that it was the writer who counted for Isorni, and it was the writer he wanted to save: "I realize that this is not the moment to speak of literature. But how not to speak of it, if only for a minute, when one has the honor of pleading before you on behalf of Robert Brasillach?" His minute was a quarter of an hour long.

While for Reboul, Brasillach was an enemy of his own country, and had used his talent to pervert the young, Isorni proclaimed that Brasillach was at the heart of French letters, he was the very soul of his generation. To seek his death was to seek the death of France's past, France's literary future:

> For us, the literature of Brasillach is a bit like a radiant morning, with its first fervor, its hopes, its eternal friendships. . . . It is he who has marvelously portrayed, with his long, supple and fulsome sentences, our waking up to life, our ecstasy faced with the richness of existence. It is he who expressed our tastes, our anguish, our combats, our first disillusionments as men. He was our youth—mine. He was the youth of my entire generation, and condemned or acquitted, tomorrow, in a half century, it is through him, through him alone perhaps that our youth will be transmitted to our children. It is through him that the legacy of our twenty-year-old selves, our thirty-year-old selves has some chance of surviving.

Who were these "we" whose legacy only Brasillach could transmit? Presumably, they were Isorni himself, along with the intellectuals, the worldly people in that audience. They were not, by any stretch of the imagination, the jurors at the tribunal—Grisonnet, Riou, Desvillettes, and Van der Beken, who were waiting for a response to Reboul's powerful indictment.

Isorni's use of the "we" was a strategic misstep. Reboul had just established that Brasillach's writing talent had nothing to do with why he was on trial. By defending that talent, Isorni was not defending his client against the real charge that had been made—the charge that he had denounced and called for murder in *Je Suis Partout*. Second, in order to defend his client successfully, Isorni needed to convince a jury composed of resistance fighters; instead he chose to craft his very first remarks for the literary-minded men and women in the courtroom audience. It was they he wanted to impress. Jacques Isorni's desire to shine rhetorically was his fatal flaw, and it would prove fatal for his client.

He read out loud from a series of letters written on Brasillach's behalf by writers: the popular short story writer Marcel Aymé; the venerable genius Paul Valéry; the Catholic dramaturge Paul Claudel; and Mauriac, pious representative of the literary resistance. He turned to the members of the jury:

> I have received letters that were written in support of our cause and I want to read a few excerpts from them to the Court. I didn't

take them from old files. They were written to me, for this trial, by people who are probably the most eminent of our era in the intellectual realm. They wrote the letters for you, jurors of the Court of Justice, so that you might know how great minds evaluate Brasillach, even today.

His tone was didactic, barely concealing his condescension. When Isorni quoted Paul Valéry's contention that "Brasillach demonstrates an incontestable talent in the critical realm and very original points of view," it sounded at best like a vague, inflated book review, at worst like a frivolous attempt to skirt the question. It made for a terrible defense of a man's life. Helsey, in the press box, saw the mistake: "This language is Greek to the jurors."

Next in his gallery of intellectuals, Isorni pronounced the name of François Mauriac, whose debate with Camus on the subject of clemency for collaborationist writers was the talk of the town. Mauriac had actually sent Isorni two letters for the defense. The first one, which Isorni didn't read, contained a strong claim: "If, as I believe, there exists no known case of a Frenchman arrested on the strength of a *Je Suis Partout* denunciation," Mauriac had written, "we can admit that Brasillach did not understand the terrible meaning his attacks took on." Here Mauriac was taking Christian charity out of the realm of common sense and into the realm of denial. Everyone believed that the denunciations in *Je Suis Partout* had been lethal. Isorni believed it, too—for if he hadn't believed it, he would have been eager to use that letter. For Mauriac's part, he must have known that praise of Brasillach's writing alone wasn't going to save him. He was trying to let Brasillach off the hook where he was most vulnerable—on the issue of denunciation. Isorni must have felt that on that ground, his client was indefensible, for he had asked Mauriac for another letter.

So Mauriac wrote a second letter, which limited itself to a nuanced but entirely literary evaluation of Brasillach's achievements. He described Brasillach's passion, his influence as a critic, and he ended by stating his own qualifications for pardoning the writer his political excesses. Isorni read this letter to the jury in its entirety:

> Robert Brasillach is one of the most brilliant minds of his generation. If the novelist in him has not yet freed himself from certain influences, the critic and the essayist have found a highly personal voice, irreplaceable, one we can certainly dislike, but which commands

our attention. . . . His best work to date is probably in his memoirs. Through Brasillach, an entire generation expresses its likes and dislikes. It is he who has given us what are probably the best pages written about the cinema between the wars, and about avant-garde theater. Each generation comes to consciousness through a very small number of writers. Brasillach has been one of these writers for men of the right.

If the Court judges that in politics, he was a passionate and blind disciple, that he was caught up in a system of ideas, an implacable logic, when he was still very young, it will perhaps attach some importance to the testimony of a man, a writer, whom Brasillach treated as an enemy and who thinks nonetheless that it will be a loss for French letters if this brilliant mind is forever extinguished.

Here Mauriac was certainly living up to Brasillach's fantasy of finding an "enemy brother," a loyal adversary in his time of need. Mauriac seemed bent on publicly forgiving, even rescuing, a man who had put him in the gravest danger during the Occupation—a man who had denounced him to German authorities and continually attacked him in print. This was not only "charity"—the word he used when he argued for forgiveness in his newspaper columns in *Le Figaro*—it was a theatrical form of charity. As for the niceties of his literary evaluation—Brasillach was a better critic and memoirist than a novelist, his opinions were controversial but memorable—these would have been lost on any jury; more important, they were beside the point.

After reading from Aymé, Valéry, Claudel, and Mauriac, Isorni lifted Brasillach onto even higher ground within the realm of letters. "There is an aspect of this man of letters that is less well known by the public—the poet—because, let's admit it, poetry has only acquired its true place in the work of Brasillach since he has experienced the rigors of prison life." We are not judging a mere journalist, Isorni was arguing here, nor even a mere writer: the man in the box of the accused was a poet, whose true art had been brought to life by the martyrdom of prison.

"Listen, gentlemen," he said, then he read a single prison poem in its entirety. This was the poem entitled "The Names on the Walls," where Brasillach pays homage to the resistance fighters imprisoned before him at Fresnes, the "brothers never known" whom he thinks about at night. For the defense lawyer, the key strophe of the poem was this one: "We hadn't the same heart, / They told us. Why should they be right? /

What does it matter what we were! / Our faces foggy in the blur /
Look alike in the dark night."

Through Brasillach's poem, Isorni was asking the jury to consider
the accused one of *their* kind, a brother, and not, in the words of
Brasillach that Vidal and Reboul had quoted, a brother or a lover to
the Nazis. He was asking them, through the images of the poem, to
look at Brasillach with misty eyes, until his face blended with the faces
of the resistance. Hadn't they all suffered for fervently held beliefs?
For Lucien Grisonnet, who had risked his life printing underground
tracts and fake IDs, who had seen the young resistance fighters of
Aubervilliers gunned down by the Germans on his own street; for
René Desvillettes, whose local hero was René Damous, the communist
resister from the Champigny electrical plant, executed as a hostage at
Mont Valérien; those faces were forever distinct. Brasillach's poem could
only offend them.

Isorni had reached the page of his notes where he had written
a single sentence in huge letters. This was a perfect moment to hold
his arms out straight in front of him, towards the jury, in the classical
form of pleading. He pronounced his grand sentence with brio: "Do
civilized people shoot their poets?" By bringing poetry and civilization
into play, he hoped to elevate the tone, make the questions as large
and humanistic as possible. Young, handsome, part bohemian artist,
part eternal student, Jacques Isorni was very much the "*premier secrétaire
de la conférence*," the brilliant orator, waiting for his ovation from the
bar. Brasillach, in his box, was studying the jurors intently, looking for
some reaction, but their faces still told him nothing. Was Grisonnet,
the resourceful printer, thinking about the paper shortages in his shop?
Had Van der Beken read Mauriac's editorials on justice in *Le Figaro?*
The journalists in that courtroom do not include the jurors in their
accounts of the trial. They scarcely mention their existence. And they
certainly don't interview them afterwards. Perhaps they felt protective of
the jury's anonymity in a case that might well have violent repercussions.
Or perhaps, with the paper shortages, the jury was the first disposable
element in their story.

Isorni continued to speak of literature. He turned back to Reboul
and, referring to one of the prosecutor's previous criminal cases (the
case of the infamous murderer, Clavier), said, "Do you realize that you
are in danger of being remembered by posterity not because of your
immense talent, but because you sought the same punishment—in this
same courtroom, in the name of the same penal code—against a horrible

dismemberer of women like Clavier, and a poet like Brasillach?" Next, veering from his immediate subject, he asked, "What punishment will you then reserve for the cannon merchants?" Isorni was referring to the businessmen who had collaborated with the Germans and bled the resources out of the country. They had not yet come to trial. His attack on the priorities of the Court of Justice was an effective change of focus away from the specific responsibility of Brasillach. Why strike down a poet when economic collaborators were going free?

Twenty minutes into his defense speech, Isorni finally reached the substance of Reboul's accusation against Brasillach: "Gentlemen, I hear the objection you'll make: [Reboul] isn't prosecuting a poet. He isn't prosecuting a writer. He is prosecuting the editor in chief of *Je Suis Partout*. I must talk to you about *Je Suis Partout*."

His first line of defense on behalf of the paper was cultural. André Bellessort, secretary of the Académie Française, had published criticism in *Je Suis Partout*. Marcel Aymé and Jean Anouilh had published literature there. He named the most literary, least political contributors to the paper. Those names, those nuances, were meaningless to the jury.

Isorni didn't even try to clear Brasillach's name in regard to his editorials in *Je Suis Partout*. Instead, he shifted blame, from *Je Suis Partout* to the court itself, from Brasillach's context, to Vidal and Reboul's. He explained to the jury that a judge named Bouchardon, unknown to them but famous in legal circles, had just been named president of the High Court of Justice—the court that was to begin trying the Vichy ministers for treason that coming summer. This Judge Bouchardon had been the subject of a friendly interview in *Je Suis Partout* during the Occupation. Of his own accord, Bouchardon had made anti-Semitic remarks in *Je Suis Partout,* when the shoe was on the other foot. Isorni quoted a letter from the journalist who had interviewed Bouchardon for *Je Suis Partout*. The letter stated that the judge had openly expressed his admiration for Brasillach, and for the newspaper. Isorni came to the point:

> Mr. Government Prosecutor, I am obliged to turn to you and tell you: you have asked for the death sentence against Robert Brasillach because of his articles in *Je Suis Partout,* and the supreme judge of treason, the man chosen over all others, declared after having given an interview to *Je Suis Partout:* "I appreciate Robert Brasillach and his paper." You have to choose.

Here Isorni got sympathy, even—especially—from the left. In its January 1945 columns, *Lettres Françaises* and *Action* were every bit as hostile to the judiciary as Isorni was in this speech. His specific jab at Bouchardon made the audience chortle and it wasn't only Brasillach's friends who were chortling—it was the young people in the courtroom, the left wingers, the communist journalists, who saw the judges as malleable bureaucrats, part of an old guard they hoped to supplant with the Liberation. Against the active collaboration of Brasillach, Isorni was positing another evil—passive collaboration—men who got along with the Germans to get by and who were now emerging with white gloves, on the other side. The judiciary, he implied, was full of such men. Was punishing Brasillach, who at least had had the courage of his convictions, a way to forget about them? It was one of Isorni's strongest moments.

"In reality, gentlemen" he persevered, capitalizing on his gain, "you understood when you heard the prosecution speech that this is nothing but a trial of opinion." *Procès d'opinion:* a case based on opinions, not on deeds. Isorni summarized succinctly. There were really only three facts in the indictment, three facts concerning Brasillach's actions, as opposed to his words. First, the charge that he was liberated by the Germans from prison camp in order to continue his propaganda. Not true, said Isorni—Brasillach was liberated because he was being considered as commissioner of cinema under Vichy. The article he wrote from the POW camp couldn't have motivated his liberation—the dates were wrong. Second, the charge that he was a member of the board of the Rive-Gauche bookstore. This is of so little importance to the case, Isorni quipped, that the examining magistrate who interviewed Brasillach in October considered it "of no importance." In fact, Isorni argued, the Rive-Gauche was a scholarly, cultural exchange—Brasillach made no money from it; he only got a few free books. And anyway, the store sold classics, not propaganda. He turned to Reboul again. "And it's for this that you're seeking the death sentence? You can't be serious."

By Isorni's account, all that remained in the way of actions in the indictment were Brasillach's two trips to Germany. Here, Isorni argued for equity: The trip to Weimar was not considered a crime for the six other writers who went, so why was it a crime for Brasillach? He added, righteously, "Don't ask me to give the names of the others. I recoil at the idea of anything that might appear as a denunciation, when it is not absolutely essential for the defense." He was taking the opportunity to distance himself—and, by extension, his client—from the denunciation charge. Lastly, he argued that Brasillach's trip with de Brinon to the Eastern front for the League of Volunteers against Bolshevism, to visit the mass graves at Katyn, was Brasillach's right and duty as a reporter.

By now Isorni was shifting directions every few minutes, turning first to Reboul, then to the jury, then back to Reboul, and back to the jury once again: "Gentlemen, these three facts have been examined. Do they merit capital punishment? I am obliged to conclude that we are in a trial of opinion." He was right that, taken out of context, these were minimal actions, especially when compared to the noxious activities of countless other political collaborators. But when he opposed these minor "actions" to the "opinions" in *Je Suis Partout,* he was ignoring Brasillach's calls for murder in his newspaper and their real consequences, which were at the heart of Reboul's case against the writer. Isorni needed to posit "mere opinions," for he was unwilling—or unable—to prove that Brasillach's calls for murder had never resulted in murder.

He admitted that, as a thinker and a writer in the violent Action Française tradition, Brasillach had been overly systematic, even erroneous in his views and their expression. This much Isorni would admit, but he would not consider his client's words as treason. To demonstrate that the treason charge was unfounded with respect to mere words, Isorni focused on the line from which Reboul had derived his most scandalous effect, Brasillach's "Frenchmen given to reflection, during these years, will have more or less slept with Germany—not without quarrels—and the memory of it will remain sweet for them."

> Look here, Mr. Prosecutor, you have not understood this text. You tried to make a facile juxtaposition to the massacres at Oradour, thinking that this would affect the jury. No, the jury deserves better than that. It deserves a serious explanation.

For Isorni, giving "a serious explanation" meant locating a source for the metaphor. Either Reboul had tipped him off during one of their many dinner conversations on the rue Geoffroy St. Hilaire, or it was obvious that the prosecution was going to use this line—so representative of Brasillach's attitude, and so outrageous—to its best rhetorical advantage. In any case, Isorni had done his homework. He had consulted Brasillach, who told him the source for "sleeping with Germany" was in Ernest Renan. Bardèche sent him to see his thesis director, Jean Pommier, a Renan specialist. In the notes laid out on Isorni's table there were four Renan quotations with full bibliographic references, including the nineteenth-century scholar's oft-quoted remark, "Germany was my mistress." Brasillach's life was on the line for treason, and Isorni had assembled footnotes. Had his desire for eloquence skewed his priorities, or did he really think that an array of literary sources would help his client?

Armed with his extensive erudition, Isorni turned to Vidal and to the jurors at the tribunal:

> What was that allusion to the bed of Germany? You see—and I apologize for saying so—how much we truly are in a trial based on opinion, I would almost say, in a philosophical trial. It is the intentional and nearly ironic (since it was, all the same, rather audacious to write during the Occupation that "we have slept with Germany," even more since it could be a rape) paraphrase of a famous line by Renan: "Germany was my mistress." This is in the preface to *La Réforme intellectuelle et morale.* It is a subtle commentary (allow me to assume that you have not understood it) on a line by Renan. . . . Forgive me for having brought this quarrel back to a little commentary by Renan, but that is the truth. You are dealing here with a man of letters who has great literary knowledge, and it so happens that not everyone has as much as he does. I was in this category, and if he hadn't explained it to me, I never would have understood.

The problem with Isorni's serious explanation was that it was pedantic; it had nothing to do with Brasillach's attitude, his situation, his state of mind. At the closing end of this exposé, Isorni threw in his lot with the jurors and declared himself as ignorant as they, hoping to compensate for his misstep in implying that the jury was without book learning. You didn't need a doctorate to sense that his afterthought was disingenuous. And in the end, whether Brasillach had been embroidering a quotation by Renan, or some other writer, was of no concern to the jury. What Isorni had communicated to them were his pretensions, his lightheartedness. He had either irritated the jurors, or simply bored them.

By now even Brasillach—who adored his defense lawyer—was beginning to think that this middle part of Isorni's defense speech was getting too long, too packed with information. From his client's verbal affection for Germany, Isorni moved to Brasillach's verbal violence against the Republic. Shouldn't the French be liberal like the English, who had freed from prison their own fascist, Oswald Mosley, in the middle of the war? In the manner of Brasillach, Mosley had savagely attacked British democracy. "What an example!" Isorni exclaimed, for only a true democracy would dare keep its harshest critics free. But England hadn't been occupied by a foreign power, and the analogy didn't carry. Mosley was no Brasillach.

Isorni admitted that Brasillach had been overly severe in asking for the death of the government officials he considered responsible for his country's defeat. But Brasillach hadn't been alone in pointing the finger, and, Isorni maintained, "there was nothing unusual about his severity except its literary form." If, in other words, when Brasillach had called for the death of his enemies by hanging, there was a voluptuous specificity to his fantasies, it was simply because he was a good writer. Good writing had gotten his client in trouble.

Of all Brasillach's calls for murder, only one moved Isorni to engage in justification. This was Brasillach's call for the execution of communists. Isorni could not ignore this aspect of the case, for he believed—mistakenly, it so happened—that the jury was composed uniquely of communists. He advanced the notion that, like the communists themselves, Brasillach had always been a social thinker, interested in "social aspirations." Furthermore, he claimed, his client had been horrified when the Germans had started executing hostages in response to communist acts of violence against the occupying soldiers. Isorni next repeated one of Vichy's antiresistance clichés. The Nazis had taken hostages in retaliation against the resistance. Vichy propaganda claimed that resistance actions invited German violence. Summing up the old argument, Isorni claimed to the jury that Brasillach had agonized over this issue, that he had believed the punishment of a few resistance activists would save the massacre of "innocent hostages." Isorni referred to passionate debates among the resistance leaders themselves about whether or not it was wise to retaliate against the hostage-taking with more violence, until it sounded as though the resistance had taken a position similar to Brasillach's.

> Well, gentlemen, in order for a moral leader of the resistance to write in the same terms as Brasillach about these facts, does this not signify a profound disarray of opinion, one where adversaries could find themselves in agreement on certain particularly burning questions?

The resistance was concerned about hostage-taking, and so was Brasillach: therefore Brasillach and the resistance were the same. Conclusion: Brasillach was not a collaborator. He was instead the moral equivalent of a resister. Isorni wanted to collapse the difference between Brasillach and his enemies whose death he had called for: It was a trick, a sleight of hand, three-fourths of the way through Isorni's speech. Though what he said was likely to infuriate the jurors, he had at least begun to talk to them.

––––––

Isorni's final tactic was to bring up one of the most humiliating episodes in the entire history of the French magistrature, the operation of the Vichy Special Section courts, which had meted out such harsh and unjust punishment to communist resisters under German duress. Isorni had great moral authority on this issue, since he had served as a defense lawyer in the Paris Special Section. It was a chance for him to cloak Brasillach, the collaborator, in his own good deeds during the Occupation. In invoking the German-controlled court, he was, by extension, trying to denounce the moral standing of Reboul and Vidal, who, although they had not themselves served in the Special Section, had been members of the larger Vichy court system of which it was a part.

"The hour has come," Isorni began. He knew this tactic was his biggest blow, his strongest move in the trial. He prefaced his attack by saying how much he regretted that Reboul was the prosecutor in the Brasillach case, for "a curious coincidence has linked the course of our existence and sometimes the beating of our hearts." Reboul, his neighbor, was sitting quietly at his elevated perch, leaning forward, his weight on his forearms. It was his way of taking the pressure off his bad hip after standing for nearly an hour and a half. For him, Isorni's phrase was more than flowery rhetoric, for they had sat together in the basement of their apartment building, their hearts beating in fear, during many an air raid alert. "If I call you my friend," added Isorni, "it is not to trivialize that word so often trivialized at this bar, but because you are—truly you are—my friend."

It was 6:15 P.M., and here it was at last, the "other trial" Reboul had been expecting—his own. There was a pause while Isorni eyed Reboul and Reboul eyed Isorni, as though no one else were in the cavernous room. Then Isorni began his diatribe:

> Your institution—the public ministry—sounds the fanfare of the resistance today. Well and good! . . . But for four years, you have stood on this floor and represented the collaboration. You are, whether you like it or not, in solidarity with this institution which, for four years, pursued and condemned Jews, pursued and condemned resisters, pursued and condemned communists!

The accusation was all the more dramatic because Isorni had just explained to the court that Reboul was his friend. He was not only challenging the moral standing of the court; he was accusing a close friend of hypocrisy.

Nothing could be more typical at the Palais de Justice than for a prosecutor and a lawyer to attack each other savagely and meet after the trial for a friendly round of drinks. That was all part of the game. Here, the game was turning serious, and one had to wonder how Reboul and Isorni's friendship could possibly emerge from these debates unscathed. The jury didn't know what we do: that in October 1944, in a case concerning illegal traffic in sugar, they had occupied the same spaces in the same courtroom. Vidal had been with them, as presiding judge.

Neither that coincidence nor Reboul's reaction were important. Isorni needed to drive his point home to the jurors. He looked at the four men from the suburbs. His bold attack on the court system had jolted them; he had their full attention as he spoke: "I have the right to turn towards the victims of the collaboration and ask them: 'What made you suffer more? the writing of a journalist or the actions of these accusers, so merciless today, and who are marked, indelibly marked, in your sorrow and in your blood!'" In other words, Isorni was asking the men at the tribunal: Who did more real harm, Brasillach and his kind, or Reboul and his kind?

He was a beat away from contempt of court when he made his abrupt about-face, composed of equal parts of charity and condescension. He turned sharply away from the jurors—confident that he now had their ear—and he stood again facing his adversary on the other side of the courtroom:

> I don't reproach you because you collaborated on this floor for four years: you, too, collaborated in order to save what could be saved. You did your duty as a magistrate. You thought that if it wasn't you who was in the business of judging the communists, it would be the Germans who did it and that there would be more deaths. You were a collaborator in order to save what could be saved in the judiciary realm, and you understand why I don't dare hold this against you: If you, a French magistrate, had refused the charge of condemning six or ten French men, the Germans would have shot fifty or sixty men. And it is for this reason that I don't hold it against you.

He was referring specifically to three scandalous death sentences pronounced by the Paris Special Section during their first week of operation, in response to the Germans' threats that they would kill sixty hostages if several men weren't put to death. "I don't reproach you"; "if you had refused": Isorni pointedly made Reboul, who had never served in the Special Section, the "you" in his sentence.

Having blasted the judiciary as hypocrites and weaklings, then forgiven them magnanimously for having given in to the lesser of two evils, Isorni turned again to the jurors and concluded that Brasillach, by comparison, was a man of courage. His evidence of that courage was the fact that Brasillach had quit *Je Suis Partout* in 1943, even though it was in his financial interests to stay. His implication: Reboul had stayed in the magistrature out of weakness, but Brasillach had left his newspaper out of strength. He reminded the jury that Brasillach had refused all opportunities to leave France as the Liberation approached. He added one final brush stroke to the romantic portrait of the writer he had begun at 5:20: "This, gentlemen, is Brasillach: fidelity to ideas, fidelity to those who support him, fidelity to those young people who wrote him and whose adviser he became; and the supreme fidelity, fidelity in danger, fidelity to his native soil." There was an argument within the portrait. Whereas Reboul had just suggested that Brasillach had merely been trying to save his skin, once the tide of the war had turned, Isorni hoped to convince the jury that Brasillach's departure from *Je Suis Partout* was based on patriotism. It was a direct challenge to the charge of treason, a bold spin on the facts of the case.

With his portrait of Brasillach complete, his concluding remarks drawing near, Isorni offered the jury a self-portrait, a touch of intimacy designed to give the jury confidence in him:

> I belong to that class of society, the bourgeoisie, often hostile, often closed off to social aspirations, but I observed up close a type of man unfamiliar to me, I saw him at close quarters in order to defend him against all odds, over the course of three years: the militant, the communist militant. I found in this militant what I found in Brasillach: sincerity, disinterestedness, purity.
>
> Which reminds me, irresistibly, of a tragic memory.
>
> I remember a twenty-year-old young man. What does his name matter! He was a woodsman from the Orgerus forest. . . . A communist, he had been condemned to death. I remember his beautiful child's face, his great stature. . . . He had just been condemned, he looked at me, and he uttered this simple phrase, "For my ideas, it's a crime!" And I, I must say that I was reduced to silence. I can still hear him: "For my ideas, it's a crime! . . ." I still see him. I know he went to his death like a Christian martyr.

This story was the kind of allegory for which Isorni was famous. Brasillach's character, his idealism, he was arguing, were exactly those of that communist woodsman. If the jury didn't trust Isorni, if they didn't trust Brasillach, he would leave them with the image of the communist woodsman. He later explained in his memoirs that there was no forest in Orgerus, but that his eloquent refrain, "the woodsman from the forest of Orgerus," had saved his client's life in the Vichy-era trial. Now, in Brasillach's trial, he went a step further in his fabulation. He pretended that the boy had gone to his death at the hands of the state and he made him into a Christian martyr. It was a lie he believed represented a deeper truth. Many years afterwards, to justify the courtroom fiction, he wrote: "For Brasillach's life, I had simply transposed that militant into a new reality. I had not seen him die, but men other than he and similar to him were dead."

That was how Jacques Isorni countered Reboul's prosecution. Reboul had labeled Brasillach, in so many words, a perverted man; Isorni countered, "No, this is a pure man." Isorni had effectively reversed his defense strategy since his opening gambit. The Brasillach of his opening was a high-minded poet, the soul of French civilization. Now, in his coda, Brasillach became as pure and simple as a country bumpkin.

Next came the rhetorical drum roll—a reference to the fact that de Gaulle's provisional government had been imposed by fiat. There had been as yet no general election. "If, Mr. Government Prosecutor, the French people disavow you tomorrow by majority, after you have brought about an irreparable death, will you have the power to resurrect?" Then, Isorni delivered the most famous line of his defense: "Mr. Government Prosecutor, you cannot ask for the eternal in the name of the provisional." In other words, a temporary government has no right to ask for something as permanent as death.

He made one more turn to the front of the courtroom. "Gentlemen of the Jury, let my last words be for you." His voice went up, deepened, softened, at just the right moment. He tried to imagine what the jurors were feeling:

> You have behind you all the pomp, the might, the apparatus of the State, you have the power, while he is all alone now and defeated, but with the pride of a soldier who never goes back on a commitment. You can strike him, you can do it without risk, but listen to me, I tell you, this is my last appeal! Death is not for him. Justice has no right to execute souls. It is not possible that this great mind described by

our most illustrious thinkers be extinguished forever and that it be extinguished forever by your hands. May your verdict, in the storm raging in our country, appear in the sky of a sorrowful France as the first sign, passionately anticipated and more than ever necessary, of France, a just and reconciled France, so that France may live.

The final words of his defense sang out in the perfect silence of the courtroom: "so that France may live" [*que vive la France*]. When the defense lawyer finished, Brasillach looked out over the audience. He saw his sister Suzanne, Jacques Tournant from the POW camp, his cartoonist friend Jean Effel. A group of right-wing students was standing in the back, and mixed throughout the audience were the many nameless supporters whom the newspapers referred to as "the Fifth Column"— men and women favorable to the collaboration and vocally hostile to the court. He saw tears on their faces.

The jury was not crying. Most of Isorni's defense was too literary and pedantic to move them. His belated attempts to acknowledge their political experience were facile, cheap: the imaginary woodsman from a forest that didn't exist. He didn't know anything about them, other than their profession and the town they lived in, as written on the jury list. Communism didn't have the hold on them he imagined. He had made mistakes. He had brilliantly assailed the justice system for collaborating, then he claimed that Brasillach had done the same as they. He couldn't have it both ways. In the shadow of his defense was an obvious line of argument he hadn't used: Brasillach had claimed far more responsibility and power than he had in fact wielded; there were a hundred, a thousand political collaborators whose actions were far, far worse than his; it was a trial of opinion because Brasillach was *merely* a writer. That such an argument might have saved his client seems obvious fifty years after the event. But to have used it would have been to lower himself, and to lower Brasillach. It would have gone against his every professional and political instinct, his sense of his client and his sense of the stakes. Jacques Isorni had spoken in lyrical gusts, as though he had prepared his defense speech already imagining that his words would appear some day in print. He was determined to elevate his client, even if it meant elevating him to martyrdom. By the time he came around to acknowledging the jury's power, hinting at his client's lack of power, it was too late.

Many years later, writer Roger Grenier summed it up in a single phrase: "Brasillach's lawyer wanted a beautiful trial."

The Questions, 6:30 P.M.

Presiding Judge Vidal asked Brasillach to stand, and asked him if he had anything to add. "No, your honor," Brasillach said. "You may be seated," Vidal said, "The debates are closed." Then he read the questions to the jury, quoting from the elaborate and turgid articles of the penal code on treason and threats to national security, as adapted for the punishment of collaborators:

1. Is Brasillach, Robert, here presently accused, guilty of having, on national territory, during the years 1941, 1942, 1943, and 1944, in any case since June 16, 1940, until the date of the Liberation, during wartime, being French, undertaken intelligence with Germany or with its agents, in view of favoring any kind of enterprise of this foreign power against France or against any one of the nations allied in war against the Axis powers?

2. Was the action specified above under question number 1 committed with the intention of favoring any kind of enterprise of this foreign power against France or against any one of the nations allied in war against the Axis powers?

The audience was suspended. Van der Beken, Riou, Desvillettes, and Grisonnet filed out of the exit marked "magistrates and jurors," to Vidal's chambers. Brasillach, too, was escorted backstage. Isorni rushed out after him. He told his client that, "no matter what happens, we have to remain steadfast and hope." Guards kept watch at the doors.

The Deliberation, 6:35 P.M.

The engineer André Van der Beken, the printer Lucien Grisonnet, the electricians Emile Riou and René Desvillettes sat in the deliberation chambers with Vidal. Here, alone with them, no longer cowed by a brilliant defendant, the presiding judge was back in his element. He explained to the gentlemen of the jury in his dignified style that unless they decided there were "extenuating circumstances" in Brasillach's favor, the result of a guilty verdict in a case of treason was going to be the death penalty. They had either to acquit Brasillach or condemn him to death. There was no middle ground.

Did André Van der Beken argue against the death sentence? Ever since the closing moments of the interrogation, when Brasillach had told how his mother had been taken hostage by the government and was held for "three weeks in a filthy prison, thirty persons to a three-by-four-meter cell, with four straw mats for the thirty," how she had been liberated the moment a letter arrived from Brasillach saying he had turned himself in, the engineer from Saint Maur had remained deeply disturbed. We learned from his daughter that when he got home that night he was outraged—morally, ethically outraged—at the treatment of Brasillach's mother by the government.

The results of a jury's deliberation are and remain, by law, secret. With the perspective afforded by a distance of fifty years, we can only speculate that André Van der Beken, the engineer from Saint Maur, was the most likely of that group of four to have argued for extenuating circumstances. He was a humanist, opposed to the death penalty; he was a Protestant among Catholics, a minority; he was the only graduate of a "Grande Ecole" on the jury, the only bourgeois. Sociologically, he had more in common with Brasillach than with his fellow jurors. What he did have in common with his fellow jurors was the experience of the resistance, which was recent, intense, life altering— and a great sociological leveler. In the resistance, Van der Beken had been in charge of "chaos management." He had gummed up the Nazi's shipping schedules, so he knew how to disturb a smoothly working system. We will never know how he actually voted in the Brasillach trial, whether or not he protested the guilty verdict, how the three other men might have responded to such a protest, if there was one. In any case, in a French court, the verdict doesn't have to be unanimous—there is no such thing as a "hung jury." However hot or tepid the debate over Brasillach's fate, it was over in twenty minutes. The ritual bell sounded, and the court was back in session.

Curtain: The Verdict, 7 P.M.

Brasillach stood at attention in his box while Vidal read the responses to the questions asked of the Court.

"Yes, by majority, on both the questions," he mumbled.

There were no extenuating circumstances.

Then he specified:

> The court, given its declaration by a majority that Robert Brasillach has rendered himself guilty of the crime of intelligence with the enemy; having heard the government prosecutor in his requisitions, the counsel of the accused, the accused himself, who has had the last word;
>
> In view of article 75, paragraphs 37, 38, 39, of the Penal Code; article 63, paragraph 3, and article 77 of the Ordinance of November 28, 1944;

In compliance with these statutes, the Court, by majority, condemns Brasillach, Robert, to death;

Says that he will be shot;

Pronounces the confiscation, to the profit of the Nation, of all the possessions of the condemned man, according to articles 37, 38, 39 of the Penal Code;

Says that the present judgment will be printed in excerpts, published and posted to conform to article 36 of the Penal Code;

Condemns Brasillach to pay State's charges.

Vidal lifted his face from his administrative papers and looked one more time at Brasillach, in the box of the accused, and at Isorni, on the defense bench below him: "Brasillach, you have twenty-four hours to contest this judgment on procedural grounds. Beyond that time, this contestation will no longer be received."

Brasillach didn't flinch. The audience booed. Vidal adjourned the court. There was pandemonium, more cries of rage, a rush of the crowd toward the condemned man. Someone—a guard? a journalist?—cried out to the tribunal that the exits should be blocked, identity cards checked, but the president of the court had already grabbed his *toque,* his ceremonial judge's hat, and made a hasty retreat to his chambers. Brasillach's sister Suzanne fought her way through the crowd to give her brother a kiss. A few friends from the audience managed to shake Brasillach's hand. The accused was smiling—an otherworldly smile. A young man from Dijon named Jacques Poillot yelled out, "Assassins! Assassins!" and, "It's a shame!" The guards seized him and arrested him for contempt of court. Brasillach had just enough time to respond with a clear and calm, "It's an honor!" Despite the chaos, everyone heard him. He turned around briefly and waved at his sister and at Isorni, then the guards cuffed him and led him from the courtroom. It was the perfect curtain call. Down the little spiral staircase he went, back through the *souricière*—the mousetrap—back to his prison van.

Brasillach had begun the afternoon, in his own mind, as in the minds of so many in that courtroom, as a bright, precocious *normalien;* he had prepared for the interrogation as carefully as an exam. By the end of the trial, after his sober, controlled performance, after these hours of listening to his words and deeds echoing back at him, he seemed to be transformed. His cutting humor was gone, replaced by a transcendent seriousness. He was a symbol now, a tragic figure in the Corneillean tradition he so admired. He was about to sacrifice his life in the name of his principles.

The trials of most of the major collaborators took several days. This time, the entire procedure had taken six hours. Six hours to condemn the "star" of the literary collaboration to death.

NINE THE WRITERS' PETITION

After his brief afternoon trial on January 19, Brasillach was moved to a solitary cell. His feet were put in chains, and he was dressed in brown burlap trousers with slits on the sides to accommodate them, as was the rule for men condemned to death. The first poem he wrote after his condemnation was called "Testament of the Condemned Man," in which he assembled around him the imaginary company of the great imprisoned martyrs of literary history: Villon, Cervantes, and Chénier. André Chénier was a poet guillotined during the Revolutionary Terror, a writer whose death remained on the French national conscience as one of that period's great excesses. He would become Brasillach's closest literary companion during the last days of his life.

On January 29, Brasillach wrote a poem about the chains on his feet. It is simple in its rhymes, in the original French as in translation—almost a nursery rime. It certainly lacks depth, and lyrical beauty, and it has none of the sense of impending tragedy one would expect from a man condemned to death. It is light, perversely so. But what is interesting about the poem is the impression it gives us that Brasillach was reacting to the rhetoric of his trial, that he was amusing himself by playing with the identity that Reboul ascribed to him in his prosecution: a courtesan, an outsider to the French masculine state, a man enslaved by his attraction to Germany. It's a poem—to make a bad pun that wouldn't work in French—about being literally "in drag," that is, tied down by chains, and at the same time, dressed up:

Jewels
I've never worn any jewelry,
Neither rings nor chains on my wrists,
This isn't done in our country:
Yet they've put my feet in iron twists.

They say it's not at all virile,
Jewels for our girls alone are sweet:
So today why is it that still
They've put more chains around my feet?

Experience is good, I suppose,
Curiosity about new things:
How strange are the clothes they've imposed
How bizarre are these double rings.

The walls are cold, the soup is thin.
I walk proud, I suffer no fools,
Resounding like a Negro King,
Adorned with his iron jewels.

Brasillach's self-proclaimed identity was as a fascist, an antiparliamentarian, a French patriot. He never claimed a homosexual identity, although others—especially his enemies—claimed it for him. But we get a glimpse here of his willingness to play with his desires, and of his desire to romanticize his experience, to the end.

His Fresnes poems can also be read in connection with the anthology of Greek poetry he had been working on in the Bibliothèque Nationale the week before the liberation of Paris. He had hidden two copies of the completed manuscript with friends in Paris and now, the day after his trial, he wrote a kind of literary will, "Instructions on the subject of my books," in which he said how important it was to him that the anthology be published, should he die. Along with the exoticism, the homoeroticism, his nationalism is apparent there, too. In italicized introductions to each poet, he compares them to poets in the French tradition. Still faithful to his fascist culture, now in a more intellectual Nietzschean or Heideggerian vein, he also compares Greek poetry in general with German poetry, the poetry of a people "whose ties to the powers of the earth are strong." The poems themselves are sensual and pagan, a sweet escape to the Mediterranean. There is Theocritus's love of youth; Herodas comically and brilliantly translated into the slang of Montmartre ("I might have forced things a little," Brasillach says in a note); Solon's "joy of having loved boys"; Sappho, of whom, "we hold it for sure, being naive, that she loved women, and that this shocked no one." Again Brasillach's sense of a desire to escape French norms is apparent. Greece, like Rome in his *Présence de Virgile,* is a place where other kinds of love were allowed.

Brasillach was linguistically gifted, sensitive to form, taking great pleasure in pastiches and imitation. The Greek anthology was the kind of virtuoso literary performance for which he had been well trained. He was a more successful translator than he was a poet.

The warm sunny Greece of the poets was remote that winter season, with the outside temperature well below freezing. Brasillach's sister wrote to him from a metro station, the only place where she was warm enough to hold a pen. Throughout December, she and her brother exchanged news about the Brasillach-Bardèche apartment on the rue Rataud, seized and requisitioned by the Liberation government. When she was finally escorted to the premises to pick up some belongings, she found that all their leather-bound Pléiade edition classics were missing from the bookshelves. They were valuable on the black market.

——

In the last week of January 1945, as Brasillach and Isorni waited for de Gaulle to decide whether he would pardon him, a group of writers decided to circulate a petition in favor of Brasillach. The effort was initiated by Jean Anouilh, author of *Antigone* (February 1944); Marcel Aymé, a literary anarchist of uncertain allegiance who had published short stories in *Je Suis Partout;* and François Mauriac, who, as soon as the war ended, had become an apologist for charity, forgiveness, and national unity in his regular front-page column in the conservative *Le Figaro.*

Mauriac's reasons for supporting Brasillach are the most complex of the three. A former Action Française supporter who had turned to the left during the Spanish Civil War, criticizing the Catholic Church for its support of Franco, Mauriac had briefly supported Pétain after France's fall, but had rallied to the resistance as early as December 1941. He was the only member of the staunchly conservative Académie Française to publish a resistance text with the clandestine Editions de Minuit.

Brasillach's attacks on Mauriac had begun in the 1930s, in the pages of the *Action Française* and *Je Suis Partout.* He blasted Mauriac much as he blasted Gide, for his pro-Republican politics and as an "esthetic elder" who needed to be surpassed. In *Notre avant-guerre,* which was published in 1941, Brasillach described Mauriac, who spoke with difficulty after a 1932 bout with throat cancer, as a "squeaky old bird" with a taste for suicidal women and tortured adolescents.

Brasillach's tone towards Mauriac in *Notre avant-guerre* is disdainful and amused, rather than vengeful. Nonetheless, after France was occupied, Brasillach went to the Propaganda-Staffel in Paris with vows to launch a veritable press campaign against Mauriac, as the example of the type of writer hostile to the new regime. *Je Suis Partout* referred to Mauriac during the Occupation as "the born antifascist"; as "the skinny Tartuffe" (as opposed to fellow Academician Georges Duhamel, the fat one); or as "the prepubescent vicar." Mauriac himself was not indifferent to these attacks. In 1941, when he learned that the administrator of the Comédie Française had asked Brasillach to lecture on Corneille to the theater company, Mauriac wrote to the man's wife, protesting his invitation to "the director of an abject newspaper that is harassing me with the most outrageous insults."

Mauriac was a founding member of the CNE, the National Writer's Committee, an organization born out of the literary resistance. In September 1944, the CNE published a list of writers compromised by collaboration, writers whom they wanted excluded from the literary community. Brasillach's name headed their blacklist.

It was one thing to criticize writers from within the literary community; Mauriac's attitude toward the punishment of literary collaborators began to change as soon as writers started appearing before the Paris Court of Justice in October; that is, as soon as writers began to be sentenced to death for treason. By the time novelist and *Gringoire* columnist Henri Béraud was condemned to death by the Paris Court of Justice in December, the newspapers were calling Mauriac "St. François des Assises" [Saint Francis of the Court of Assizes] for his stance of Christian forgiveness. After Mauriac's strong editorial protest of the Béraud verdict, de Gaulle pardoned Béraud. It looked as though Mauriac's intervention had been decisive.

Meanwhile, in his columns in *Le Figaro,* Mauriac was engaging in a vigorous polemic with Albert Camus, in *Combat*. It was front-page call and response: Mauriac called for charity; Camus responded by calling for justice. The young editor of *Combat* did not understand how Mauriac could love traitors; the venerable columnist for *Le Figaro* did not see how hatred could heal France's wartime wounds. The motto of *Combat* was "from resistance to the revolution." Camus did not understand how French society was going to remake itself if the corrupt, mediocre elements of the elite were left in place. He accused Mauriac of asking him to choose between hatred and forgiveness. Prompt justice, he replied, was neither.

Much as Reboul would do rhetorically in his prosecution of Brasillach, Camus referred to collaboration itself as a foreignness within France. Here Camus was not the defender of the outsider, the champion of the condemned man, so familiar to us from *The Stranger,* he was the patriot, attacking the collaboration as a tumor on the body politic:

France carries within her, like a foreign body, a minority of men who caused her unhappiness and who will continue to do so. These are men of treason and injustice.

Be careful, "young master," was the gist of Mauriac's reply to Camus, whom he considered something of an upstart; be careful of what the world looks like "from the great heights of your oeuvre to come."

Brasillach's mother wrote to Mauriac in January 1945, asking if he would intervene for her son's pardon. François Mauriac's subsequent support of Brasillach, which grew in intensity and purpose up until the day of execution, was a supreme act of Christian forgiveness that probably astonished no one as much as it did Brasillach himself.

———

Mauriac's son Claude was one of de Gaulle's personal secretaries in January 1945, and it was he who prepared a first version of the petition. It began:

The undersigned intellectuals, all belonging in various capacities, to the French resistance . . .

This was a claim that very few fervent Brasillach supporters, apart from François Mauriac himself, could make in 1945.

The statement went on to argue that although Brasillach had committed crimes, these crimes did not merit a death sentence. Building on the notion of the "two Brasillachs"—the political writer and the esthete—it argued for a recognition of Brasillach's contribution to France:

He loved, as they should be loved, the best of all that our French civilization and culture have given. . . . The man capable of the intelligence and the sensitivity that the nonpolitical part of his work reveals could not truly be towards himself—and towards God, those of us who have faith would add—a traitor.

It concluded by rejecting the "eye for an eye" argument of justice, and by speculating about Brasillach's future.

It is terrible to fell a thinking head, even if it thinks badly. Who knows the future of a poet?

From bad thinker of the present, to poet of the future. The future Brasillach, it implied hopefully, would no longer write political editorials, but poems.

Acknowledging the notion in the air of "the writer's responsibility," the statement concluded by warning against the dangers of martyrdom: "Bad causes need no martyr: the martyrdom of their authors gives the ideas that we have so rightly fought against an influence that makes them even more dangerous." A living Brasillach, in other words, would do less harm than a dead one.

The statement was unworkable. It claimed active membership in the resistance for the signers, severely limiting the number of people who could sign it in good conscience. It was religious in tone if not in content, implying a faith in transcendent nonpolitical values—a faith that was very hard to sustain in such a profoundly political moment. Worse, the argument was convoluted. It wasn't clear if the goal was to save a good writer for his potential, or prevent a bad writer from becoming a martyr.

So the petition was rewritten. The final version said nothing more than that Brasillach's father had given his life for France in 1914, and asked that the son of a fallen war hero be spared:

> The undersigned, remembering that Lieutenant Brasillach, the father of Robert Brasillach, died for his country on November 13, 1914, respectfully request that General de Gaulle, head of the government, consider with favor the pardon request addressed to him by Robert Brasillach, condemned to death on January 19, 1945.

It was a classic argument directed at the General: the Brasillach family has already given a father to save our country; please spare his son.

———

The petitioners went out in search of signatures. Anouilh talked to the theater crowd; Mauriac, to his fellow members of the Académie Française and its affiliate Institutes; Aymé, to novelists and artists on the left. Brasillach's sister Suzanne and Thierry Maulnier also contacted potential signers.

Several different versions of the list of those who signed have been published over the years. Confusion was inevitable, since the names were gathered in haste by letter, by telegram, and door to door, through the efforts of each member of the organizing team. The list de Gaulle saw, the list sent to him by Jacques Isorni with the official request for pardon, was a typewritten list containing fifty-seven names, with two names added in pen at the last minute. There was most certainly never an actual physical petition with all the signatures on it.

We have accounts of a few of the refusals to sign. Brasillach's correspondence tells us that Sartre, who was touring New York around the time of the trial, was sent a telegram. A chronicler of life in Paris after the Liberation, he was already a central figure on the postwar scene. He didn't sign and never explicitly explained why, but he referred in much of his writing of the period to the responsibility of the writer and to the idea that a writer must be prepared to die for what he puts on paper. Simone de Beauvoir wrote twice about why she hadn't signed the petition—once in her essay on the Brasillach trial in *Les Temps Modernes,* a year after the fact, and once in her 1963 memoirs, *La Force des choses.* Sylvia Bataille, a Jewish actress famous for her roles in prewar films by Jean Renoir, and who was married to Georges Bataille and later to Jacques Lacan, was asked to sign. She refused. Picasso refused, citing the desires of the French Communist Party. Claude Roy signed, then withdrew his signature, citing pressure from the Communist Party. In 1947, reading a veiled attack on him in Isorni's introduction to *Le Procès de Robert Brasillach,* Roy wrote to Isorni to justify his decision after the fact. He explained that his father-in-law had been killed on the strength of a denunciation in *Je Suis Partout.* His best friend, too, had been shot because of a denunciation in that newspaper where, in 1940, he himself had woken up "on the brink of treason." The men to whom he owed having emerged from the war with his conscience intact—his comrades in the Party—had convinced him not to sign for the life of his former comrade. In a terse, bitter response, Isorni reminded Roy that he had come to his office freely, given his signature loyally, and withdrawn it in cowardice. He reminded Roy that, once he had withdrawn his signature, he had promised to send cigarettes to Brasillach in prison. Had his friends also forbidden that? Isorni later published both Roy's letter of justification, and his own angry, ironic response.

André Gide, whom Brasillach had buried prematurely in his 1931 "Funeral Oration for André Gide," received a letter from Brasillach's mother, pleading with him to support the pardon—the same type of letter Mauriac had received. He did not follow Mauriac's lead. Gide wrote to his colleague Jean Schlumberger, cofounder of the *Nouvelle Revue Française,* on January 28, 1945:

> I received a letter from Brasillach's poor mother, begging me to intervene to try and get her son pardoned. But I only know him from the articles that used to leave me indignant, and, even if there wasn't exactly "commerce with the enemy" on his part, he still

remains one of the worst poisoners of yesterday—and of tomorrow
if he is pardoned.

While Mauriac worried about killing off a poet, Gide was more worried
about letting the vicious polemicist live.

In addition to those who refused, there were clearly many Brasillach
supporters who were too compromised to be asked for a signature. Their
names would have done more harm than good. These included *Je Suis
Partout* writers on the lam, writers in prison awaiting trial, and those
blacklisted by the CNE.

Still, two men who signed the petition, Henry Bordeaux and the
painter Maurice de Vlaminck, had themselves appeared on the CNE
"blacklist" of 1944. Bordeaux had written a hagiographic book about
Pétain and had attacked the decadence of Popular Front materialism
throughout the Occupation in classic Vichyssois style. Vlaminck, with
cosigner Derain, was blacklisted for having traveled to Nazi Germany
on a propaganda tour. He himself had written an ideological and savage
critique of Picasso in *Comoedia* in 1942, calling the artist impotent and
corrupt. Yet his work had been included by the Nazis, along with
Derain's, in one of their exhibits of "degenerate" art. Vlaminck wrote
to Isorni on January 28, 1945, "Dear Maître, Placing myself outside all
political errors committed, I associate myself with those who ask for the
pardon of Robert Brasillach."

Others who signed the petition weren't too compromised to be
asked, but had a reason to identify with Brasillach's situation. One might
say that they were in the "there but by the grace of God go I" group.
Among these signers, we would have to count Arthur Honegger, the
French-born Swiss composer, who accepted the Nazis' invitation to
Vienna for the 150th anniversary of the death of Mozart, and Jean
Cocteau, who, with the cream of Parisian collaborators, had attended
the opening of the sculpture exhibit by Nazi artist Arno Breker and
praised him in a front-page article, "Salut à Breker."

Eight petition signers had been associated with *Je Suis Partout* in
one way or another—they had contributed a short story, a translation,
or a single article, usually before the Occupation. Marcel Aymé, one of
the originators of the petition, had written short stories for the paper
as late as 1944.

François Mauriac, Albert Camus, Claudel, Colette, Valéry, Cocteau
were the most prominent signers, along with painters Derain and
Vlaminck.

Among the famous writers, Cocteau had the most double-edged position. His support of the Nazi sculptor Breker was infamous. At the same time his companion, Jean Marais, an actor who had distinguished himself in the resistance, was the target of vicious homophobic attacks by Alain Laubreaux, the *Je Suis Partout* theater critic. Cocteau himself was a "bête noire" of both Vichy propaganda and *Je Suis Partout,* because of his flamboyant homosexuality. Cocteau wrote in his diary about the petition:

> I find Brasillach absurd and harmful, but I will sign because I'm fed up that they're sentencing writers to death and leaving the people who furnished the German army in peace. The ridiculousness of the lawyer is to make an issue out of talent. Brasillach is not André Chénier.

What Cocteau didn't know was that as he wrote this entry, Brasillach was finishing a thinly veiled literary testament in the form of an essay on Chénier. In this, his last work of literary criticism, Brasillach contrasted the charming, lightweight writer—what the guillotined poet might have meant to literary history if he hadn't been killed by the revolution——with the mythical figure he had become, by virtue of his execution.

————

The first draft of the petition to save Brasillach had claimed that its signers "all belonged in various capacities to the French resistance." In the end, the only true resistants to join François Mauriac in signing were Jean Paulhan, cofounder, with Jacques Decour, of the underground *Lettres Françaises,* and Albert Camus, from *Combat.* Their reasons for signing the petition are particularly complex and interesting.

When Paulhan wrote to Jean Guéhenno about the petition in late January 1945, he was of two minds. It seemed to him equally impossible to provide an argument in favor of pardon and to decide in favor of execution. "Who am I to condemn a man to death, even if it's Brasillach?" He added:

> So the modest petition seems to reconcile everything for me. It is *true* that Brasillach's father died for us. It is also true that we had too many dead in 1914, due to lack of preparation, due to (democratic) refusal to believe in war. It is therefore possible that Brasillach's father was one of those "excessive" deaths and Brasillach an orphan through the fault of democracy, through our fault.

The terse language of the second draft, insisting on Brasillach's status as a son of a man who died for France in 1914, was the only argument for pardon Paulhan could endorse. But in fact, Brasillach's father was not a casualty of the First World War itself; he was killed in a colonial skirmish in Morocco.

Camus's signature came as a particular surprise, given his firm stand in support of a purge and his public opposition to Mauriac's politics of pardon.

Camus wrote to Marcel Aymé, the writer who lobbied him on behalf of the Brasillach cause, that he had spent a sleepless night making up his mind to sign. He had no sympathy for Brasillach, whom he was sure would never have signed a petition to save him or any of his friends. His was a strict anti–death penalty position:

> I've always held the death penalty in horror and judged that, at least as an individual, I couldn't participate in it, even by abstention. That's all. And this is a scruple that I suppose would make Brasillach's friends laugh. It is not for him that I join my signature to yours. It is not for the writer, whom I consider of no significance. Nor for the individual, whom I disdain with all my might. If I had even been tempted to be interested in him, the memory of two or three of my friends who were mutilated or gunned down by Brasillach's friends while his newspaper encouraged them to do it would have prevented me. You say that there is an element of chance in political opinion and I don't know about that. But I know there is nothing accidental about choosing to do what dishonors you and that it is not by accident that my signature will exist alongside yours, whereas Brasillach never acted in favor of Politzer or of Jacques Ducour [resistance intellectuals shot by the Germans].

Camus's passion puts a harsh light on Brasillach's poetic tenderness towards the resistance. How dare he fantasize forgiveness from those he had betrayed?

––––––

Among other surprising signatures on the petition were those of two intellectuals of Jewish origins, Gustave Cohen, the former Sorbonne professor and man of the theater, and Jean-Jacques Bernard, a dramatist whose father, the well-known playwright Tristan Bernard, had been arrested and incarcerated at Drancy during the Occupation. Tristan Bernard was released after several actors with social connections to the Nazis in Paris intervened with them in his favor.

Gustave Cohen was a Belgian Jew converted to Catholicism as well as a veteran of World War I who had taught medieval theater at the Sorbonne and whose troupe of student actors, the "Théophiliens," had charmed Brasillach in the 1930s. In his *Animateurs du Théâtre,* Brasillach said that Cohen had resuscitated the Middle Ages "in heart and soul." Cohen had been stripped of his professorial post and his French citizenship by the Vichy anti-Jewish laws. He spent the war years teaching at Yale. By the fall of 1944, he had returned to Paris and begun his campaign to become one of the "immortals" of the Académie Française. He wanted to replace André Bellessort, the Action Française intellectual who had inspired Brasillach in his classes at Louis-le-Grand. Brasillach's sister is sarcastic and repulsed about her maneuvers to charm him into signing:

> At least I didn't have to kiss him! But I had to discuss the collaboration with him! Explain the collaboration to Cohen! I think I'm the only one to whom things like this happen! And I looked at him, and I answered him in my sweetest voice, excusing myself for being obligated to explain these things to him, since he was asking me!

In signing the Brasillach petition, Cohen joined a large cohort from the Académie he wanted to join. François Mauriac had great success lobbying the Académie and its affiliate institutes for signatures. Of the sixty-three signers mentioned in various versions of the petition, twenty-seven were Academicians or Institute members in January 1945. Another eight were future members of the Académie. Many of these men had links to Brasillach; he had reviewed their work favorably, or they had taught him at the Sorbonne. One signer, Marcel Bouteron, was a librarian at the Académie Française, a specialist on Balzac who had helped Maurice Bardèche with his thesis research.

The theater was well represented, too, thanks to Anouilh: six dramatic authors, decorators, and directors, including Jean-Louis Barrault from the Comédie Française, Jacques Copeau, and Charles Dullin. Dullin and Copeau were much lauded in Brasillach's *Animateurs de théâtre.* During the Occupation, Dullin had administered the former Théâtre Sarah Bernhardt—Aryanized by the Nazis. He had miraculously escaped the Purge.

———

The Brasillach petition became an event in and of itself, with consequences that went beyond Brasillach's individual case. In the CNE and in *Lettres Françaises,* more and more closely identified with the

Communist Party, Louis Aragon and Paul Eluard, the toughest-minded of the purgers, were setting the tone: no sympathy for the traitors! Among the writers who had signed the original CNE manifesto with them in September 1944, Camus, Mauriac, Paulhan, Schlumberger, Gabriel Marcel, Georges Duhamel, and the Tharaud Brothers all signed the petition in favor of Brasillach. It was a dissident move within the organization. All but Mauriac resigned from the CNE a year later, and he was excluded from the group in 1948. For these men, the Brasillach petition was a turning point. The decision to sign was the germ of a position Paulhan would dub "the writer's right to error" and which he would represent at length in two influential essays, "De la paille et du grain" [The wheat and the chaff] (1947) and *Lettre aux directeurs de la résistance* [Letter to the directors of the resistance] (1952), both deeply critical of the judicial purge. Perhaps it was Paulhan's position, more than anyone else's, which has led critics to understand the Brasillach petition as a protective, "corporative" response to the purge of collaborationist writers. Paulhan's argument could be summed up this way: Whatever one might think of a particular writer, when a writer's life is in danger, fellow writers must band together to save him. This is not so much a freedom of speech argument, but an argument for freedom of speech *for writers.*

To represent the Brasillach petition as a corporative, protective response on the part of all French writers is misleading. Well over half of those who signed were members, or would become members, of France's most conservative cultural institutions, the Académie Goncourt, the Académie Française, the Comédie Française; even the several writers connected to Gallimard's *Nouvelle Revue Française* were conservative and well established. Camus, in this company, was the exception who proved the rule.

Age tells a similar story. Only seven out of the fifty-nine who signed in favor of Brasillach's pardon were under forty years old. In other words, very few of Brasillach's intellectual supporters were members of his own generation. Among the writer's friends from his student years at the Ecole Normale, only two, Thierry Maulnier from Louis-le-Grand and the Ecole Normale, and Jean Effel, the cartoonist and family friend, signed. Anouilh, the organizer of the petition, was in his thirties, as was the poet Patrice La Tour du Pin, much celebrated by Brasillach in his criticism, and Henri Pollès, a proletarian writer also well reviewed by Brasillach. Jean-Louis Barrault, from the theater milieu, was thirty-five, Brasillach's age. Camus was the youngest signer, at thirty-two. But the average age of the petition signers was sixty-two. Brasillach did not have the support of his peers.

For every signature there is a story to be reconstructed, a form of identification, or sympathy, a debt to Brasillach, or, more rarely, as in the case of Camus, a moral stance. If there is any generalization to be made on the basis of this list of fifty-nine, it is that a majority of them were members of a generation who had forged their careers long before the start of the Occupation, men too old to have seen combat even in the First World War. Their support of Brasillach was part of their attachment to a prewar France that no longer existed, and to another century.

TEN NO PARDON

It was surprising how fast it went. Since the French abolished the death penalty in 1981, we can't compare a contemporary French case. Certainly in American terms, it is unfathomable that a person of public repute could be sentenced and executed so quickly. But again, it was wartime, and this death sentence was a public and symbolic act of war.

Just as in the regular criminal courts of law, there was no possibility of an appeal in the Court of Justice. Jacques Isorni filed his request that the verdict be overturned on procedural grounds. When his request was turned down, the only step remaining was for Isorni to make a direct request for pardon to General de Gaulle.

The Pardon File

A man's life hung in the balance, and it all came down to a file and an executive signature. In the French judicial system, when a condemned prisoner comes up for pardon, the government assembles a dossier to assist the head of state in making the irrevocable decision. This one is an ordinary looking administrative file, kept in a "chemise," or paper folder. Inside are other paper folders, with a standard administrative sheet detailing the contents. Brasillach's file was put together in the days following his trial by de Gaulle's immediate staff, with official documents from the Court of Justice of the Seine, the Ministry of Justice, the Bureau of Criminal Affairs, and from Brasillach's defense lawyer, along with whatever unofficial letters were received by de Gaulle from the public at large. The file is thick, surprisingly thick, given that there were only eighteen days between Brasillach's trial and his execution. The sense of de Gaulle's power and personality is everywhere in Brasillach's pardon file, from his modest signature on the actual death sentence, to the tens of letters beginning "Mon Général," recognizing his life-and-death power over the condemned man, extolling his virtues as the savior of France.

Eerily, because the file is organized in reverse chronological order, the last document received is the first piece of paper one sees. This first piece of paper is prosecutor Reboul's memo informing the Minister of Justice that the execution has taken place without incident on February 6, 1945.

Then come many official pieces of letterhead—from the Paris Court of Appeals, the Ministry of Justice, the Division of Criminal Affairs. Memos on official stationery are headed: "Capital Punishment" and "Opinion of the Pardon Commission" and "Opinion of the Judges." One learns the opinions on the verdict held by the president of the court, Vidal; by the prosecutor, Reboul; by the Prosecutor General of the Paris Court of Appeals, Boissarie; and by the Director of Criminal Affairs for France, M. Patin. The court secretary's account of the trial is also included. Following these government documents are a few pages sent in by Isorni for the defense, including his request for an audience with de Gaulle. From the public at large are nearly sixty hand- and typewritten letters, on scrap paper, because paper was scarce in 1945, letters on feminine blue stationery, letters with Lorraine crosses drawn at the bottom, claiming allegiance to the Resistance—all of them pleading for Brasillach's life. When these letters came in, during the period from January 20, the day after the trial, until February 5, the day de Gaulle finalized his decision, they were stamped "cabinet de Gaulle" [office of de Gaulle], dated, and placed in the file by subcategories: letters from students, letters from "personalities," petitions.

In the section of the file marked "Avis des Magistrats" [Opinion of the Judges], the judicial opinions ranged from unequivocal to doubtful about the necessity of carrying out the death sentence. A handwritten letter from Vidal, president of the court, was pro forma. Although he had been present during the jury's deliberations, he gave no sense in his memo of the details of their debate. He simply referred to the "gravity of the facts," and recommended that the sentence be carried out.

Prosecutor Reboul, in a much longer, typewritten analysis, summarized the case in his shrewd, concise style. He insisted that Brasillach's treason was a proven fact. He detailed the pro-German, anti-Allied propaganda that had appeared in *Je Suis Partout* and *Révolution Nationale* under Brasillach's signature. He insisted on Brasillach's denunciations of political figures and resistance fighters, "general and schematic but quite sufficient for the Gestapo to be able to profit from them." He reviewed Brasillach's visits to Germany, and his involvement with the Franco-German bookstore, which he considered a form of espionage. Furthermore, Reboul argued, pointing his remarks toward de Gaulle himself, Brasillach had insulted de Gaulle and had condemned the Free French who lost their lives for their cause. Reboul recommended a rejection of the "recours en grâce" [request for pardon].

Even though Reboul recommended execution, he was aware of the political consequences of the death sentence. He understood that there was much public sympathy for Brasillach, based on what he had felt from the audience in the courtroom. In a dramatic conclusion to his memo, Reboul reflected on this sympathy, pointing out that Brasillach's powerful personality, his literary value, his intellectual attraction, were highly effective in certain high classes of society; that the writer had a powerful effect on a part of French opinion, and that the audience in the courtroom had been almost completely on the side of the accused. Reboul had this impression from the laughter, the shouting, and from other interruptions during the trial. One gets the same impression of an audience sympathetic to Brasillach in the press coverage of the trial. Reboul knew that if Brasillach were shot, there would be an emotional outcry from the public. The way he put it was: "If justice followed the path indicated by the treasonous acts committed, a certain 'emotion' could be expected among those classes of society." In other words, there might be trouble. In the long term, as we shall see, his remarks were prophetic.

The Prosecutor General of the Paris Court of Appeals, André Boissarie, agreed with the court's death sentence, but noted that there was a parallel between Brasillach's case and that of writer Henri Béraud. It is useful to look at the case of Béraud, where de Gaulle did grant a presidential pardon. The contrast with Brasillach is both surprising and instructive.

Several journalists had been condemned to death in the first months of the Purge, but Henri Béraud was the only other writer of stature among them. He was arguably even more prominent than Brasillach, having won a Prix Goncourt in 1922 for *Le Vitriol de lune* and *Le Martyre de l'obèse*. Béraud was a jolly, brilliant polemicist and a well-known Anglophobe, rather than a fascist. The bulk of his polemics were directed against the English, with sideswipes at the Jews. A typical comment, quoted in his pardon file, is: "Yes, we've been 'Churchilled,' and we can affirm without lying that this has not brought us happiness, [that it] has injected us with an Anglo-Russian bellicosity maintained by the Judaic virus and we've nearly croaked from it."

Prosecutor Raymond Lindon sought and obtained a death penalty against Béraud in a Court of Justice trial on December 29, 1944. De Gaulle pardoned Béraud on January 13, a week before the Brasillach trial. Béraud's court files include interviews with his chauffeur and with restaurant owners in Lyon and an audit of his bank accounts, to show that he got rich during the Occupation. If Robert Brasillach was condemned for idealism, Béraud was saved by greed. We might conclude that ideology was understood in 1945 as more dangerous and significant than personal corruption.

In Béraud's pardon file, prosecutor Lindon summarized his reasons for recommending that the death sentence be carried out. He wrote that he considered the Court of Justice to be a "war counsel" and that the death of Béraud was "indispensable from the point of view of exemplariness." He was arguing, in other words, that France needed a symbolic punishment, and that such a punishment could bring France closer to victory in the war. Meanwhile, in *Le Figaro,* Mauriac was blasting the courts for condemning a man on charges of treason, who, despite his polemics, had had virtually no contact with the Germans. There is nothing in Béraud's pardon file that tells us why de Gaulle made the decision to pardon. Béraud himself believed that Mauriac's passionate intervention saved his life.

When it came time to decide whether Brasillach should be pardoned, Prosecutor General Boissarie said that he shared Reboul's belief that the sentence was justified. But he added a note of doubt: "The information I must provide on this affair would not be complete if I did not signal the parallelism with the case of Henri Béraud, whose propaganda in the free zone was at least as harmful as that of Brasillach in the occupied zone. My opinion of the execution of the sentence cannot be unaffected."

Boissarie's parting lines in his report to the Brasillach pardon commission shows that, at the highest level of the judicial system, there was real doubt about carrying out Brasillach's death sentence. De Gaulle could have used Boissarie's argument as a precedent for a presidential pardon of Brasillach, but he didn't. Someone was still needed to fill the symbolic role, the death sentence that, in Lindon's words, would be "indispensable from the point of view of exemplariness."

———

In Brasillach's pardon file, after the opinions of Reboul and Boissarie, came a memo from Jacques Isorni, Brasillach's defense lawyer, requesting an audience with de Gaulle. Attached to his request is the most surprising document in the entire pardon file: a letter handwritten by Brasillach himself to de Gaulle, asking the general to save his life.

Brasillach's letter, simple and direct, follows the strategy both of Isorni's defense and of the writers' petition in its insistence on Brasillach as the son of a soldier who fell for France, in its reminder that

Brasillach turned himself in voluntarily, and that the state had held his
mother hostage.

"My General," began Brasillach, the reserve lieutenant, as though he
were still a part of the French army, addressing his commander in chief:

Fresnes, January 28, 1945

Mon Général,

*I was condemned to death the 19th of January by the Court of Justice of
Paris, after having turned myself in as a prisoner last September, when I learned
of the arrest of my mother.*

*Thirty years ago, my mother learned of the death of my father, Lieutenant
Brasillach, who fell in the battle of El Herri in Morocco on the 13th of November,
1914, in the Laverdure column.*

It is for her that I have the honor of asking that you pardon me.

I beseech you, my General, to accept this expression of my duty.

Robert Brasillach

This sober, handwritten letter has never been described or quoted
by Isorni in his memoirs, probably because Brasillach's lawyer, a lifelong
anti-Gaullist, would never want to admit that Brasillach had asked de
Gaulle for anything.

———

Next, in the pardon file, came the letters from the public, nearly sixty of
them. All but three or four were signed. All were favorable to Brasillach.

Many of them gave literary arguments for pardon. There was a
letter from Marcelle Tassencourt, the wife of Brasillach's school chum
Thierry Maulnier. She was a well-known actress, but she pretended
to be an "unknown," representing many "unknowns" who wished for
Brasillach's pardon. She compared the death sentence of Brasillach to
the death of two poets who had died in deportation and whom she
called "poets with pure hands": "Must we also lose Robert Brasillach,
an authentic poet, as guilty as he might be?" There were many letters
from readers of Brasillach: "Have pity on this unhappy young man who
has written such beautiful books. He enchanted our youth." There was
a letter from an unemployed former typesetter at the Action Française,
arguing how much more patriotic Brasillach was than the worst of the *Je
Suis Partout* gang, Lesca and Laubreaux. Many of the letters mentioned
the qualities of specific Brasillach books. Fellow POW officers wrote in
praise of *Bérénice*, the play that had provided a night of entertainment
in the Oflag at Soest. Other letter writers mentioned *Les Sept couleurs*

and *Comme le temps passe.* They argued that de Gaulle needed to save Brasillach because he was a writer, because France needed the prestige of her thinkers in the postwar era. Brasillach's editor at Plon wrote to say that during a time when paper shortages radically curtailed publishing, Brasillach had never asked the Germans for extra paper supplies and was content to have his work published in very small print runs.

There was a smaller number of letters more political in nature, by people with obvious Gaullist credentials, hoping to influence the General in this weighty affair. Maurice Schumann, distinguished *résistant* and the voice of Free France in London, had written Isorni to report that he had been able to confirm a rumor: Brasillach had indeed contributed to preventing the execution of Jean Cavaillès, the great mathematician affiliated with the Ecole Normale. No one knew yet that Cavaillès was finally shot by the Nazis in 1944. Schumann's letter was forwarded by Isorni to de Gaulle and included in the pardon file. A similar letter from the wife of Georges Bruhat, head of the Ecole Normale, arrested by the Gestapo and deported in 1944, informed de Gaulle directly that she believed a member of Brasillach's family who had informed her that Brasillach had attempted to prevent the deportation of her husband, out of feelings of solidarity for his old school. It wasn't yet known that Bruhat died in 1944, at Buchenwald.

Brasillach's commanding officer in the prison camp described the writer's patriotism, his disinterestedness, along with his "misplaced zeal." He gave de Gaulle his own patriotic credentials: three brothers killed by the enemy, a cousin shot by the Germans in the resistance, another cousin tortured and shot, another cousin tortured and deported, three other cousins, deported. Fourteen citations, a military medal, and two Legions of Honor among them. In the name of his family, he asked for Brasillach's pardon.

Then there were the petitions. A typed copy of the famous petition in Brasillach's favor signed by fifty-nine writers and intellectuals was forwarded by Isorni, along with a memo saying he would bring the actual signatures when he met with de Gaulle. There were several other petitions as well, one sent by students, two sent by fellow prisoners of war, and one by right-wing supporters of Brasillach, blaming the Third Republic for the fall of France.

The first prisoner-of-war petition describes how "by our side, in a noisy room, [Brasillach] wrote one of his most beautiful novels, without a single cross-out," how indifferent he was to material life, how badly he dressed, how he gave his packages away to the needy of the camp.

A separate petition signed by officers in the camp described his literary and intellectual contribution to camp life, through his public lectures.

A petition from students was less credible since almost every signature emanated from the same address, in the fifth arrondissement near the Ecole Normale. The repetitive addresses did not support the claim made by one student in a letter, that Brasillach had the support of "the entire student milieu."

In addition to the literary defense, based on Brasillach's qualities as a writer, the letters were full of moral and historical arguments. Many of them referred to the fact that the other members of *Je Suis Partout,* far more guilty than Brasillach, had fled to Germany to avoid justice, whereas Brasillach turned himself in out of patriotism. Others referred to Brasillach's father.

———

In favor of pardon, de Gaulle had before him the petition from writers and intellectuals, the petition from Brasillach's fellow prisoners of war, the mass of letters from the public about Brasillach's courage and literary achievements, the two letters indicating that Brasillach had tried to save Cavaillès and Bruhat, affiliated with the Ecole Normale. De Gaulle must also have felt pressure to pardon from his personal secretary, Claude Mauriac, François Mauriac's son. On de Gaulle's desk were Boissarie's remarks about the resemblance of the Brasillach case to the Béraud case, where he had granted a pardon several weeks earlier. Against pardon, he had the powerful arguments of the magistrature and the Pardon Commission, and his own sense of justice and history.

The night of February 3, Isorni was called by the Director of Criminal Affairs and driven for his visit to General de Gaulle in a small house—a *pavillon*—bordering the Bois de Boulogne. The final act in any pardon procedure is this formal visit by the condemned man's lawyer to the President of the Republic, a ritual left over from the old monarchist tradition of royal mercy. In February 1945, there was as yet no President of the Republic, but as provisional head of the Liberation government, de Gaulle filled the role.

Isorni described the visit minute by minute, in a text he published twice—first in the *Cahiers des amis de Robert Brasillach,* then in his memoirs. His is the only eyewitness account of this decisive event we shall ever have. He remembers that he spoke for thirteen minutes without much more than a nod from the General. He spoke first in the name of Brasillach's mother, reminding the General that Brasillach's father had died for France. De Gaulle answered, "I know." He argued that there was neither money nor blood involved in Brasillach's case, and that a pardon could be a sign of national reconciliation. He remembers thinking at first that de Gaulle looked touched by his argument, and then wondering whether it wasn't he, Isorni, who was moved by his own words. He asked de Gaulle if he wished any further information and he remembers that de Gaulle answered, "*Ce n'est pas la peine*" [it's not worth the trouble]. He remembers that when he offered to leave a copy of the writers' petition, de Gaulle said it wasn't necessary and asked, nonchalantly, if Abel Hermant had signed. Isorni took this as an insult, since Hermant, a notorious collaborator, was imprisoned in Fresnes awaiting judgment. "The petition is mainly signed by adversaries," Isorni answered. It was something of an exaggeration.

It sounds from his account as though de Gaulle refused to look at the petition. What Isorni neglects to say is that he had already sent a typed version of the petition to the pardon commission on February 1. It was part of the dossier de Gaulle had in front of him on February 3, and it is still in the pardon file today.

What Isorni remembered vividly from his interview was de Gaulle's face, his narrow forehead, his blue eyes set too close together, his slack chin, and his cigar. And the cigar smoke that blew in Isorni's face. What stayed with Brasillach's defender for the rest of his life was de Gaulle's silence in that moment, the silence of a king. In his typed notes on the meeting, though not in his memoirs, Isorni wrote: "I can't say that I was in the presence of a wall—rather a sphinx—or rather still a man full of a sense of his own dignity whose will—rather than his nature—inspired him to remain inscrutable."

———

After reviewing all the material, de Gaulle refused the request for pardon. The decree to carry out the death sentence, signed by de Gaulle and his Minister of Justice, carries the date of February 3, 1945. One can't know for sure—the document could have been signed between 10:30 P.M. and midnight, after Isorni left—but it is possible that de Gaulle had made up his mind about Brasillach before Isorni even arrived at his office.

———

On the morning of February 6, the prison barber came to the cell to cut Brasillach's hair. Brasillach said his last confession to a priest. Reboul arrived representing the state, along with Isorni and Mireille Noël for the defense. Madame Reboul and Madame Isorni went to mass together at St. Nicolas du Chardonnet church that morning. Brasillach asked

Reboul, as a last wish, if he would free Bardèche from prison for the good of his family. To his defense lawyers, Brasillach said, "Today is February 6; you will think of me and you will think, too, of the others who died the same day, eleven years ago." He was carefully marking the coincidence of his death with the nationalist riots of 1934.

Then a transport vehicle came to take Brasillach to the fort at Montrouge.

The firing squad of twelve lined up. Brasillach refused to tie a scarf around his eyes. As they fired, he cried out, "Vive la France quand même" [long live France anyway]. It was a perfect last line for Brasillach, typical in its combination of ideological fervor and a taste for the joke and "bon mot"—saying the right thing at the right time.

Brasillach had put his few possessions in a bag, to which he attached a note: "Please give this bag and its contents to Maurice Bardèche." When the firing squad had finished, Isorni gathered a drop of Brasillach's blood on a handkerchief for his loved ones.

By now, the story of de Gaulle's refusal to pardon Brasillach has reached mythical proportions. Everyone in France who knows anything about the Brasillach trial has heard the following story about the contents of the pardon file.

It is said that de Gaulle simply made a mistake, that a complicated story of mistaken identity and a false piece of information in a judicial file led to Brasillach's execution. The story has all the elements of a good conspiracy theory. De Gaulle is supposed to have refused to pardon Brasillach because there was a photograph in Brasillach's file showing him wearing a German uniform.

The photograph that did Brasillach in, according to legend, came from the cover of the magazine *Ambiance*—a kind of postwar socialist *Life*—where it had been published two days before the Brasillach trial, on January 17, 1945. It was a photo taken when Brasillach had accompanied Jacques Doriot and members of the collaborationist press to the Eastern front, an anti-Soviet propaganda trip where they visited the site of the massacre of Polish officers at Katyn. In the center of the photo we see Jacques Doriot, leader of the major French fascist political party, the Parti Populaire Français. He is wearing the uniform of the league of French volunteers in the German army—a Nazi uniform. To his left is Brasillach, in civilian clothes; to his right another *Je Suis Partout* writer, Claude Jeantet. The caption reads:

> The ignoble smile of a sad individual: Doriot, in German masquerade, looks delighted, as do his two companions in shame: Jeantet and Brasillach. It is not a smile guaranteed to last for long.

The legend, recounted at length by Brasillach's biographer, Pierre Pellissier, has it that a government official slipped this magazine cover into the Brasillach file before it was sent to Charles de Gaulle for his consideration of pardon, and that a hasty look at the image convinced de Gaulle that Brasillach—not Doriot—was the man wearing the Nazi uniform. Any French writer donning a German uniform was proof enough of treason, de Gaulle is supposed to have said to an aide. Doriot bore little resemblance to Brasillach—he was a bear of a man, Brasillach a lamb by comparison. The only similarity was that they both wore the same standard issue, black owl round glasses. Thus, the right-wing legend goes, Brasillach, one of the few French witnesses to the Soviet massacre at Katyn, was put to death, and the mystery of Katyn would remain unsolved until after the demise of the Eastern bloc in the 1980s.

It is a neat story and it is grandiose. It also has the ideological advantage of substituting the single incident at Katyn for the sum of Nazi war crimes.

There is no such photo in the official administrative pardon file, which was put in a safe at the Archives Nationales in 1965 and which I consulted in 1998. The photo could have been removed, but it's not there now.

Alain Peyrefitte, one of de Gaulle's closest advisers, tells in a book published in 1997 that when he looked at Robert Brasillach's pardon file in the 1960s, he noticed that de Gaulle had pencilled in the margins, "Brasillach wouldn't have wanted it [the pardon]." This second myth about the pardon file is more suggestive than the first: it resonates with the theme of Brasillach's self-sacrifice. This remark was nowhere in the file I saw. Of course, there could be another file containing the photo or the pencilled remark, in de Gaulle's personal archives, which are closed to the public until the year 2005. There is always another file somewhere, always a missing piece.

In writing about his decisions during the Purge in his war memoirs, de Gaulle never mentions Brasillach by name. He does pause to justify a single decision he made not to pardon an unnamed writer. This writer can be no other than Brasillach:

> If they hadn't served the enemy directly and passionately, I com-
> muted their sentence on principle. In the opposite case—the only
> one—I didn't feel I had the right to pardon. For in literature as
> in everything, talent confers responsibility [*le talent est un titre de
> responsabilité*].

Brasillach's talent and intelligence, the argument made in the bulk of the letters in the pardon file and the very cornerstone of Isorni's defense, seem to have decided de Gaulle in favor of the death sentence.

———

We know that much about de Gaulle's attitude. What about the nation at large? A public opinion poll was taken shortly after the Brasillach verdict. Although later there would be revulsion against the execution of a writer, the poll, published in March 1945, was based on a survey begun on January 25, six days after the trial, and completed February

3, three days before the execution. It concluded that 52 percent of the French public approved the Brasillach condemnation; 11 percent opposed it.

Dossiers were moving through the Paris Court of Justice at an amazing speed. As of January 1945 the court had seen 106 trials and had declared 18 death sentences, of which 12 were carried out. In the month of February alone, there were 32 trials in Paris, and 1 death sentence carried out—that of Brasillach. The winter of Brasillach's trial was the apogee of the court's short life; the staff was functioning at an almost impossible pace, especially difficult since the Court of Justice was a brand-new jurisdiction with all new rules and procedures.

A year later, in April 1946, Pierre-Henri Teitgen, Minister of Justice, gave a lecture defending the actions of the Court of Justice. He told his audience that he was often criticized for the court's leniency. 108,338 cases had been opened as of March 1946; 19,000 cases were left to judge. "Haven't you let too many get away?" he claimed he was frequently asked. To respond to this charge, he cited figures from the French Revolution. The revolutionary tribunals of 1793, he reported, had condemned 17,500 people, a paltry sum compared to the numbers judged by the Court of Justice.

That fall, the trial known as the "*Je Suis Partout* trial" took place in Paris. The defendants were Pierre-Antoine Cousteau, Lucien Rebatet, and Claude Jeantet, Brasillach's "hard-line" fascist colleagues at the newspaper he left in 1943. The day of Brasillach's execution, these colleagues were hiding from justice at Sigmaringen, Germany, where they dreamed of forming a French fascist government in exile. In reaction to Brasillach's death, Cousteau broadcast the following comments on the radio station he had set up, Radio-Patrie:

> They shot Robert Brasillach. They dared to do it. They killed a thirty-three-year-old [sic] boy, whose mischievous glance was full of all the hope of youth. Robert Brasillach was one of the most talented of our times, one of the most intelligent, one of those who best honored French letters and honored France, period. He was shot by General de Gaulle. . . . The Jews demanded the blood of this righteous man.

This was the state of mind of the man who was returned to France and tried with his colleagues on November 18, 1946. In the *Je Suis Partout* trial Jeantet got forced labor. Cousteau and Rebatet were condemned to death, then pardoned. Their sentences were commuted to forced labor. Eventually, they were all amnestied. When he was interviewed on French radio in 1969, a free man since 1952, Lucien Rebatet said that Brasillach had "saved our lives by dying first."

The pardoning of Rebatet and Cousteau came nearly two years after Brasillach's execution. Despite the myth that "writers took the fall" for collaboration, very few writers had actually gone to their deaths, and those who did—Chack, Suarez, Ferdonnet, Luchaire, and Brasillach—were tried as propagandists. Among them, Ferdonnet was the most classic traitor: married to a German woman, living in Germany, broadcasting anti-French propaganda over the German airwaves, he had been totally identified with the Nazi cause since the 1930s. Luchaire, head of the syndicate of the French press during the Occupation, was part of the high society of the collaboration. Chack and Suarez, like Brasillach, were ideologues, writing in favor of collaboration in pro-German newspapers. Among influential literary figures who might have gone on trial, two of the most important escaped Brasillach's fate. Drieu la Rochelle, dedicated fascist theorist and wartime editor of the *Nouvelle Revue Française,* committed suicide on March 15, 1945, the evening he received a mandate for his arrest. Céline, deeply involved in French anti-Semitic movements and author of incendiary pamphlets, fled to Germany, then to Denmark, where he was detained. In 1949 the Paris Court of Justice condemned him in absentia to one year in prison, and gave him a fine. After the Court of Justice was dissolved, a military court found him eligible for amnesty as a wounded veteran of the First World War.

By the time of the *Je Suis Partout* trial in late 1946, the hottest moment of the Purge was over. The public had begun to criticize the harsh sentencing, and amnesty was already in the air. Many analysts of the trial have wondered: If Brasillach had fled, if Isorni had delayed, if the procedure could have been slowed down by even six months, might he have lived? Would he be sitting with his cohorts in the Académie Française today, a venerable eighty-eight-year-old writer?

TWELVE AFTER THE TRIAL

The Brasillach trial affected all who participated in it, and many who only thought about it. From the Parisian intellectuals who debated the consequences of the death sentence, to Brasillach's own family, his prosecutor, his defense lawyer, and the members of the jury, the event set lives on a new course. It was a trauma, an opportunity, a crisis of conscience.

The Writers
Whether they had signed in his favor or vehemently refused to sign, French writers were eager to exchange opinions about Brasillach's execution. He was one of them. For at least a year following the execution, one can say with no exaggeration that the death of Robert Brasillach was at the forefront of every French writer's mind.

A month after the execution, the newspaper *Carrefour* ran a series of articles by prominent intellectuals on "The responsibility of the writer." Brasillach was mentioned in nearly every column. The overall message of the series was that writers were indeed responsible for the political consequences of their words, and that the Brasillach verdict was justified. Pierre Seghers, a resistance poet, was one of the most specific:

> If a writer writes in a pro-Nazi newspaper in the presence of Germans, "It seems that Pierre Emmanuel is a communist and I'm the only one who doesn't know it," he's no longer a writer but an informer. When, on the same day, another "collaborator" signs his name to this suggestion: "To bring France back to life [*relever*], we have only to lead the communists to the moat at Vincennes"; he is putting the blood of patriots on his conscience. If Brasillach is dead in this same moat, if he fell in turn, this is justice.

In echoing the state in its judgment of writers like Brasillach, intellectuals like Seghers set the moral tone for the postwar republic of letters. Sartre made a similar claim in his polemical introduction to the first issue of *Les Temps Modernes* in October 1945: Ideas mattered more than words. Along with ideas come political responsibility, ethics, moral rectitude.

Jean Paulhan was the first to punch holes in the Sartrian vision. For him there was something nonsensical about the fact that it was Brasillach, of all people, who had come to stand for the crimes of the intellectual during the Occupation:

> The fact that a person as frivolous as Brasillach could behave in a manner as to be, one day, justly worthy of death, this says much about a profound incoherence of our mores.

As Cocteau put it, Brasillach was "absurd *and* harmful." They were both trying to understand the transformative power of the trial: through the magic of Isorni's defense, and through Brasillach's own performance, he had entered the Salle des Assises harmful but frivolous, and emerged from it condemned, and dignified.

Paulhan's sense of the incoherence of Brasillach's verdict evolved into an ironic, then critical, attack against the Purge itself. In May 1945, Paulhan quipped in *Lettres Françaises* that if the collaborationist writers were blacklisted they would have too much free time to write: "In five or ten years they'll return in force with ripe works . . ." A year later he resigned from the CNE and became a leading spokesperson for what he called the "writer's right to error." His position was both theoretical and specific: Paulhan was instrumental in helping Céline, exiled in Denmark, get his start on the postwar literary scene. By 1951, in his fiercely polemical *Lettre aux directeurs de la résistance,* he attacked the judicial purge, the constitution of juries using militants from the resistance, the text of article 75 with its insistence on the illegality of the French government from 1940 to 1944. The Liberation, he claimed, had "400,000 victims" to its name.

By 1948, his tone was one of disgust at the violent positions writers had taken against one another during the Purge. He wrote: "I have great respect for judges and for the men of the police, but in the end, I'm not one of them." He concluded that writers should conduct themselves towards one another neither as judges nor as snitches: "ni juges, ni mouchards." It was the view of a writer and an editor who had seen writers get in trouble politically on the left and on the right, and finally, it was Paulhan's way of retreating to higher ground. He was known at Gallimard in the postwar years as "the pope of literature."

Albert Camus's position on the Purge also evolved as a consequence of the Brasillach condemnation. In the intense months of 1944–1945, he was neither as disdainful towards the Purge as Paulhan, nor as certain of harsh postwar justice as Seghers and Sartre. In 1948 he stated publicly that Mauriac had been right in emphasizing forgiveness, rather than punishment. The Brasillach case had presented him with the kind of "neither-nor" moral dilemma that often sparked his best writing. In a diary where he wrote about his work-in-progress and planned new work, Albert Camus notes, in 1946:

> Prepare a book of political texts around Brasillach.

Camus never started the Brasillach book. Instead, in 1947, he published *The Plague,* his allegory of life in occupied France. The Brasillach case remained a paradigm for him of the limits of violence to fight violence. As the conflict in Algeria was heating up, putting him in a political quandary that surpassed even what he had experienced during the Purge, he wrote a short story called "The Guest," about a *pied-noir* schoolteacher who is asked to escort an Arab, a petty murderer, to the police station: "That man's stupid crime revolted him, but to hand him over was contrary to honor."

———

"Oeil pour oeil," [Eye for an eye] Simone de Beauvoir's account of the Brasillach trial in *Les Temps Modernes,* published in February 1946, exactly a year after the event, was the first extended reflection on the Brasillach verdict. With none of Paulhan's irony, Beauvoir insisted on Brasillach's worthiness at the moment of his trial, the bravery with which he acknowledged responsibility for his acts. She pointed out, too, that the theatrical nature of a trial could seduce you into forgetting why it needed to happen in the first place. Brasillach's crimes, in her view, were not adequately covered by the charge of treason for which he was condemned by the court. Brasillach was accountable for a more profound crime, "the degradation of man into a thing." For this crime of treating men as less than human, she says, "no indulgence is permissible." In Beauvoir's prose, the analysis of Brasillach's crimes of denunciation— so pointed in the prosecution at the trial—could now take on a more general, philosophical slant. Even twelve months' perspective had made a difference in the sense of who Brasillach had been.

How the world had changed in those twelve months! Pétain and Laval had been tried—one pardoned, the other executed; the concentration camps were liberated, the few survivors home, barely alive. The excesses of the Purge—the summary executions of members of the Milice in the first months of the Liberation, the surfeit of unfounded arrests, the blacklists of writers—were starting to be criticized. The Nuremberg trials of the major Nazi war criminals, underway since November 1945, had introduced a new legal concept, "crimes against humanity." These crimes, distinct from war crimes, focused on the death camps, on the murder, extermination, enslavement, and deportation of civilian populations. Persecution on political, racial, and religious grounds was the criterion for crimes against humanity; the mass murder of the Jews by the Nazis was its demonstration. Yet the judges at Nuremberg found it difficult to distinguish these crimes from regular war crimes, and limited their jurisdiction to what had taken place after the start of the war. Janet Flanner, writing for *The New Yorker,* complained that the concept of crimes against humanity was "the most nebulous possible charge." With her rather startling phrase—"degradation of man into a thing," Simone de Beauvoir was echoing the articulation of crimes against humanity taking place at the Nuremberg trials during the months when she drafted her essay. However nebulous their first legal articulation, crimes against humanity—the idea that humanity itself might be endangered by human will and action—had a profound effect on Beauvoir's essay and on all subsequent thinking about the Second World War.

Seventeen years later, Beauvoir felt that time had done nothing to attenuate her anger, or her sense that the death sentence for Robert Brasillach had been just: "There are words as murderous as gas chambers. . . . In the case of Brasillach, there was no question of a mere 'offense of opinion'; his denunciations, his advocacy of murder and genocide constituted a direct collaboration with the Gestapo."

Maurice Bardèche

Technically, the Brasillach trial was about treason against the nation, not about race or genocide. Beauvoir was the first analyst to suggest that what Brasillach had done might be considered a kind of crime against humanity of the pen. The Holocaust played a relatively minor role in this as in other Purge trials, in part because the world was still numb and relatively uninformed about what had happened. Today, on the contrary, the trial and execution's importance is far more connected to issues of race and the Holocaust than it is to treason. At the heart of this legacy is the activism of Maurice Bardèche, Brasillach's brother-in-law.

The day of Brasillach's execution, Reboul had made a promise to Brasillach that he would release his brother-in-law so that he could take care of his family. Bardèche was released from Fresnes prison in April. The evidence gathered—a few literary and film articles from *Je Suis Partout*—was deemed insufficient to warrant a trial. For Maurice Bardèche, the death of Brasillach meant the loss of his brother-in-law, his housemate, his best friend. A Purge commission in the university had stripped him of his teaching post at Lille. The apartment where he had lived with Brasillach was requisitioned. His brother, Henri, would die in forced labor. Bardèche's world was shattered. He says in his *Souvenirs* that he can't even remember the months following Brasillach's execution. What he does say is that he felt an overwhelming sense of failure, a sense of having deserted his best friend by not having been able to save him. Loss of memory, he writes, "was like a balm, a dressing, by which nature, without consulting us, helps us to tolerate the burning of our conscience."

It was in this state of protective amnesia that Bardèche began his career as a polemicist. After finishing an academic book on Stendhal, filtering his experience of the 1945 Purge through his reading of Napoleon's defeat at Waterloo, Bardèche wrote a defense of the legality of Vichy in the form of a letter to François Mauriac. He asked Mauriac, who had lobbied so selflessly for Brasillach's pardon, to admit he had been wrong, wrong to have participated in the resistance, wrong to have supported de Gaulle, wrong to have been a member of the Comité National des Ecrivains.

Then came *Nuremberg ou la terre promise* [Nuremberg or the promised land], an attack on the Nuremberg trials. To publish it he set up his own private publishing operation, calling it "Les Sept Couleurs," a reference to Brasillach's 1939 fascist novel. The judgment at Nuremberg, he argued, was a setup, a publicity scam, an "assembly of Negro Kings." The people deported for their resistance activities should never have defended the cause of the Jews. Whatever had befallen the Jews was just punishment for the world war they had wanted. Postwar concentration camp museums, with their representations of a holocaust, were orchestrated by Jewish technicians. Extermination itself was nothing but the consequence of a new technology of war. The true victims of World War II were the Germans, not the Jews.

A resistance group and a federation of Jewish veterans filed a civil suit against Bardèche under a legislation outlawing "apology for murder." Bardèche was tried and acquitted. The plaintiffs appealed the verdict. Waiting for the decision of the appeals court, Bardèche launched his public career as a neofascist, appearing as the French representative at the first international meeting of European neofascists, in Malmö, Sweden. A year later, the judge in the appeals court said, "I consider this trial serious . . . , because M. Maurice Bardèche today, is a leader." He fined Bardèche 50,000 francs for "apology for murder" and sentenced him to a year in prison. Existing copies of his book were ordered destroyed.

Bardèche's lawyer, in both trials, was Jacques Isorni, who, in June 1951, had been elected as a representative to the National Assembly on a new extreme right-wing ticket.

1952, the year of the appeals court trial, Bardèche created a magazine called *Défense de l'Occident* [Defense of the West]. For thirty years, the magazine would provide him with a platform for airing his political beliefs. Its managing editor was Jacques Poillot, the boy who had shouted "It's a shame!" at the conclusion of the Brasillach trial.

———

By 1961 Bardèche was well established in France as the leading intellectual proponent of a neofascism. That year, he published a manifesto called *Qu'est-ce que le fascisme?* arguing that fascism had nothing to do with the politics of extermination, that fascism and anti-Semitism needed to be separated, and that the youth of the postwar world, if given a chance, would recognize their own hopes and aspirations in the fascist doctrines of the 1930s—i.e. Brasillach's doctrines. It was fascism with a smiling face.

After his legal battle over *Nuremberg ou la terre promise,* he appeared to leave the dirty work of blatant Holocaust denial to others. His own position was that Germany could not be held responsible for the horrors of the camps. At the same time, throughout the 1960s and 1970s, he published a whole gamut of negationist articles in his *Défense de l'Occident:* a series of articles by Paul Rassinier, the originator of the genre; Harwood's "La Vérité sur les camps de concentration allemands" [The truth about the German concentration camps], and finally, Robert Faurisson's "Le Problème des chambres à gaz" [The problem with the gas chambers], the 1978 article that would give rise to a violent public protest and would put Holocaust denial on the map. By the 1980s, Holocaust denial had become such a widespread phenomenon that historians and critics were forced to confront it—despite their fear that any attention might give the deniers credence. Bardèche was the quiet dean and mentor of the movement.

Meanwhile, Bardèche continued on his way as a literary critic, publishing *Stendhal, romancier* (1947); *Une lecture de Balzac* (1964); *Marcel Proust, romancier* (1971); *Balzac* (1980); and *L'Oeuvre de Flaubert* (1974). In the 1970s, if you picked up a mass-market paperback edition of Balzac's *Le Père Goriot* or Flaubert's *Madame Bovary,* you could read the preface by Maurice Bardèche. He was a clear, didactic writer, an excellent presenter of texts.

And so from 1947 until his death in 1998, Maurice Bardèche, emulating his brother-in-law, maintained a "double personality"—judicious, conservative literary critic on the one hand, extreme right-wing polemicist on the other.

———

We might conclude, in a vast emotional shorthand, that Bardèche expressed his mourning for Brasillach in the form of Holocaust denial. Brasillach's death sentence—on top of the loss of a brother, the loss of an academic career—gave birth in Bardèche to a fury so great that he could not take in the reality of Nazism, the genocidal program of Hitler, because taking it in would be admitting there was something just in the punishment of Brasillach. Brasillach's recommendation that Jews be deported from France, "*en bloc,* without keeping any little ones"; his denunciation of Jewish officers in a prisoner-of-war camp; the extent to which Brasillach had colluded in crimes against humanity were, for Bardèche, unthinkable truths. Holocaust denial kept pure the sullied cause for which Brasillach had died.

Marcel Reboul

In 1945, Marcel Reboul's daughter Bernadette contracted a serious illness, scarlet fever, which was followed by a double mastoid trepanation. It was then that Marcel Reboul decided to move his family to Aix, for the air; he believed later that the move had saved his daughter. He was promoted to "procureur général" in Aix, but it was a far cry from his role in the capital. He had left Paris at the height of his glory.

Reboul's role in the Brasillach trial, as well as his prosecution of Vichy's militiamen and members of the French Gestapo, made him a target after the war. There was always a discreet police protection looking after him. Bernadette remembers the little red coffins coming in the mail, delivered each day by the concierge. She remembers when they stopped coming. By the time her father moved back to Paris in 1956 to serve in the appeals court, the fuss was over. He still insisted on an unlisted number. "We received letters, tons of letters, letters of insult, for years: always anonymous, where my father was accused of having his hands covered with blood. The Brasillach trial weighed on us our whole lives."

How did the rumor get started, among Brasillach's friends, that the Brasillach trial made Reboul go mad? It was wishful thinking. One of Brasillach's schoolmates from the Ecole Normale, Thierry

Maulnier, the fellow Action Française enthusiast who had quit *Je Suis Partout* in time, and who, in 1964, would be elected a member of the Académie Française, moved into the apartment building on the rue Geoffroy St. Hilaire vacated by the Rebouls when they moved to Aix for Bernadette's health. There were any number of exchanges about phone bills, etc. But in 1985, nine years after her father's death, Bernadette Reboul picked up a book of essays about writers and their cats, called *Chat plume: 60 écrivains parlent de leurs chats* [Cat pen: 60 writers talk about their cats], and in an essay by Thierry Maulnier about his wife's collection of strays from the Jardin des Plantes, she read the following:

> When the little studio on the rue de Bellechasse got too small for us, we looked for an apartment. Jacques Isorni offered us one that had just become vacant, under dramatic circumstances. They had to take the occupant away to a rest home, he'd become half insane: this was the poor prosecutor Reboul, fallen into a terrible nervous depression after having sought the death penalty for Robert Brasillach, whom Jacques Isorni was defending. Reboul thought he'd be pardoned.

In 1996, I heard the same rumor from the owner of a bookstore on the rue St. Martin specializing in right-wing literature.

Throughout his career, Marcel Reboul maintained the dignified "silence of the magistrature" concerning his role in the Purge trials. As for the much-assailed hypocrisy of the magistrature in its smooth passage from Vichy to the Liberation, he expressed himself on this point most clearly in his prosecution of Alexandre Angeli, an administrative prefect for the Vichy region who was sentenced to death in Lyon, then retried in Paris in 1946 and sentenced to four years in prison. Reboul acknowledged how many French administrators had chosen to stay at their posts under Vichy. It was an oblique way of saying that he was one of them. He argued fervently that they could not use Vichy law to justify their actions. They had been duty bound to subvert those laws, or to refuse to obey them, whenever their refusal might serve the French nation. He gave examples: A policeman could refuse to arrest a resistance fighter; a doctor could refuse to deliver a certificate of Jewish identity that would send the bearer to a concentration camp. Everyone had a margin of initiative.

His career wasn't waylaid, even by the move to Aix. He went on to become Procureur in Toulouse, Procureur Général in Nancy, then a judge of the appeals court in Paris. His last position was as the first dean at the new University of Toulon law school. His legs, which had never been strong, had failed him. His students had to carry him in their arms up a flight of stairs so he could teach. The strength of his voice remained.

Jacques Isorni

The Brasillach trial set Jacques Isorni on a political path from which he never strayed. Seven months later, someone young was needed to defend the Marshal Pétain; Isorni's defense for Brasillach had distinguished him. One of a team of three defense lawyers, Isorni pronounced his "plaidoirie" for Pétain in the High Court of Justice before thirty leading figures of the resistance. Against those who wanted to paint the hero of Verdun as senile, no longer responsible for his actions, Isorni argued proudly that Pétain's Vichy government had saved France from a much worse fate. Isorni's "plaidoirie" was considered a great success. Believing that de Gaulle would commute Pétain's death sentence to life in prison, Isorni told his client that "more than a moderate sentence, [the death sentence] would contribute to the grandeur and influence of his legend." The Brasillach case had strengthened his belief in the dignity of martyrdom. De Gaulle did commute the death sentence, and Pétain spent his remaining days interned on the Ile d'Yeu. Isorni's campaign for a retrial failed.

In 1946, Isorni published the transcript of the Brasillach trial with a sentimental preface and an epilogue recounting the day of the execution. "A tragedy from antiquity in three voices," his editor told him. He signed a copy for Marcel Reboul: "To Marcel Reboul, to the loyal adversary, who in his heart, I am sure, would have preferred a defeat. This sign of friendship, Jacques Isorni."

In 1951, Isorni was elected deputy to the National Assembly on an extreme right-wing ticket. His election represented the first political breath of life for the far right since the Purge. He would be a key figure in pushing through legislation amnestying collaborators. There were approximately 40,000 people imprisoned for collaboration; by early 1964, everyone had been released.

Pétain died in his island prison in 1951, the year Isorni was elected. Isorni's commitment to Pétain didn't end there. He devoted the remaining years of his own life to the effort to get Pétain's remains moved from the prison on the Ile d'Yeu to Verdun, the battlefield that had made Pétain's military reputation in World War I. He never succeeded.

In the 1960s Isorni's sympathies went with the OAS, the splinter group in the French army who plotted to keep Algeria French. Isorni defended a group of soldiers, sympathizers with the OAS, who had

attempted to assassinate de Gaulle at Petit-Clamart in 1962. The ring
leader of the group—defended by another lawyer—was executed. Isorni
managed to save his own clients from the death sentence. It cost him.
His venomous rhetoric against the special military court convened to
hear the charges earned him a three-year suspension from the Paris bar.
It was during this suspension that he wrote his memoirs.

In a bizarre incident in 1973, Pétain's remains were stolen and
recovered in a Paris garage—at least one version of the story has it that
the garage was owned by Isorni. Isorni suspected that the political stunt
was the work of his colleague Tixier-Vignancour, the lawyer who had
represented Céline in the Purge and another bastion of the postwar right.

Isorni devoted an entire book, *La Fièvre verte* [Green fever], to his
quest to be elected to the Académie Française. When he failed, he
concluded that the Académie was still intimidated by the Purge. On
the contrary, the Académie had elected Carcopino, former Minister of
Education under Vichy, as early as 1955. Paul Morand, ambassador to
Romania under Vichy who had taken refuge in Switzerland in 1944,
entered the Académie in 1968. Gaxotte, the founding editor of *Je Suis
Partout,* became an *académicien* as well. They shared the floor with men
of the resistance, Guéhenno and Paulhan. It was Isorni himself who
was still fighting the battles of the Purge, Isorni who still saw every
conflict as a consequence of 1945. His struggle over Pétain's remains,
his burning desire to be accepted by the Académie, embittered him, and
the more embittered he was, the more he clung to his two famous lost
causes: Pétain and Brasillach. His reputation in Paris was as a brilliant
man obsessed, a gadfly. He was always admired by his colleagues at the
bar, who spoke of him with enormous affection.

When he died, in 1995, an obituary in the London *Economist* quoted
one of his favorite sayings. Perhaps it was apocryphal:

> Any fool can defend an innocent man. It requires talent to defend a
> guilty one.

The Jurors

After the Liberation, the printer Lucien Grisonnet had a contract with
the township of Aubervilliers. His shop produced the announcement of
the return to school on October 2, 1944, the instructions for the first
important postwar election, the mayor's advertisement for a municipal
adult education course, the poster explaining to residents of damaged

buildings that they could declare themselves disaster victims and receive reparations from the state. His house was listed on the 1946 tax rolls as an official "resistance group." Postwar Aubervilliers cleaned up its rubble, restored its township, built low-income housing. It was a solidly communist culture, voting on issues such as whether to name a new housing project the "Cité Ethel et Julius Rosenberg." The township was especially proud of the first electric lights on its city streets. In 1947, Lucien Grisonnet ran for the Aubervilliers city council for the first time and lost. In 1952, at age sixty-four, he received the Legion of Honor for his heroism in the First World War. In 1953 he ran again for city council, part of an anticommunist coalition whose campaign propaganda said, "We don't want a mayor who isn't ours, who is the plaything of a secret party leadership. We simply want our commune to be administered in a healthy manner." Grisonnet was no longer on the election rosters in 1959, and he disappears from the Aubervilliers phone book in 1966. His death is duly recorded on his birth certificate: September 17, 1968.

André Van der Beken, much like Lucien Grisonnet in his own community, was elected to the St. Maur city council after the war, running with the MRP, the Mouvement Républicain Populaire—a French version of the Christian Democratic Parties formed in postwar Italy and Germany, and which fared less well in France than elsewhere in Europe. Hostile to communism all his life, Van der Beken was a man of the right wing, but never the extreme right. He remained a pillar of the community, an elder in his church. He liked to read Mauriac's paper *Le Figaro,* the Protestant magazine *Réforme,* and *Le Christianisme au 20e Siècle* [Christianity in the twentieth century]. The novelists he preferred were Henry Bordeaux and Mauriac—two académiciens who had signed the petition to save Brasillach from execution—as well as classic authors such as Balzac. He didn't read modern literature. André Van der Beken died in 1991, in June; he was nearly ninety. His son Jacques described his father's difficulty towards the end of his life after a failed cataract operation left him blind in both eyes—"he who had lived for the vision of things . . ."

After his death, his children cleaned out the house on the avenue de la République. In the attic, they found a collection of newspapers from the Occupation: *Gringoire,* where Henri Béraud had published his columns, and *Je Suis Partout,* Brasillach's newspaper. Did André Van der Beken read them after the events of 1945, trying to understand

Brasillach, the man he had condemned to death, and Béraud, the man de Gaulle had spared? Or had he read them during the war, curious about the enemies of the resistance?

After his appearance in the census of 1954 as "master worker electrician," Emile Jean-Marcel Riou disappears in my paper chase. An electrician, a simple man from a rural township, a member of the FFI. He wasn't on the city council. He didn't have any children. He died in 1964. We don't know much more.

Of all the jurors, René Desvillettes has the only sensational postwar history. Duty on the Purge jury was one of many political acts that would help Desvillettes along in his political career and lead to his victory as mayor of Champigny-sur-Marne in 1947. His deputy mayor, Yvonne Laffargue, the wife of a metro employee, became his mistress. When Yvonne Laffargue's husband Jean learned of his wife's affair, he confronted Desvillettes. The mayor offered Laffargue a visa for Poland so he could start life anew there, but before the arrangements could be made, Laffargue surprised the lovers and shot Desvillettes to death with a German Mauser, a gun that was probably left over from the German Occupation.

"It's very simple," Jean Laffargue testified at his murder trial, "ever since my wife became deputy mayor, my socks weren't mended. Then I learned that our mayor was taking advantage of gold wedding anniversaries or the sale of our newspaper [*L'Humanité*] on Sunday morning to cheat on me with my wife." Or, as one of the newspapers put it, "Madame Yvonne Laffargue found in the years that followed the Liberation a whole new distraction for French women: politics. And from a simple Party affiliate she soon became a local militant."

The trial of René Desvillettes's murderer took place in the same courtroom of the Palais de Justice where Desvillettes himself had sat five years earlier on the Brasillach jury. Alex Ancel, who had covered the Brasillach trial, covered the Desvillettes murder for the same newspaper, *Le Parisien Libéré*. The prosecutor in the trial was Raymond Lindon, the man who had prosecuted Henri Béraud and so many other collaborators during the Purge. The murder of René Desvillettes by Jean Laffargue was considered a crime of passion. Laffargue was sentenced to five years in prison, with a suspended sentence. The day the decision was rendered, July 24, 1951, was the same day the papers announced the death of Marshal Pétain, on the 23rd, in his exile prison on the Ile d'Yeu. The political dramas of the Purge had given way to a suburban scandal, a *fait divers*. An era had come to an end.

THIRTEEN JUSTICE IN HINDSIGHT

Every few years, on the February 6 anniversary of Brasillach's death, the French daily newspaper *Le Monde* runs a commemorative page about the case. People send in letters debating the issues, and the polemic flames up again. The issues are profound and irresolvable. Why was a writer punished for what happened in France between 1940 and 1945? Why this writer and not others? When are words as noxious as actions? Did Brasillach deserve to die for what he wrote? Certainly we cannot judge this trial today the way we would have judged it in 1945, when the Second World War was still going on and when France was in the midst of its immense suffering.

The execution of Brasillach, which fulfilled a symbolic function in 1945, served, in the long run, to obfuscate the issues. The burning question became, in the years after the verdict, "Should Brasillach have been shot?" The real question—"Was Brasillach guilty?"—has proved much more difficult to keep at the center of the debate.

What Brasillach wrote was treasonous according to article 75 of the penal code. He had used his talent as a journalist to support the presence of an enemy on French soil. Treason, in 1945, was punishable by death. As critics, at a safe distance of over fifty years, we can judge his trial excessive and unfair. The jury was composed of partisans; the judges had been judges at Vichy; Brasillach was convicted for writing. In particular, there was no way that the government could prove a strict cause-effect relationship between Brasillach's violent sentences and the murders and deportations that did take place in France. Reboul said in his report to the pardon commission that Brasillach's denunciations were "sufficient for the Gestapo to be able to profit from them." He couldn't prove it absolutely. What Reboul did and could prove was desire and intent.

Brasillach was no Eichmann. The most disturbing aspect of his case is precisely that he was *not* following orders. He was acting out of his own will, volition, imagination, racism, dream of a French fascism and a France cleansed of democrats and foreigners. Both the defense and prosecution could agree on that point, and that's precisely what made him an appropriate candidate for a trial that was also a symbolic reckoning.

Is there a time in the life of a nation when such a symbolic punishment is absolutely necessary for a nation's recovery? France was shattered in 1945, depleted of its resources, with hundreds of thousands of people deported, imprisoned, missing, dead. The country had been humiliated, its people murdered, for four years, and Brasillach was publicly identified as having aided and abetted that humiliation, those murders. The war was not yet over when he was tried; his death sentence was an act of war. If Brasillach was a scapegoat, he was an important scapegoat. He represented the unreality of the intellectual elite, the ability of a man of great talent to use his talent to do harm. Of all the men who were executed for propaganda—Chack, Suarez, Ferdonnet, Luchaire— Brasillach, at age thirty-five, was both the youngest writer among them, and the only man to die with a significant literary oeuvre beyond his polemics, the only one with a conceivable posterity as a writer. This fact alone gave him a special status, though, as we saw, it did not protect him.

Although Brasillach was certainly small fry in comparison with other symbolically executed men throughout French history—the beheaded Louis XVI being the most obvious comparison—one can also argue that, for the period of the Purge, his trial was loftier in tone than any other. In Brasillach, the nation had before it a young man whose youth was caught up in the adventure of fascism; he seemed to have no other reason for being. Personal greed and corruption did not interfere with the political issues in the case. From our own distant perspective of fifty years after the fact, it seems obvious that no trial with this much symbolic weight could be entirely fair. Why was Brasillach killed when René Bousquet, the head of the Paris police who masterminded the massive roundup of Jews at the Vél d'Hiv, got only two years of "national degradation," which were suspended on the grounds that he had aided the resistance? Bousquet was not punished in 1945 because his crime—crimes against humanity, complicity in deportations to the death camps—did not yet have a name or a place in the French legal code. The purpose of the Purge was to rebuild a nation and restore its dignity. The crimes against humanity trials that have taken place in France in the 1980s and 1990s represent France's very different attempt to take responsibility for a horror that was only understood after the Purge.

Even if Brasillach had lived and were retried again today on new charges, it is an open question whether or not his written denunciations, his incitements to the extermination of Jews, could be said to constitute "crimes against humanity." The recent French trials have turned around issues of direct administrative or executive responsibility for racially motivated murder.

Looking at the trial from Brasillach's point of view gives us a very different kind of critical perspective on his death sentence. By claiming, throughout his ordeal, that he was willing to pay for his actions, eager to accept his responsibility, Brasillach was both elevating his importance and encouraging his own guilty verdict. As Roger Grenier points out in *Le Rôle d'accusé,* grand speeches are always bad for the accused. The best strategy is to say as little as possible. Both Brasillach and his lawyer had too much to say, they were arguing for an entire point of view, an interpretation of history, for posterity, for their own dignity in a future where Brasillach had already been executed. From the heroic perspective of both Isorni and Brasillach, the defendant was a figure in a tragedy by Corneille who must take responsibility, in order to die with honor. Even the right-wing anarchists at *Crapouillot* seem to acknowledge the danger of this strategy in a 1955 special issue on the Liberation trials: "Isorni's defense speech is beautiful, but it is profoundly painful to read, since, like too many speeches from that era, it was delivered in full view of the firing squad."

Finally, in looking back at what happened in 1945, it is important to remember that although the Brasillach verdict was symbolic, it was also highly efficacious—for both sides. With Brasillach's punishment, the government committed an irrevocable act, an execution that consolidated de Gaulle's power and proved the might of his newly conceived Court of Justice only four months into its operations. Brasillach's death sentence had a legitimating function. In the literary realm, too, the Brasillach death sentence reinforced the seriousness of the written word at a time when France needed to rebuild its intellectual elite. Writers knew that words counted in a court of law. This was both an intimidating and an empowering knowledge: they mattered. Thus, Brasillach's execution served the Republic he hated, and it served the literary world he had disgraced. In the long run, his execution also served his own cause—the extreme right.

FOURTEEN THE BRASILLACH MYTH

Brasillach is buried in the same grave with his mother in the Charonne cemetery, one of the few remaining village cemeteries in Paris, several green acres attached to a neighborhood church in the twentieth arrondissement. His neighbors wouldn't have pleased him. Dominating the tombs in the middle of the cemetery is the statue of Begue, known as "Magloire," who claimed to have been Robespierre's personal secretary. Along an interior wall are the unmarked graves of members of the Paris commune, shot along the "Mur des Fédérés" bordering the Père Lachaise cemetery and moved to Charonne decades later. Closer still to Brasillach is the tomb of the writer Gérard Bauer, a columnist for *Le Figaro* who liked to remind his friends that he had been denounced in *Je Suis Partout* as "half Negro, half Jew." Brasillach's eternal company also includes the family members of André Malraux, who, as one of the revolutionary writers of the 1930s, wrote his ode to Spanish Republicanism at a time when Brasillach was writing fervently in support of Franco. Malraux became everything Brasillach hated and everything he was not: world-renowned novelist, man of state, Minister of Culture under de Gaulle. Malraux is now in the Pantheon.

What place to give the Brasillach legacy today, what connection to the rise of the National Front in the 1980s and 1990s? Is he really a precursor of the new extreme right? Has he been resurrected?

A May 1998 article in France's major news magazine, *Le Nouvel Observateur,* entitled "Le Pen and His Uncles," is accompanied by a picture of Brasillach speaking at a political meeting during the Occupation. The caption reads:

> In 1944, he [Brasillach] predicted the return of the extreme right in France for the 1960s.

Brasillach never "predicted" the return of the far right. In his prison essay called "Lettre à un soldat de la classe '60," written to justify his racism and fascism, he fantasized that in the distant future, young people might read his political texts with sympathy. In 1960, a manifesto of the extreme right paid homage to Brasillach by echoing the title of that essay in a manifesto called "Manifesto of the Class of '60."

Brasillach was not a predictor, but he has been an instrument, used by the extreme right to claim a fresh intellectual genealogy in the postwar period. This genealogy was all the more necessary because of the fact that, since 1945, respectable right-wing thinking in France has been predominantly Gaullist and Republican. The extreme right, with roots in the Republic-hating Action Française, was devastated and discredited by Vichy. Its figurehead, Charles Maurras, made his exit from history as the decrepit deaf old man who cried out, "It's the revenge of Dreyfus," after he was condemned by the Lyon Court of Justice in 1945. He had his sights on the past, not the future, until the bitter end. In Brasillach, on the contrary, the extreme right has found a figure for their future: an imaginary hero, forever young, killed by the Republic he hated. The Brasillach trial provides the extreme right with a story of origins, the possibility of rebuilding itself on high esthetic ground.

Jean-Marie Le Pen, founder of the National Front party, former French deputy and member of the European parliament, has shown a consistent devotion to Brasillach's memory that is sentimental, almost familial. In the late 1960s and early 1970s, Le Pen produced a series of long-playing records giving his revisionist version of the history of World War II. On one of these LPs we hear the rare ten-second recording of Brasillach from "Voice of the Reich," decrying the massacres at Katyn. In this same period of Le Pen's flowering as an extreme right pundit, he produced a recording of Brasillach's Fresnes prison poems read by Pierre Fresnay, the beloved star of Renoir's *Grand Illusion*.

Another connection between Le Pen and Brasillach comes through Le Pen's long-standing political association with François Brigneau (born Well Allot) who was at Fresnes with Brasillach and who has been, since 1945, one of the primary Brasillach mythmakers. In 1993, Brigneau published a collection of portraits called *La Mort en face* in which he juxtaposed martyrs of the collaboration with martyrs of the resistance. It was Algeria, Brigneau explains in a preface to the book, that taught him the unity of resistance and collaboration, for in Algeria, former Free French resisters were charged with keeping Algeria French. It is an astonishing distortion of an historical tragedy. The French military in Algeria, among whom were former members of the anti-Nazi resistance, were given full police powers to suppress the Algerian revolution, and used torture methods once used on them by the Nazis to torture members of the Algerian independence movement. Brigneau turned a scandal of the Algerian conflict into a reason for celebration.

The afterword to *La Mort en face* is by Le Pen. The founder of
the National Front focuses on two of the portraits in the book, that of
Brasillach and that of d'Estienne d'Orves, a naval officer with roots in
the Action Française who became one of the first Gaullists and was shot
by the Wehrmacht in 1941. Both, says Le Pen, died at the "martyr age"
in their early thirties, like Christ:

> I made the connection between Robert Brasillach and d'Estienne
> d'Orves on the occasion of another speech at the Mutualité, last
> February 6 [on the anniversary of Brasillach's death]. I addressed
> the young people to tell them they have to get beyond the quarrels
> of their historic past, so rich in confrontations and ruptures—and
> never give up on associating in their minds and in their hearts the
> names that History has divided but that their piety must reunite. I
> quoted Robert Brasillach and d'Estienne d'Orves because, as Robert
> Brasillach wrote in one of his poems, "blood that has flowed is
> always pure blood" and the ideal served is the ideal we take into
> consideration along with the sacrifices that were made.

Le Pen thus recommends to young people that they rewrite history,
embracing within the same pious vision men who were once enemies:
As long as these men have spilled their blood for what they believed in,
they are equally worthy of respect. Brasillach equals d'Estienne d'Orves;
collaboration equals resistance; all spilled French blood is equally pure.

This transformation of the Brasillach legend has been willed onto
his memory by an extreme right that is no longer anti-Republican and
fascist so much as Catholic, patriotic, anachronistic, and ready to use
any available tradition, from fascist populism to medieval revivalism, to
reach its goals, which are electoral, rather than revolutionary. In Le Pen's
vision, what is left of fascist ideology is this desire to empty opposing
political figures of their content, leaving only symbols of reconciliation.
This is the legacy of Brasillach's notion of fraternal adversaries.

In 1965, Brasillach's complete works were published by the Club
de l'Honnête Homme in twelve volumes, compiled and edited by
Maurice Bardèche. As we have seen, many of Brasillach's most damning
statements are edited out of the volumes. A publicity brochure for the
collection states the desire of the publishers to move beyond a political
view of the writer: "The case is closed, the verdict rendered, it is useless
to keep pleading or prosecuting. We can now forget everything about
Brasillach that isn't exclusively literary." The Club de l'Honnête Homme
edition was an opportunity to move Brasillach beyond his fascist milieu,

putting him in the company of Colette, Camus, and Sartre, among the other writers published in the collection.

Despite the ambition of the complete works project to make Brasillach exclusively literary, despite the efforts of a *Société des amis de Robert Brasillach* to claim his work for a disinterested literary history, Brasillach is more marked politically today than he has been at any other time since the Occupation. He is lauded regularly in *Présent,* the weekly newspaper of the Catholic branch of the Front National, where Anne Brassié, his most enthusiastic biographer, writes a regular literary column. The political program of *Présent* is based on opposition to what the newspaper calls "false, official history," and "moral, intellectual, and physical genocide." In the ideological lexicon of *Présent,* abortion constitutes physical genocide; the "Loi Gayssot," the French legislation outlawing written expressions of Holocaust denial, is the equivalent of moral and intellectual genocide. The Loi Gayssot has been criticized by intellectuals in the Ligue des Droits de l'Homme, among others, on free speech grounds. The attack on the Loi Gayssot by *Présent,* however, is not based on a commitment to free speech. Calling the Gayssot law "intellectual genocide" is racially motivated rhetorical insolence, typical of Le Pen—and very much in Brasillach's own tradition.

To understand the political use being made of Brasillach today, nothing is more useful than watching a short videotape entitled *Il s'appelait Robert* [His name was Robert]. *Il s'appelait Robert,* advertised regularly in *Présent,* was produced by a group called "Christianity and Solidarity," whose motto is: "Against racism and for the respect of French and Christian Identity." Every twist and turn of the contemporary Brasillach myth is deployed here, in a series of soft-focus images, quick juxtapositions, religious music, and evocative quotations. We hear Pierre Fresnay reciting Brasillach's Fresnes poem, "The Judgment of the Judges," which tells us, in so many words, that Brasillach's judges are guilty and he isn't. Mood-setting images include glowing votive candles and images of the sky and beach near Brasillach's birthplace in Perpignan. We see documentary photographs of young collaborators rounded up at the Liberation, juxtaposed in a blink of the eye with photos of resistance heroes on a firing squad, followed in another blink of the eye by a fictional Brasillach facing his own execution. Here, no words are necessary. The sequencing of these images makes all these men—the nameless collaborators, the resisters, and Brasillach—equally heroic at the moment of their punishment. It is the perfect translation of Jacques Isorni's defense into film. What we have here, through images, is a vision of Brasillach so misty that his face blends with the faces of the resistance. . . . With the proper montage, a man who called for the arrest of his fellow writers in 1942 can become, in 1998, a martyred Christian, a brother to the men who were executed by the Nazis for resistance.

And his literature? In the 1970s, Brasillach's novels still bore the imprint of his 1930s publisher, the conservative, mainstream Editions Plon—publisher of Charles de Gaulle, among others. That, too, has changed. Since 1995, Robert Brasillach's books have been reissued by the tiny Editions Godefroy de Bouillon, named after the anti-Saracen crusader of the eleventh century. The political trademark of this nationalist, Catholic publisher is already present in the name. Along with Brasillach, Editions Godefroy de Bouillon publishes books with titles like *The Baptism of Clovis: Should We Burn the Arabs in France?* and *The Duty of Memory: Justice for Marshal Pétain*. Brasillach has found a home with his political descendants.

He takes his place in a political family where he is part of a whole network of positions: so-called free speech support for Holocaust revisionism; pure French ethnicity perceived as "cultural difference"; hostility to North African immigration; in a nutshell, "France for the French." For the cultural wing of the National Front, Brasillach remains the cult figure so eloquently created by Jacques Isorni: the poet of innocent awakenings, unfairly accused but willing to die for his principles—the James Dean of French fascism. The smart aleck; the ambitious, nasty, and violent writer; the denouncer, burying his own demons in sentiment and nostalgia—that reality of Brasillach has had to be revised in order for the mythical Brasillach to come to life.

The trial and execution of Brasillach, like any event with a political afterlife, tugs at us to judge, to second guess after the fact, however unscientific it is to do so. Was Brasillach guilty? Yes. Should he have been shot? No. In 1945, it was Brasillach's fascist vision that France hoped to destroy along with the man. Today, the myth of a martyred, innocent Brasillach gives sustenance to the extreme right. We can say with hindsight that this myth would not exist if Brasillach had not been put to death; that is the price exacted by de Gaulle's exemplary gesture of February 6, 1945.

I am grateful to the John Simon Guggenheim Memorial Foundation for their generous support of my research in France. A fellowship from the Stanford University Humanities Center provided a stimulating scholarly environment in the early stages of this project. The Maison Suger in Paris was my home away from home during the most intense period of my research, and I thank Jean-Luc Lory, its director, for his welcome. I also thank Dr. and Mrs. Maurice Sitomer, Vassar College, the Duke Center for European Studies, and Duke University for their support.

At the Archives Nationales de France, Section du 20ème siècle, Paule René-Bazin assisted me generously at all stages of my work. I am also grateful to Yvonne Poulle, and to Christelle Noulet, Jean Pouëssel, and Cécile Simon for their help. At the *Nouvelle Revue Française,* Editions Gallimard, I thank Nicole Aboulker for her guidance.

My thanks go to the following:

Helen Solanum, Western European Curator of the Hoover Library; Helen Baumann and Linda Purnell, Perkins Library Interlibrary Loan (Duke University); Jean-Marc Dabin, Aubervilliers municipal archives; Daniel Lancia, Aubervilliers Historical Society; Daniel Guerin, Archives Départementales de l'Yonne; Hélène Dupont, Municipal Library, Villetaneuse; Marie-Thérèse Guthauser, Archives Communales de Champigny-sur-Marne; Marie-Pascale Boreux, Archives Communales de St. Maur; Emmanuelle Jouin, Maison de la Radio; Valérie Jourdan and Anne Ducret, French Ministry of Justice; Jean Astruc, Institut d'Histoire du Temps Présent; Luce and Marion Fieschi, Club de l'Honnête Homme; Christine Petillat, Centre des Archives Contemporaines de Fontainebleau; and Yves Ozanam, Paris Bar Association (who helped me find my way to Brasillach's pardon file).

Henry Rousso showed me how to go about the complex process of obtaining access to archival sources. His critical and exacting analyses of the Purge have been my constant guides. Alain Bancaud educated me about the history of the magistrature, and helped me decipher Marcel Reboul's career dossier. Philippe Burrin helped me unravel the history of Brasillach's liberation from POW camp. Jean-Pierre Bertin-Maghit answered many questions about the Vichy film archives. Stephen Kargère steered me towards the Brasillach trial papers in the Archives de Paris. For interviews on the year 1945 and on the Brasillach trial jurors, I thank Denise Altenbourger, Stéphane Israël, André and Madeleine Mauny, Frédéric Pottecher, René Rémond, Jean-Pierre Sirinelli, Jacques Van der Beken, and Janine Van der Beken Steenkiste.

Michel Laval introduced me to the Palais de Justice and generously shared the experience of his research on the Brasillach trial. Laurent Mayali gave precious guidance on French legal research. Alain David enabled me to sit in on a trial at the Salle des Assises, and helped me locate the Isorni archives. Philippe Lejeune was my guide in Villetaneuse.

My thanks go to Linda Orr, for our conversations and our co-teaching on the period of occupied France over many years.

Among those who remember Brasillach's trial, I am especially grateful to Bernadette Reboul-Bertone for opening her father's papers and sharing her childhood memories. Arlette Grebel made the world of journalists come alive for me.

For research assistance, I thank Alden Bumstead, Alex Galloway, Beth LaMacchia, and Daniel Villanueva.

I am grateful to David Auerbach, Jane Tompkins, Marianna Torgovnick, Janice Radway, Cynthia Herrup, and Ann Smock for their criticism and encouragement in the early stages of this project. Mary Louise Roberts, Aron Rodrigue, and the Stanford History Workshop responded insightfully to "Court," as did Anne F. Garréta.

Philippe Burrin, Donald Reid, Henry Rousso, Kristin Ross, Philippe Roussin, David Schalk, Philip Watts, and Edmund White each gave me the benefit of a critical reading of the entire manuscript. Russell Harper, at the University of Chicago Press, was a talented and meticulous copyeditor. I have also benefited greatly from the keen eye and the support of Alan Thomas, my editor.

Laurel Goldman taught me the value of reading a draft out loud and using the insights of fiction along with the values of nonfiction. I am grateful for the critical insight of the members of her writing workshop: Alex Charns, Mia Bray Faulkner, Kathy O'Keeffe, Martha Pentecost, and Susie Powell.

Roger Grenier has been my guide to 1945 and my inspiration, both for thinking about this period he knows so well, and for his example as a writer. He read several manuscript drafts, and helped me see a context through the names, dates, and details surrounding the case of Brasillach.

Finally, Cathy N. Davidson has been a brilliant and demanding reader of rough drafts at every step of the process. She changed the shape of this book. I can't thank her enough.

Preface

x **the published transcript of the hastily prepared Brasillach trial:** Jacques Isorni, ed., *Le Procès de Robert Brasillach* (Paris: Flammarion, 1946).

xi **incorporated . . . crimes against humanity into internal French law:** On crimes against humanity in a French legal context and on the recent retrospective trials in France, see Richard J. Golsan's excellent collection, *Memory, the Holocaust, and French Justice* (Hanover and London: University Press of New England, 1996), especially the afterword by Bertram M. Gordon, pp. 179–198.

xii **has sharpened public interest in the Occupation:** The first book to deal with the Purge was Robert Aron's voluminous *Histoire de l'Epuration* (Paris: Fayard; tome 1, 1967; tome 2, 1969; tome 3, 1975), a passionate and ideologically marked indictment of the postwar trials by a Vichy apologist. Peter Novick's *The Resistance versus Vichy: The Purge of Collaborators in Liberated France* (New York: Columbia University Press, 1968), a scholarly study based on government documents and statistics, did not appear in French translation until 1985. Herbert R. Lottman's *The Purge* (New York: William Morrow, 1986) is a valuable synthesis. Henry Rousso's 1992 article "L'Epuration en France: Une Histoire inachevée" (*Vingtième Siècle. Revue d'Histoire*, no. 33, January–March 1992, pp. 78–105) has launched a new generation of research. Rousso's "Une Justice impossible: L'Epuration et la politique antijuive de Vichy" (*Annales*, 48ème année, no. 3, mai–juin 1993, pp. 743–770) analyzes the surprising absence of the issue of anti-Semitism from Purge trials. Rousso and Bancaud's "L'Epuration de la magistrature à la Libération (1944–1945)," in *Histoire de la justice*, Paris, no. 6 (no. spécial), 1994; and Jean-Pierre Bertin-Maghit's *Histoire du cinéma sous l'occupation: Le Monde du cinéma français de 1940 à 1946* (Paris: Olivier Orban, 1989) provide vital information on the Purge within professional groups. In the world of letters, two important studies have set the groundwork and stimulated debate. Gisèle Sapiro's "Complicités et anathèmes en temps de crise: Modes de survie du champ littéraire et de ses institutions, 1940–1953 (Académie Française, Académie Goncourt, Comité National des Ecrivains)" (Thèse de Doctorat de Sociologie, Ecole des Hautes Etudes en Sciences Sociales, 2 vols., December 19, 1994), is a sociological study of three literary institutions reacting to the Occupation and Purge. Literary critic Philip Watts's brilliant *Allegories of the Purge* (Palo Alto: Stanford University Press, 1999) argues that the Purge had a decisive effect, not only on French writers (Céline, Sartre, Blanchot, and Eluard are his examples), but on their conception of the literary enterprise itself.

xii **Varaut quoted, out of context, from an essay . . . Henry Rousso wrote:** *Plaidoirie de Jean-Marc Varaut devant la cour d'assises de la Gironde au procès de Maurice Papon, fonctionnaire sous l'occupation* (Paris: Plon, 1998). "In the trial of Robert Brasillach, editor in chief of *Je Suis Partout* . . . his 'anti-Semitic action' is well placed in the prosecution speech. . . . This attention given to Brasillach's radical anti-Semitism is even more remarkable in that this was before the shock of the liberation of the camps" (p. 67); and, "The trial of Robert Brasillach . . . where the prosecutor speaks only of 'exceptional camps in Poland' . . . shows us that the question of the racial deportations was not completely ignored" (p. 137).

xii **Reboul . . . specified that Brasillach was on trial for his treason:** "[The Republic] will not put you on trial for your tragic errors, for your deadly intolerance, for your subversive opinions, but she will, in the context of article 75 of the Penal

Code, with all the evidence assembled, put you, the clerk who has betrayed, on trial for your treason." Isorni, ed., *Le Procès de Robert Brasillach* (Paris: Flammarion, 1946), p. 137.

xiii **an intense polemic in France over access to World War II archives:** See Sonia Combe, *Archives interdites: Les Peurs françaises face à l'histoire contemporaine* (Paris: Albin Michel, 1994), and Eric Conan and Henry Rousso, "Les Archives: On nous cache tout, on nous dit rien," in *Vichy: Un Passé qui ne passe pas* (Paris: Fayard, 1994).

xiii **the ministries gave permission for me to study the files:** With one exception: my request to study the dossier of writer Céline, amnestied in 1951 by a military court, was refused by the Ministry of Defense.

xiii **the National Archives published an exhaustive guide:** Direction des Archives de France, *La Seconde guerre mondiale: Guide des sources conservées en France, 1939–1945* (Paris: Archives Nationales, 1994), under the direction of Brigitte Blanc, Henry Rousso, and Chantal de Tourtier-Bonazzi.

One   The Making of a Fascist Writer

1 **Brasillach's earliest, most romantic memory:** The Moroccan episode became the source for Brasillach's last novel, *La Conquérante.*

2 **he sent his future stepfather a letter full of insults:** Pierre Pellissier, *Brasillach . . . le Maudit* (Paris: Denoël, 1989), p. 25, refers to the letter, but does not quote it.

2 **Brasillach and Suzanne . . . delighted at putting on plays:** Ibid., pp. 26–27.

3 **stood on chairs and recited verses of poetry at one another:** In Bardèche's reconstructions of the scene, Vailland and Brasillach are reciting either Baudelaire with the poet-lovers Rimbaud and Verlaine (*Ecrits à Fresnes* [Paris: Plon, 1967], p. 12); or Baudelaire and Tristan Corbière (*Souvenirs* [Paris: Editions Buchet/Chastel, 1993], p. 31).

3 **Brasillach described Bardèche . . . as a tough fellow:** Brasillach, *Notre avant-guerre* (Paris: Plon, 1941), p. 26.

3 **Bardèche described Brasillach:** "He was very brown-skinned . . .": Bardèche, *Ecrit à Fresnes*, p. 12.

3 **Low in rank—26 out of 28, but he made it in:** Archives Nationales. Brasillach, dossier de l'Ecole Normale Supérieure. 6A AJ 255. 1928 Lettres, Brasillach, Robert.

4 **Jules Romains . . . had fictionalized the spirit of the Ecole:** Paul Gadenne, a friend from those years, published a novel after the war called *La Plage de Scheveningen* (Paris: Gallimard, 1952). Its main character, Hersant, was clearly inspired by Brasillach. Condemned to death in 1945 for fascist journalism at a newspaper called *Le Jeune Européen* [the young European], Hersant was a lighthearted sort of boy, for whom the Ecole corresponded to a desire to play a hoax on life: "What Hersant loved at the School was, of course, its uselessness, its relic-like quality, its luxury. This involved certain delusions, the pleasure of communal life without its severity, the nearly daily use of mystification and what was called the 'canular,' a practice he'd transport later into his journalism and that would constitute, finally, a notable part of the intellectual climate of *Le Jeune Européen*" (p. 45).

4 **the entire world was like a vast high school:** See Brasillach's pages on Jules Romains in *Les Quatre jeudis, Oeuvres complètes,* vol. 8 of 12 (Paris: Club de l'Honnête Homme, 1964 [vols. 1–4, 1963; vols. 5–8, 1964; vols. 9–11, 1965; vol. 12, 1966]), pp. 203–208.

5 **Brasillach was a boy who . . . :** Georges Pelorson, a classmate of Brasillach's at the Ecole Normale, described Brasillach, in an interview for a 1993 book on the history

of the school, as "a terribly feminine boy who needed a master"; he remembered being in the next room and through the thin walls, "hearing Brasillach crying and Bardèche leaving, slamming the door" (François Dufay and Pierre-Bertrand Dufort, *Les Normaliens: De Charles Péguy à Bernard-Henri Lévy, un siècle d'histoire* [Paris: Lattès, 1993], p. 150). It is difficult to evaluate how much a memory such as this one, seventy years after the events, may be tainted by reflection on Brasillach's subsequent career and death sentence. Or how Pelorson's own career as a minor official in the Vichy government might influence his critique of a fascist. One also finds the stereotype of Brasillach as a sissy in texts by Céline and Etiemble (see note to page , below). Twenty-five years after the fact, what Brasillach's one-time friend Claude Roy remembers are the writer's beginnings as an esthete: "I had gotten hooked up with a young writer from the *Action Française* that my friends thought had a wretched head for politics; he was a sweet amateur of poetry, a moderate 'humanist' and, in their opinion, not sufficiently interested in the *social* . . ." (*Moi je* [Paris: Gallimard, 1969], p. 234).

5   **"I, too, wanted to write 'in tight, voluptuous little paragraphs' ":** *Notre avant-guerre,* p. 46.

6   **a man who kept people at a "magic lantern's distance":** Roy, *Moi je,* p. 255.

6   **"You talk about staying with us or going off to the Far East":** Unpublished letter from Robert Brasillach to Maurice Bardèche, October 1, 1932, quoted by Pellissier, *Brasillach . . . le Maudit,* p. 109.

6   **Brasillach's sexuality has been the subject of much speculation:** Dominique Fernandez, in "Chemises brunes et pulsions roses" [brown shirts and pink instincts] in *Le Nouvel Observateur* (October 26—November 1, 1989, p. 190) criticizes two recent biographies of Brasillach by Pierre Pellissier and Pascal Louvrier for completely ignoring what he refers to as a "secret de polichinelle"—a well-known secret: "his homosexuality, probably repressed but all the more harmful for that." Piere Senarclens's analysis of specific homoerotic passages in Brasillach's writing provides a textually based study ("Brasillach, le Fascisme et l'Allemagne: Essai d'interprétation," Colloque international du CNRS: Les Relations Franco-Allemandes, Strasbourg, October 7–10, 1975 [Paris: Editions du CNRS, 1976], pp. 179–208). Francine de Martinoir's reflections on a Brasillach "fleeing what he felt was his true sexuality" are also suggestive [*La Littérature occupée: les années de guerre (1939–1945)* (Paris: Hatier, 1995), pp. 95–98]. Fernandez, Senarclens, and Martinoir are the only critics I have found who have explored the link between Brasillach's homoeroticism and fascism seriously. The link is often assumed: Pascal Ory, at the moment of the Barbie trial, published a capsule portrait of Brasillach, among other French collaborators, in *Le Nouvel Observateur* (April 17–23, 1987, p. 40). "Hobby: amitié virile," he notes elliptically. The best writer on the Brasillach trial, Michel Laval, avoids any discussion of his personal life, as well as any consideration of his literary reputation (*Brasillach ou la trahison du clerc* [Paris: Hachette, 1992]).

7   **His contemporaries . . . refer to him repeatedly as a homosexual:** Homophobic slurs on Brasillach occur regularly in Drieu la Rochelle's diary, published posthumously. October 24, 1939: "Certainly, there are fags, pods, and opium addicts on the right: Gaxotte, Brasillach, and others, Bernard Fäy . . ."; May 18, 1940: "As far as Brasillach goes, he is the blabbermouth of the Barcelone faggots"; June 21, 1940: "[should I] make ties to Céline, Giono (?), Malraux (?). Look for new ones especially, train them. Brasillach? No. Neither fags nor half-Jews." Céline's animosity towards Brasillach was equally homophobic. Céline was furious when, on May 26, 1939, *Je Suis Partout* accused him of having "wimped out" because he had agreed to let his two pamphlets be removed from bookstores after a lawsuit. His June 1939 response to Brasillach was aimed directly at the writer's sexuality: "Brasillach, you're quibbling, I don't accuse you of being a faggot, or a whore; if I wanted to, I wouldn't

use a pretext. I'd tell you man to man. Come tell me and we'll see. . . . I told you we're already dealing with two lawsuits. Do we need to take on thirty-six of them to make you come, little girl?" (*Cahiers Céline 7. Céline et l'actualité, 1933–1961* [Paris: Gallimard, 1986], p. 57). In a March 17, 1949, letter to Albert Paraz, Céline referred to Brasillach as "a zealous little employee of the Propaganda-Staffel, ambitious, political, neronian faggot" (*Cahiers Céline 6. Lettres à Albert Paraz, 1947–1957,* Jean-Paul Louis, ed. [Paris: Gallimard, 1980], p. 140). Etiemble's "brasillèche et bardache" is from "L'Ecrivain et la collaboration: Justice pour les 'collabos,' " in *Hygiène des lettres,* vol. 2, *Littérature dégagée, 1942–1953* (Paris: Gallimard, 1955), p. 167. The essay was first published in *Evidences,* June–July 1952.

7   **"Why so many pederasts among the collaborators?":** Jean Guéhenno, *Journal des années noires (1940–1944)* (Paris: Gallimard, 1947), p. 123.

7   **When historians . . . talk about the homoerotic pull of fascist culture:** See especially George Mosse, "Fascism and Sexuality," in *Nationalism and Sexuality: Respectability and Abnormal Sexuality in Modern Europe* (New York: Fertig, 1985), pp. 153–223: "[T]he love stories in [Brasillach's] novels usually place the woman in a triangle between two close male friends, reflecting perhaps his own feelings toward Maurice Bardèche, whose sister he married" (p. 175). Despite the mistake about who married whose sister, his remarks are perspicacious. For a now classic theoretical treatment of these plots, see Eve Sedgwick's *Between Men: English Literature and Male Homosocial Desire* (New York: Columbia University Press, 1985). In *Male Fantasies* (Minneapolis: University of Minnesota Press, 1987), Klaus Theweleit studies the sexual fantasies of Nazi Freikorps officers. Harry Oosterhuis, ed., *Homosexuality and Male Bonding in Pre-Nazi Germany: The Youth Movement, the Gay Movement, and Male Bonding before Hitler's Rise* (New York: Haworth Press, 1991), provides important historical analysis of the uneven attitude towards homosexuality among the Nazis. In 1931 and 1932, when Röhm was attacked by the left for homosexual decadence, Hitler said he preferred not to interfere with private life. He later used the issue of homosexuality to justify purging Röhm and dismantling the SA. Himmler, leader of the SS, considered homosexuality a grave danger. In 1940, as chief of police, he decreed that all convicted homosexuals who had seduced more than one partner would be deported to a camp. Oosterhuis underlines the contradiction: German national socialism radiated homoeroticism and the idealization of male friendships. Nazi ideology itself was characterized by a constant conflict between the exaltation of male bonding—the "Männerbund"—and the traditional symbols of the party—home, the family, etc. But of course, the realization of a Männerbund and celebration of masculine beauty in National Socialism was accompanied with severe persecution of homosexual men. According to Oosterhuis, between 5,000 and 15,000 men primarily identified as male homosexuals perished in the camps.

8   **It was a mock obituary for André Gide:** "Oraison funèbre pour M. Gide," *La Revue Française,* 25th year, no. 48, November 30, 1930, pp. 520–522, reprinted in *Les Cahiers Mensuels 1930,* December 1930, and again in *Les Quatre jeudis: Images d'avant guerre* (Paris: Editions Balzac, 1944).

8   **Brasillach . . . announced that Gide, once a profound influence on him:** In a postwar essay on literary collaborators cited above (see page and note to page), the polemicist Etiemble, Brasillach and Bardèche's classmate at the Ecole Normale, was violently critical of what he saw as the hypocrisy inherent in their disapproval of Gide: "As for Brasillach and Bardèche (whom we called, more precisely, 'Brasillèche and Bardache') *they* were both intelligent, they didn't have the alibi of [Alain] Laubreaux: stupidity. They gave us several good books. Still, what creeps, as early as 1929 or 1930! Their eyes still black from the amorous thrashings they inflicted upon one another (which is no one's business but their own and might have given me some sympathy for them in a rather stupid hypocritical era, where unnatural acts are concerned), you had

only to hear them insult Gide for being an infamous catamite and sing in the press the praises of that religion and that monarchy which, together, would have surely burned them both at the stakes for sodomy." Etiemble, "L'Ecrivain et la collaboration."

8 **this article had earned him a mention in Gide's famous diary:** Gide's journal was published in France in 1939, and widely read by his contemporaries (Paris: Gallimard/Bibliothèque de la Pléiade, 1939). See the entry for January 12, 1931: "In the *Cahiers du mois* [sic], a new 'Funeral Oration for André Gide,' which recognizes that I have some talent but that I'm tired out: that is, I've ceased to do any harm" (André Gide, *Journal, 1926–1950*, vol. 2, ed. Martine Sagaert [Paris: Gallimard: 1997], p. 242). See also Brasillach's reprint of the Gide article in his 1944 collection of literary criticism, *Les Quatre jeudis: Images d'avant guerre*, with this note:

> I was barely twenty years old when I wrote this impertinent funeral oration. If I allow myself to reprint it here, only correcting a few phrases, it is not out of respect for what I thought then; it is because, on many points, I would not know how to write anything different and because, in spite of a few injustices, this first judgment seems to me rather equitable. And then also because André Gide speaks about these pages in his *Journal*. (reprinted in Brasillach, *Oeuvres complètes*, vol. 8, p. 171)

9 **The Action Française . . . schooled Brasillach in an approach:** Jeannine Verdès-Leroux argues that as a model, the Action Française was important to the extreme right for its negativity, its insistence on refusal, more than for any constructive political program. *Refus et violences: Politique et littérature à l'extrême droite des années trente aux retombées de la Libération* (Paris: Gallimard, 1996), pp. 50ff.

9 **In June of 1931, Brasillach published his first book:** Robert Brasillach, *Présence de Virgile* (Paris: Editions Rédier, 1931).

9 **"He [Virgil] loved to surround himself with young people":** *Présence de Virgile*, in Brasillach, *Oeuvres complètes*, vol. 7, pp. 111–112.

10 **Brasillach failed the agrégation twice . . . and never took it again:** Laval, *Brasillach ou la trahison du clerc*, p. 33.

11 **The "end of the postwar" survey was another Brasillach "coup":** Brasillach's series appeared in *Candide*, August 27, 1931; September 3, 1931; September 10, 1931; September 17, 1931; September 24, 1931. See Pellissier, *Brasillach . . . le Maudit*, p. 95, on the controversy. In André Gide's correspondence with Paulhan (*Paulhan-Gide: Correspondance 1918–1951* [Paris: Gallimard, 1998], pp. 112–114, letters 99 and 100) we learn that Marcel Arland was mortified to see his interview in print; he felt that Brasillach had put words into his mouth about Gide. Here is how Brasillach recorded their exchange:: "Brasillach: 'Gide?' Arland: 'Ah yes, Gide! He is one of the two men who has had the most profound influence on me; the other is Barrès. However, something about him has always bothered me, something false, unnatural. . . .' Brasillach: 'That is more or less my own opinion'" (*Candide*, September 10, 1931).

11 **he was impressive, at first . . . and he wrote whatever he felt like:** Paul Léautaud, *Journal Littéraire* (Paris: Mercure de France, 1961), vol. 11., January 1935—May 1937, entry for September 5, 1935, reporting a conversation with Benjamin Crémieux: "One day they gave him a review to write. He proved himself to be extremely brilliant. So they gave him the literary column. At first he wrote whatever he pleased, the way he thought, not minding the standard situations in forming his opinion. They ended up telling him that it wasn't what was wanted, he had to speak

this way about this one, that way about that one, etc. etc. Which is what he does today" (p. 62).

11 **There was nothing automatic about this evolution:** The routes to fascism for a young Frenchman in the 1930s were various: reactionary populism, hatred of communism, a belief in racial or cultural purity, disgust with parliamentary politics, a longing for authoritarian rule. Brasillach came to his fascism rather conventionally, through fervent right-wing nationalism. However, not all Action Française intellectuals ended up as fascists. The movement was virulently anti-German; during the German occupation, the few Action Française adepts who did choose resistance were naturally drawn to de Gaulle's conservative nationalism.

12 **returned to the site each subsequent year with a bouquet of violets:** Pellissier, *Brasillach . . . le Maudit,* p. 45

12 **Brasillach would refer to the martyrs of February 6:** Brasillach himself was executed on the eleventh anniversary of these riots, a coincidence underlined with great emotion both by him, on the eve of his death in 1945, and by his supporters.

12 **Henceforth . . . two camps were in place:** Following the scare of February 6, the left reorganized into a Popular Front for Defense against Fascism and triumphed in the 1936 elections. They were led by Léon Blum, a Jewish intellectual. Meanwhile, on the far right, French fascist parties emulating Mussolini and Hitler, more populist than monarchist in inspiration, were claiming a small space in the French political constellation. They responded to Blum's victory with high pitched reactionary anti-Semitism. There is a huge bibliography on this marginal but stubborn French fascism phenomenon. Historians such as Sternhell (*Ni droite, ni gauche: l'idéologie fasciste en France.* Paris: Le Seuil, 1983) argue that France was a laboratory for fascist doctrine, well before the first world war; Robert Soucy locates French fascism in two distinct periods between the wars (*French fascism: the first wave, 1924–1933* [New Haven: Yale University Press, 1986]; *French fascism: the second wave, 1933–1939* [New Haven: Yale University Press, 1995].)

12 **Brasillach reacted to the victory of the left in classic extreme right style:** See his "Lettre aux Cocus de la droite" [Letter to the Cuckolds of the Right] in *Combat,* March 1936. The Popular Front was defeated in 1937, giving way to a series of right-wing and radical party governments; Brasillach remained hostile to the moderate right.

13 **he . . . wrote a romantic portrait of Degrelle's "Rex-Appeal":** *Léon Degrelle et l'Avenir de "Rex"* (1936), reprinted in *Oeuvres complètes,* vol. 5.

13 **Annie Jamet, a militant right-winger and mother of six:** Letter from Roger Grenier, October 1997: "Before the war, Claude Roy was the lover of a woman whose sister, Annie Jamet, is the only mistress attributed to Brasillach. It seems that he wasn't homosexual, but without sexuality. The friendship between Claude Roy and Brasillach was heightened by their attachment to these two sisters."

13 **lectures . . . on the topic "Will Europe Be Fascist?":** Archives Nationales. Centre des archives contemporaines, Fontainebleau: "Conférence de M. Robert Brasillach sur 'L'Europe sera-t-elle fasciste' organisée sous les auspices du groupe 'Rive Gauche' au Studio Bonaparte, Place Saint-Sulpice, le 20 novembre 1936." A Report on Brasillach's lecture is in a file marked "Robert Brasillach," Archives de la direction de la Sûreté (archives repatriated from Russia). Dossier 1/2/48364, cote 940434/580.

14 **" . . . a great, strange country, further from us than India and China":** "Cent heures chez Hitler: Le Congrès de Nuremberg," *La Revue Universelle,* October 1937, pp. 56–74. The last sentence of the quotation is cut from the reprise of the essay

in *Notre avant-guerre,* published in 1941, when the Germans were no longer very far away. On *Notre avant-guerre,* see chapter 2, "Brasillach's War."

15 **The spectacle of young men working together for mother Nazi Germany:** By now it is a commonplace to argue that many European intellectuals were misled by the theatrical aspects of fascism, and that, in Walter Benjamin's immortal phrase, fascism was an "estheticization of politics." Brasillach is a case in point, probably the most perfect case in point for Benjamin's theory. For a discussion of theories of fascism, see my *Reproductions of Banality: Fascism, Literature and French Intellectual Life* (Minneapolis: University of Minnesota Press, 1986). To Benjamin's sense of the willful theatricality of Nazism we can add the importance of homoerotic spectacle to which Brasillach was specially sensitive. The homoerotic element of fascism has been studied, in the German context, by Klaus Theweleit (*Male Fantasies* [Minneapolis: University of Minnesota Press, 1987]). Whatever Brasillach's political fears about German hegemony might have been, the Nazified country, with its flags, its parades, its beautiful young men in work camps, was a feast for Brasillach's eyes. In his study, Theweleit also investigates the negative fantasies of fascist males: fear of communism or "red flood" and deep-seated misogyny. This negative element is oddly lacking from Brasillach's writing about Germany.

15 **lectures on the classical tragedian Pierre Corneille:** Robert Brasillach, *Pierre Corneille* (Paris: Fayard, 1938).

15 **tried to make Corneille's famous "will" . . . Hitlerian:** In the *Nouvelle Revue Française,* Roger Caillois, an anthropologist and member of the prestigious *Collège de Sociologie,* was disdainful of Brasillach's "cheap tricks" to make Corneille a "now" writer, accessible to a wide audience. It wasn't the fascism he objected to, it was the vulgarization, which he found brilliant but empty. He confessed that he would rather read a pedant. Roger Caillois, "Résurrection de Corneille," *Nouvelle Revue Française,* October 1938, no. 301, p. 659–666, 1938, vol. 2.

16 **"Did you know that Corneille was . . .":** *Je Suis Partout,* February 11, 1938.

16 **"reflected . . . like high cliffs in a hand mirror":** First published as "L'Age critique de M. Mauriac," in *Je Suis Partout,* July 2, 1937, p. 6; reprinted in *Les Quatre jeudis: Images d'avant guerre* (Paris: Editions Balzac, 1944), pp. 319–326. By Brasillach's own request, none of his articles on Mauriac were republished in the *Oeuvres complètes,* so as not to insult Mauriac's heroic efforts to save his life in 1945.

16 **he described Julien Benda . . . as a "circumcised diplodocus":** "La fin de l'après-guerre: Vieilles Maisons, Vieux Papiers," *Je Suis Partout,* January 14, 1938. The context for this cut on Benda is a mockery of the entire *Nouvelle Revue Française.*

16 **"Mr. Brasillach will perhaps remain more faithful to his antipathies":** André Bellessort, in a review of Brasillach's first collection of literary criticism, *Portraits* (Paris: Plon, 1935), in *Je Suis Partout,* February 27, 1937.

17 **They had moved from right-wing nationalism to fascist internationalism:** For a comparison of Brasillach with other French writers of the 1930s identified with fascism, see my *Reproductions of Banality.* Vast differences separate Brasillach from Céline and Drieu la Rochelle, to name the two writers most frequently associated with literary fascism. Drieu comes to fascism through a kind of embittered left wing dandyism; Céline through an anti-semitic populism. Both are veterans of World War I; neither of them have a background in the Action Française nor any connection to the Ecole Normale. For an analysis of fascist themes and concepts in figures as diverse as Péguy, Maurras, Brasillach, Céline, and Thierry Maulnier, see David Carroll, *French Literary Fascism* (Princeton: Princeton University Press, 1995). On Brasillach, William R. Tucker, *The Fascist Ego: A Political Biography of Robert Brasillach* (Berkeley: University of California Press, 1975) remains a useful intellectual history.

See also Luc Rasson, *Littérature et fascisme: les romans de Robert Brasillach* (Paris: Minard, 1991) for close reading of ideology within Brasillach's novels.

17 **"For me, who perhaps hasn't had a true friendship":** *Notre avant-guerre* (Paris: Plon, 1941), p. 230.

17 **Eventually, he hired her as his typist:** One of the sources for Pierre Pellissier's biography, *Brasillach . . . le Maudit* is Brasillach's letters to Marguerite Cravoisier.

18 **one half—the critic—disapproves of the other half—the writer:** See, for example, Edmond Jaloux's remarks in his review of *L'Enfant de la nuit,* in *Les Nouvelles Littéraires,* December 1, 1934: "I see in the excellent literary column that M. Brasillach writes that, though he recognizes its qualities, he is hostile to literature that we might call 'fairy-like' or 'magic,' or whatever word one might use to christen it. Yet it is this very element that gives *L'Enfant de la nuit* its value."

18 **He constructed this first novel around a typical nationalist theme:** René Lalou, in a November 5, 1932, review for *Nouvelles Littéraires,* lauds Brasillach's ability to turn his nationalist theme with more charm than polemic: "As for ideology, these adventures . . . obey the teachings of Barrès and Maurras. Still, the true charm of *Le Voleur d'étincelles,* which renders it appealing in a juvenile sense, is that the itinerary of Lazare Mur is not a dogmatic cruise, but a true journey of discovery" (p. 3). Lalou also sees in Brasillach a "precious" version of Jean Giraudoux, a *normalien* twenty years his elder and a leading literary figure in the France of the 1930s, for whom French identity was a constant theme.

18 **the narrator invokes nostalgia for his own lost youth:** On Brasillach's nostalgia, see Edmond Jaloux's review of *L'Enfant de la nuit* in *Les Nouvelles Littéraires,* December 1, 1934, p. 5: "You can tell he is twenty-five years old. This is a twenty-five-year-old who, on every page, says that his youth is dead and gathers up his memories with a somber and delicate poetry. It is part of youth to get nostalgic about lost youth."

19 **One early critic warns that he's in danger of becoming formulaic, insipid:** See Edmond Jaloux's review of *Le Marchand d'oiseaux* in *Les Nouvelles Littéraires,* July 11, 1936, p. 5: "[His novels] are threatened by a gracious blandness, which quickly risks becoming a tick; but, as an excellent critic, showing great wisdom in his reasoning and an unshakeable lucidity in his responses, M. Robert Brasillach always remains the first to know his weaknesses and to remedy them." This review tells us that Brasillach was respected first and foremost as a critic, someone other critics were watching with great curiosity to see if he could transfer his talents successfully to fiction. The *London Times,* in particular, spoke enthusiastically of his "elfin" qualities, calling Brasillach "the most interesting accession of youthful talent to the French literary Right of recent years." The *London Times'* review of Brasillach, an untranslated French writer, denoted a certain literary *succes* (*Times Literary Supplement,* no. 697: Saturday August 29, 1936.)

19 **Thierry Maulnier . . . complained in his review of *L'Enfant de la nuit:*** Maulnier reviews *L'Enfant de la nuit* in Action Française, November 29, 1934, p. 5; and *Le Marchand d'oiseaux* in the *Action Française,* July 16, 1936, p. 3.

19 **He wondered if he'd ever make it:** Letter to Jacques Brousse, dated August 22, 1938, in Brasillach, *Oeuvres complètes,* vol. 10, p. 507: "I thank you for what you say about my books, and I am happy that you liked *Comme le temps passe . . .* Still, you are right to think that the two heroes don't have enough weightiness [épaisseur]. It is a very difficult thing, and I don't think I'll succeed for several more years, if I ever do. . . . Don't put too much hope in *Les Sept couleurs.*"

20 **"Sometimes there are admirable pages, analyses, and descriptions":** Denis Saurat, *Nouvelle Revue Française,* 1933, no. 233, p. 348.

20 **"Then gradually, [Chaplin] evolved an individual comic style":** Maurice

Bardèche and Robert Brasillach, *The History of Motion Pictures*. (New York: Norton, 1938), translated and edited by Iris Barry, p. 126. In this paragraph, I've restored the reference to Henri Bergson, which was eliminated from the translation, and slightly altered the translation.

21 **In later editions . . . the authors added anti-Semitic quips:** For a study of various editions of *Histoire du cinéma,* see "The Movies: Bardèche and Brasillach," in Kaplan, *Reproductions of Banality,* pp. 142–160. For example, the 1935 edition reads: "Through these films the Germans found expression for that profound romanticism, that fascination with cruelty and fear and horror, that marrying of sex with death which were to intoxicate so many of her sons after the war" (p. 200); the same passage in the 1943 edition was changed to: "Germany satisfied her profound romanticism, and that taste for sadism, fear, shock, that junction of sexuality and death, which intoxicated so many of her *Jews* after the war" (p. 150). Native German sons became Jews: Brasillach and Bardèche's critique of German expressionism, typical of an Action Française anti-German position, evolved during the Occupation to become a philo-German anti-semitism. Bardèche, in an interview, insisted that these changes were not made by the German censor, but by Brasillach and Bardèche. The censor did ask that several pictures— Chaplin and Eisenstein—be removed in the wartime edition (see "The Late Show," in *Reproductions of Banality,* p. 171.)

21 ***Triumph of the Will* is "monotonous and occasionally magnificent":** "This monotonous but occasionally magnificent *Triumph of the Will,* a film without a narrative plot, a film of massed crowds and processions (some of which are impressive), presumably represents the supreme effort to create a mass ideology inspired by Hitler; an ideology opposed to Marxism, but which produces the same effects" (*Histoire du cinéma* [Paris: Denoël, 1935], p. 370). I've altered Barry's translation, *The History of Motion Pictures,* which softens the ideology of the original. Compare the 1943 edition (*Histoire du cinéma* [Paris: Denoël, 1943], p. 358): " . . . the greatest artist of the Third Reich, the beautiful Madame Leni Riefenstahl . . . *Triumph of the Will* (1943), a simple account of the Nuremberg rallies, will live on as the testimony of the festivals of the regime. Historians will consult it, and perhaps it will be the essential instrument of the Hitlerian regime and legend after the death of the Fuehrer." Brasillach, *Oeuvres complètes,* vol. 10, reproduces the 1935 edition.

21 **"He lifted himself up onto his heels":** *Comme le temps passe* (Paris: Plon, 1937), p. 179, reprinted in *Oeuvres complètes,* vol. 2, p. 156.

22 **At least one of his contemporaries admired the scene:** See Edmond Jaloux's review of *Comme le temps passe* in *Nouvelles Littéraires,* December 25, 1937, p. 4.

22 **"a love and excessive respect (if you can say that) for one's mother":** *Comme le temps passe,* p. 302, reprinted in *Oeuvres complètes,* vol. 2, p. 255.

22 **It's an implausible plot, made of equal parts of romance . . . :** Jean Vaudal's review of *Comme le temps passe* in the *Nouvelle Revue Française* (January 1938, no. 292, pp. 130–132) complained that the novel was indeed charming, "féerique," the details sensual, but that Brasillach hadn't succeeded in plotting a real narrative, only in putting together a series of scenes and exercising his love for atmosphere.

22 **it was one of ten books sent to Hitler on his birthday:** Gérard Loiseaux, *La littérature de la défaite et de la collaboration.* (Paris: Fayard, 1995), p. 111.

23 **"We don't want to kill anyone":** "La Question Juive," first special issue of *Je Suis Partout* on "The Jewish Question," edited by Lucien Rebatet, April 15, 1938.

24 **"What tribunal would dare to condemn us":** "La Question singe," *Je Suis Partout,* March 31, 1939. The article was published during the period when the Marchandeau Decree was being debated in the National Assembly; it passed into law in April.

26 **"I'm getting to know Germany . . . which may be useful in the future":** *Les Sept couleurs* (Paris: Plon, 1939), p. 95; reprinted in *Oeuvres complètes,* vol. 2, p. 419.

26 *Les Sept couleurs* **. . . would never be published in English translation:** Of all Brasillach's fiction, only *Comme le temps passe* was translated into English: *Youth Goes Over: A Novel,* Warre Bradley Wells, trans. (London: Chatto and Windus, 1938).

26 **"Brasillach's sympathy with nascent fascism":** *New York Times,* August 6, 1939, p. 17.

26 **"The young fascist, involved with his race and his nation":** "Réflexions," *Les Sept couleurs,* p. 149, reprinted in *Oeuvres complètes,* vol. 2, p. 463.

26 *Les Septs couleurs* **appeared on the list for the Goncourt Prize:** See René Benjamin's enthusiastic minority report on the 1939 Goncourt, "Un Livre rayonnant" in *Candide,* December 13, 1939, p. 4: "The soul flames in Brasillach! Which is to say that his book is the most anti-Bolshevik in the world. And I know of nothing, at the present moment, more precious." Only he and Sacha Guitry voted for Brasillach.

26 **Léon Daudet . . . had voted for a Jew:** Letter to Maurice Bardèche, December 16, 1939, in Brasillach, *Oeuvres complètes,* vol. 10, p. 523. See the announcement of the prize in *Je Suis Partout,* December 8, 1939: "Robert Brasillach kept the two faithful votes of René Benjamin and Sacha Guitry. Léon Daudet's vote went, as he had announced, to Mme Simone, born Benda, actress and wife of M. François Porché."

Two   Brasillach's War

29 **"Who would ever have wanted to die for Reynaud . . . ?":** *Je Suis Partout,* September 6, 1941. Quoted by Reboul, *Le Procès de Robert Brasillach,* ed. Jacques Isorni (Paris: Flammarion, 1946), p. 136.

29 **"Ah! Certainly, . . .":** *Je Suis Partout,* April 18, 1942. Quoted by Reboul, *Le Procès de Robert Brasillach,* p. 136.

29 **"I make to France the gift of my person":** Quoted in Richard Griffiths, *Marshal Pétain* (London: Constable and Company, 1970), p. 240.

30 **After 1942 . . . Vichy was nothing more than a puppet government:** The best of account of diplomatic and political relations between Vichy and Nazi Germany remains Robert Paxton's *Vichy France: Old Guard and New Order, 1940–1944* (New York: Knopf, 1972).

30 **around 22,000 officers and staff:** The statistics are from Philippe Burrin, "The Machinery of Occupation," in *France under the Germans: Collaboration and Compromise* (New York: The New Press, 1997), pp. 87–88.

31 **Was the personal always political?:** Two million French men were away in prisoner-of-war camps. According to Robert O. Paxton (*Vichy France: Old Guard and New Order, 1940–1944,* p. 368), 3.3 percent of the total population was drafted into so-called "voluntary" labor camps in Germany. Women were not drafted, but there were female volunteers. See the extensive discussion of forced and voluntary labor service, including a breakdown by gender, in Burrin, *France under the Germans.*

32 **"We remember the warmongering Jew Charles Ruff":** *Je Suis Partout,* August 18, 1941. The Comtat Venaissin is the region around Avignon and Carpentras. Under the reign of Philippe Le Bel, the Papacy moved from Rome to Avignon; the Avignon Popes were known for their protective stance toward the Jews. Jews of the Comtat are thus called "the Pope's Jews."

32 **"The Jew David Rubiné":** *Je Suis Partout,* July 7, 1941.

32 **Often their exact addresses were given:** In his introduction to a partial reprint of Brasillach's *Je Suis Partout* articles in Brasillach's *Oeuvres complètes,* vol. 12 (Paris: Club

de l'Honnête Homme, 1963–1966), Maurice Bardèche argues that as editor in chief of the paper, Brasillach's powers were more limited than one would expect and that, in particular, "the 'echoes' [gossip column] in the paper escaped his jurisdiction" (p. 319). It is hard to imagine how Brasillach could have served as editor of the newspaper and published in it regularly without endorsing the "Partout et ailleurs" column, whether or not he contributed to writing it.

32 **76,000 Jews were deported from France:** For a discussion of statistics, see Michael R. Marrus and Robert O. Paxton, *Vichy France and the Jews* (New York: Schocken, 1983), p. 344. For an exact account of the deportation of Jews from France, see Serge Klarsfeld, *Le Calendrier de la persécution des juifs en France, 1940–1944* ([Paris]: Editions Klarsfeld, 1993), and *Memorial to the Jews deported from France, 1942–1944: Document* (New York: Klarsfeld Foundation, 1983). On the number of French deported for nonracial reasons, Jean-Pierre Azéma, *De Munich à la Libération, 1938–1944: Nouvelle Histoire de la France contemporaine* (Paris: Le Seuil, 1979), p. 189, estimates approximately 63,000 nonracial French deportees, of whom some 41,000 were deported specifically for acts of resistance.

33 **Others accommodated:** Burrin's *France under the Germans* makes a useful distinction between accommodation and active collaboration. On the value of Burrin's contribution from a literary perspective, see my review essay, "France on German Time," in *Modernism/Modernity,* vol. 5, no. 3, 1998, pp. 99–105.

33 **Lucien Febvre, the *Annales*-school historian:** On the *Annales* during the Occupation, see Burrin's somber analysis in *France under the Germans,* as well as the ensuing debate by Bertrand Müller and Peter Schöttler in *Le Monde,* February 8, 1995, p. 13 ("Faut-il brûler Lucien Febvre?"). The booing of Febvre by *normaliens* is reported by Stéphane Israël in his thesis, *L'Ecole normale supérieure et la Seconde Guerre Mondiale,* dir. Sirinelli, Paris, 2 vol. (Mémoire de DEA, Histoire contemporaine, Lille III, fall 1993), vol. 1, p. 282.

33 **Roger Leenhardt . . . describes a radio program at Vichy:** Roger Leenhardt, *Les Yeux ouverts: Entretiens avec Jean Lacouture* (Paris: Le Seuil, 1979).

34 **he [Roy] was making fun of fascist writers:** See for example, *Poésie 43,* no. 5, July–September 1943, "Le Goût du jour: Essai d'examen," where Roy mocks an article in the *Cahiers Français* by Jean Turlais called "Introduction à l'histoire de la littérature fasciste." Roy's sardonic report tells us that the latest definition of the fascist writer was his "purity" and that Turlais's up-to-the minute list of "true fascist writers" included Corneille, Stendhal, Homer, Jean Genet, Jules Verne, Brasillach. . . . One mustn't despair of somehow finding a way to annex Proust to the list, Roy concluded.

34 **"with tears in his eyes":** Anne Brassié, *Robert Brasillach ou Encore un instant de bonheur* (Paris: Laffont, 1987), p. 234.

34 **Roy declined to sign a petition:** See "The Writers' Petition," below.

34 **Eluard wrote Cocteau a letter reprimanding him:** The text of Eluard's July 2, 1942, letter is reproduced in Jean Cocteau, *Journal 1942–1945,* ed. Touzot (Paris: Gallimard, 1989), p. 174: "My dear Cocteau, Freud, Kafka, Chaplin are forbidden by the same people who honor Breker. We saw you among the forbidden. How wrong you were to appear suddenly among the censors! The best of those who admire you and who love you were painfully surprised. Give us back our confidence in you. Nothing should separate us."

35 **The interrogation of Brasillach . . . became the cornerstone:** Charles Lesca's *Quand Israël se vengea* (Paris: Grasset, 1941) dramatized the arrest for propaganda purposes.

35 **he blamed democratic, parliamentary France:** Brasillach, *Oeuvres complètes,* vol. 6, *Journal d'un homme occupé,* p. 388.

36 **He even acknowledged Jewish heroism:** "Les Français devant les Juifs," *Je Suis Partout,* February 17, 1939. See chapter 1, "The Making of a Fascist Writer."

36 **"I'm with seven officers":** Letter to Suzanne and Maurice Bardèche, July 29, 1940, in Brasillach, *Oeuvres complètes,* vol. 10, p. 563.

36 **"I created a scandal by publicly forbidding a Jew to speak":** Brasillach, *Oeuvres complètes,* vol. 10, letter to his mother, November 20, 1940, p 570.

37 **"Naturally, you should cut what is no longer of value":** *Oeuvres complètes,* vol. 6, p. 345.

37 **"We won't surprise the readers of *Je Suis Partout*":** "Les Universités des camps," *Je Suis Partout,* May 26, 1941.

38 **Camp life . . . was deeply satisfying for him:** Archives Nationales Z6 255, No. 2999, *Je Suis Partout* trial dossier. Lucien Rebatet, interrogated before his own 1946 trial by examining magistrate Alexis Zousman (October 19, 1945), underlines Brasillach's difficulty: "Brasillach seemed to me during my first contacts with him [after his liberation from POW camp in April 1941] badly readjusted to civilian life . . ."

38 **"One was asked to point out the Jews":** *Je Suis Partout,* July 3, 1943: "Revolution nationale et captivité romantique: Souvenirs par Robert Brasillach." The bilingual pun is typical of Brasillach: Dreyfus = drei fuss = trépied or trois pieds; three feet in English.

39 **At least one historian of the French captivity:** Yves Durand, *La Captivité: Histoire des prisonniers de guerre français, 1939–1945* (Paris: FNCPG, 1982), pp. 354–355.

39 **Bardèche also insists in his 1955 editor's notes:** *Journal d'un homme occupé* (Paris: Les Sept Couleurs, 1955), p. 153. See also Bardèche's introductory notes to the *Je Suis Partout* articles from the war years in Brasillach, *Oeuvres complètes,* vol. 12: "These are pieces of a literary and political dossier. . . . Speaking as an editor, it seems to us that it would be a very grave attack on historical probity to voluntarily dissimulate an entire aspect of a writer whose complete works one is presenting. Such a mutilation would be contrary to all the rules of criticism and even, it seems to us, those of honesty. It also seemed to us that it was important to make the file of articles on the basis of which Robert Brasillach was condemned available to the public" (p. 321).

39 **we see the mark in this writing of an actual public denunciation:** A former prisoner of war who had been in the same camp with Brasillach sent this letter to *Le Monde* in 1957, at the moment of the polemic around the production of Brasillach's play, *Bérénice:* "I was at Oflag VI A, in Soest (Westphalia), prisoner number 5085, a French officer among 2,000 others that the temporary defeat had united in a barracks of Wehrmacht cadets. It was in this camp that I saw Brasillach take, in the month of August 1940, a leadership role in an anti-Jewish, Maurrassien (i.e., Action Française) movement, whose goal was to reject the Jews and freemasons from our community. This movement scapegoated our army's defeat, and pursued them with a hatred that reached its height when these 'exclusive patriots' asked the enemy, who held us under the permanent threat of its weapons and its wardens, to assemble our Jewish comrades in a particular spot so that they would cease to corrupt the purity of the atmosphere in which the 'aryans' were living. I quote the names of the officers who were the victims of this scandalous discrimination due to an act of Brasillach: Lieutenant Rothschild, Lieutenant Hauser, Lieutenant Menasset, Captain Friedmann, in particular. These officers, denounced as Jews by Brasillach, were then sent to a reprisal camp at Lübeck. . . . I remember only too well the poisoned atmosphere of the Oflag VI A during the period when the disciples of Brasillach, strengthened by the support and the advice of their master, dared to pin 'Jews do not enter here' on the door of their 'Zimmer.'" His accusation of official denunciation is serious,

especially when matched with Brasillach's own comments. However, the details in his letter can't be corroborated, and we need to read his charges with skepticism. For example, the camp at Lübeck was not opened until after Brasillach's release from Oflag VI A. A similar accusation appeared in 1976 in an interview with writer Dominique Aury for the 1976 André Halimi documentary, *Chantons sous l'occupation*. Aury said Brasillach didn't deserve the death sentence for anything he wrote. She believed that he was condemned unjustly for his opinions and for his errors in judgment. But she added: "I would have condemned him to death for his behavior in the prison camp." She spoke of his denunciation, not of Jewish officers, but of Gaullist officers to the German camp administrators, who were then sent to "reprisal camps."

40 **According to the penal code:** In November 1944, by special ordinance, the jurists who designed the Courts of Justice modified articles 75–86 of the 1939 Penal Code on treason, in order to take into account the occupation of France by a foreign power and the role of the de facto Vichy government in supporting that occupation. The modified penal code specified that denunciation was to be considered a crime. See Henry Rousso, "L'Epuration en France: Une Histoire inachevée" (*Vingtième Siècle. Revue d'Histoire*, no. 33, January–March 1992), p. 87; and *Code pénal annoté par Emile Garçon*, new edition by Marcel Rousselet, Maurice Patin, and Marc Ancel, eds., vol. 1 (Paris: Recueil, Sirey, 1952), pp. 244–414.

40 **Jacques Tournant, who wrote to de Gaulle:** The letters to de Gaulle are part of Brasillach's pardon file. Archives Nationales, Recours en grâce de Robert Brasillach, 1945, S.2977. See chapter 10, "No Pardon."

40 **fellow officers read the play out loud:** Pierre Pellissier, *Brasillach . . . le Maudit* (Paris: Denoël, 1989), p. 268.

41 **Brasillach chose a theme treated famously . . . :** For a cultural study of French classical treatments of the Bérénice figure, see Michèle Longino, "Orienting the World: Competition and Gendered Geography: *Tite et Bérénice, Bérénice,*" forthcoming in *The French Turban: Staging Exoticism in Seventeenth-Century France* [manuscript]. Longino mentions well-known Latin versions of the Bérénice story by Suetonius, Tacitus, Flavius Josephus, and Juvenal.

41 **"I imagine that this woman must have been beautiful; but the Orientals fade quickly":** Brasillach, *Oeuvres complètes,* vol. 4, pp. 140, 147–148, and 150, respectively. Brasillach waited until the last months of the Occupation to publish the text of *Bérénice* (*La Chronique de Paris,* no. 6–7, April/May 1944).

41 **"an old syphilitic whore, stinking of patchouli and yeast infection":** *Je Suis Partout,* 7 février 1942; for the full quotation, see chapter 4, "Jail."

42 **After he has finished addressing a crowd:** Brasillach, *Oeuvres complètes,* vol. 1, *Les Captifs:* "The crowd looked at him with sympathy and he looked with sympathy at the crowd. . . . He felt tired and happy, exactly as if he had just made love" (p. 616).

42 **someone else was in fact named as Commissioner of Cinema:** Francis Courtade, in *Les Malédictions du cinéma français: Une Histoire du cinéma français parlant (1928–1978)* (Paris: Editions Alain Moreau, 1978), quotes a document from Maurice Bardèche's archives marked "May or June 1941," in the form of a report by Brasillach on the situation of French film. Brasillach writes like a fervent nationalist, protective of French interests and suspicious of German interference in matters such as exportation, distribution, production. Courtade concludes that Brasillach actually served as Commissioner of Cinema but resigned due to Vichy incompetence and German interference. Brasillach's biographer, Pellissier, goes a step further. Quoting Courtade's document as his source, he claims that Brasillach served as a commissioner of cinema upon his return from POW camp, but was forced to leave his post when he refused to solicit the endorsement of the Germans in Paris. It is more likely that

when he was a candidate for the position, Brasillach wrote the report or "projet" in a nationalist vein to please the men in Vichy—specifically Paul Marion, Minister of Information—who were in a position to give him the job. Jean-Pierre Bertin-Maghit, author of *Le Cinéma sous l'Occupation: Le Monde du cinéma français de 1940 à 1946* (Paris: Editions Orban, 1989), based on a careful study of the voluminous archives concerning the administration of cinema under Vichy (Archives Nationales, series F42), and who, in the course of his research, conducted many interviews with the chosen commissioner, Galey, found no evidence that Brasillach was anything other than an unsuccessful nominee for the post. (Interview with J.-P. Bertin-Maghit, Paris, June 26, 1998. See also Bertin-Maghit, *Le Cinéma sous l'Occupation*). But Brasillach's desire to serve as Commissioner was well-known on the Paris scene. In his postwar correspondence, Céline comments: "He would have left for London if he could have landed in a ministry of cinema there—his ambition" (March 17, 1949, letter to Albert Paraz in *Cahiers Céline 6, 1947–1957*. [Paris: Gallimard, 1980], p. 140).

43 **He was released by official request of the German Embassy in Paris:** The initial date of request for Brasillach's release was October 1, 1940. The request was made by Schleier, the number two man in the Nazi embassy in Paris. The reason: "press work." An internal memo of December 19, 1940, explains that "in connection with the most recent visit of Ambassador Abetz in Berlin, Lieutenant General Reinecke agreed to furlough or release the following French POWs (a list followed including Brasillach). These POWs are going to be politically active in the interests of Germany after their furlough or release" (Germany Foreign Ministry Archives, Document R29259, Bonn, Germany). Brasillach's release was delayed only because there was some difficulty locating him in his specific camp. The Spanish embassy also requested Brasillach's release in a document dated December 9, 1940, and received December 17, 1940—over two months after the initial German request (Foreign Ministry Document R28671). On October 1, 1941, Brasillach's name again appears on a list of furloughed POWs "Who Are Active in Public or Political Life" (Unnumbered Foreign Ministry Document, Germany Foreign Ministry Archives, Bonn, Germany). Philippe Burrin first identified these documents concerning the release of politically useful POWs in his *France under the Germans*, pp. 373 and 516, note 1.

43 **the German Propaganda-Staffel in Paris:** The 1941 German Propaganda-Staffel list of works considered valuable for the Nazi propaganda effort in France is published in Pascal Fouché, *L'Edition française sous l'Occupation, 1940–1944*, vol. 1 (Paris: Bibliothèque de Littérature Française Contemporaine de l'Université de Paris, 1987), pp. 163–173.

44 **"We have to give to youth the cult of the hero":** Pierre Masteau, "Un quart d'heure avec Maurice Bardèche," *Jeunesse,* September 28, 1941. *Jeunesse* was linked to the Vichy youth ministry, whose "Chef de la propagande" was Georges Pelorson, an Ecole Normale classmate of Brasillach and Bardèche's (see chapter 1, "The Making of a Fascist Writer," note to page). In 1942 the newspaper merged with Doriot's Parti Populaire Français, then disappeared. Bardèche's connection to *Jeunesse* was first signaled by Claude Singer, *L'Université libérée, l'université épurée, 1943–1947* (Paris: Les Belles Lettres, 1997). On Georges Pelorson, see Vincent Giroud, "The Transition to Vichy: The Case of Georges Pelorson" (paper delivered at the Whitney Humanities Center, Yale University, September 18, 1998, at the conference "The Avant-Garde in Transition: Eugene and Maria Jolas and Their Contemporaries").

44 **under the giant photo of Marshal Pétain:** Roger-Viollet Photo Agency, "Manifestation au Magic City, Paris, May 1942": Robert Brasillach, Maurice Bardèche (second plan), Georges Blond et Charles Lesca. Photo No. LAPI 7548.

45 **Brasillach's *Trial of Joan of Arc:*** Joan of Arc—woman of the people, peasant, and

religious seer—is a symbol deployed both by the French left and the French right. Most recently, she has been appropriated by Le Pen's Front National, who stage an annual demonstration in her honor.

45 **"We must leave behind the sterile verbosity of dead ideologies":** Pierre Leforestier, *Nouvelle Revue Française,* September 1941, no. 332, pp. 495–497.

45 **He mentioned in particular François Mauriac:** Mauriac was a subject of ridicule in "Partout et ailleurs" as well as in Brasillach's own literary criticism. On the Heller meeting, see Fouché, *L'Edition française sous l'Occupation,* vol. 3, p. 180. In 1943, Mauriac expressed his horror of Nazism in *Le Cahier noir,* which he published underground with the Editions de Minuit using the pseudonym Forez. His style was nonetheless utterly recognizable; it was a dangerous and courageous act.

46 **"In a Paris eaten away, sucked dry":** L'Ubiquiste, "La Guerre des rats," *Je Suis Partout,* April 25, 1941.

46 **In July 1942 came the Vél d'Hiv roundup:** *Je Suis Partout,* where Brasillach's pro-German columns were appearing weekly, did not report Vél d'Hiv—nor did anyone in the collaborationist press.

46 **the Germans began executing hostages in reprisal:** The first German ordinance concerning hostages is dated August 22, 1941. Fifty hostages, including 27 communists, were shot at Chateaubriant, in the Loire-Atlantique region, on October 23, 1941.

46 **The Allies had begun bombing Paris:** The first major air raid on Paris targeted the Renault factory; there were 500 casualties when the bomb missed its target. See David Pryce-Jones, *Paris in the Third Reich* (New York: Holt, Rinehart and Winston, 1981), p. 173.

47 **the "practice and poetry of fascism":** From a speech at Magic City, 1942, quoted by Brasillach's examining magistrate and summarized in *Je Suis Partout,* May 7, 1943, p. 3: "It is because fascism has taken on the form of a practice and a poetry at the same time, the form of a politics that carries the most exalting images of our time, that youth can give itself to fascism." The Magic City speech does not appear among Brasillach's *Je Suis Partout* articles reproduced in the complete works.

47 **Jean Grenier, in a 1941 entry in his occupation diary:** Jean Grenier, *Sous l'Occupation* (Paris: Editions Claire Paulhan, 1997), p. 114.

47 **"those whose lack of character":** Jean Guéhenno, *Journal des années noires* (Paris: Gallimard, 1947), p. 166. Guéhenno was a target of particular scorn in Brasillach's 1930s journalism. See, for example, Brasillach's review of Guéhenno's *Jeunesse de France* in the *Action Française,* April 9, 1936 (Brasillach, *Oeuvres complètes,* vol. 11, pp. 660–663), which begins: "Despite what badly intentioned people may think, we have no antipathy towards M. Jean Guéhenno. He is, however, neither a very frank man nor a very subtle intellect," and ends: "He is one of the last representatives of a zoological type doomed to extinction. What zoo is going to welcome him?"

47 **The anti-Jewish legislation of 1941:** Stéphane Israël, *L'Ecole normale supérieure et la Seconde Guerre Mondiale.* Mémoire de DEA, Histoire Contemporaine, Lille III (Paris: 1993), 2 volumes. In the French universities, a quota system allowed 3% of Jewish students to enroll during the Occupation. At the Ecole, admission was strictly closed, but Jewish students who had matriculated before 1941 could finish their studies (vol. 1, p. 183).

48 **Students used to boo him regularly:** Israël, *L'Ecole normale supérieure,* vol. 1, p. 151.

48 **He [Bruhat] died at Buchenwald:** Israël, *L'Ecole normale supérieure,* p. 170.

49 **the heartthrob of the collaborationist homosexual milieu:** David Pryce-Jones,

Paris under the Third Reich (New York: Holt, Rinehart and Winston, 1981): "Epting's assistant included Karl-Heinz Bremer, a minor writer whose blond good looks caused tremors in the homosexual milieu of Paris. . . . 'You will always arise for us like a young Siegfried conquering evil spells,' was a characteristic phrase coined by Brasillach, who seems to have had feelings akin to hero worship for Bremer" (p. 39). The quotation is from Brasillach's September 18, 1942, obituary in *Je Suis Partout*.

49 **"Dear Karl Heinz, we had made plans together":** Brasillach, "Sur la mort d'un ami allemand," *Je Suis Partout,* September 18, 1942.

49 **the column he wrote the day after the Bremer obituary:** At least one historian has offered a very different reading of the relationship between the Bremer obituary and "Les Sept Internationales contre la patrie": Fred Kupferman, Laval's biographer, argues that Brasillach was simply distracted by Bremer's death and barely gave a thought to the phrase about deporting the Jews in a block. See the chapter entitled "On ne badine pas avec le destin," in *Robert Brasillach et la génération perdue,* no. 2 in the series *Les Cahiers du Rocher* (Paris: Editions du Rocher, 1987), pp. 227–235.

50 **Brasillach made his second trip under German auspices:** "A l'est vers une aube possible: choses vues," *Je Suis Partout,* July 23, 1943: "Crossing these plains, I imagined that a little to the north, in similar plains, in an unknown field, lies the only German friend I have had, Karl-Heinz Bremer, who died in the month of May last year. I have often thought about him during this trip, I have often sought his lively and charming shadow among these military trains he must have taken, I remember the only letter I received from him from the front, where he spoke of this common destiny which, for better or worse, was ours . . ." reprinted in Brasillach, *Journal d'un homme occupé, Oeuvres complètes,* vol. 6, p. 517.

50 **It is a serious but boyish tenor:** Maison de la Radio, Archives Politiques, July 7, 1943. 13 minute, 40 second recording entitled "Reportage au charnier de la forêt de Katyn. A la fin quelques mots de Robert Brasillach."

50 **the most widely read newspaper in the occupied zone:** The numbers are from Pierre-Marie Dioudonnat, *Je Suis Partout (1930–1944)* (Paris: La Table Ronde, 1973), p. 173.

50 **Brasillach was caught in a fundamental contradiction:** Philippe Burrin, *La Dérive fasciste: Doriot, Déat, Bergery, 1933–1945* (Paris: Le Seuil, 1986), traces this contradiction in three political figures associated with French fascism.

51 **"All that was left for this strange [political] house . . .":** Robert Brasillach, "De l'épopée aux décombres," *Je Suis Partout,* September 4, 1942.

51 **he means . . . that the Action Française movement was finished:** Robert Belot in *Lucien Rebatet* (Paris: Le Seuil, 1994), situates the break of the *Je Suis Partout* team at the moment when *Je Suis Partout* resumes publication in occupied Paris, February 1941. Dioudonnat, in *Je Suis Partout (1930–1944),* quotes Brasillach's qualms about the reappearance of his newspaper in an October 11, 1940, letter to his mother: "I'd like to get permission from old Charles, in any case, we must be prudent and dignified" (Brasillach, *Oeuvres complètes,* vol. 10, p. 569). A witness at Maurras's trial testified that Maurras was hostile to the reappearance of *Je Suis Partout* and quoted him as saying, "How can a nationalist paper think about reappearing in Paris and asking for the authorization of the Germans, under a German censor? It's completely impossible" (Yves Chiron, *La Vie de Charles Maurras* [Paris: Perrin, 1991], p. 427). When Brasillach visited Lyon in February 1942, Maurras announced his refusal to see him in the pages of the *Action Française:* "Just as we have already had the opportunity to do as far as his paper is concerned, we reply that we no longer have any relationship with Robert Brasillach" (quoted in Chiron, *La Vie de Charles Maurras,* p. 428). On the relationship of the Action Française to French fascism, see Eugen Weber's classic

Action Française: Royalism and Reaction in Twentieth Century France (Stanford: Stanford University Press, 1962).

51 **"It is not about transporting the German way of life here":** "La Guerre et la paix," *Je Suis Partout,* March 19, 1943.

51 **how does one collaborate with the Nazi occupiers . . . :** Philippe Burrin gives a vivid analysis of what he calls "the collaborationist nationalists" and their demise in *France under the Germans:* "For this minority, the physical nation was of small account compared with the ideal nation that needed to be created. The occupier was at once a national partner and a political model: by creating the new France, they would at the same time be saving the French nation. But for that the occupier needed to be a real partner and the alliance of nationalists needed to be something other than wishful thinking that concealed the reality of men who had simply become turncoats serving a new colonial power" (p. 457).

52 **He was a highly conciliatory intellectual:** Anatole de Monzie, *La Saison des juges* (Paris: Flammarion, 1943), p. 151. For information on the role of de Monzie during the Occupation, see Burrin, *France under the Germans,* and Jean-Louis Crémieux Brilhac, *Les Français de l'an 40* (Paris: Gallimard, 1990). Crémieux-Brilhac describes him as the ultimate pragmatist, tolerant, generous, hoping, in the last days of the Occupation, to help negotiate a peaceful transfer of power from Pétain and Laval to de Gaulle. Brasillach's review, entitled "Pour Saint Louis contre Brid'oison," appeared in *Je Suis Partout* on August 6, 1943.

52 **De Monzie recommended blanket political amnesty:** Reboul, in his prosecution speech, would use Brasillach's argument against de Monzie's theory of amnesty to argue against amnesty for Brasillach. See Isorni, ed., *Le Procès de Robert Brasillach* (Paris: Flammarion, 1946), p. 133.

53 **Why was Brasillach wasting his column on de Monzie?:** Archives Nationales, dossier Pierre-Antoine Cousteau Z6 253, no. 2974, interrogation concerning the internal crisis at *Je Suis Partout:* "Brasillach having persisted in his resolution to orient *Je Suis Partout* toward literature and having, consequentially, written an article on the front page about a book by M. de Monzie, just at the moment where fascism was disappearing in Italy and where our readers were expecting us to analyze the event, the crisis blew up." See also the file on the *Je Suis Partout* trial, Rebatet, Z6 255, no. 2999.

53 **Brasillach said . . . that *Je Suis Partout*'s net profits:** Interrogation of Brasillach by Inspector Galey of the Paris police, October 13, 1944. Copies of this document were found in Prefecture of Police Archives and in Isorni's papers at the Ordre des Avocats. "The provisional accounting for the paper's profits for the first seventh months of 1943, once all the expenses were paid, came to four and a half million francs. *Je Suis Partout* was the most important business concern of the northern zone. . . . My revenues during the occupation were from two sources, first, the revenues from my books published by the editors Plon, Denoël, and Gallimard, and my journalism and salary as editor. In addition to *piges* [payments for articles], *Je Suis Partout* gave a regular bonus at the end of the year which had become rather large because of the company's profits. In 1941 it was 20,000 francs, in 1942 it was 90,000 francs, and in 1943 it was 120,000 francs; in all, the amounts I earned year to year varied from 150 to 250,000 francs, the payments were always made by check, the account is available at the Société Générale, 27 boulevard Saint-Michel. I had the same life style during the Occupation as before the war." This is a healthy, but not extravagant, salary for a leading journalist. Before the war, a reporter might have earned between 6,000 and 10,000 francs a month. Note that, in the published version of the trial, where the same question was asked by the president of the court, Isorni's transcript has Brasillach

naming the amount of the bonus for 1943 as "20,000" francs instead of "120,000" francs—a significant typographical error.

54 **"I don't think there are many prisoners who haven't . . ."**: *Six heures à perdre* (Paris: Plon, 1953), p. 66, reprinted in *Oeuvres complètes*, vol. 3, p. 395.

54 **their tearful farewell scene at the gates of the camp:** See *Six heures à perdre*, chapter 4, "La porte ouverte," pp. 114–131 in the 1953 edition; reprinted in *Oeuvres complètes*, vol. 3, pp. 433–447. Bardèche transposes much of this chapter in his construction of a posthumous wartime memoir by Brasillach, *Journal d'un homme occupé*. See part 1, chapter 3, Oflag VI A, "La port ouverte," pp. 147–150 (Paris: Les Sept Couleurs, 1955), reprinted in *Oeuvres complètes*, vol. 6, pp. 461–464.

54 **Jean Zay . . . was taken out of his prison cell and shot:** On the extreme right press campaign against Jean Zay, see Linda Orr, "Céline, Jean Zay, and the Mutations of Hate," in *Céline, USA,* Kaplan and Roussin ed., spring 1994, vol. 93, no. 2, pp. 333–344.

54 **fascist radio star and Minister of Information Philippe Henriot:** Henriot contributed regularly to *Je Suis Partout* during the period 1943–44.

54 **Victor Basch . . . was . . . shot in the back:** See Françoise Basch, *Victor Basch: De l'Affaire Dreyfus au crime de la Milice* (Paris: Plon, 1994).

55 **"Nous ne sommes pas des dégonflés":** *Je Suis Partout,* January 16, 1944.

55 **"French more than national socialist, really":** Robert Brasillach to Lucien Rebatet, August 14, 1943. The letter was entered as state's evidence at his trial but Brasillach would quote from it during his interrogation, in his own defense. A carbon copy of the letter was in prosecutor Marcel Reboul's private papers (courtesy Bernadette Reboul). Jacques Isorni, *Mémoires, 1911–1945* (Paris: Laffont, 1984), leaves out the damaging conclusion from his own lengthy quotation of this letter, pp. 290–291.

56 **a series of editorials for *Révolution Nationale:*** During this period, Brasillach also wrote literary and theater criticism for the *Chronique de Paris* and *L'Echo de France.*

56 **Anne Brassié, his biographer, reports:** Anne Brassié, *Robert Brasillach ou Encore un instant de bonheur* (Paris: Laffont, 1987), p. 275.

56 **He told a police inspector:** Robert Brasillach, interview with Inspector Galey, Commissaire de Police, October 13, 1944 (Archives of the Paris Préfecture de Police): "The Propaganda-Staffel were upset about this departure and even recounted the incidents at *Je Suis Partout* in a confidential bulletin, strictly reserved for the German censors and which was reproduced eight days later in a clandestine journal of the resistance. All the same, I figured I had no obligation toward the Propaganda-Staffel. I therefore abandoned my role at *Je Suis Partout* as editor in chief and at the same time I stopped contributing to the newspaper and resigned as a member of the board of administrators, thus abandoning a financial situation that had become very lucrative as a result of the sales of the paper." A second copy of this police interview is part of the Isorni archives, Paris Bar Association.

57 **"Brasillach, editor of the courageous political weekly *Je Suis Partout*":** "Der Fall Brasillach" *Spiegel der Französischen Presse: Bericht der Gruppe Pressse der Propaganda-Abteilung Frankreich,* October 1943, p. 1. From the full text of the report, courtesy Christine Arnothy and the Bellanger Foundation (translated from the German by Cordula Guski and Daniel Villanueva): "The events of these weeks in September have accelerated the separation of the courageous journalists from the lazy and fearful journalists in French press circles. The overall grouping of the French populace into German-friendly, German-unfriendly and/or hesitant elements and those who do not care one way or the other is also plainly visible here. The case of Brasillach

is an example of this. Brasillach, editor of the courageous political weekly *Je Suis Partout,* who had just returned from a trip to the French Volunteer Legion in the East, suggested to the editorial board of his paper that they should retreat from coverage of current political issues and in the future offer only literature—this under the influence of news of Mussolini's 'resignation.' Discouraged by the military developments as he saw them, and strongly influenced by the secretly published book of the unreliable collaborator Fabre-Luce, his opinion was that French interests dictated a greater reticence in the political domain as he could already perceive it in certain newspapers in the southern zone, particularly *Gringoire.* He hesitated in response to the aggressive and open attacks on America and thought they were unwelcome, even dangerous. During the meeting of the editorial team, opinions clashed. Brasillach's proposal to flee politics was rejected by a majority. Brasillach left the editorship. As if they needed to be forgiven, the remaining editors redoubled their political credo. The general director Lesca found strong words to express a 'final objective.' It was out of the question to let oneself be intimidated by the numbers and materials deployed in the mathematical war strategy of the English and the Americans. To the gentlemen in the propaganda service, they made excuses and expressed their steadfastness. A call by the [Nazi] press group to the Parisian journalists not too cowardly abandon their fight was perceived in these circles. The number of courageous articles, signed personally, increased. Brasillach, motivated by a sort of shame, published an article in *Révolution Nationale* on the collaboration of hearts between Germany and France. Encouraged by his entourage, he has resumed his valuable political work. . . . In view of the constant attacks of which several pro-German journalists have been victims, the question of personal protection becomes more and more urgent. Globally, the French press, in many of her positive elements, has demonstrated that it is equal to the great challenges of the past weeks." An excerpt from this report was published by Claude Bellanger in his *La Presse clandestine: 1940–1944* (Paris: Colin, 1961), p. 186.

58 **"When I see German soldiers, on the street or in the countryside":** Brasillach, "La Naissance d'un sentiment," *Révolution nationale,* September 4, 1943, reprinted in *Oeuvres complètes,* vol. 12, p. 579.

58 **"It seems to me that I've contracted a liaison with German genius":** Brasillach, "Lettre à quelques jeunes gens," *Révolution nationale,* reprinted in *Oeuvres complètes,* vol. 12, p. 612.

Three   The Liberation of Paris

60 **Bernadette Reboul . . . tells about the week of August 19:** Interviews with Bernadette Reboul, April 1996.

63 **His modest journal:** "Transcription d'une sorte de journal tenu en août–septembre 1944, pendant la Libération de Paris" [Unpublished transcript of a diary of sorts, kept from August to September 1944, during the Liberation of Paris]. This text is one source for Grenier's 1957 novel, *Les Embuscades* (Paris: Gallimard, 1957), translated by Linda Ascher as *Years in Ambush* (New York: Knopf, 1963).

65 **the headquarters of Paris's administrative prefect:** In 1944, Paris had no single mayor. The city was governed by a central prefect with jurisdiction over the entire Parisian region, including the suburbs. Each arrondissement, or neighborhood district, had its own city hall and mayor.

65 **there weren't enough members of the CDLR to go around:** The joke among its members was that the CDLR was so small, it wasn't "Ceux de la Résistance" [those of the resistance], but rather "celui de la résistance" [he of the resistance]. In the heat of the moment, Grenier said, he didn't realize there was a battle going on, on every Committee of Liberation, for political control between the communists and the Gaullists.

66 **each city hall was liberated by a "Committee of Liberation":** The CDLs were composed of "representatives of resistance movements, trade unions, and parties affiliated with the Conseil National de la Résistance." There were committees of liberation in every state (what the French call "départements"), county, and town in France (Herbert R. Lottman, *The Purge* [New York: William Morrow, 1986], p. 49).

67 **an "immense rumor that crossed Paris":** Arlette Grebel, *Vous disiez donc, matelot: Récit.* (Paris: Gallimard, 1972), p. 157. Interviews with Arlette Grebel, Saint Germain des Champs, March 1996.

67 **The gardens were teeming with people making love:** Perhaps she was remembering Claude Roy's lyrical passage on the lovers of postwar Paris: "Around Paris, at night, a belt of lovers. From the bois to Notre-Dame, parading down the Champs-Elysées, on the quais, under the bridges, in the squares, in the Tuileries, under the arches of the Louvre, on the lawns, in the jardins, on the porches of houses, on the metro steps, lovers. Happy lovers." "Les Yeux fermés dans Paris apaisé," in *Saison violente: Journal d'un témoin, 1944–1945* (Paris: Julliard, 1945), p. 232.

68 **The anarchist diarist Jean Galtier-Boissière:** *Mon journal pendant l'occupation,* p. 163, quoted in Pierre-Marie Dioudonnat, *Je Suis Partout (1930–1944)* (Paris: La Table Ronde, 1973), p. 379.

68 **A new press corps had organized itself . . . by August:** Marc Martin, "La Reconstruction de l'appareil d'information en France à la Libération," in *Matériaux pour l'histoire de notre temps,* juillet–décembre 1995, no. 39/40, pp. 35–38.

69 **"The Joy of Paris":** "Le Général de Gaulle à Paris," *France-Libre,* August 26, 1944.

70 **"It seems to me a good thing in and of itself":** Brasillach, *Oeuvres complètes,* vol. 9 (Paris: Club de l'Honnête Homme, 1963–1966), Letter from Brasillach to Maurice Bardèche, January 28, 1945, p. 300.

70 **The seven-story building . . . housed the major resistance dailies:** See Yves-Marc Ajchenbaum, *A la vie, à la mort: L'Histoire du journal Combat, 1941–1974.* Paris: Le Monde Editions, 1994, p. 93.

70 **he certainly wasn't going to leave his country now!:** Brasillach, *Oeuvres complètes,* vol. 6, *Journal d'un homme occupé,* p. 541.

71 **"We stayed chatting in the garden for a long time":** Ibid., p. 542.

71 **"Jews have lived in cupboards for nearly four years":** Ibid., p. 539.

71 **Meanwhile, Sens . . . was aflame with Liberation fever:** For a history of the liberation of Sens, see Joël Drogland, *Histoire de la résistance sénonaise, 1940–1944* (Auxerre: A.R.O.R.Y., 1997). There is an administrative paper trail in the departmental archives concerning the arrest of Brasillach's stepfather, Dr. Maugis. An October 23, 1944 list entitled "traitors" reads, "Docteur Maugis: honorary president of the RNP [Rassemblement National Populaire, the political party of Marcel Déat], father-in-law of the traitor Brasillach, was released for so-called reasons of health, but in fact continues his consultations" (Archives Départementales de l'Yonne 1W322, "Liste des personnes faisant l'objet d'un arrêt d'internement"). Dr. Maugis was arrested, interned in the Sens hospital, released for health reasons, then arrested a second time on the strength of a denunciation by the Mayor of Saint-Martin du Tertre, who accused him of having given a speech encouraging voluntary work service in Germany. According to the records, the mayor later took back his accusation. In a letter dated December 1, 1944, Dr. Maugis's lawyer writes to the examining magistrate of Sens to ask for Dr. Maugis's release (Archives Départementales de l'Yonne 6Wsc25477). Although Maugis's name appears on several lists of arrested collaborators, there is no administrative trace of Madame Maugis's arrest—which never resulted in an interview with an examining magistrate—in the records. My

information on the arrest of Madame Maugis comes from Isorni's memoirs, from the notes to Brasillach's *Oeuvres complètes,* and from Brasillach's correspondence.

72 **"I discovered the smug accounts of German atrocities":** Brasillach, *Oeuvres complètes,* vol. 6, *Journal d'un homme occupé,* p. 557. See also Andrée Viollis, *Indochine S.O.S.,* preface by André Malraux (Paris: Gallimard, 1935). Viollis was one of the first and strongest critics of French colonialism.

73 **"I did what I thought was right for four years":** Brasillach, *Oeuvres complètes,* vol. 9, "Lettres écrites en prison," Letter from Brasillach to his mother, dated September 6 through September 14, 1944, p. 173.

73 **"Not I," . . . "I find it rather funny":** Brasillach, *Oeuvres complètes,* vol. 6, *Journal d'un homme occupé,* p. 562.

73 **a leader in the Sens resistance named Lieutenant Germain:** Germain was the "nom de guerre" for François Grillot, who had served as the commissioner for regional operations (COR) of the Francs-Tireurs Partisans and who became, at the liberation, the adjunct to Lieutenant Kléber, in charge of the local Purge (Drogland, *Histoire de la résistance sénonaise, 1940–1944*).

74 **"the shame of this country":** "Critique de la nouvelle presse," *Combat,* August 31, 1944, reprinted in Albert Camus, *Essais* (Paris: Gallimard/Bibliothèque de la Pléiade, 1977), p. 263.

74 **"To be twenty or twenty-five in September of '44":** Simone de Beauvoir, *Force of Circumstance,* trans. Richard Howard (New York: Putnam's Sons, 1964), p. 9.

Four Jail

75 **"This time, I was going to learn about prison":** Brasillach, *Journal d'un homme occupé, Oeuvres complètes,* vol. 6 (Paris: Club de l'Honnête Homme, 1963–1966), p. 580.

75 **linked by prosecution speeches that referred to one another:** See chapter 8, "Court."

76 **Levillain . . . dreamed of becoming the head of the police:** Archives Nationales, Z6 414.

76 **Levillain was a slightly ridiculous Philistine:** Pierre Pellissier, *Brasillach . . . le Maudit* (Paris: Denoël, 1989), p. 366.

76 **Henri Bardèche had been arrested . . . for "notorious collaboration":** Henri Bardèche's trial took place on June 1, 1945. His family tie to Brasillach counted as heavily against him as his involvement in the bookstore. He was sentenced to five years forced labor and ten years of "national degradation" (amounting to the loss of basic civil rights, including the right to vote or to hold public office and the right to own a company); he died in forced labor (Dossier Z6 46, no. 787, Archives Nationales).

76 **"You wanted France to take lessons from a foreign power":** Brasillach, "Mémorandum écrit par Robert Brasillach pour la préparation de son procès," *Oeuvres complètes,* vol. 5, pp. 615–645. It is interesting to note how few questions Brasillach anticipated on the subject of his anti-Semitism. The few questions he did imagine were couched in terms of foreign influence: "Your anti-Semitic campaigns were inspired by Germany"; "Isn't anti-Semitism German and Hitlerian?"; "Shouldn't you have avoided bringing up this problem during the German occupation?" It is obvious here that he was preparing to defend himself under the assumption that he was being tried for treason, not for ideological crime.

76 **"Like the accused of 1793":** Robert Brasillach to Jacques Isorni, November 2, 1944, quoted in Isorni, *Mémoires, 1911–1945* (Paris: Laffont, 1984), p. 281.

77 **"I mistrust witnesses terribly"**: Brasillach, "Lettres écrites en prison," *Oeuvres complètes,* vol. 9, December 16, 1944, p. 242.

77 **For the prosecution, Reboul counter-proposed Zousman:** Interview with Bernadette Reboul. Brasillach referred to Zousman in his January 14, 1945 letter to Maurice Bardèche as "a Jew from Odessa, with whom I was in captivity, and who hates me" ("Lettres écrites en prison," *Oeuvres complètes,* vol. 9, p. 280).

77 **from what Bernadette Reboul learned from her father:** Interview with Bernadette Reboul, March 1996. She remembers her father explaining that the prosecution's witnesses were extremely damming—perhaps concerning Brasillach's behavior in the oflag, toward Jewish officers. But she is not sure. "My father and Isorni decided by mutual agreement not to use witnesses on either side, but to fight it out 'face to face.'"

77 **"Finally, I'll have no witness"**: Brasillach to Maurice Bardèche, January 14, 1945, "Lettres écrites en prison," *Oeuvres complètes,* vol. 9, p. 281.

77 **he must have written all day long:** Sixty-four prison letters are published in the *Oeuvres complètes.* Geneviève Maugis published Brasillach's prison letters to her in *Mon demi-frère, Robert Brasillach; (suivi de) Il fallait bien vivre quand même: Mémoires* (Paris: la Pensée Universelle, 1981).

78 **new jurisdictions for the punishment of collaborators:** The Courts of Justice were established by an ordinance of June 26, 1944; the crime of national indignity by an ordinance of August 26, 1944. See Henry Rousso, "L'Epuration en France: Une Histoire inachevée," *Vingtième Siècle: Revue d'Histoire,* no. 33, January–March, 1992, p. 87.

78 **they settled on articles 75–86 of the penal code:** See Michel Laval, *Brasillach ou la trahison du clerc* (Paris: Hachette, 1992), pp. 161–166, for a useful exposé of the legal planning for the Purge and a clear explanation of the legal codes applied to collaboration. See *Code pénal annoté par Emile Garçon,* new edition by Marcel Rousselet, Maurice Patin, and Marc Ancel, eds., vol. 1 (Paris: Recueil Sirey, 1952), for an analysis of each separate article.

79 **chosen within the realm of professional magistrates:** In regular French courts, the examining magistrates, or "juges d'instruction," the judges who studied the dossier to determine whether a case should go to trial, were extremely powerful. In the Purge courts, their power was reduced to that of collecting information. The examining magistrates were not empowered, for example, to call a "mistrial"— only the Commissaire du Gouvernement (the government prosecutor) could do this. See Rousso, "L'Epuration en France," p. 88.

79 **The Courts of Justice operated . . . until January 31, 1951:** Ibid.

79 **They condemned 6,763 people to death:** The figures on sentencing are from Olivier Wieviorka, "Les Mécanismes de l'Epuration," *L'Histoire,* no. 179, July–August 1994, pp. 44–51.

79 **taken up residence in the castle at Sigmaringen:** On Sigmaringen, see Henry Rousso, *Pétain et la fin de la collaboration: Sigmaringen, 1944–1945* (Paris: Editions Complexe, 1984).

81 **"an old syphilitic whore, stinking of patchouli and yeast infection"**: "La Conjuration anti-fasciste au service du Juif," *Je Suis Partout,* February 7, 1942. Discussed in chapter 2, "Brasillach's War," in connection with *Bérénice.*

82 **"We must separate from the Jews *en bloc* and not keep any little ones"**: Brasillach, "Les sept Internationales contre la patrie," in *Je Suis Partout,* September 25, 1942, reprinted in *Oeuvres complètes,* volume 12, p. 479. On Laval's policy to separate Jewish children from their parents, see Michael Marrus and Robert O. Paxton,

Vichy France and the Jews (New York: Schocken, 1983), and Kupferman, *Laval* (Paris: Flammarion, 1988). For the details of police arrests of parents and children, see Serge Klarsfeld, *Le Calendrier de la persécution des juifs en France, 1940–1944* ([Paris]: Editions Klarsfeld, 1993).

82 **during the year 1942, 1,032 children under the age of six:** Marrus and Paxton, *Vichy France and the Jews,* p. 269.

83 **"deporting children to Auschwitz would improve his image":** Marrus and Paxton, *Vichy France and the Jews,* p. 269.

83 **Parents were deported immediately:** For an exact and detailed chronological account, with a breakdown by age and location, see Klarsfeld, *Le Calendrier de la persécution des juifs.*

83 **"That children, women, men, fathers and mothers":** For the speeches of the Archevêque de Toulouse, criticized by Brasillach, see Monseigneur Saliège's speech of August 23, 1942, "Sur la personne humaine" [On the human person], published in Monseigneur Saliège, Archevêque de Toulouse, *Témoignages, 1939–44* (Paris: Editions du Témoignage Chrétien, 1944), p. 117.

84 **"Like many Frenchmen of all tendencies":** From Isorni archives, Paris Bar Association. Statement by Brasillach, undated, marked "déposition préalable au procès destinée au juge d'instruction." In the transcript of his October 27, 1944, interrogation, Brasillach is quoted as announcing, "Please find attached my memorandum in response to the charges against me." This document is probably the memorandum to which he refers.

84 **"I approve of no physical violence":** Brasillach, *Oeuvres complètes,* vol. 5, p. 640.

85 **"I am an anti-Semite":** "Lettre à un soldat," *Oeuvres complètes,* vol. 5, p. 596. The first part of the passage is especially twisted, and difficult to render in English: "Je suis antisémite, je sais par l'histoire l'horreur de la dictature juive, mais qu'on ait si souvent séparé les familles, jeté dehors les enfants, organisé des déportations qui n'auraient pu être legitimes que si elles n'avaient pas pour but, à nous, caché, la mort pure et simple, me paraît, et m'a toujours paru inadmissible."

85 **Even Germany's actions, he explains in this passage:** Bardèche, introducing the Brasillach collection entitled *Ecrit à Fresnes* (Paris: Plon, 1967), which included "Lettre à un soldat," ignored this paragraph and claimed that Brasillach had had no idea about the death camps, because, according to him, no one did: "The concentration camps, which weren't discovered by the American army until April 1945, were completely unknown. I can only presume . . . that he would never have associated himself with a politics of extermination, or even cruelty." Jeannine Verdès-Leroux, in her *Refus et violences* (p. 434), called my attention to this inconsistency. (Later, of course, Bardèche would become infamous for his role in promoting Holocaust revisionism.)

85 **deportation . . . had as its goal "death, pure and simple":** In 1978, Klarsfeld's patient research finally allowed the French to count and identify the people who died in deportation from France. See, in English translation, his *Memorial to the Deportation of the Jews of France, 1942–1944: Document* (New York: Klarsfeld Foundation, 1983).

86 **"The Expiation Is Starting":** "Partout et ailleurs," subtitled "L'Expiation commence," in *Je Suis Partout,* July 17, 1942. In an article entitled "Que savaient les collaborationnistes" (in Stéphane Courtois and Adam Rayski, eds., *Qui savait quoi? L'Extermination des juifs, 1941–1945* [Paris: La Découverte, 1987], pp. 67–77), Philippe Burrin argues convincingly, quoting passages from *Au Pilori,* the most virulently anti-Semitic of the collaborationist papers in Paris, that the "ultra" collaborationists knew very well about the plan for a final solution, referring to it in veiled, but excited, "insider's" terms, in their columns.

86 **starting to "run in all directions like poisoned rats":** "Partout et ailleurs," *Je Suis Partout,* January 10, 1943, p. 2.

87 **an article on the liberation of Maïdanek:** *Le Choc: 1945, la presse révèle l'enfer des camps nazis* (Paris: Fédération Nationale des Déportés, Internés, Résistants et Patriotes, 1985).

87 **"We all know":** "Assemblée Consultative Provisoire—Séance du 6 Décembre 1944," in *Débats de L'Assemblée Consultative Provisoire,* tome 1, November 7—December 28, 1944 (Paris: Imprimerie des Journaux Officiels, 1945), refers to prison camps and deportation camps, to Auschwitz, and to gas chambers as widely shared knowledge: "We all know that French people in large numbers have fallen executed in Poland, [and] have perished in gas chambers" (p. 442).

87 **"The Names on the Walls":**

Les Noms sur les murs
D'autres sont venus par ici
Dont les noms sur les murs moisis
Se défont déjà, et s'écaillent.
Ils ont souffert et espéré
Et parfois l'espoir était vrai,
Parfois il dupait ces murailles.

Venus d'ici, venus d'ailleurs,
Nous n'avions pas le même coeur,
Nous a-t-on dit: Faut-il le croire?
Mais qu'importe ce que nous fûmes!
Nos visages noyés de brume
Se ressemblent dans la nuit noire.

C'est à vous, frères inconnus,
Que je pense, le soir venu,
O mes fraternels adversaires!
Hier est proche d'aujourd'hui.
Malgré nous nous sommes unis
Par l'espoir et par la misère.

Je pense à vous, vous qui rêviez,
Je pense à vous qui souffriez
Dont aujourd'hui j'ai pris la place.
Si demain la vie est permise,
Ces noms qui sur les murs se brisent
Nous seront-ils nos mots de passe?

88 **in magazines such as *Poésie 42–43,* . . . :** These magazines were the medium through which Brasillach's friend Claude Roy made the transition from critic at *Action Française* and *Je Suis Partout* to intimate of the unofficial poet laureate of the communist literary resistance, Louis Aragon. On Roy's career, see chapter 2, "Brasillach's War."

88 **Poems by Eluard ("Liberté") and Aragon ("La Rose et le réséda"):** See also the anthology *Ecrivains en prison* ["In memoriam. Poèmes des absents. Sortis des liens," August, 1945] (Paris: Seghers, 1945), which includes resistance poems from Fresnes and from the concentration camps. For a reading, with photographic illustrations, of the resistance graffiti in Fresnes prison, see Henri Calet, *Les Murs de Fresnes* (May 1945; Paris: Editions Viviane Hamy, 1993, new edition).

89 **He applauded the arrest of Emmanuel Mounier:** Emmanuel Mounier was one of forty people arrested on January 15, 1942; the group included carriers of the

underground newspaper *Combat*. For details of his detention and trial, see Michel Winock, *"Esprit": Des intellectuels dans la cité, 1930–1950* (Seuil: Points/Histoire, 1975), pp. 248 ff.

89 **"All it would take would be ten suppressions":** "A travers Lyon dans les brumes de l'attentisme," *Je Suis Partout,* February 28, 1942.

89 **"The young poets aren't worth much more [than Aragon]":** Brasillach, "Y a-t-il un renouveau de la Poésie?" *Je Suis Partout,* July 31, 1942. The article is omitted from the collection of Brasillach's *Je Suis Partout* articles in the *Oeuvres complètes.*

89 **Every sentence encouraging the arrest of writers has been cut:** In addition, the word "Jew" has been changed throughout the article to "émigré." A sentence that reads, "There are Jews everywhere [in Lyon, in the unoccupied zone], we're stepping on them—or rather, they'd happily step on us," is cut. A pious pro-Vichy statement has been moved from the middle of the article to become the last sentence of the chapter: "Thus even the thinking of the chief of state has been betrayed." See "A travers Lyon dans les brumes de l'attentisme," *Je Suis Partout,* February 28, 1942. The article is not included in the first published version of *Journal d'un homme occupé* (Paris: Les Sept Couleurs, 1955). The truncated version of the article appears in *Oeuvres complètes,* vol. 6, pp. 469–473.

90 **an anthology of resistance poetry called *L'Honneur des poètes:*** For a history of *L'honneur des poètes,* see Anne Simonin, *Les Editions de Minuit 1942–1955 Le devoir d'insoumission* (Paris: IMEC, 1994), pp. 114 ff. *L'Honneur des poètes* was the object of a famous literary attack by a surrealist, Benjamin Péret, in 1945 (*Le Déshonneur des poètes* (Paris: Pauvert, 1965).

90 **Gallois wrote a letter in favor of Brasillach:** Personal collection of Bernadette Reboul, Letter from Daniel Gallois to Jacques Isorni, November 3, 1944: Gallois explains in his letter that he belonged to the OCM, which was a right-wing resistance organization.

90 **Brasillach made gestures in favor of several other people:** Cavaillès, Bruhat, and Colette's husband Goudeket. See Pellissier, *Brasillach . . . le Maudit,* p 362. See also the correspondence in Brasillach's pardon file, Archives Nationales, Recours en grâce de Robert Brasillach, 1945, S.2977.

Five   Marcel Reboul: Government Prosecutor

92 **[Mornet] had served under Vichy as the president of a commission:** Fred Kupferman, *Laval, 1883–1945* (Paris: Flammarion, 1988), p. 498.

92 **Roy . . . remarked that Laval was being judged not by France:** Claude Roy, "Accusé, ne vous levez pas," in *Les Lettres Françaises,* 5th year, no. 77, October 13, 1945. Quoted by Kupferman, *Laval, 1883–1945,* pp. 498–499.

92 **Grenier . . . wrote bitterly about the old men:** Roger Grenier, *Combat,* October 6, 1945, p. 1: "And Laval cried out: 'You were at the Government's disposal.' France should not put herself in the situation of letting such a thing be said to those who represent Justice in a trial such as this one. The score to be settled is not between these inadequate old men and this imperious criminal. It is between Laval and the country. That is why a popular tribunal, with no salaried magistrate on it, might have shown more dignity and more force in this affair."

92 **Marcel Reboul . . . had been in charge of the repression of terrorism:** Pascal Copeau, "Châtiment, épuration et politique," *Action,* January 20, 1945, quoted in Michel Laval, *Brasillach ou la trahison des clercs* (Paris: Hatchette, 1992), p. 226: "Perhaps we will see the prosecutor general Reboul, who under Vichy was given the special function of prosecutor in charge of 'repression of terrorism,' asking for the death

sentence. The self-righteous will return home to bed reassured, for 'force will remain with the law.' For us for, the red blush of shame will race to our faces and we will start to doubt our country."

92 **suspicious of the continuity of power between Pétain and de Gaulle:** People like to tell the story that de Gaulle wanted Pétain to be his son's godfather but Madame de Gaulle refused because Pétain had been divorced.

93 **"Yesterday, members of the jury":** Procès Georges Suarez, October 23, 1944, Sténographie Bluet, 334 AP8. Plaidoirie de Maître Boiteau, p. 100.

93 **"I argued behind this bar during the Occupation":** Lucien Felgines, Cour de Justice de la Seine, October 27 and November 3, 1944. Archives Nationales, Sténographie Bluet, plaidoirie de Maître Ribera, pp. 5–7.

94 **It was he in particular who defined the notion of "national indignity":** For a good discussion of Rolland's role, see Herbert R. Lottman, *The Purge* (New York: Morrow, 1986), pp. 41–43.

94 **The magistrature was like many other institutions:** See Alain Bancaud and Henry Rousso, "L'Epuration des magistrats à la Libération (1944–1945)," pp. 117–144 in a special issue of *Histoire de la justice,* no. 6, 1994, entitled "L'Epuration de la magistrature de la révolution à la Libération: 150 ans d'histoire judiciaire," including an analysis of the Purge commissions. For a long-range history of the tradition of political purges in the magistrature—including Vichy's purge of Jews and freemasons—see same issue of *Histoire de la justice,* esp. Christian Bachelier and Denis Peschanski, "L'Epuration de la magistrature sous Vichy," pp. 103–115.

94 **sins of the magistrature:** See Bancaud and Rousso, "L'Epuration des magistrats à la Libération (1944–1945)."

95 **they would be tried in a criminal trial in the Salle des Assises:** Jean Favard, *Au coeur de Paris, un palais pour la justice* (Paris: Gallimard, 1995), p. 86.

95 **there were simply too many constraints built into the system:** Interview with legal historian Alain Bancaud, Paris, April 1996.

96 **"His words fell, like the blades of a guillotine":** *Combat,* December 10, 1944, in the coverage of the trial of the rue Lauriston gang, known as the "French Gestapo."

96 **Reboul was "tall, black-haired, bony":** *Le Figaro,* December 2, 1944.

96 **"M. Reboul roars," read the headline in *Libres-soir:*** André Marianne, "Lafont pleure, Delval sourit, M. Reboul tonne," *Libres-soir: Organe du mouvement national des prisonniers de guerre et déportés,* December 10, 1944.

96 **A caricature drawn of Marcel Reboul:** Caricature dated December 25, 1944, by Socrate Broffoni, courtesy Bernadette Reboul.

99 **with the exception of a man named Paul Didier:** On Didier and his administrative context, see Marc-Olivier Baruch, *Servir l'Etat français: L'Administration en France de 1940 à 1944* (Paris: Fayard, 1997), p. 312.

100 **joined forces to get one of their neighbors . . . released:** Interview with Bernadette Reboul, March 1996.

101 **the most notorious . . . were the explicitly political Special Sections:** Law of April 24, 1941, published in "Lois et decrets," *Gazette du Palais,* 1941, p. 849. There were Special Sections in each Court of Appeals district.

101 **After 1942, when Reboul started prosecuting there:** Interview with Alain Bancaud, based on his work-in-progress on the magistrature during the Occupation.

102 **A magistrate's charge is . . . "to loyally serve the regime in place":** In Bancaud and Rousso's view, Vichy did not make major changes in the judicial apparatus, except for the oath of loyalty to Pétain and a certain lessening of the

independence of the sitting judge. French Judges considered Pétain's government legal. Reboul would have considered himself a representative of the French state he served, not the Vichy state. However, it's important to remember that this same Vichy regime purged Jews and freemasons from the magistrature in 1940, considering them unreliable. Such purges have taken place in the French magistrature since the nineteenth century (see Bachelier and Peschanski, "L'Epuration de la magistrature sous Vichy").

102 **Reboul would send them to their deaths in 1944:** Along with the rue Lauriston gang, the defendants in the trial included Delval, made famous in Marguerite Duras's story, "Pierre X, dit Rabier" (*La Douleur*). In her story, she describes cultivating a friendship with a Gestapo agent to get information about her husband, Robert Antelme. Duras testified against Delval in the case prosecuted by Reboul. For the transcript of the trial, see Archives Nationales, AO 334/9: "Bonny, Lafont et autres." For a fascinating account of the Duras-Delval relationship, and Duras's testimony in the trial, see Laure Adler, *Marguerite Duras* (Paris: Gallimard, 1998).

102 **his black market decisions go back to October 1940:** See *Dalloz,* the *Gazette du Palais,* and the *Semaine Juridique* for the period October 4, 1940 through May 10, 1944.

104 **"From that moment on, he knew":** Bernadette Reboul, June 11, 1987, letter to Alain Decaux in response to his June 10, 1987, television broadcast, "Le Dossier d'Alain Decaux. Brasillach: La Mort en face" (produced by Jean-Charles Dudrumet).

104 **Reboul family legend tells how the men in Sigmaringen:** Interview with Bernadette Reboul. French Ministry of Information transcripts of the Sigmaringen radio broadcasts are available at the Hoover Library, Stanford University, although I found no trace of the broadcast she describes.

105 **"Look, I could have been in the dry goods business like my grandfather":** Interview with Bernadette Reboul, Toulon, April 1996.

105 **"Justice is god, but you're not allowed to say so":** Interview with Frédéric Pottecher, Paris, June 1997.

106 **"While, from an economic point of view":** Transcript of the Maubourguet trial, Archives Nationales 334AP/8, November 3, 1944.

106 **The wife of the prosecutor found it a very strange gesture:** Interview with Bernadette Reboul, April 1996.

106 **"a grotesque character in the style of Joseph Prudhomme":** Robert Brasillach to Maurice Bardèche, December 21, 1944, in Brasillach, *Oeuvres complètes,* vol. 9 (Paris: Club de l'Honnête Homme, 1963–1966), p. 244.

106 **"If only Isorni would let me say two or three funny things":** Robert Brasillach to Maurice Bardèche, January 9, 1945, in ibid., p. 268.

107 **"If he lets out a line like that about me":** Brasillach to Bardèche, December 21, 1944, in ibid., pp. 244–245.

Six   Jacques Isorni: Counsel for the Defense

108 **performed the most brilliant verbal tricks in the trial:** Bernadette Reboul called the trial a "concours d'éloquence" (interview, Toulon, April, 1996).

110 **Charles Maurras . . . "Socrates teaching his disciples":** Jacques Isorni, *Mémoires, 1911–1945* (Paris: Laffont, 1984), p. 53.

110 **he threw himself on his bed and wept in disappointment:** Ibid., p. 57.

110 **"I understood what the strength of a successful oration":** Ibid., p. 63.

110 **"My adolescence . . . was devoured by the need":** Ibid., p. 77.

111 *L'Insurgé* . . . **only existed for one year, from 1936 to 1937:** The short life span of *L'Insurgé* corresponded to the period that Charles Maurras spent in prison for having called for the murder of Léon Blum in the *Action Française*—October 1936 to July 1937. Maurras attacked the representatives who signed a petition asking for sanctions against Italy, after the Italian invasion of Ethiopia: "Do you have an automatic pistol, a revolver or even a kitchen knife? Whatever weapon it is, it must be used against the assassins of peace whose list you have." Attacking Léon Blum more generally in May 1936 for his attitude towards Mussolini, he wrote: "He's going to be the master of power? It is possible. He will not be the master for sending the French people to the slaughterhouse. If necessary, he will be the first killed," and, in the next issue, he wrote, "It is as a Jew that this Blum must be seen, conceived of, listened to, fought and taken down." See Jean Favard, *Au coeur de Paris, un palais pour la justice* (Paris: Gallimard, 1995), p. 79.

111 **The article that targets Isorni:** *L'Insurgé,* no. 17, May 3, 1937. With no date to go on, Alex Galloway located the article on microfilm.

113 **For Maulnier . . . it would have been an embarrassment:** By 1968, Maulnier had become a member of the Académie Française, the august institution Isorni longed to enter. Isorni wasn't even sure that Maulnier supported him. See chapter 12, "After the Trial."

113 **"Being a lawyer in order to remain a free man":** Isorni, *Je suis avocat* (Paris: Editions du Conquistador, 1951), p. 11.

113 **"Sometimes I feel profoundly revolted":** Ibid., p. 12.

114 **"the beginning of hope":** Isorni, *Mémoires, 1911–1945,* p. 206.

114 **"To tell the truth, I felt like a Jew":** Ibid., p. 211.

115 **Isorni was quickly restored:** Robert Badinter, *Un Antisémitisme ordinaire: Vichy et les avocats juifs (1940–1944)* (Paris: Fayard, 1997), p. 62. The legislation was dated September 10, 1940. It excluded 203 lawyers from practice. Badinter estimates that at least 60 of these were Jewish. In addition, 10 lawyers born of foreign parents were maintained because they were veterans or descendants of veterans; 25 were reinstated by special decision of the Minister of Justice, due to their professional merits. Jacques Isorni was one of these.

116 **The inaugural session of the Paris Special Section:** For a dramatization, see Costa Gavras's 1974 film *Section Spéciale.*

116 **The judiciary did comply:** See for example, the memoirs of Joseph Barthélemy, *Ministre de la justice: Vichy, 1941–1943* (Paris: Pygmalion, 1989); Bertram M. Gordon, ed., *Historical Dictionary of World War II France: The Occupation, Vichy, and the Resistance, 1938–1946* (Westport, CT: Greenwood Press, 1998); and Hervé Villeré, *L'Affaire de la Section spéciale* (Paris: Fayard, 1973).

116 **prosecutors and presiding judges who sought the death penalty:** See Alain Bancaud and Henry Rousso, "L'Epuration des magistrats à la Libération (1944–1945)," in *Histoire de la justice,* Paris, no. 6 (special issue), 1994, pp. 133. On November 16–21, 1944, the magistrates who had served in the Paris Special Section went before a Purge commission composed of magistrates and members of the resistance. In all, ninety-seven magistrates who had served in a Special Section were brought up before this commission; a third of them were sanctioned. The most sensitive cases were those involving the repression of resistance fighters. Magistrates were punished, not for serving in these courts, but for not using their margin of independence to minimize the damage. Then in June 1945, six months after the Brasillach trial, the prosecutors and presiding judges of the Special Section were tried for treason in the

Salle des Assises, with sentences ranging from forced labor in perpetuity to prison and acquittal. The *Procureur* [Prosecutor General] who had imposed the Special Section legislation was condemned to death in absentia. (See Favard, *Au coeur de Paris, un palais pour la justice*, p. 86).

117 **"Remember . . . this is the woodsman from the forest of Orgerus":** See Isorni, *Mémoires, 1911–1945*, p. 229, and Isorni, *Les Cas de conscience de l'avocat* (Paris: Librairie Académique Perrin, 1965), p. 224.

119 **"Most of the deportees died because of what the enemy did to them":** Isorni, *Mémoires, 1911–1945*, p. 267.

119 **"Article 75 . . . was ravaging France":** Ibid., p. 266.

120 **He and Reboul spent hours talking about the case:** Interview with Bernadette Reboul.

120 **"Yes, you'll all be meeting up again, and I'll be playing dead":** Isorni, *Mémoires, 1911–1945*, p. 303: "Et je ferai le mort."

120 **"The one whose name shines":** Isorni, *Je Suis Avocat*, p. 37.

120 **"If the man exists who is ready to sacrifice his ideas":** Ibid., p. 99.

Seven   Missing Persons: Brasillach's Suburban Jury

122 **The legal designers of the new Courts of Justice:** On the choice of jurors, see *Code pénal annoté par Emile Garçon*, new edition by Marcel Rousselet, Maurice Patin, and Marc Ancel, eds., vol. 1 (Paris: Recueil, Sirey, 1952), pp. 268: "The legislators wanted the popular character of the Courts of Justice to be more accentuated than in the Courts of Assizes, the courts that tried criminal cases. Therefore, while there were seven members of the jury and three magistrates in the Court of Assizes—that is, a proportion of one to two—in the Courts of Justice the proportion of magistrates to members of the jury was one to four. It looks as though the legislators wanted to react against the Vichy regime which, in special sections of the courts of appeal, had instituted jurisdictions composed solely of professional magistrates."

122 **Vichy's "exceptional courts":** See the passionate speech by Laurent Bonnevay in the *Provisory Consultative Assembly*, December 5, 1944, p. 416: According to his account, twenty-six laws were passed under Vichy to establish nine new categories of "exceptional tribunals" including the Riom Supreme Court, the Special Tribunals, the Special Sections, and the special criminal courts for punishing terrorist—i.e. resistance—activities. For a useful summary of the court system under Vichy, see Marc Olivier Baruch, *Le Régime de Vichy* (Paris: La Découverte, 1996), pp. 78–79.

122 **"who had not ceased to show proof of national sentiments":** The French phrase is: "n'ayant pas cessé de faire preuve de sentiments nationaux." Garçon, *Code pénal annoté par Emile Garçon*, no. 174, article 8, paragraph 5, of the ordinance of November 28, 1944.

122 **committees . . . set in motion during the dramatic week of liberation:** See chapter 3, "The Liberation of Paris."

122 **In Champigny-sur-Marne, for example:** Archives of the city of Champigny-sur-Marne. City Council minutes, August 22, 1944: "By order of the National Committee of Resistance and the Paris Committee of Liberation, the representatives of the Union des Syndicats du Front National, the Forces Unies de la Jeunesse, the Resistance of the Communist Party, accompanied by representative groups from the Union des Femmes Françaises, des Veuves de Guerre, des Prisonniers . . ." On August 24, the Committee of Liberation was enlarged to include representatives from the group "Libération" and the Socialist Party.

123 **What remained intact, even after December 1945:** Garçon, *Code pénal annoté par Emile Garçon,* p. 268. The law was amended on December 14, 1945. From then on, representatives from the Committees of Liberation no longer participated in drawing up lists of jurors. The lists were to be drawn up solely by the President of the Tribunal along with two representatives designated by the departmental Commissioner of the Conseil Général du Département (and in the Seine by the Conseil Général).

123 **The phrase is key for understanding the period:** See ibid., pp. 175–176.

123 **the trial of the anti-Jewish administrator Xavier Vallat:** Vallat was in charge of the Commissariat aux Questions Juives.

123 **"The jurists were drawn at large from a list of the resistance":** Brasillach, *Journal d'un homme occupé, Oeuvres complètes,* vol. 6 (Paris: Club de l'Honnête Homme, 1963–1966), p. 587. See also Brasillach to Maurice Bardèche, December 11, 1944, "Lettres écrites en prison," *Oeuvres complètes,* vol. 9, p. 337: "I also understood from the [Chamber of Deputies] report that it is Midol, a commie, who made up the list from which jurors are chosen."

123 **there was a famous Midol family in the resistance:** According to Jean Maitron, *Dictionnaire biographique du mouvement ouvrier français* (Paris: Les Editions Ouvrières, 1986), vol. 4, pp. 361–364: Lucien Midol (1883–1979) was a member of the political bureau of the Communist Party from 1924 to 1959 as well as a *député* representing the Seine et Oise. In 1939, he was arrested for attempting to revive the outlawed communist party and condemned to five years in prison; he was transferred from the Puy to the Maison-Carrée in Algeria. Liberated by Allied troops in February 1943, he helped reorganize unions in Algiers. Midol was proposed to de Gaulle as a commissioner for industrial production for the Comité Français de Libération Nationale; instead, he was put in charge of the repatriation of French exiles remaining in Algeria. He returned to Paris in September 1944. His two sons, Maurice and René, were also active in the resistance.

123 **Isorni had brought the published minutes of that discussion:** Letter from Robert Brasillach to Maurice Bardèche, December 11, 1944, *Oeuvres complètes,* vol. 9, p. 237: "I saw the report in the *Officiel* of the session on the Purge in the Chamber [of Deputies]." A page torn from this document is conserved in the Isorni archives, along with his preparatory notes for the Brasillach trial. The entire debate on the Purge is part of the published records of the *Assemblée Consultative Provisoire: Débats,* vol. 1, November 7—December 28, 1944 (Paris: Imprimerie des Journaux Officiels, 1945), December 5, 1944, session, pp. 417–424. In response to challenges from the floor, Francis de Menthon, Minister of Justice, passionately defended the resistance credentials of Rolland, as well as those of other magistrates in charge of the Purge, and he described the careful purge that had taken place within the magistrature. He explained the choice of jurors for the Courts of Justice: "The Court of Justice is composed of four jurors named by two representatives of the departmental Committee of Liberation, in consultation with a magistrate. For example, the CPL [Parisian Committee of Liberation], in Paris, was represented by M. Midol, from the union, and by Mme Schmidt, representing the widows of men who were executed.... It was M. Midol who established the list that the first President [of the court] was happy to ratify. The jurors who are chosen, whose names are drawn from the lists thus established, pronounce the variety of condemnations which may surprise or scandalize you. These are the jurors, this is a popular tribunal, a tribunal of the resistance."

124 **the CNE published a list of writers tainted by the collaboration:** The CNE also had a newspaper, *Lettres Françaises,* that commented on the trials of collaborationist journalists.

124 **"I've seen some of them, some of those jury members!":** Jean Paulhan, *Lettre aux directeurs de la Résistance* (Paris: Editions de Minuit, 1951), p. 46.

125 **French women had finally received the right to vote:** See *Vingtième Siècle,* no. 42, April–June 1994, special issue on the fiftieth anniversary of women's right to vote, *Clio,* no. 1, 1995, "Résistances et libérateurs: France, 1940–1945."

125 **"For the first time in the judicial annals of France":** Alex Ancel, *Le Parisien Libéré,* October 23, 1944, p. 1: "Devant la Cour de Justice, Georges Suarez ouvrira le procès de la trahison."

125 **"Members of the jury, two officer workers . . .":** Madeleine Jacob, "Première audience de la Cour de Justice," *Franc-Tireur,* October 24, 1944.

126 **"Women, full partners in the jury, came to court untamed":** Marcel Perthus, "Les Cours de Justice sont-elles des Cours d'injustice?" *Esprit,* August 1947, pp. 195– 211.

126 **many suburban jurors were from the working class:** Christian Chomienne, "Juger les Juges," in *Juger sous Vichy,* special issue of *Le Genre humain* (Paris: Seuil, 1994), p. 14, argues that Vichy modified the composition of juries in criminal courts so as to effectively exclude manual workers, but I was unable to find any trace of such a reform.

126 **The myth of Paris's "red suburbs" . . . was more than a myth:** Annie Fourcaut, "Banlieue rouge, au-delà du mythe politique," *Banlieue rouge, 1920–1960* (Paris: Editions Autrement, 1992), p. 27.

127 **the suburb would no longer be a vague countryside:** For a portrait of the suburbs in postwar France, see Blaise Cendrars, *La Banlieue de Paris,* photos by Robert Doisneau (Paris: Seghers, 1949). On *Mon Oncle* (1958) and *Rue des Prairies* (1959), see Christian-Marc Bosséno, "Les Environs de Paris au fil du cinéma," *Banlieue rouge, 1920–1960,* pp. 242–251: "One has to wait for the end of the 1950s for the appearance of a new discourse on the periphery: the birth, on screen, of the suburb."

127 **" . . . poor people's memory is less nourished":** Albert Camus, *The First Man,* trans. David Hapgood (New York: Knopf, 1995, Vintage edition), p. 80.

128 **the alphabetical lists of jury members . . . of the Cours:** Archives Nationales. C.J. 896. Listes de jurés. Z6896 et 897. Including "Sommiers juridiques du 23 décembre 1944" (summons); "Services des Assises. ler trimestre. Liste par ordre alphabétique des jurés désignés par le sort pour siéger pendant la session de la Cour d'Assises, dont l'ouverture est fixée au 4 janvier 1945"; "tirage des jurés pour la 2ème sous-section de la Cour de Justice qui s'ouvrira le 4 janvier 1945 et sera présidée par M. le conseiller Vidal" (list of twenty). For the final four, see *L'Arrêt* for January 19, 1945: "Messieurs Riou, Grisonnet, Desvillettes, et Van der Beken, jurés titulaires de jugement, membres de ladite Cour de Justice . . ."

129 **Printers . . . play a big role in our imagination of the resistance:** On printers in the resistance, see Henri Noguères, *La Vie quotidienne des résistants de l'armistice à la Libération, 1940–1945* (Paris: Hachette, 1984), pp. 161–162.

129 **the documented resistance stories of Aubervilliers:** Chronology on the resistance in Aubervilliers by Joël Clesse and Sylvie Zaidman, in preparation for their *La Résistance en Seine Saint-Denis, 1940–1944* (Paris: Syros, 1994), courtesy Aubervilliers Historical Society.

130 **People lived in shacks, on "the zone," the periphery:** Jean-Jacques Karman, *Des histoires (extra)ordinaires d'Aubervilliers* (Rome: Lito Service di p. Fiorani, 1993), p. 127, courtesy Aubervilliers Historical Society.

130 **"The hands are nothing; imagine what is going on inside":** *Aubervilliers* (1945), short film. Director: Eli Lotar; commentary and lyrics: Jacques Prévert; photography: Eli Lotar; music: Joseph Kosma.

130 **races, where enormous rats were pursued by dogs:** "Le Ratodrome," in Jean-Jacques Karman, *Des histoires (extra)ordinaires d'Aubervilliers,* pp. 93–87.

130 **Today, the rue Heurtault . . . is one of the most run-down streets:** Information on the rue Heurtault and the rue du Moutier, below, is from Jacques Dersain, C. Fath, and J.-J. Karman, *Histoire des rues d'Aubervilliers: Supplément au Journal d'Aubervilliers,* undated, vol. 1, p. 43 (rue Heurtault), and p. 49 (rue du Moutier).

131 **Manigart was commander of the vast CDLR sector:** See Marie Granet, *Ceux de la Résistance, 1940–1944* (Paris: Les Editions de Minuit, 1964), pp. 220–221.

131 **The rue du Moutier was one of the trouble spots:** "Rue du Moutier," in Dersain, Fath, and Karman, *Histoire des rues d'Aubervilliers,* vol. 1, p. 49.

133 **"Laval was an ideal scapegoat":** Robert O. Paxton, *Vichy France: Old Guard and New Order, 1940–1944* (New York: Norton, 1972), pp. 25, 27.

134 **He was a successful student, who knew both German and English:** Telephone interview with Jacques Van der Beken, February 9, 1994, and correspondence with Janine Van der Beken Van Steekiste.

136 **Riou's niece . . . remembers him as a small man:** Telephone interview with Denise Altenbourger, Paris, 1977. The photographs of Riou discussed in this chapter were made available to me by Denise Altenbourger.

137 **"This essentially working-class population":** All from Seine Saint-Denis: Archives de Villetaneuse, 3H5, memos to the Kreiskommandantur of Seine Saint-Denis from the Mayor of Villetaneuse.

137 **a tricolor French flag . . . was hung on an electrical wire:** Clesse and Zaidman, *La Résistance en Seine Saint-Denis, 1940–1944,* p. 254. They refer to Archives Nationales F7 14881.

137 **The township was liberated on August 26–27:** Ecole Communale de Jeunes Filles (Villetaneuse), Rapport sur les opérations de la Libération, Tuesday, September 12, 1944. Library of the Institut d'Histoire du Temps Présent.

138 **Champigny was and is a communist stronghold:** Interview with André and Madeleine Mauny, Champigny-sur-Marne, March 2, 1996.

138 **the names of political leaders victimized by the far right:** Roger Salengro committed suicide in 1936 after a right-wing press campaign accused him falsely of desertion; Marx Dormoy was assassinated in 1941 by members of the nationalist "Cagoule"; Jean Jaurès, a founding father of French socialism, was assassinated in 1914 by a militant nationalist.

139 **The history of the Champigny resistance:** Jean Morlet, *Champigny: Hier aujourd'hui* (Paris: Temps Actuels, 1981), p. 178.

139 **"I wish to give homage to all the authors of our liberation":** Champigny-sur-Marne city council minutes, October 15, 1944, Champigny-sur-Marne archives.

142 **Both the prostitute and the draftsman were accused:** Both trials took place in the Salle des Assises on January 18, 1945: Dossiers de justice Z6, no. 83, for the prostitute; Z5181, no. 7054, for the draftsman.

142 **The jury . . . sentenced her to "national degradation":** For a definition of the crime of "national indignity," resulting in a punishment of "national degradation," see Herbert R. Lottman, *The Purge* (New York: Morrow, 1986), p. 134.

142 **The draftsman . . . was acquitted of all charges:** In 1947 he was called before a lesser Purge court, the Chambre Civique, accused of membership in the RNP.

Eight Court

143 **"Bakery closed for lack of flour and lack of wood":** "Les Actualités françaises, 1945." January–February 1945 (18 minutes), Vidéothèque de Paris.

143 **"Existence in Paris is still abnormal with relief, with belief":** Janet Flanner (pseudonym: Genêt), *Paris Journal,* vol. 1, 1944–1965, William Shawn, ed. (New York: Atheneum, 1965), entry for December 15, 1944.

144 **His defense lawyer, Jacques Isorni, left home earlier than usual:** Isorni, *Mémoires, 1911–1945* (Paris: Laffont, 1984), p. 304. In his 1948 *Le Rôle d'accusé* [The role of the accused] (Paris: Gallimard), inspired by his coverage of the postwar Purge trials, Roger Grenier argued that the accused party in the courtroom is like the new boy in school; everyone else knows one another, and he's the odd man out. This was certainly the case in the Brasillach trial. The government itself had changed, but the legal personnel was the same as ever.

145 **wild-eyed Alexandre Astruc covered the trial for Camus's *Combat:*** Astruc did not replace Grenier—any number of reporters at *Combat* covered the Purge trials: Jean-Pierre Vivet, Georges Altschuler, Albert Palle, etc.

145 **there was Madeleine Jacob for *Franc-Tireur:*** For their recollections of the trial, see Madeleine Jacob, *Quarante ans de journalisme* (Paris: Julliard, 1970), pp. 161–164, and Alexandre Astruc, *Le Montreur d'ombres: Mémoires* (Paris: Bartillat, 1996).

146 **"Like a bull leaving his pen" . . . "A wild beast":** Robert Brasillach to Maurice Bardèche, January 20, 1945, *Oeuvres complètes,* vol. 9 (Paris: Club de l'Honnête Homme, 1963–1966), p. 285; Francine Bonitzer, *L'Aurore,* January 20, 1945.

147 **Brasillach gave them all a shy little wave:** According to "Les Professeurs de haine," unsigned, *Lettres Françaises,* January 27, 1945.

147 **a naughty schoolboy brought up before the principal:** Edouard Helsey, *Le Figaro,* January 20, 1945: "When the guard sits him down on the bench of the accused, Robert Brasillach is no longer the jovial, privileged, noisy and cutting boy we've known. He's a student in trouble, about to appear before the school principal."

147 **"Deferential," "irreproachable," and especially *"courtois"*:** Maurice Vidal, 890147, art. 141 (B3721), Centre des Archives Contemporaines, Fontainebleau.

147 **still hoarse from the freezing air outside:** Robert Brasillach to Maurice Bardèche, January 20, 1945, *Oeuvres complètes,* vol. 9, p. 286: "It allowed me to see people, things, to clear my voice by replying sagely to questions about my identity."

147 **It was a bright and gaudy backdrop for the scene:** Henri Pelletier's plan to paint a sixty-square-meter fresco on one wall of the Paris Cour d'Assises is described in "Un Lit de justice à la Cour d'Assises," *Le Cri du Peuple,* March 9, 1941. (Article courtesy M. Ozanam, Ordre des Avocats, Palais de Justice.) The fresco, which remains in the courtroom today, is signed "Henri Pelletier, 1945."

147 **he had been dreaming of Julien Sorel:** Letter from Robert Brasillach to Maurice Bardèche, 16 December 1944, *Oeuvres complètes,* vol. 9, p. 236: "I'm calling up the spirit of our seventeen years and of Julien Sorel."

148 **a house painter from La Courneuve and a mechanic:** Edmond Fourquignon from La Courneuve and Henri Blanchard from Kremlin-Bicêtre.

148 **Noël, . . . who had visited Brasillach almost daily at Fresnes:** Isorni/Noël archives, Mireille Noël's *"permis de communiquer"* with Brasillach is stamped seventeen times.

148 **"So ugly she's scary":** Robert Brasillach to Maurice Bardèche, January 20, 1945, *Oeuvres complètes,* vol. 9, p. 285.

149 **Brasillach . . . observed that the *greffier* stumbled over these sentences:** Ibid., p. 286.

149 **Vichy was to be considered a parenthesis in French history:** See Dominique

Rousseau, "Vichy-a-t-il existé?" in "Juger sous Vichy," *Le Genre humain* (Paris: Le Seuil, November, 1994), pp. 97–106, for an analysis of this paradox.

150 **"Short fingers" . . . "tiny little hands":** Bonitzer, *L'Aurore,* January 20, 1945; Helsey, *Le Figaro,* January 20; see also Astruc in *Combat,* January 20: "He gripped the bar with his small hands."

151 **Beneath the perfect diction of the *normalien:*** Alexandre Astruc, *Combat,* January 20, 1945: "He speaks with a light southern accent . . ."

151 **"Very nondescript, but impartial, to be fair":** Letter from Robert Brasillach to Maurice Bardèche, January 20, 1945, *Oeuvres complètes,* vol. 9, p. 286: " . . . he interrupts himself from time to time and I push him out of the way to insert the longest possible tirade. . . . I always throw myself into the interstices of a sentence in order to speak as much as I can. Which must have disgusted the poor President, who suddenly wrapped up his interrogation." A week later, Brasillach writes Bardèche: "What was both useful and embarrassing was that the President didn't react at all. He read his little excerpts from the indictment with a gloomy eye, listened to me launch into a tirade, and continued on. Perhaps he did it to be useful, for I never had the impression that he wanted to condemn me" (letter to Maurice Bardèche, January 27, p. 297).

152 **Brasillach quoted well-chosen passages of a private letter:** On the letter to Rebatet, see chapter 2, "Brasillach's War," pp. 55–56.

153 **He questioned neither the source of the evidence, nor its content:** On Brasillach's liberation from the POW camp, see chapter 2, "Brasillach's War."

153 **a colloquium in Weimar with six other writers:** The other six were: Drieu la Rochelle, Marcel Jouhandeau, Jacques Chardonne, Abel Bonnard, Ramon Fernandez, and André Fraigneau. See Philippe Burrin, "The Signing-up of the Muses," in *France under the Germans: Collaboration and Compromise* (New York: The New Press, 1997), pp. 342–357, for a discussion of this and other propaganda trips organized by the Germans for French artists, musicians, and writers.

154 **Reboul . . . now understood how hostile the audience was:** See "Avis des magistrats," Recours en grâce de Robert Brasillach, 1945, S.2977.

155 **"the tenacious resistance of antifascist intellectuals":** Quoted in Pascal Fouché, *L'Edition Française sous l'occupation 1940–1944,* vol. 1 (Paris: Bibliothèque de littérature française contemporaine de l'Université Paris 7, 1987), p. 189.

156 **the French colonial atrocities . . . were much worse:** Brasillach was referring to Andrée Viollis, *Indochine S.O.S.,* preface by André Malraux (Paris: Gallimard, 1935), the book he had read while hiding in the maid's room on the rue de Tournon. His strategy—to excuse the Nazi terror by attacking France's colonial terror—was used by Vergès, forty-four years later, in defending Klaus Barbie.

157 ***Lettres Françaises* complained that Vidal was "lamentable":** George Adam, *Lettres Françaises,* January 20, 1945: "Was it the trial of the traitor Brasillach or a reception at the Académie Française that took place last Friday?"

158 **"I wasn't part of the Action Française":** The emphasis (on "responsibility/ies") is mine.

159 **He thought they looked wooden:** Letter from Robert Brasillach to Maurice Bardèche, January 20, 1945, *Oeuvres complètes,* vol. 9, p. 287.

159 **"I can regret nothing of what I have been":** "Je ne puis rien regretter de ce qui a été moi-même," or, literally, "I can regret nothing of what has been myself."

160 **His colleagues had told him he ought to put on the red gown:** Interview with Bernadette Reboul, Toulon, April, 1996.

160 **Isorni had delivered the book to the rue Geoffroy St. Hilaire:** Reboul had read *Les Quatre Jeudis,* and he had discussed Brasillach's writing over many evenings with his friend Isorni. Telephone interview with Bernadette Reboul, November 4, 1998.

161 **"Can we believe . . . that the pen that dissected":** In his 1996 memoirs, Alexandre Astruc, whose political orientation had shifted to the right since he covered the Brasillach trial for *Combat,* wrote, "This trial was a lesson for me: Brasillach had been shot because he had written 'the Republic with its dripping buttocks.' It was adjectives, not acts, that led to the firing squad" (*Le Montreur d'ombres,* p. 49).

161 **"[The Republic] will not put you on trial for your tragic errors":** See the analysis by Henry Russo, "Une Justice impossible: L'Epuration et la politique antijuive de Vichy," in *Annales,* 48th year, no. 3, May–June 1993, pp. 745–770. Rousso argues that anti-Semitism played a small role in postwar Purge trials precisely because they were treason trials. The phrase "treason of the clerk" was a reference to Julien Benda's famous essay *The Treason of the Clerks.*

162 **"If you want to know my entire opinion":** Brasillach, "Lettre à quelques jeunes gens," *Révolution Nationale,* February 19, 1944.

162 **"this feeling that dare not say its name":** A sodomy charge was brought against Oscar Wilde by his lover's father.

162 **Reboul was accusing Brasillach . . . of homosexual desire for Germany:** In empirical legal terms, Vichy's most explicit act concerning homosexuality was its ordinance of August 6, 1942, reinforcing legislation concerning sexual aggression against a minor—the punishment was to be more severe if aggressor and aggressee were of the same sex. This statute was retained in postwar law. See Frédéric Martel, *Le Rose et le noir: Les Homosexuels en France depuis 1968* (Paris: le Seuil, 1996).

163 **"in the salons of the Stülpnagels":** A reference to Otto von Stülpnagel and Heinrich von Stülpnagel, military governors headquartered in the Majestic Hotel in Paris. Otto von Stülpnagel, who ordered the first hostage executions, was eventually brought down by internal political conflicts and was replaced by his cousin Heinrich von Stülpnagel, known for both for his intellectual predilections and for his role in the unsuccessful plot to assassinate Hitler.

163 **he was using Oradour to introduce the standard trope of a prosecutor:** The ruins of the burned-out town of Oradour have been preserved as a monument to Nazi barbarism. See the fascinating study by Sarah Farmer of the Oradour massacre and its aftermath, *Oradour: Arrêt sur mémoire* (Paris: Calmann-Lévy, 1994). The Oradour legacy was complicated in 1953 when it turned out that fourteen members of the SS division who destroyed the town were French Alsatians drafted into the SS; of these men, thirteen claimed to have been forcibly drafted.

163 **He thought Reboul was fudging the dates:** Letter from Robert Brasillach to Maurice Bardèche, January 20, 1945, *Oeuvres complètes,* vol. 9, p. 287: "Then Reboul pleaded. He bored me a lot. I find him ridiculous. Full of bad faith and ignorance. Organizing things to make it seem as though I wrote my most Germanophile articles at the time of Oradour, for example."

163 **Nothing like this . . . exists in any other trial of the period:** Homosexuality plays a role in two Purge trials, but without dominating the rhetoric of the prosecution to the extent that it does in the trial of Brasillach. The charge of homosexuality is part of the indictment read at the trial of Marcel Bucard, the leader of a small Nazi party, the Francistes. Bucard recruited spies for the Nazis and led his men in acts of violence in France and again in Germany, as French members of the Waffen SS. He was accused during his February 1946 trial of misleading his young recruits, who were called to court to testify. In his speech to the jury, state prosecutor Vassart does not talk

about homosexuality per se but rather about the youth who venerated Bucard like a father, calling the defendant "a spider in the middle of his web." Bucard's defense lawyer countered that combat in the First World War had weakened Bucard physically and morally; he had lost his critical judgment. *(Quatre procès de trahison devant la Cour de Justice de Paris. Paquis, Bucard, Luchaire, Brasillach. Réquisitoires et plaidoiries* [Paris: Editions de Paris, 1947].) See also the press coverage: Roger Grenier, "Bucard lets the kids accuse themselves to save him," *Combat,* February 20, 1946: "Bucard protests the insinuation that he is a homosexual . . ." and Madeleine Jacob: "[Bucard is] the one known, in his crowd, as 'Big Marcelle.' The indictment specifies: 'The information on his private life is favorable; nonetheless, he had a reputation as a homosexual.' Big Marcelle' casts some discreet smiles at a few of the strong men, standing at the back of the courtroom" ("Bucard in Court," *Le Franc-Tireur,* February 19, 1946, p. 1). Homosexuality was a minor issue in the trial of Le Vigan (born Robert Coquillaud) the actor who had participated in Radio-Paris, the German radio in Paris. He fled France for Germany in August 1944, joining his friend Céline in Baden-Baden, then Sigmaringen, where he became an announcer for the French fascist radio "Ici la France." Witnesses in Le Vigan's trial argued that he was "betwitched" by the anti-semitic, pro-fascist tendencies of his friend Céline. A psychiatric expert included homosexuality in his description of the defendant's symptoms: "Coquillaud is not mentally ill, but only psychically unstable, susceptible, emotional, fatigued, a little bit perverse, homosexual and addicted to drugs." Le Vigan was condemned to ten years of forced labor and released on parole in 1949, when he fled France for Spain, then Argentina, where he spent the rest of his life. (The quotation from the trial was found in Jean-Pierre Bertin-Maghit, *Le cinéma sous l'occupation: le monde du cinéma français de 1940 à 1946* [Paris: O. Orban, 1989], pp. 236–238.)

163 **"He sleeps with Germany, and the day after that fornication":** "Fornication," in French as in English, implies illegal sexual acts, prostitution.

164 **Reboul's speech touched on a crisis of masculinity:** Jean-Paul Sartre uses a similar rhetorical strategy in "What is a collaborator?" *(La République Française,* no. 8, August 1945, pp. 14–17, and reprinted in Sartre, *Situations III* [Paris: Gallimard, 1949], pp. 43–62), first published the summer after Brasillach's execution: "Everywhere in articles by Chateaubriant, Drieu, and Brazillach [*sic*] are curious metaphors that present the relationship of France and Germany under the aspect of a sexual union where France plays the role of the woman." His essay thus plays out a heterosexual version of the argument advanced by Marcel Reboul in this prosecution of Robert Brasillach. Sartre wrote about the *Je Suis Partout* team, the ones who had begun as Action Française royalists; these were men, he argued, who, having more or less refused everything that had taken place in France since the Revolution, were "without real ties to contemporary France, with our great political traditions, with a century and a half of our history and our culture." Sartre was denying that the right-wing, Action Française tradition of Maurras had anything to do with modern France. Therefore, "nothing protected them against the attractions of a foreign community." It was a polemical move, but not an historically accurate one, since the right wing had a long history in France, a centuries-old foundation in royalism. Like Sartre, Reboul focused his rhetorical energy on showing that Brasillach was an outsider, vulnerable to sexual and political penetration. By insisting on the homosexual quality of his rhetoric, Reboul went a step further than Sartre would go in marginalizing Brasillach.

165 **"I find him ridiculous":** Letter from Robert Brasillach to Maurice Bardèche, January 20, 1945, *Oeuvres complètes,* vol. 9, p. 287.

166 **He wasn't a particularly dramatic gesturer:** Telephone interview with Bernadette Reboul, November 8, 1998.

166 **But the evidence of mass murder was growing:** "Que savaient les Français?"

in Stéphane Courtois and Adam Rayski, eds., *Qui savait quoi? L'Extermination des juifs, 1941–1945* (Paris: La Découverte, 1987), p. 91. On the BBC, July 8, 1943, Paul Bouchon spoke of "this systematic extermination carried out in cold blood. It is the first time in modern history that an entire people has been thus condemned to disappear completely from the surface of the earth."

166 **Struthof . . . liberated by American troops on November 23, 1944:** Roger Vailland, "Au Struthof," in *Action*, December 15, 1944; Georges Soric, "Maïdanek, vision d'épouvante," in *Ce Soir*, January 10, 1945, both quoted in *Le Choc: 1945, la presse révèle l'enfer des camps nazis* (Paris: Fédération Nationale des Déportés, Internés, Résistants et Patriotes, 1985).

167 **thought he saw a little saliva forming at the corner of his mouth:** Edouard Helsey, *Le Figaro*, January 20, 1945.

168 **Having claimed his own moral ground, with Parodi:** Parodi was arrested and tortured but he refused to give the names of the *résistants* in his group. He died in his cell at Fresnes on April 15, 1942. See Jean Favard, *Au coeur de Paris, un palais pour la justice* (Paris: Gallimard, 1995), p. 85.

168 **infected with this propaganda that you distilled at *Je Suis Partout*":** Claude Maubourguet trial, November 3, 1944, Archives Nationales, Sténographie Bluet, 334 AP/8, p. 37ff.

169 **he modulated his booming voice into an intense whisper:** Madeleine Jacob, *Quarante ans de journalisme* (Paris: Julliard, 1970), p. 165: "This 'why wait?'—the government prosecutor didn't proclaim it, he pronounced it in a whisper."

169 **"What I was looking for was just one word of pity or regret":** See Michel Laval's evocative description of this moment in *Brasillach ou la trahison du clerc* (Paris: Flammarion, 1992): "The day, in its waning, had slowly plunged the courtroom into a sort of unreal half-light, from which there emerged the immense black silhouette of the government prosecutor, his voice becoming progressively heavier and deeper" (p. 253).

172 **"This language is Greek to the jurors":** In French, the metaphor is "like Hebrew." Edouard Helsey, *Le Figaro*, January 20, 1945.

172 **he had asked Mauriac for another letter:** Isorni quotes the letter in part in *Mémoires, 1911–1945*, and explains, "I informed him that I couldn't use his text. You could not defend Brasillach by damning him" (p. 286). The full text of the letter is in the Isorni archives, Paris Bar Association.

173 **Mauriac seemed bent on publicly forgiving:** For details, see chapter 9, "The Writers' Petition."

174 **Isorni had reached the page of his notes:** The Brasillach trial courtroom notes are part of the Isorni collection in the Paris Bar Association.

174 **Brasillach, in his box, was studying the jurors intently:** Letter from Robert Brasillach to Maurice Bardèche, January 20, 1945, *Oeuvres complètes*, vol. 9, p. 286.

175 *Lettres Françaises* and *Action* were every bit as hostile to the judiciary: See for example, Pascal Copeau's attack on the magistrature—and Reboul in particular—in the next day's issue of *Action*, January 20, 1945.

176 **Isorni was positing another evil—passive collaboration:** See Philippe Burrin's *France under the Germans* for a study of collaboration as accommodation. On the civil service under Vichy, see Marc Olivier Baruch, *Servir l'Etat français: L'Administration en France de 1940 à 1944* (Paris: Fayard, 1997).

176 **The article he wrote . . . couldn't have motivated his liberation:** On the reasons for his liberation from the POW camp, see chapter 2, "Brasillach's War."

177 **In the notes laid out on Isorni's table there were four Renan quotations:** In remembering Brasillach's February 1944 sentence about "sleeping with Germany," Isorni writes, "What an exploitation could be made of it, when it was only literature!" Isorni consulted with Jean Pommier, Bardèche's thesis director at the Sorbonne, who had written his own doctoral thesis on Renan, and who supplied the various possible sources in Renan for the quotation. But "how could the jurors be sensitive to this philosophic exegesis?" Isorni concluded (*Mémoires, 1911–1945*, p. 298). Pommier's sources are conserved in a folder in Isorni's archives for the trial, under the heading "textes de Renan sur l'Allemagne." They are: Preface to *La Réforme intellectuelle et morale* (1872), p. 6: "Germany had been my mistress; I was conscious of owing her what was best in me"; Letter from Renan to Charles Ritter, March 11, 1871: "I had made the purpose of my life to work for the intellectual, moral, and political union of France and Germany"; and "Réponse au discours de réception de M. Cherbuliez à l'Académie française," May 25, 1882: "In our intellectual education, both of us have cited this great German school . . . as a new ideal." Years later, Isorni recalls, he realized that Jean Giraudoux's *Siegfried* contained the line, "They're catching me, flagrante delicto, in the act of adultery with Germany. Yes, I've slept with her, Siegfried." He decided that the real literary source for Brasillach's phrase was Giraudoux, not Renan, but that Brasillach was so close to Giraudoux's writing that he hadn't been conscious of it. For Isorni, finally, what counts is the play of literature—not Brasillach's affectionate support of Germany in the violent last year of the Occupation.

178 **The problem with Isorni's serious explanation:** If you read it very closely, Isorni's use of Renan in the trial is a clever response to Reboul, because it takes a turn of phrase ("We have slept with Germany") that Reboul had interpreted as homoerotic, and restores it to heterosexuality. If Germany was Brasillach's mistress, as she had been Renan's, France is once again the man, Germany the woman. Normalcy and power are restored. If that was the reinterpretation Isorni meant to impose, it was a clever countermaneuver, but far too subtle to influence the debates.

178 **this middle part of Isorni's defense speech was getting too long:** Letter from Robert Brasillach to Maurice Bardèche, January 27, 1945, *Oeuvres complètes*, vol. 9, p. 297: "The middle, to read it, seems more indecisive, because he wanted to respond to just about everything, and so it appears not to have much unity. But this is not his fault, it's the fault of the subject."

179 **whether or not it was wise to retaliate against the hostage-taking:** See Pierre Laborie, *Opinion française sous Vichy* (Paris: Le Seuil, 1990), pp. 254–255, for the effect of the hostage-taking on public opinion under Vichy. For a useful summary of the debates within the resistance, see Jean-Pierre Azéma, *De Munich à la Libération, 1938–1944* (Paris: Le Seuil, 1979), p. 241.

180 **the operation of the Vichy Special Section Courts:** See chapter 6, "Jacques Isorni: Counsel for the Defense."

180 **He knew this tactic was his biggest blow:** Isorni, *Mémoires, 1911–1945*, p. 306. See also the letter from Brasillach to Maurice Bardèche, January 27, 1945, *Oeuvres complètes*, vol. 9, p. 297: "Very good, too, naturally, what [Isorni] said about the prosecution and the magistrature, which made a great impression at the Palace of Justice."

181 **they had occupied the same spaces in the same courtroom:** See chapter 6, "Jacques Isorni: Counsel for the Defense."

183 **"For Brasillach's life, I had simply transposed that militant":** Isorni, *Mémoires, 1911–1945*, pp. 228–229.

183 **de Gaulle's provisional government had been imposed by fiat:** The official provisional government was established on June 3, 1944, by a vote of the advisory

congress (Assemblée Consultative) of the Comité Français de Libération Nationale in Algiers. A standard history of the period, Azéma's *De Munich à la Libération, 1938– 1944,* refers in its chronology to a "popular coronation" of Charles de Gaulle on August 26, 1944, the day of his parade down the Champs Elysées. The first national election in postwar France did not take place until October 21, 1945. It involved the election of an Assemblée Constituante, a parliamentary body, and included a referendum to repeal the constitution of 1875 (that is, of the Third Republic) and make room for a Fourth Republic, whose constitution would be adopted by a subsequent referendum of October 1946. Vichy was a nonentity.

183 **His voice . . . softened, at just the right moment:** Isorni made an LP recording of his defense speech several years after the event. Available in the video collection of the Bibliothèque Nationale, AP 1304-5: Jacques Isorni, *Fragment de la "Plaidoirie au Procès de Robert Brasillach en 1945."*

184 **He saw tears on their faces:** Letter from Robert Brasillach to Maurice Bardèche, January 27, 1945, *Oeuvres complètes,* vol. 9, p. 297, in response to Bardèche's reading of a transcript of the trial: "As for the defense speech, the effect it had doesn't come through on the page. Imagine that people were crying at the end, there was truly an extraordinary emotion. Isorni delivered it with an admirable warmth."

184 **"Brasillach's lawyer wanted a beautiful trial":** "Son avocat a voulu plaider un beau procès." Interviewed in the film *Les Messagers de l'ombre,* directed by Michèle Van Zèle, part 2, "De la Libération à l'Epuration," 1991 documentary, France 3 Television.

185 **"no matter what happens, we have to remain steadfast and hope":** Letter from Robert Brasillach to Maurice Bardèche, January 20, 1945, *Oeuvres complètes,* vol. 9, p. 287.

187 **but the president of the court had already grabbed his *toque:*** Francine Bonitzer, *L'Aurore;* Dominique Pado, *Maurras, Béraud, Brasillach: Trois condamnés, trois hommes, trois générations* (Paris: Pathé, 1945), p. 57, "President Vidal, horrified, escapes. . . ."

188 **This time, the entire procedure had taken six hours:** Pencilled on the stenography of the trial: "début à 13 h; fin à 19h/à mort." Sténographie Bluet, Archives Nationales, 334 AP/10. Bardèche, in his *Souvenirs,* remembers it lasted only two hours; Alain Decaux, in a June 10, 1987, television broadcast on the trial, reports five hours ("Le Dossier d'Alain Decaux. Brasillach: La Mort en face").

Nine   The Writers' Petition

189 **It's a poem . . . about being literally "in drag":** The postwar French term for drag queen is *travesti* or *travelo.*

189 **"Jewels":**

Bijoux
Je n'ai jamais eu de bijoux,
Ni bagues, ni chaîne aux poignets,
Ce sont choses mal vues chez nous:
Mais on m'a mis la chaîne aux pieds.

On dit que ce n'est pas viril,
Les bijoux sont faits pour les filles:
Aujourd'hui comment se fait-il
Qu'on m'ait mis la chaîne aux chevilles?

Il faut connaître toutes choses,
Etre curieux du nouveau:

Etrange est l'habit qu'on m'impose
Et bizarre ce double anneau.

Le mur est froid, la soupe est maigre.
Mais je marche, ma foi, très fier,
Tout résonnant comme un roi nègre,
Paré de ses bijoux de fer.

190 **a people "whose ties to the powers of the earth are strong":** Brasillach, *Anthologie de la poésie grecque,* in *Oeuvres complètes,* vol. 9 (Paris: Club de l'Honnête Homme, 1963–1966), p. 323.

191 **Brasillach's sister wrote to him from a metro station:** Letter from Suzanne Bardèche to Robert Brasillach, [Thursday], December 1944, in ibid., p. 231.

191 **all their leather-bound Pléiade edition classics were missing:** Letter from Robert Brasillach to Suzanne Bardèche, December 22, 1944, in ibid., pp. 248–249.

191 **Mauriac's reasons for supporting Brasillach:** For Marcel Aymé, support for Brasillach may have been an expression both of his anarchism—his opposition to the state—and his sympathy for his former editor at *Je Suis Partout.* Jean Anouilh seemed to be acting out of a kind of bitter anti-institutionalism. In 1963, looking back at his efforts on Brasillach's behalf, he wrote, "The young man Anouilh, whom I had remained until 1945, left one morning, insecure (understandable in those deceptive times) but on his left foot, to go get signatures from his colleagues for Brasillach. He went door to door for eight days and he returned home old—as in a Grimm's Fairy Tale." Reprinted in *Robert Brasillach et la génération perdue* (Paris: Les Cahiers du Rocher, ed. Pierre Sipriot, 1987), pp. 179–182.

191 **a "squeaky old bird" with a taste for suicidal women:** See the first edition of *Notre avant-guerre* (Paris: Plon, 1941), p. 173: "Mauriac continued to assemble his bourgeois women à la Bovary, and his tormented adolescents . . ."

191 **vows to launch a veritable press campaign against Mauriac:** It is not clear whether Brasillach asked Gerhard Heller, the man in charge, to censor Mauriac's new novel, *La Pharisienne,* or whether Heller requested of Mauriac's publisher, Grasset, that the print run be limited. According to Rebatet, the novel appeared without censure, to the annoyance of the entire *Je Suis Partout* team. Rebatet, *Les Mémoires d'un fasciste,* vol. 2, p. 56: "We begged him vehemently to censor the horrible twisted asshole François Mauriac, who was able to publish new books, to our great indignation." Both sources quoted in Jean Touzot, *Mauriac sous l'occupation* (Paris: La Manufacture, 1991). See also the chapter of Gisèle Sapiro's thesis contrasting the wartime activities and attitudes of two members of the Académie Française, Mauriac and Henry Bordeaux. A copy of Mauriac's *La Pharisienne* with an inscription to Lieutenant Heller, thanking him for his interest in the novel, was much joked about after the war in ex-collaborationist circles.

192 **protesting his invitation to "the director of an abject newspaper":** Quoted in Touzot, *Mauriac sous l'occupation,* p. 41. On Brasillach's invitation to lecture to the Comédie Française in June 1941, see Marie-Agnès Joubert, *La Comédie-Française sous l'Occupation* (Paris: Tallandier, 1998), p. 79.

193 **"France carries within her, like a foreign body":** Quoted by Michel Winock in "Fallait-il fusiller Brasillach?" *L'Histoire,* no. 179, July–August 1994. Camus is writing in *Combat,* October 25, 1944, in the aftermath of the death sentencing of Georges Suarez on October 23. His first gesture is to oppose the death penalty: "We have no taste for murder. And the human person represents all that we respect in this world. Our first reaction to this death sentence is repugnance. It would be easy for us to think that our business is not to destroy men, but that it is only to do something for

the good of this country. But in fact, we have learned, since 1939, that we would thus be betraying the very good of this country. France carries within her . . . ," etc.

193 **The undersigned intellectuals:** This first version of the Brasillach petition is from the Isorni papers, Paris Bar Association. A slightly different version of the text is quoted by Jean-François Sirinelli, *Intellectuels et passions françaises: Manifestes et pétitions au XXème siècle* (Paris: Fayard, 1990), pp. 241–242.

194 **Several different versions of the list of those who signed:** The pardon file includes a carbon copy of a typed list of fifty-seven names; then a directly typed copy with two names added by hand: Claude Farrère and Mgr. Bressolles, Vice Rector of the Institut Catholique. A slightly different version of this petition is reproduced in Sirinelli's *Intellectuels et passions françaises;* it also includes the financier Jacques Léon Rueff, the painter Louis Latapie, the stage set designer André Barsacq, and Max Favalelli, a sometime contributor to *Je Suis Partout* known for his crossword puzzles and sports reporting. The version published in the *Cahiers des amis de Robert Brasillach,* reproduced in Pellissier's biography of Brasillach, omits Bressolles and Farrère. The press agency Tallendier has in its archives a photograph of the typewritten text of the Brasillach petition followed by ten signatures of men who were all members of the Académie Française in January 1945 (Valéry, Mauriac, Duhamel, Bordeaux, Jérôme Tharaud, Madelin, Laforce, Chevrillon, Louis de Broglie, and one illegible signature, possibly Farrère, Lacaze, or Lecompte). This was presumably the copy of the petition circulated at the Académie by François Mauriac.

194 **There was most certainly never an actual physical petition:** See for example, Vlaminck's note to Isorni, below, note to page 196.

195 **Brasillach's correspondence tells us that Sartre . . . was sent a telegram:** Letter from Brasillach to his mother and sister, January 26, 1945, *Oeuvres complètes,* vol. 9, pp. 296.

195 **a writer must be prepared to die for what he puts on paper:** See Phil Watts, *Allegories of the Purge* (Palo Alto: Stanford University Press, 1999), for a study of Sartre's relationship to the Purge. Sartre mentions Brasillach explicitly in his summer 1945 essay "What Is a Collaborator?" (see chapter 8, "Court," note to page 164).

195 **Simone de Beauvoir wrote twice:** "Un oeil pour un oeil," in *Les Temps Modernes,* February 1945, *La Force des choses* (Paris: Gallimard, 1963), p. 32. For a discussion of Beauvoir's retrospective views of Brasillach's sentencing, see chapter 12, "After the Trial.".

195 **Sylvia Bataille . . . was asked to sign:** Conversation with Sandra Basch, Paris, January 1997.

195 **Isorni later published both Roy's letter of justification:** Letter from Claude Roy to Jacques Isorni, January 7, 1947; and letter from Jacques Isorni to Claude Roy, January 9, 1947, in Isorni archives, L'Ordre des Avocats. Both letters are reproduced in Isorni, *Mémoires, 1911–1945* (Paris: Laffont, 1984), pp. 302–303.

195 **"I received a letter from Brasillach's poor mother":** André Gide, Jean Schlumberger, *Correspondance, 1901–1950,* ed. Pascal Mercier and Peter Fawcett (Paris: Gallimard, 1993), p. 975.

196 **Bordeaux had written a hagiographic book about Pétain:** On Bordeaux's career, see Gisèle Sapiro's thesis, "Complicités et anathèmes en temps de crise: Modes de survie du champ littéraire et de ses institutions, 1940–1953 (Académie Française, Académie Goncourt, Comité National des Ecrivains)," (Thèse de Doctorat de Sociologie, Ecole des Hautes Etudes en Sciences Sociales, 2 vols., 19 December 1994).

196 **an ideological and savage critique of Picasso in *Comoedia:*** Jean Cocteau,

Journal, 1942–1945, ed. Jean Touzot (Paris: Gallimard, 1989), p. 144. Vlaminck, June 6, 1942, reprinted in *Portrait avant décès* (Paris: Flammarion, 1943). He called Picasso "impotence made man" and "the Stavisky of painting."

196 **"Dear Maître, Placing myself outside all political errors committed":** Vlaminck's note to Jacques Isorni, reproduced in facsimile in *Présent,* April 6, 1996, was on sale at the Galerie Jean-Emmanuel Raux in Saint-Germain-en-Laye in April 1996 for 10,000 francs.

196 **Jean Cocteau . . . praised him in a front-page article:** Jean Cocteau, "Salut à Breker," *Comoedia,* May 23, 1942, p. 1, reprinted in *Journal, 1942–1945,* p. 133.

196 **Marcel Aymé . . . had written short stories for the paper:** Other petition signers who had written for *Je Suis Partout* included Anouilh; Henry Bordeaux; Paul-Henri Michel; Firmin Roz, a right-wing historian who had contributed a few articles on the U.S. in 1930 and 1931; Jean and Jérôme Tharaud; and finally, Thierry Maulnier, Brasillach's school chum. Maulnier had been an active literary critic at *Je Suis Partout* until 1940, when he was condemned as a "traitor" by the rest of the staff for having helped produce an issue during the *drôle de guerre,* when the others were being interrogated by the government on suspicion of treason. Maulnier emerged from the war a solid right-wing columnist at *Le Figaro* and an ally of Mauriac's. He was in a safe position to support his friend. See Jean-Marie Dioudonnet, *Les 700 rédacteurs de 'Je Suis Partout,' 1930–1944* (Paris: Sedopols, 1993). Aymé's political trajectory is exceedingly complex. He wrote before the war for *Je Suis Partout* as well as for the left-wing *Marianne.* Brasillach lauded his novels as early as 1930. During the Occupation he protested anti-Semitic legislation in *Aujourd'hui.* After the war, he became a noted satirist of the Purge in texts such as *Uranus* and the play *La Tête des autres.*

196 **François Mauriac, Albert Camus, Claudel, Colette . . . :** Brasillach had been a Colette fan since his school days, when he invited her to the Ecole Normale for tea. In his correspondence, he claimed to have intervened to get her Jewish husband, Maurice Goudeket, freed from detention in Drancy. Colette contributed in 1943 to *Combats,* the newspaper of the Vichy Milice (not to be confused with Camus's *Combat*): was this another gesture to insure her husband's protection? She hesitated to sign the petition for Brasillach; Cocteau, her neighbor, convinced her. Claudel was one year from membership in the Académie Française; the diplomat-writer was famous for having written an ode to Pétain, followed by an ode to de Gaulle. Paul Valéry, seventy-eight years old in 1945 and a few months from death, had been at de Gaulle's side the week of the Liberation.

197 **the target of vicious homophobic attacks by Alain Laubreaux:** See Laubreaux, "Une Semaine tragique," *Je Suis Partout,* May 26, 1944. He described Marais in *Andromaque* as "l'Homme au Cocteau entre les dents" [the man with Cocteau between his teeth]. Cocteau, in French, is one letter away from "couteau" which means "knife." The expression was used to refer to communists. Laubreaux's article is reprinted in Cocteau, *Journal, 1942–1945,* pp. 699–700.

197 **"I find Brasillach absurd and harmful, but I will sign":** Cocteau, entry for January 25, 1945, in *Journal, 1942–1945,* pp. 613–614.

197 **In this, his last work of literary criticism:** Brasillach, *Chénier,* in *Oeuvres complètes,* vol. 9, pp. 147–168.

197 **"So the modest petition seems to reconcile everything for me":** Letter no. 353 from Jean Paulhan to Jean Guéhenno, dated Sunday [before February 6, 1945], in Jean Paulhan, *Choix de lettres,* vol. 2: *Traité des jours sombres, 1937–1945,* ed. Aury et al. (Paris: Gallimard, 1992), pp. 402–403.

198 **"I've always held the death penalty in horror":** Quoted in Jean-François Sirinelli, *Intellectuels et passions françaises,* p. 247.

198 **Tristan Bernard . . . arrested and incarcerated at Drancy:** Bernard was arrested in the south of France on October 10, 1943, and sent to Drancy by train. Sacha Guitry and Arletty intervened with the German embassy; Bernard was transferred to the Rothschild Hospital in Paris (Cocteau, *Journal, 1942–1945,* p. 387). See also Jean-Pierre Bertin-Maghit, *Le cinéma français sous l'Occupation* (Paris: Presses Universitaires/Que sais-je, 1994). The actress Arletty testified before a cinema Purge commission that she and Sacha Guitry had intervened with the Propaganda Abteilung on Tristan Bernard's behalf (p. 69); witnesses in Sacha Guitry's treason trial also described his actions in favor of Bernard (p. 100).

199 **Brasillach said that Cohen had resuscitated the Middle Ages:** Brasillach, *Animateurs du théâtre, Oeuvres complètes,* vol. 8, p. 81. On Cohen in a larger intellectual and cultural context, see Helen Solterer, "The Waking of Medieval Theatricality, Paris, 1935–1995," *New Literary History* 27, no. 3 (summer 1996), pp. 357–390; as well as her book in progress, *Playing the Dead.*

199 **"At least I didn't have to kiss him!":** Letter from Suzanne Bardèche to Robert Brasillach, undated [late January 1945], *Oeuvres complètes,* vol. 6, p. 301.

199 **twenty-seven were Academicians or Institute members:** Bardoux, Henry Bordeaux, Marcel Bouteron, Emile Bréhier, Duc de Broglie, Prince de Broglie, Albert Buisson, André Chevrillon, Emile Dard, Georges Desvallières, Georges Duhamel, Claude Farrère, Firmin-Roz, Armand Duc de la Force, Pierre Janet, Emile Jordan, André Lalande, Amiral Lacaze, Georges Lecompte, Louis Madelin, Germain Martin, François Mauriac, Paul-Henri Michel, Pichat, Charles Rist, Jérôme Tharaud, Paul Valéry.

199 **Another eight were future members of the Académie:** Marcel Achard, Jean Anouilh, Paul Claudel, Daniel-Rops, Thierry Maulnier, Wladimir d'Ormesson, Jean Paulhan, Jean Tharaud.

199 **The theater was well represented, too:** From the theater world: Jean-Louis Barrault, André Barsacq, Jean-Jacques Bernard, Jacques Copeau, Charles Dullin, André Obey.

200 **Among the writers who had signed the original CNE manifesto:** From the Editions Gallimard and the *Nouvelle Revue Française,* the milieu of André Gide, were Copeau, Schlumberger, Jean Paulhan. Sapiro's thesis lists the members of the CNE by year of membership. For the period prior to April 1945, CNE members who also signed the Brasillach petition were: Jean-Jacques Bernard, Paul Claudel, Gustave Cohen, Georges Duhamel, Gabriel Marcel, François Mauriac, André Obey, Jean Paulhan, Simone Ratel, Jean Schlumberger, Jérôme et Jean Tharaud, Paul Valéry. Duhamel, Paulhan, Schlumberger, and the Tharaud Brothers all resigned from the CNE in 1946; Gabriel Marcel, that same year, did not renew his membership. (Claudel resigned in 1948, Cohen in 1949 or 1957, Obey in 1953. Ratel, in 1953, didn't renew. François Mauriac was excluded from the CNE in 1948, Obey resigned in 1953, Paulhan resigned in 1946.)

200 **All but Mauriac resigned from the CNE a year later:** This information is from Gisèle Sapiro's "Complicités et anathèmes en temps de crise."

Ten   No Pardon

202 **This one is an ordinary looking administrative file:** Recours en grâce de Robert Brasillach, 1945, S.2977.

204 **One gets the same impression of an audience sympathetic to Brasillach:** The

title of Pierre Lambelin's article in *France-Soir* is "Brasillach Lost the Match before the Elite of the Fifth Column"; *Les Lettres Françaises* reports that "partisans of Brasillach came in a crowd to his trial"; *L'Aube* describes the "protests that greeted his verdict"; Madeleine Jacob, *Franc-Tireur,* writes, "The room, where the Fifth Column and all of *Je Suis Partout* is crowding, boos the speech by government prosecutor Reboul . . ." (all articles dated January 20, 1945).

204 **"If justice followed the path indicated by the treasonous acts":** Report dated January 20, 1945, "à Monsieur le Garde des Sceaux, Ministre de la Justice, Paris." A typed carbon of the report is item no. 3 in Dossier Brasillach, Archives de Paris, 1320W.C74/no. 22 (folder marked: Cours de Justice, condamnations capitales); another copy is in the Brasillach dossier de grâce (2277 S 45) under the rubric "Avis des Magistrats."

204 **It is useful to look at the case of Béraud:** Archives Nationales, dossier de grâce no. 515 S 45 (dossier Henri Béraud).

204 **Henri Béraud was the only other writer of stature among them:** Charles Maurras, Brasillach's mentor, was declared guilty of treason by a court in Lyon, but he was given life in prison for extenuating circumstances.

204 **"Yes, we've been 'Churchilled' ":** From *Gringoire,* quoted in the Béraud pardon file under the rubric "Against the Allies."

204 **Béraud's court files include interviews with his chauffeur:** Béraud, dossier de justice Z 6/7, no. 102. Although venality was not always a saving grace in the Purge trials. Jean Luchaire, editor of *Les Nouveaux Temps* and head of the syndicate of the press under Vichy, was condemned to death and executed in 1946, after a trial that concentrated on exposing his flashy, corrupt, sexually promiscuous life.

205 **He was arguing . . . that France needed a symbolic punishment:** Lindon invokes the possibility of a presidential pardon, but he does so in language that is extremely veiled, so much so that it is difficult to say if he is recognizing that a pardon is a foregone conclusion or whether he is simply being ironic: "This present report is not the place to pay attention to efforts that might be made in view of obtaining a pardon for Béraud, because these would certainly, without a doubt, be founded on the most noble motives. But it is far from sure that a measure of clemency inspired by the fact that Béraud was a brilliant man of letters would correspond to the sentiment of the larger fraction of public opinion and notably of those among that crowd of patriots who had to resist Béraud's propaganda before they could triumph over the enemy."

205 **"The information I must provide on this affair":** In the "Avis des Magistrats," Recours en grâce de Robert Brasillach, 1945, S.2977.

206 **whom she called "poets with pure hands":** Max Jacob and Saint-Pol Roux.

206 **"Have pity on this unhappy young man":** Letter dated January 27, from a woman whose husband had been in Brasillach's prison camp since 1940.

208 **Isorni described the visit minute by minute:** Typescript, Isorni archives, "Audience du Général de Gaulle le 3 février 1945 à 22 heures," reprinted in *Cahiers des amis de Robert Brasillach,* vol. 2, p. 12, and in Isorni, *Mémoires, 1911–1945* (Paris: Laffont, 1984), p. 314.

209 **could have been signed between 10:30 P.M. and midnight:** This is the chronology of paperwork detailed in the pardon file: January 20: Vidal and Reboul report to the Minister of Justice, recommending that the death sentence be carried out. February 1: Boissarie, the Prosecutor General of the Paris Court of Appeals, writes to the Minister of Justice about the case. February 2: The Pardon Commission decides in favor of execution. February 3: The Director of Criminal Affairs and Pardons

summarizes Brasillach's case, as well as the positions of Vidal, Reboul, and Boissarie. De Gaulle and Francis de Menthon, Minister of Justice, sign a decree refusing pardon and requesting that the death sentence be carried out. February 5: The Minister of Justice reports back to the Attorney General that de Gaulle has refused pardon and asks for the execution to be scheduled. February 6: Reboul reports to the Minister of Justice that the execution has taken place without incident. (Isorni visited de Gaulle the night of February 3; he received word that the pardon had been refused on February 5, the day before the execution.)

209 **Madame Reboul and Madame Isorni went to mass together:** Interview with Bernadette Reboul. It was their neighborhood church. In recent years, Saint Nicolas du Chardonnet has become known as the headquarters of Monseigneur Lefevre's "integral Catholicism"—a reactionary form of Catholicism opposed to Vatican policies.

210 **"you will think of me and . . . of the others who died the same day":** As reported by Jacques Isorni, *Le Procès de Robert Brasillach* (Paris: Flammarion, 1946), p. 26.

Eleven Reactions

211 **they visited the site of the massacre of Polish officers at Katyn:** On the visit to Katyn, see chapter 2, "Brasillach's War." The Soviets lied and said the Poles were assassinated by German occupation forces. The Soviets recognized responsibility for the massacre in June 1991. See Louis FitzGibbon, *Katyn: A Crime without Parallel* (New York: Scribner's, 1971).

212 **"Brasillach wouldn't have wanted it [the pardon]":** Alain Peyrefitte, *C'était de Gaulle* (Paris: Fayard, 1997), p. 187.

212 **This remark was nowhere in the file I saw:** All documents at the Fondation de Gaulle concerning the year 1945 are closed to researchers until the year 2005.

212 **"If they hadn't served the enemy directly and passionately":** De Gaulle, *Mémoires de guerre,* tome 3, p. 141, quoted by Pierre Assouline in *L'Epuration des intellectuels, 1944–1945* (Paris: Editions Complexe, 1990), pp. 83–84.

213 **52 percent . . . approved . . . ; 11 percent opposed:** Philippe Butor, "Les Premières décisions du pouvoir," in *Paris 1944: Les Enjeux de la Libération. Actes du colloque, 2–4 février 1994,* Christine Levisse-Touzé, ed. (Paris: Albin Michel, 1994), p. 391. Source Note, "Bulletin d'informations de l'Institut français d'opinion publique."

213 **As of January 1945 the court had seen 106 trials:** Statistics are from a March 1945 report from the Cour de Justice of Paris to the Prosecutor General's office. Archives de la Ville de Paris, document no. 1320W/85, folder marked "Statistiques Cour de Justice." Conditions in the Court of Justice are described in a November 1944 memo, Archives de la Ville de Paris, document no. 1320W/85.

213 **Teitgen . . . gave a lecture defending the actions of the Court of Justice:** Pierre-Henri Teitgen, "Les Cours de Justice" (Paris: Editions du Mail, 1946), p. 34 [text of a speech given at the Théâtre Marigny, April 5, 1946].

213 **"They shot Robert Brasillach":** Chronique de Pierre Antoine Cousteau, *Radio-Patrie,* February 7, 1945, 5 P.M. bulletin in *Bulletin des écoutes radiophoniques* (Paris: Ministère de l'Information, 1945) [monitoring radio broadcasts in the Allied and enemy countries, including "Radio-Patrie" in Germany]. Courtesy Hoover Library collections, Stanford University.

214 **Brasillach had "saved our lives by dying first":** Jacques Chancel interviews Lucien Rebatet, in "Radioscopie," October 12, 1969 (Paris: Maison de la Radio [tape archives]).

214 **Drieu la Rochelle . . . committed suicide on March 15, 1945:** *Franc-Tireur,* March 15, 1945, complains about the mysterious delay in Drieu's arrest: "M. Berny of the Court of Justice has been charged with opening the case for intelligence with the enemy against the journalist Drieu la Rochelle, who published articles in *La Gerbe, Je Suis Partout,* and *Le Cri du Peuple.* Before charging Drieu la Rochelle, they patiently waited until he had time to flee." Drieu's suicide is announced on March 17: "Drieu la Rochelle was forgotten. Only today was a mandate drawn up against him. But Drieu la Rochelle beat the mandate. He turned on the gas . . ."

214 **if the procedure could have been slowed down by even six months:** See François Mauriac, "L'Affaire Brasillach," in *L'Express,* no. 336, November 28, 1957, reprinted in *Bloc-notes,* tome 1, 1952–1957 (Paris: Le Seuil, 1993), pp. 544–547: "If Brasillach had been able to disappear for six months, perhaps today his friends would be offering him the beautiful sword of the Academy."

Twelve   After the Trial

215 **"If a writer writes in a pro-Nazi newspaper":** *Carrefour,* March 17, 1945, p. 5. Other columns in the series were by Gabriel Marcel, Claude Aveline, Emmanuel Mounier, Emile Henriot, Max Pol Fouchet, Georges Duhamel. Henriot, Marcel, and Duhamel had signed the petition for Brasillach.

216 **"The fact that a person as frivolous as Brasillach":** Letter no. 354 from Jean Paulhan to Armand Petitjean, [Friday], February 9, 1945, in Jean Paulhan, *Choix de lettres,* vol. 2, *Traité des jours sombres, 1937–1945* (Paris: Gallimard, 1992), p. 403: "Let us add that Brasillach, in his newspaper, *recommended* certain executions (of communists, of French hostages) which then took place. All the recommendations and all the petitions (one of which I signed, which simply recalled that Brasillach's father was killed in 1914) could do nothing to counter that. That said, the fact that . . . ," etc.

216 **As Cocteau put it, Brasillach was "absurd *and* harmful":** See chapter 9, "The Writers' Petition."

216 **Paulhan's sense of the incoherence of Brasillach's verdict:** See also letter no. 114, Jean Paulhan to Louis Aragon, March 1945, in Louis Aragon, *Correspondance générale, Aragon-Paulhan-Triolet,* "Le Temps traversé: Correspondance, 1920–1964 / Louis Aragon, Jean Paulhan, Elsa Triolet" (Paris: Gallimard, 1994), Bernard Leuilliot, ed., p. 178: "The first letter of protest, when the *Nouvelle Revue Française* published your poems in 1940, was addressed to me by Brasillach. 'That candidate,' he said, 'for the moat at Vincennes. . . .' It was a slight error." The moat at Vincennes refers to the military fort where traitors were executed—including Mata Hari.

216 **"In five or ten years they'll return in force with ripe works . . .":** May 12, 1945.

216 **The Liberation, he claimed, had "400,000 victims" to its name:** Jean Paulhan, *Lettre aux directeurs de la résistance* (Paris: Editions de Minuit, 1951), p. 12.

216 **"I have great respect for judges and for the men of the police":** Paulhan, *De la paille et du grain: Essai* (Paris: Gallimard, 1948), p. 54.

216 **In 1948 he stated publicly that Mauriac had been right:** Albert Camus, "L'Incroyant et les Chrétiens," in *Essais* (Paris: Bibliothèque de la Pléiade, 1965), pp. 371–375. Text of a 1948 lecture at a Dominican convent of Latour-Maubourg: "Three years ago, a controversy set me against one of you, and not one of the least significant. The fever of those years, the difficult memory of two or three assassinated friends, gave me that pretension. I can testify, however, that despite a few excesses of

language on the part of François Mauriac, I never stopped reflecting on what he was saying. At the end of this reflection—and I am giving you here my opinion on the utility of dialogue between believers and nonbelievers—I came to recognize in myself, and I state publicly now, that, in the end, and on the precise point of our controversy, M. François Mauriac was right, not I." Cited by Roger Grenier in "Camus and the Post War," seminar at Duke University, September 1998.

217 **"Prepare a book of political texts around Brasillach":** Camus, *Carnets: janvier 1942–mars 1951,* vol. 2 (Paris: Gallimard, 1962), p. 188.

217 **"That man's stupid crime revolted him":** Camus, "The Guest," in *Exile and the Kingdom,* trans. Justin O'Brien (New York: Vintage, 1991 [original publication 1957]), p. 105.

217 **"the degradation of man into a thing":** Simone de Beauvoir, "Oeil pour oeil," *Les Temps Modernes,* no. 5, February 1, 1946, pp. 812–830. The Nuremberg trials of the major war criminals began in November 1945 and lasted until October 1946.

218 **crimes against humanity was "the most nebulous possible charge":** Janet Flanner [pseudonym: Genêt], "Letter from Nuremberg," *The New Yorker,* January 5, 1946, pp. 46–50: "It would seem that we Americans, prosecuting the most nebulous possible charge—crimes against humanity—have, ever since our own Chief Prosecutor Jackson's precise, idealistic, impressive opening, weakened our case, already difficult because the charge lacks precedence, by our irrelevancies and redundancies." On the legal invention of crimes against humanity, see Alain Finkielkraut, *Memory in Vain: The Klaus Barbie Trial and Crimes against Humanity,* intro. Alice Kaplan (New York: Columbia University Press, 1992), and Alice Kaplan, "When War Goes on Trial," in *Civilization,* October–November 1997, pp. 60–65.

218 **However nebulous their first legal articulation:** Crimes against humanity remained a subset of war crimes. It was only two decades later, when Eichmann went on trial in Israel for his role in administering the death camps, that the crucial idea of genocide, separate from the waging of war, came into its own. But the definition of crimes against humanity in the Nuremberg indictment blended genocide, political prosecution, and murder of civilian populations. See Alice Kaplan, "When War Goes on Trial."

218 **"There are words as murderous as gas chambers":** Simone de Beauvoir, *Force of Circumstance,* trans. Richard Howard (New York: Putnam's Sons, 1964), p. 22.

218 **The evidence gathered . . . was deemed insufficient:** Maurice Bardèche, dossier de justice Z6 NL5182. Bernadette Reboul believes her father engineered his release, to honor his promise. Bardèche was arrested September 1, 1944; his release is dated March 31, 1945. In a separate, university Purge commission proceeding, Bardèche was removed from his position as a tenured professor at the University of Lille (see Claude Singer, *L'Université libérée, l'université épurée, 1943–1947* [Paris: Les Belles Lettres, 1997]).

219 **Loss of memory . . . "was like a balm, a dressing":** Maurice Bardèche, *Souvenirs* (Paris: Editions Buchet/Chastel, 1993), p. 197.

219 **Bardèche wrote a defense of the legality of Vichy:** Maurice Bardèche, *Lettre à François Mauriac* (Paris: La Pensée Libre, 1947).

219 **a legislation outlawing "apology for murder":** Precursor to the current "Loi Gayssot" outlawing Holocaust revisionism. The French have also ratified the United Nations legislation against "incitement of racial hatred."

219 **Existing copies of his book were ordered destroyed:** Cour d'Appel de Paris, XIe Chambre, Arrêt rendu dans l'Affaire Bardèche, Audience du 19 mars 1952. Marcel

Reboul papers, Courtesy Bernadette Reboul. On the two trials, see Florent Brayard, *Comment l'idée vint à M. Rassinier* (Paris: Fayard, 1996), p. 236.

220 **a whole gamut of negationist articles in his *Défense de l'Occident*:** Analysis of *Défense de l'Occident* by Ghislaine Desbuissons, "Maurice Bardèche, un précurseur du révisionnisme" in *Relations Internationales,* no. 65, 1991, quoted in Florent Brayard, *Comment l'idée vint à M. Rassinier,* p. 238.

220 **Holocaust denial had become such a widespread phenomenon:** See Pierre Vidal-Naquet, *Assassins of Memory: Essays on the Denial of the Holocaust,* trans. Jeffrey Mehlman (New York : Columbia University Press, 1992). For a history of negationism, see Florent Brayard, *Comment l'idée vint à M. Rassinier.* On Rassinier's trajectory, see also Nadine Fresco, *Fabrication d'un antisémite* (Paris: Editions du Seuil, 1999), which came out as this book was going to press.

220 **In the 1970s . . . you could read the preface by Maurice Bardèche:** Bardèche prefaced the following mass-market paperbacks: Flaubert, *Education sentimentale* (Paris: Le Livre de Poche, 1972); Flaubert, *Madame Bovary* (Paris: Le Livre de Poche, 1972); Flaubert, *Trois contes* (Paris: Livre de Poche, 1972), Balzac, *Père Goriot* (Paris: Presses Pocket, 1978).

222 ***Chat plume: 60 écrivains parlent de leurs chats:*** Paris: Pierre Horay, editeur, 1985.

222 **he expressed himself on this point most clearly in his prosecution of Angeli:** Cour de Justice, Audience du 17 Mai 1946, Ministère Public contre M. Angeli, Requisitoire de M. le Commissaire du Gouvernement Reboul. Sténographie René Bluet. Courtesy Bernadette Reboul.

223 **"would contribute to the grandeur and influence of his legend":** Jacques Isorni, *Souffrance et mort du Maréchal* (Paris: Flammarion, 1951), p. 158.

223 **"A tragedy from antiquity in three voices":** Isorni, *Mémoires, 1911–1945* (Paris: Laffont, 1984), p. 305.

223 **"To Marcel Reboul, to the loyal adversary":** *Le Procès de Robert Brasillach,* Jacques Isorni, ed. (Paris: Flammarion, 1946). Signed copy from Jacques Isorni to Marcel Reboul in the collection of Bernadette Reboul.

223 **by early 1964, everyone had been released:** Peter Novick, *The Resistance versus Vichy* (New York: Columbia University Press, 1968), pp. 297–298, describes three amnesty laws, in 1947, 1951, and 1953. By 1956 only sixty-two collaborators remained in prison; in 1958, nineteen; by 1964, not a single prisoner.

224 **Isorni devoted an entire book . . . to his quest to be elected:** Jacques Isorni, *La Fièvre verte* (Paris: Flammarion, 1975).

224 **"Any fool can defend an innocent man":** *The Economist* (London) vol. 335, no. 7915 (May 20–26, 1995), p. 113.

224 **His shop produced the announcement of the return to school:** Municipal Archives of Aubervilliers, poster collection.

225 **His house was listed on the 1946 tax rolls:** Aubervilliers archives. 1946 Tax Rolls. "Contributions Directes," call number 1G48.

225 **In 1952, at age sixty-four, he received the Legion of Honor:** Too old to have been drafted in 1940, he had fought in the trenches in 1914–1918 (second-class infantry) and was lucky to have survived. His decoration described him as a "Soldat de 2ème classe d'Infanterie recrutement de la Seine 1er bureau" (quoted in a letter to the author from the Grande Chancellerie de la Legion d'Honneur, August 28, 1996).

225 **"We don't want a mayor who isn't ours":** Municipal archives of Aubervilliers, electoral list for city elections of April 26, 1953.

225 **His death is duly recorded on his birth certificate:** Registre des Actes de

Naissance pour l'an 1888. Département de la Seine. Arrondissement communal de Saint-Denis, Commune d'Aubervilliers. No. 207, Grisonnet, Lucien Albert. Aubervilliers municipal archives.

226 **"It's very simple," Laffargue testified at his murder trial:** Both quotations from Alex Ancel, *Le Parisien Libéré,* July 24, 1951, p. 1: "Jean Laffargue—mari bafoué de Mme l'adjointe—avait tué M. le Maire . . . 5 ans de prison avec le bénéfice du sursis."

Thirteen Justice in Hindsight

227 **Did Brasillach deserve to die for what he wrote?:** In 1975, a young historian named Pascal Ory published a column in *Le Monde* saying that, although he was opposed to the death penalty, he would have been proud, in 1945, to serve on the firing squad that executed Brasillach. See Pascal Ory, "Apologie pour un meurtre," *Le Monde,* February 6, 1975. In 1977 Ory published *Les Collaborateurs* (Paris: Le Seuil) and *La France allemande* (Paris: Gallimard). See also Michel Winock's vivid synthesis on the question of Brasillach's guilt, "Fallait-il fusiller Brasillach?" *L'Histoire,* no. 179, July–August 1994, pp. 62–67.

228 **one can also argue that . . . his trial was loftier in tone than any other:** Henry Rousso's comments on the Brasillach trial in "L'Epuration: Une Histoire inachevée" (*Vingtième Siècle. Revue d'Histoire,* no. 33, January–March 1992, pp. 78–105) give a useful sense of the way this event has been put into a larger context by contemporary historians of the Purge: "That a notable part of the intellectual milieu took loud and public positions in favor of [ideological] 'collaborationism' played a large role in the French postwar imaginary. Hence the importance granted after the war to the trials of intellectuals, of which the archetypal trial was that of Robert Brasillach. Even though this type of collaboration was marginal, it contributed to hardening the debates around the Purge, since intellectual commitments in France traditionally carry a strong symbolic charge" (p. 79).

228 **Why was Brasillach killed when René Bousquet . . . got only two years . . . ?:** Bousquet was indicted for crimes against humanity in the 1980s, but was assassinated before he came to trial.

228 **Even if Brasillach had lived and were retried again today:** The case of Julius Streicher, sentenced for crimes against humanity at Nuremberg for "the incitement of the persecution of the Jews" in his newspaper *Der Stürmer,* makes an interesting analogy with the Brasillach case. In his *Anatomy of the Nuremberg Trials* (New York: Knopf, 1992), Telford Taylor, the prosecutor at Nuremberg, wrote that the death sentence against Streicher was "hasty," "unthinking," and "callous" . . . "not an episode to be proud of" (p. 562, p. 631). "Proof was thin" against Streicher, and "the charges in the Indictment were brought against a private newspaper owner and journalist to punish him for publishing statements in which he believed" (p. 378). Unlike the youthful and charming Brasillach, Streicher performed the role of hideous ogre and pervert at the trial. For an analysis of Taylor's critique of the decision against Streicher, see Donna E. Arzt, "Nuremberg, Denazification and Democracy: The Hate Speech Problem at the International Military Tribunal," in *New York Law School Journal of Human Rights,* vol. 13, part 3, Symposium 1995, pp. 689–758.

228 **The recent French trials:** Klaus Barbie, Butcher of Lyon, was indicted for the torture and deportation of 730 Jews and resistance fighters; Bousquet, Prefect of Police, for his responsibility in the Vél d'Hiv roundup. The trial of Touvier, head of the Milice, revolved around a massacre by that militia of Jewish resistants at Rillieux-la-Pape; the trial of Papon, prefect of the Gironde, around the administrative papers he had signed sending convoys of Jews to Drancy.

229 **"Isorni's defense speech is beautiful":** Pierre Dominique, "Les Procès célèbres. Trois procès de la Libération: Béraud, Brasillach, Laval," *Crapouillot,* no. 31, November 1955, p. 50.

Fourteen   The Brasillach Myth

230 **Brasillach is buried in the same grave with his mother:** After the execution, Brasillach's body was taken to the cemetery at Thiais, to the graves reserved for people put to death by the state. In April, his family moved him to Père Lachaise. Twelve years later, Brasillach's body was moved to his final resting spot.

230 **denounced in *Je Suis Partout* as "half Negro, half Jew":** Interview with Roger Grenier, June 15, 1998. See, for example, *Je Suis Partout,* July 7, 1941, "Indiscretions": "*Le Figaro* still counts among its collaborators the anglophile Wladimir d'Ormesson and Guermantes, that is to say the Jew Gérard Bauer"; April 7, 1944, "Partout et ailleurs": "L'Ami Guermantes, is, we know, the Jew Gérard Bauer. The aforementioned Gérard Bauer tried, after the armistice, to pass himself off as an Aryan and did not hesitate—one is subtle or one isn't—to proclaim that his mother had cheated on his father with a goy." Bauer's father, Henri Bauer, was the illegitimate son of Alexandre Dumas père.

230 **"In 1944, he [Brasillach] predicted the return of the extreme right":** *Le Nouvel Observateur,* May 7–12, 1998, p. 52. The article is a review of a book by Jean-Christophe Cambadélis and Eric Osmond called *La France blafarde* [Pallid France] (Paris: Plon, 1998). Highly critical of the development of the extreme right, Cambadélis and Osmond trace today's National Front back through Le Pen's beginning and link him to the network of men who founded the extreme right in the twilight of the Purge years. The first chapter of their book is a portrait of Brasillach at Fresnes, writing his "Lettre à un soldat de la classe '60."

230 **a manifesto called "Manifesto of the Class of '60":** Cambadélis and Osmond, *La France blafarde,* p. 43.

231 **On one of these LPs we hear . . . Brasillach:** Jean-Marie Le Pen, director of production, *Histoire sonore de la Deuxième Guerre Mondiale* [Sound history of the Second World War], record no. 8, "La Guerre totale." Conférence de Presse sur "L'Affaire de Katyn," July 6, 1943, Fernand de Brinon et Robert Brasillach (Paris: S.E.R.P., 1972). On Katyn, see chapter 2, "Brasillach's War."

231 **he produced a recording of Brasillach's Fresnes prison poems:** *Robert Brasillach, Poèmes de Fresnes, lus par Pierre Fresnay* [sound recording] (Paris: S.E.R.P., 1964). Fresnay was investigated at the Purge. He remained a lifelong supporter of Pétain. His nephew, Roland Laudenbach, became a director of La Table Ronde, orienting that publisher towards right-wing, even extreme right-wing, literature.

231 **Le Pen's long-standing political association with François Brigneau:** François Brigneau, born Well Emmanuel Allot, met Brasillach in the last months of the Occupation. He was imprisoned at Fresnes for his last-minute participation in the Milice. He married the niece of Georges Suarez, the first journalist executed by the Cour de Justice. After the war, he wrote for *France-Dimanche* under the name Julien Guernec. He has been associated with any number of extreme right newspapers of the postwar era, including *Rivarol, Minute, Présent,* and *National Hebdo,* the weekly newspaper of the Front National. He is the author of a self-published three-part brochure entitled "At Fresnes with Robert Brasillach."

231 **In 1993, Brigneau published a collection of portraits:** *La Mort en face,* ed. Marcel Hasquenoph, Philippe Vilgier, François Brigneau, with an afterword by Jean-Marie Le Pen (Paris: Publications François Brigneau, 1993).

232 **"blood that has flowed is always pure blood":** The allusion is to Brasillach's "Psaume IV," *Poèmes de Fresnes:* "Father, here flows the blood of our land. / The blood that has flowed is never anything but pure blood, / And here it is, blended, the blood of adversaries . . ." [*Seigneur voici couler le sang de notre terre. / Le sang qui a coulé n'est jamais qu'un sang pur, / Et le voici mêlé, le sang des adversaires . . .*]

232 **"The case is closed, the verdict rendered":** Announcement and order form for the Brasillach complete works, courtesy Luce Fieschi.

234 **reissued by the tiny Editions Godefroy de Bouillon:** Richard Haddad, founder of the Editions Godefroy de Bouillon, is a thirty-year-old Lebanese Christian whose early career in Beirut included a reedition of the classic anti-Semitic tract of the Dreyfus period, Drumont's *La France Juive.* Close to the editors of *Présent,* the Catholic branch of Le Pen's Front National, he has been criticized by some in the movement because he is Arab; he has recently taken some distance from the National Front. Interview with Pierre-André Taguieff, June 1998.

234 **Brasillach has found a home with his political descendants:** Revisionist accounts of Brasillach also occur in mainstream publications. A dictionary of French literature, edited by two university professors of French literature, refers to Brasillach's "Lettre à un soldat de la classe '60" as "poignant" and argues that, during his trial, "he assumed responsibility for a newspaper which he never effectively directed." The entry on Brasillach is signed by Anne Brassié, the literary critic for *Présent.* See *Le XXème siècle: Dictionnaire des Lettres Françaises,* ed. Martin Bercot and André Guyaux (Paris: Le Livre de Poche, 1998), pp. 182–184.